Cher Stéphane,

Je te souhaite une
très bonne lecture,
cher collègue mcgillien !

Hugo

Canadian Federalism and Treaty Powers

Organic Constitutionalism at Work

P.I.E. Peter Lang

Bruxelles · Bern · Berlin · Frankfurt am Main · New York · Oxford · Wien

Hugo CYR

Canadian Federalism and Treaty Powers

Organic Constitutionalism at Work

"Diversitas" Series
No.2

© P.I.E. PETER LANG s.a.
Éditions scientifiques internationales
Brussels, 2009
1 avenue Maurice, B-1050 Brussels, Belgium
info@peterlang.com; www.peterlang.com

Printed in Germany

ISSN 2031-0331
ISBN 978-90-5201-453-1
D/2009/5678/15

Library of Congress Cataloging-in-Publication Data
Cyr, Hugo.
Canadian federalism and treaty powers : existential communities, functional regimes and the organic constitution / Hugo Cyr.
p. cm.
Includes bibliographical references.
ISBN 978-90-5201-453-1
1. Exclusive and concurrent legislative powers—Canada. 2. Treaty-making power—Canada. 3. Federal government—Canada. 4. International and municipal law—Canada. 5. Canada—Foreign relations—Treaties. I. Title.
KE4275.C97 2008   342.71'0412—dc22   2008044786

CIP also available from the British Library, GB.

Bibliographic information published by "Die Deutsche Bibliothek". "Die Deutsche Bibliothek" lists this publication in the "Deutsche National-bibliografie": detailed bibliographic data is available on the Internet at <http://dnb.ddb.de>.

À Thanh-Tram et Héloïse-Thanh

Contents

PART II. TRYING TO FIND OUR OWN PATH
BEYOND THE *LABOUR CONVENTIONS* CASE

Preface

A few years ago, Professor Michael Byers (formerly professor at Duke University and now at the University of British Columbia) and the Center for Canadian Studies at Duke University invited me to lead a seminar on "American and Canadian Federalism and Foreign Affairs". I produced for the occasion a short discussion paper on the topic. However, it soon became clear to me that an in-depth study of the constitutional law applicable to treaty powers and Canadian federalism was truly lacking. Someone needed to go back to all the original sources and needed to re-examine the often mistaken assumptions lying underneath what had passed for too long as constitutional truths in many Anglo-Canadian circles. I thus would like to thank Michael, the Center for Canadian Studies and, in particular, the participants to my seminar (Stéphane Beaulac, Gerry Boychuk, Bernard Duhaime, Joanna Harrington, Vicki Jackson, Andrew Petter, David Schneiderman and Debora VanNijnatten) for having challenged me to undertake this large research project.

Since I began researching this field connecting Canadian constitutional law, international law and international relations and political theory, many people have contributed in helping me clarify my ideas through discussions and debates (Mark Antaki, Bruce Broomhall, Bernard Duhaime, Paul W. Kahn, Lucie Lamarche, Pierrick Choinière-Lapointe, François Soucy and Pierre Ducasse) or have read draft versions of this book and have made constructive comments (Bruce Broomhall, François Chevrette, John Gould, Jula Hughes, William Hughes, Jean Leclair and Alejandro Lorite). I would like to thank them all for their immense generosity. Also, I would like to thank the members of the jury who evaluated a previous version of this book that was submitted as a doctoral thesis at the Université de Montréal (Suzanne Lalonde, Alain Noël, Danielle Pinard, and Guy Tremblay) for their very insightful suggestions. I have also had the chance to present certain ideas developed here at a seminar jointly organised by the Faculty of Law at McGill University and the Federal Department of Justice, at a meeting of the Canadian Law and Society Association held at Harrison Hot Springs (British Columbia) and at a conference organised by Chi Carmody at the Faculty of Law at the University of Western Ontario. I would like to thank those who attended those events for their useful comments. Obviously, my students, especially those taking my Introduction au droit interne et international course, have been a great source of inspiration in the preparation of this book.

I would also like to thank those whose financial support made this project possible: the Université du Québec à Montréal (U.Q.A.M.), the Center for Canadian Studies at Duke University, the Centre de recherche interdisciplinaire sur la diversité au Québec (C.R.I.D.A.Q.), the Centre d'études sur le droit international et la mondialisation (C.É.D.I.M.) and the Département des sciences juridiques, U.Q.A.M. Without their help, this book would not have existed. In particular, I would like to thank my colleague Alain-G. Gagnon.

Special thanks go to Valérie Scott for her amazing editorial work.

That being said, the two people who have influenced me the most over my young academic life have been Justice Ian Binnie and Professor François Chevrette. Justice Binnie has taught me the patient ways of common law thinking and has offered me a prime example of what a *phronimos* is. Likewise, François has shown to generations of Québec jurists what it means to be a true scholar. His encyclopedic knowledge of public law and political theory, his meticulous reading, his incisive comments, his wit and his sincerity have made him a reader of choice for anyone who wants a serious appraisal of his or her work. These qualities and their extreme generosity make Justice Binnie and François Chevrette the perfect mentors.

Finally, I would like to thank Thanh-Tram and Héloïse-Thanh for their love and patience. May we keep growing happily in our "existential community".

Introduction

On a brisk April 12th 1965, in Montréal, a man braved the rain.[1] He had something very important to do. He knew that a storm might ensue but he believed that it was necessary to face the rain for the future to be brighter. There had already been an important political storm a little more than a month earlier because of what he did in Paris and he needed to clear the air. With his conference notes under his arm – notes that he had prepared meticulously with the help of a visionary statesman[2] –, he walked confidently into a room filled with foreign dignitaries. He – and the People who were going to speak through his voice – was literally stepping on the world stage. After expressing his pleasure at hosting the Consular Corps, he told them something that is still not totally understood today. He spoke clearly but many who heard him could not make sense of what he said. Blinded by their own assumptions, many believed that his speech was, if not revolutionary in character, at least revolutionary in its intent. But interpreting intents is a risky business, particularly in moments of anxiety.

So what did Paul Gérin-Lajoie tell the Consular Corps? The constitutional law scholar turned Vice-President of the Québec Executive Council of the Liberal government of Jean Lesage told them, in short, that Québec, while still being a federated state of Canada, had both the capacity and the desire to engage herself[3] on the world stage in order to

---

[1]   Canada, Environment Canada, *Daily Data Report for April 1965*, online: Environment Canada <http://www.climat.meteo.ec.gc.ca/climateData/dailydata_f.html>.

I will often refer to Internet webpages in this document. We all know that such webpages have a variable lifespan. However, it is often possible to retrieve web pages that have been taken down by searching the Internet Archive, *Wayback Machine* found at <http://www.archive.org/web/web.php>. The Internet Archive apparently contains over 55 billion web pages archived since 1996.

[2]   Robert Aird, *André Patry et la présence du Québec dans le monde* (Montréal: VLB, 2005) at 57-73.

[3]   The use of the feminine in relation to a "state" might seem dated to the contemporary reader. However, I have decided to revert to the older English usage of feminising states and countries to better highlight the fact that such collective entities are conceived as "persons" in our political culture. I will address in more depth the issue of the personification of states in section II.A.2.iv. However, I will use neuter words to refer to "governments", "Parliament" and "legislatures" because those entities are not personalised in the same way as are states and countries. While "governments", "Parliament" and "legislatures" are collective decision mechanisms, they are not necessarily considered *to be the collective* itself.

fulfil her governmental missions. That assertion explained the agreement that Québec had concluded with France, in the previous month, on education.[4] Paul Gérin-Lajoie's speech was luminous in its pragmatism and far from being revolutionary; it was in the pure British tradition of constitutional evolution and continuity.

Unfortunately, many could not imagine that Québec's position on her capacity to conclude international agreements was anything but a demand for secession or, at least, a step in that direction. While they tried to understand Québec's position on her capacity to conclude international agreements, they were prisoners of their own conceptual prejudices. Too many listeners had forgotten that other forms of political institutions existed before we imagined the "sovereign nation-state". In effect, the long history of pluralistic arrangements between ecclesiastical, imperial and local governments that covered the European continent from the Middle Age on was a good source of examples as to the different ways one could distribute exclusive, concurrent or complementary jurisdictions between autonomous or semi-autonomous authorities.[5] But

---

[4]   See Québec, Ministère des relations internationales, *Échange de lettres entre le ministère de la Jeunesse du Québec et l'Association pour l'organisation des stages en France (ASTEF) concernant un programme de coopération technique*, 1964-01, online: Ministère des relations internationales du Québec <http://www.mri.gouv.qc. ca/fr/informer/ententes/pdf/1964-01.pdf>. See also Jacques-Yvan Morin, "La conclusion d'accords internationaux par les provinces canadiennes à la lumière du droit comparé" (1965) 3 Can. Y.B. Int'l Law 127 at 173-76 [J.-Y. Morin, "La conclusion d'accords internationaux par les provinces canadiennes"] for a discussion of the reactions to that agreement. Morin's article is also quite instructive on the way different federations dealt with treaty-making powers until the mid-1960s.

[5]   The German legal historian and theorist Otto Friederich von Gierke had done much to keep alive the memory of the pluralist structure of the Medieval political order in Europe with his four volumes *Das deutsche Genossenschaftsrecht* (Berlin: Weidmann, 1868-1913). At the turn of the 20th century, the famous Downing professor of the laws of England at Cambridge, Frederic William Maitland, introduced to the English-speaking world part of Gierke's opus. He translated a section of volume 3 of *Das deutsche Genossenschaftsrecht* and wrote an introductory note to the German scholar's work. See Otto Friederich von Gierke, *Political Theories of the Middle Age*, trans. and introd. by Frederic William Maitland (Cambridge: Cambridge University Press, 1900) [Gierke, *Political Theories of the Middle Age*]. Frederic William Maitland's work also dealt significantly with the issue of political pluralism and the multiplicity of superimposed forms of government that constitute the history of political order in England and Europe. In general, one can consult the essays collected in Herbert Albert Laurens Fisher, ed., *Collected Papers of Frederic William Maitland* (Cambridge: Cambridge University Press, 1911) Vol. 3. Political pluralism was also widely discussed in England in the first half of the 20th century thanks to the works of George Douglas Howard Cole, John Neville Figgis and Harold Joseph Laski. Laski taught at McGill from 1914 until 1916 when he left for Harvard. On the intellectual relations between Harold Laski and Vicount Haldane, see David Schneiderman's very instructive article, "Harold Laski, Viscount Haldane and the Law of the Canadian Constitution in the Early Twentieth Century" (1998) 48 U.T.L.J. 521 [D. Schneider-

these arrangements were somehow forgotten and replaced by the concept of the "sovereign nation-state". Probably influenced by a decolonization movement that was in full swing, many listeners became somehow amnesiac. Their forgetfulness brought with it an incapacity to imagine that alternative institutional arrangements might better describe contemporary and future political arrangements. To put it differently: the revolution was not to be found in Gérin-Lajoie's speech but in the fearful and forgetful minds of others. All this seems clear when one takes a sober look at the main lines of Paul Gérin-Lajoie's speech.

Gérin-Lajoie proceeded by reminding his guests that the consular function consists in encouraging the development of relations between the represented state and the state of residence, i.e. the state of Québec. Because Québec's status as a "state" might have been a point of contention, he elaborated on that point. First, he recognized that Québec, being a member of the Canadian federation, is not sovereign in all domains. But after reviewing the criteria of statehood, he concluded that Québec nonetheless met the characteristics of a state. Gérin-Lajoie went further and argued that, beyond simply meeting those criteria, Québec had a unique vocation in North America: she was the "political expression of a people distinguished, in a number of ways, from the English-language communities inhabiting North America", "the political instrument of a cultural group, distinct and unique in all of North America."[6] Thus, the Québec statehood had to be viewed as one possible institutional embodiment of a particular People.

Once he had established that Québec was the institutional embodiment of a particular political community, he went on to describe the needs of that community. These needs were the ones of a political community which was coming of age. He described with excitement the *Québécois* of the "Quiet Revolution" as overflowing with a superabun-

---

man, "Harold Laski, Viscount Haldane and the Law of the Canadian Constitution in the Early Twentieth Century"].

[6] The address by Paul Gérin-Lajoie, Vice-Président of the Executive Council and Québec's Minister of Education was delivered, as I noted earlier, in Montréal to the Consular Corps on April 12, 1965. For a complete version of this address, see Québec, *Ministère des Relations internationales, Paul Gérin-Lajoie's speech delivered at the Montreal to the Consular Corps on April 12, 1965*, trans. by *Ministère des Relations internationales*, online: *Ministère des Relations internationales* <http://www.mri.gouv.qc.ca/en/ministere/documentation/textes/discours_paul_gerin_lajoie.asp> [Paul Gérin-Lajoie, *Address to the Consular Corps*]. The original French version of this speech is available in Québec, Ministère des relations internationales, *Discours de Paul Gérin-Lajoie devant le corps consulaire de Montréal le 12 avril 1965*, online: Ministère des relations internationales http://www.mri.gouv.qc.ca/fr/ministere/documentation/textes/discours_paul_gerin_lajoie.asp [Paul Gérin-Lajoie, *Discours de Paul Gérin-Lajoie devant le corps consulaire de Montréal*].

dant energy and engaged in a wide range of productive activities.[7] He described a Québec determined to take her "rightful place in the contemporary world" and eager "to provide, in external as well as internal affairs, all the means necessary for the realization of the aspirations of the society for which it stands."[8] And to optimise the results of those endeavours, to attain their destiny, the *Québécois* knew that they needed the appropriate "material and constitutional means".[9]

It is important to note that Gérin-Lajoie was convinced that the fulfilment of those needs was within reach.[10] While he thought that major constitutional revisions were needed in relation to, *inter alia*, the division of legislative powers and the institutional structures of the Canadian state,[11] he was, however, convinced that Québec *already* had the constitutional powers to engage in international affairs related to her own fields of legislative powers. Therefore, Gérin-Lajoie was not advocating for constitutional changes to allow Québec to take her place on the world stage. Rather, he claimed that Québec was simply awakening a latent power that already lay in the Constitution of Canada.[12] A power that was simply a logical consequence of a series of already accepted constitutional imperatives.

The legal grounds for Gérin-Lajoie's argument were presented in a clear and succinct manner. First, Gérin-Lajoie stated that "the constitution which Canada was given in 1867 ... assigns to Canadian provinces the status of states fully and absolutely sovereign in certain definite

---

[7]   Gérin-Lajoie said, *ibid.*:

    [t]he Quebecer has assumed his responsibilities and has taken his fate [in] his own hands. The economy, natural resources, education, community and social organization have been the main fields of action of the new Québec citizen. I shall note simply by way of landmarks the creation of the Departments of Education, of Natural Resources, and of Cultural Affairs, the setting up of the General Finance Corporation, the nationalization of electricity, the approaching creation of a siderurgical complex, of a universal pension plan and its investment fund which will soon be a reality, along with the introduction of hospitalization insurance as a forerunner to a complete system of sickness insurance ...

[8]   *Ibid.*

[9]   *Ibid.*

[10]   He was confident that the Québec society knew "that from now on the realization of its own ends and aspirations l[ay] within its reach." *Ibid.*

[11]   See Paul Gérin-Lajoie, *Constitutional Amendment in Canada* (Toronto: University of Toronto Press, 1950).

[12]   In the French version of Paul Gérin-Lajoie's address, this point is made in unequivocal terms: "C'est dire que l'activité débordante que manifeste l'État du Québec depuis cinq ans dans les domaines qu'il n'avait pas jusqu'alors abordés ne doit apparaître en aucune façon comme révolutionnaire sur le plan constitutionnel." (Paul Gérin-Lajoie, *Discours de Paul Gérin-Lajoie devant le corps consulaire de Montréal*, *supra* note 6).

domains."[13] He cited the famous judgment of the Privy Council in *Hodge v. R.* to support his claim:

> [The provincial legislatures] are in no sense delegates of or acting under any mandate from the Imperial Parliament. When the British North America Act enacted that there should be a legislature for Ontario, and that its legislative assembly should have exclusive authority to make laws for the Province and for provincial purposes in relation to the matters enumerated in sect. 92, it conferred powers not in any sense to be exercised by delegation from or as agents of the Imperial Parliament, but authority as plenary and as ample within the limits prescribed by sect. 92 as the Imperial Parliament in the plenitude of its power possessed and could bestow. Within these limits of subjects and area the local legislature is supreme, and has the same authority as the Imperial Parliament, or the Parliament of the Dominion, would have had under like circumstances ... [14]

Second, he highlighted the fact that "[i]n the matter of international competence, the Canadian constitution is silent. With the exception of Article 132, which has become a dead letter since the *Statute of Westminster*, in 1931, there is nothing which says that international relations are solely under the jurisdiction of the federal state."[15] What he meant here by "the Canadian constitution" was the series of entrenched enacted constitutional texts. He wanted to remind the audience that the federal authorities did not enjoy plenary powers over international matters. "Therefore", he added, "it is not by virtue of written law, but rather by repeated practice over the past forty years, that the Federal Government has assumed an exclusive role with regard to relations with foreign countries."[16] But those times were past and Québec wanted to step in and take her rightful place.

Having first established that Canadian provinces had "the status of states fully and absolutely sovereign in certain definite domains"[17] and, second, that nothing conferred to the federal authorities exclusive jurisdiction over international affairs, Gérin-Lajoie argued that provinces already enjoyed such constitutional powers in relation to the subject-matters of their jurisdictional domains.

He reminded his audience that the implementation of treaties in Canada, when it required modifications to domestic law, had to be undertaken by the legislature that has power over the subject-matter involved

---

[13] *Ibid.*

[14] *Hodge v. R.*, [1883-84] 9 A.C. 117, 132. [*Hodge v. R.*]

[15] Paul Gérin-Lajoie, *Address to the Consular Corps, supra* note 6.

[16] *Ibid.*

[17] *Ibid.*

in the treaty obligation.[18] This rule was the result of the very important decision of the Privy Council in what is known as the *Labour Conventions* case.[19] From there, he moved on to three legal conclusions.

1) Gérin-Lajoie claimed that Québec possesses "a limited 'jus tractatum'",[20] that is, a limited treaty-making power, and that she had no intention to give away that power to the federal Parliament. In effect, Gérin-Lajoie commented on the absurdity that would characterise a system in which the authority charged with the execution of an obligation would not be able to sign and negotiate that obligation. He said: "Is an agreement not concluded with the essential purpose of putting it into application, and should those who will have to implement it not have the right to work out the conditions in advance?"[21] While Gérin-Lajoie was speaking to a crowd of diplomats, he did not get into the details of the argument in favour of recognizing a *jus tractatum* for Québec apart from arguing that it would be absurd to attribute to separate authorities the power to make and the power to execute international obligations. The "absurdity" argument was obviously not sufficient since it could cut both ways: if treaty-making and treaty implementation ought to belong to the same authority, why shouldn't they belong to the federal authority?[22] If the federal executive has the power to conclude treaties on all and any subjects, why couldn't the federal Parliament execute the obligations thus created? The answer to that objection lies in the fact that, in the Canadian federation, it is the legislative jurisdiction that determines the primordial scope of the executive powers and not the other way around. This argument would be fleshed out a few years later.[23]

---

[18] *Ibid.*

[19] *Canada (A.G.) v. Ontario (A.G.)*, [1937] A.C. 326, [1937] 1 W.W.R. 299, [1937] 1 D.L.R. 673 (P.C.) [*Labour Conventions* case with references to A.C.].

[20] Paul Gérin-Lajoie, *Address to the Consular Corps*, *supra* note 6.

[21] *Ibid.*

[22] Gerald R. Morris, "The Treaty-Making Power: A Canadian Dilemma" (1967) 45 Can. Bar Rev. 478 at 490 [G.R. Morris, "The Treaty-Making Power: A Canadian Dilemma"].

[23] See for example, Lorne Giroux, "La capacité internationale des provinces en droit constitutionnel canadien" (1967-1968) 9 C. de D. 241 [L. Giroux, "La capacité internationale des provinces en droit constitutionnel canadien"] who referred to the Privy Council decision in *Bonanza Creek Gold Mining Co. v. R.*, [1916] 1 A.C. 566 (P.C.) [*Bonanza Creek Gold Mining Co.*] where it was stated that "[i]t is to be observed that the British North America Act has made a distribution between the Dominion and the provinces which extends not only to legislative but to executive authority. ... [T]he distribution under the new grant of executive authority in substance *follows the distribution under the new grant of legislative powers*" (at 479-80. Emphasis added). Jacques-Yvan Morin, in his article "La conclusion d'accords internationaux par les provinces canadiennes", *supra* note 4 at p. 180, had hinted at the argument by refer-

2) Having affirmed Québec's limited *jus tractatum* and capacity to intervene on the world stage to achieve her objective, Gérin-Lajoie added that it was inadmissible "for the federal state to exert a kind of supervision and adventitious control over Québec's international relations."[24]

3) In parallel to these conclusions, Gérin-Lajoie claimed a right for Québec to "participate in the activity of certain international organizations of a non-political character."[25] What he meant by "international organizations of a non-political character" was "interstate organizations ... founded for the sole purpose of bringing about a solution, by international cooperation" to "problems which up to now have been purely local in nature".[26]

It is not because Québec or other provinces had not made great use of their powers that they had lost them. If there was a time when an almost exclusive participation of the federal authorities in international affairs was not detrimental to provinces because such affairs were fairly limited, Gérin-Lajoie's address was meant to say that those days were over[27]: "Interstate relations now touch *every aspect of social life.*"[28]

In effect, international relations were no longer dominated by issues of war and peace but dealt increasingly with issues traditionally characterized as "domestic" such as labour conditions, education, family, etc. In many ways, being able to cooperate with other jurisdictions was becoming, for provinces, necessary if they were to fully accomplish their missions. This is why Gérin-Lajoie argued that the *"collectivités membres"* of the federation ought to be able "to participate actively and directly in the preparation of international agreements with which they are immediately concerned."[29] Gérin-Lajoie noted that a "large number of interstate organizations have been founded for the sole purpose of bringing about a solution, by international cooperation, [to] problems which up to now have been purely local in nature"[30] and it made good sense for those responsible for dealing with those issues to participate in those organizations.

---

ring to *Liquidators of the Maritime Bank v. New Brunswick (Receiver-General)*, [1892] A.C. 437 [*Liquidators of the Maritime Bank*] where the Privy Council stated that the Lieutenant-Governor is as much the representative of Her Majesty for provincial purposes as the Governor General is for the Dominion.

[24] Paul Gérin-Lajoie, *Address to the Consular Corps, supra* note 6.

[25] *Ibid.*

[26] *Ibid.*

[27] *Ibid.*

[28] *Ibid.* (emphasis added).

[29] *Ibid.*

[30] *Ibid.*

The "Gérin-Lajoie doctrine" – or, as it is often called, the doctrine of "the external extension of internal competence"[31] – has been accepted by all subsequent Québec governments.[32] Recently, for example, Liberal Premier Jean Charest declared:

> Il est d'ailleurs intéressant de constater que les gouvernements qui se sont succédé au Québec depuis ce temps ont agi, en matière internationale, avec une remarquable constance. Tant les gouvernements souverainistes que les gouvernements fédéralistes ont trouvé normal et nécessaire de pousser toujours plus loin l'engagement du Québec sur la scène internationale. Cette unanimité de la classe politique québécoise autour de l'engagement international du Québec trouve sa source dans ce qu'on a appelé la doctrine Gérin-Lajoie, dont le principe demeure toujours aussi actuel aujourd'hui que lorsqu'elle a été formulée pour la première fois en 1965 par Paul Gérin-Lajoie, alors ministre du gouvernement de Jean Lesage. Pour bien comprendre la portée de cette doctrine, il faut savoir que, contrairement à l'idée reçue, la compétence en matière de politique étrangère n'est pas attribuée à l'un ou l'autre des ordres de gouvernement dans les textes constitutionnels. Je n'ai pas l'intention de m'étendre sur ce sujet, déjà bien documenté, si ce n'est que pour préciser que nous croyons que lorsque le gouvernement du Québec est le seul gouvernement compétent pour appliquer un engagement international, il est normal qu'il soit celui qui prenne cet engagement. En somme, il revient au Québec d'assumer, sur le plan international, le prolongement de ses compétences internes. Par ailleurs, les divers gouvernements ont tou-

---

[31] The Government of Québec, *Ministère des Relations internationales* website summarizes the Gérin-Lajoie doctrine in the following terms:

> In areas in which the Government of Québec is the only government empowered to keep a commitment, it is normal that such commitment be made by the Government of Québec and that any foreign agreement in this area be made by the Government of Québec.

> In short, Québec is responsible for the international extension of its domestic areas of jurisdiction.

See Québec, *Ministère des Relations internationales, Gerin-Lajoie's doctrine presentation*, online: *Ministère des Relations internationales* <http://www.mri.gouv.qc.ca/en/politique_internationale/fondements/fondements.asp#doctrine>.

[32] The Government of Québec states:

> Following the change in government in the wake of the 1966 Québec general election, the new government solemnly confirmed the political legitimacy of the Gérin-Lajoie doctrine and the legal foundations of Québec's international involvement. This position was further confirmed by a debate on April 13, 1967, in the Legislative Assembly (today's National Assembly) leading up to the unanimous adoption of an act creating the Ministère des Affaires intergouvernementales.

Ibid. All subsequent Québec governments have adopted this line of thought and have worked to endow Québec with the appropriate institutional structures for her participation in international relations. See Daniel Turp, "La doctrine Gérin-Lajoie et l'émergence d'un droit québécois des relations internationales" in Stéphane Paquin, ed., *Les relations internationales du Québec depuis la Doctrine Gérin-Lajoie (1965-2005)* (Québec: Presses de l'Université Laval, 2006).

jours pris soin d'exercer cette compétence dans le respect de la politique étrangère canadienne. En d'autres mots, ce qui est de compétence québécoise chez nous, est de compétence québécoise partout.[33]

Not only did subsequent Québec governments accept the three conclusions that Gérin-Lajoie teased out of his constitutional analysis, but they ultimately added a fourth: federal authorities cannot bind Québec to an international agreement without the latter's consent. This fourth conclusion would ultimately be arrived at by the Québec National Assembly when it formalised Québec's positions by adopting declaratory legislation stating that:

The Québec State is free to consent to be bound by any treaty, convention or international agreement in matters under its constitutional jurisdiction.

No treaty, convention or agreement in the areas under its jurisdiction may be binding on the Québec State unless the consent of the Québec State to be bound has been formally expressed by the National Assembly or the Government, subject to the applicable legislative provisions.

The Québec State may, in the areas under its jurisdiction, establish and maintain relations with foreign States and international organizations and ensure its representation outside Québec.[34]

L'État du Québec est libre de consentir à être lié par tout traité, convention ou entente internationale qui touche à sa compétence constitutionnelle.

Dans ses domaines de compétence, aucun traité, convention ou entente ne peut l'engager à moins qu'il n'ait formellement signifié son consentement à être lié par la voix de l'Assemblée nationale ou du gouvernement selon les dispositions de la loi.

Il peut également, dans ses domaines de compétence, établir et poursuivre des relations avec des États étrangers et des organisations internationales et assurer sa représentation à l'extérieur du Québec.

---

[33] Québec, Cabinet du Premier ministre, "Address of the Premier of Québec to ÉNAP, February 25th, 2004", *Discours du mois de février 2004*, online: Premier ministre du Québec
<http://www.premier.gouv.qc.ca/general/discours/2004/fevrier/dis20040225.htm>.
The phrase "ce qui est de compétence québécoise chez nous, est de compétence québécoise partout" was also used by Premier Charest in his speech "Pour redécouvrir l'esprit fédéral" (Address pronounced at the occasion of the 40th anniversary of the Confederation Centre of the Arts in Charlottetown (P.E.I.), November 8, 2004), online: Premier ministre <http://www.premier.gouv.qc.ca/general/discours/2004/novembre/dis20041108.htm>.

[34] *An Act respecting the exercise of the fundamental rights and prerogatives of the Québec people and the Québec State*, R.S.Q. c. E-20.2, s. 7.

The legislature of Québec also adopted *An Act respecting the Ministère des Relations internationales*[35] in which it specified that the Government of Canada can negotiate international agreements with foreign governments or international organisations on matters within the constitutional jurisdiction of Québec if authorized by that province. In effect, following Québec's traditional claim that executive prerogatives parallel legislative jurisdiction, s. 22.1 provides that:

The [Québec] Minister [of International Relations] may agree to the signing of such an accord by Canada.	Le ministre [des Relations internationales du Québec] peut donner son agrément à ce que le Canada signe un tel accord.
The Government must, in order to be bound by an international accord pertaining to any matter within the constitutional jurisdiction of Québec and to give its assent to Canada's expressing its consent to be bound by such an accord, make an order to that effect. The same applies in respect of the termination of such an accord.	Le gouvernement doit, pour être lié par un accord international ressortissant à la compétence constitutionnelle du Québec et pour donner son assentiment à ce que le Canada exprime son consentement à être lié par un tel accord, prendre un décret à cet effet. Il en est de même à l'égard de la fin d'un tel accord.

However, most of these positions were not entirely new. Other provinces had made similar claims in the past. For example, Ontario had argued to the Privy Council that the only "authority competent to sign a treaty creating obligations is the King or some authority specially delegated to do so by the King ..."[36] and that "[t]here are no grounds whatever for saying that the parties to advise His Majesty in matters relating to the jurisdiction of the provinces have in some way come to be the Dominion Ministers."[37] Therefore, Ontario claimed that she had jurisdiction to conclude treaties on matters within her jurisdiction.[38] Whether or not this position was "new" it still caused a certain amount of fear. As mentioned above, it is probable that the decolonisation movement that was sweeping the World at the time had something to do with the anxiety of some of Gérin-Lajoie's listeners.

The most spectacular way in which colonized peoples exercised their newfound right to self-determination was secession from the old metropoles. Thus, secession might have appeared as the paradigmatic act of decolonisation. While in the 1960s, Canada was already autonomous

---

[35] *An Act respecting the Ministère des Relations internationales*, R.S.Q. c. M-25.1.1, s. 22.1 [*An Act respecting the Ministère des Relations internationales*].

[36] *Labour Conventions* case, *supra* note 19 at p. 333.

[37] *Ibid.*

[38] See I.C.1. below.

from the British Parliament, it still required the formal participation of the latter to amend certain parts of the *Constitution Act, 1867*.[39] The fact that the Canadian constitution had not been entirely given back to Canadians – and, in some Québec nationalist circles, the fact that the Head of State was still the same individual as the Head of State of the United Kingdom – was seen as evidence that the colonial ties had not been completely broken yet. And, according to many Québec nationalists, the decolonisation paradigm appeared to fit their situation. Thus, there were fears that Québec was not simply making claims about having rights to participate in international affairs but that she was rather taking steps towards fuller claims of independence from both the United Kingdom *and* the rest of Canada. In fact, thinking that possession of an "international legal personality" or of a power to make treaties were exclusive attributes of completely sovereign states, some thought that recognizing Québec's claim was equivalent to recognizing Québec's secession![40]

More generally, those opposed to the Gérin-Lajoie doctrine often shared a conception of an independent Canada that must speak with one voice and in which that voice came from the same place as where Canadian sovereignty lay: in the federal authorities. The absence of an express constitutional enactment explicitly distributing powers over international relations and diverging visions of the respective roles of Canada and the provinces on the world stage had been, early in the withdrawal process from the declining British Empire, an important cause of tensions between the federal and provincial governments. Accordingly, the question of the creation and implementation of treaty obligations in Canada has been the subject of a great number of debates that are still ongoing.[41] In effect, the succeeding federal governments

---

[39] *Constitution Act, 1867* (U.K.), 30 & 31 Vict., c. 3, reprinted in R.S.C. 1985, App. II, No. 5 [*Constitution Act, 1867*]. This statute was originally entitled *British North America Act*. The name of this statute was changed by the *Canada Act 1982* (U.K.), 1982, c. 11, Sch., item 1.

[40] See for example: Bora Laskin, "The Provinces and International Agreements" in Ontario, Ontario Advisory Committee on Confederation, *Background Papers and Reports*, Vol. 1 (Toronto: Queen's Printer, 1967) at 108 [B. Laskin, "The Provinces and International Agreements"]; Jean-Yves Grenon, "De la conclusion des traités et de leur mise en oeuvre au Canada" (1962) 40 Can. Bar Rev. 151 [J.-Y. Grenon, "De la conclusion des traités et de leur mise en œuvre au Canada"]; G.R. Morris, "The Treaty-Making Power: A Canadian Dilemma", *supra* note 22.

[41] See for example, the following classical articles on those issues: Clarence W. Jenks, "The Present Status of the Bennett Ratifications of International Labour Conventions" (1937) 15 Can. Bar Rev. 464 [C.W. Jenks, "The Present Status of the Bennett Ratifications of International Labour Conventions"]; W. Ivor Jennings, "Dominion Legislation and Treaties" (1937) 15 Can. Bar Rev. 455 [W.I. Jennings, "Dominion Legislation and Treaties"]; Norman A.M. Mackenzie, "Canada and the Treaty-Making

Power" (1937) 15 Can. Bar Rev. 436; Richard J. Matas, "Treaty Making in Canada" (1947) 25 Can. Bar Rev. 458; David C. Vanek, "Is International Law Part of the Law of Canada?" (1949-50) 8 U.T.L.J. 251 [D.C. Vanek, "Is International Law Part of the Law of Canada?"]; John Peter Nettl, "The Treaty Enforcement Power in Federal Constitutions" (1950) 28 Can. Bar Rev. 1051; Jean-Yves Grenon, "De la mise œuvre du futur Pacte international des droits de l'homme dans l'État fédératif canadien" (1951-52) 1-2 R.J.T. 195; George J. Szablowski, "Creation and Implementation of Treaties in Canada" (1956) 34 Can. Bar Rev. 28; Ivan C. Rand, "Some Aspects of Canadian Constitutionalism" (1960) 38 Can. Bar Rev. 135 [I.C. Rand, "Some Aspects of Canadian Constitutionalism"]; Gerald V. La Forest, "May the Provinces Legislate in Violation of International Law?" (1961) 39 Can. Bar Rev. 78 [G.V. La Forest, "May the Provinces Legislate in Violation of International Law?"]; J.-Y. Grenon, "De la conclusion des traités et de leur mise en œuvre au Canada", *ibid.*; J.-Y. Morin, "La conclusion d'accords internationaux par les provinces canadiennes", *supra* note 4; Edward McWhinney, "The Constitutional Competence within Federal Systems as to International Agreements" (1964-68) 1 Can. Legal Stud. 145 [Edward McWhinney, "The Constitutional Competence within Federal Systems as to International Agreements"]; G.R. Morris, "The Treaty-Making Power: A Canadian Dilemma", *ibid.*; B. Laskin, "The Provinces and International Agreements", *ibid.*; Edward McWhinney, "Canadian Federalism and the Foreign Affairs and Treaty Power: The Impact of Québec's Quiet Revolution" (1969) 7 Can. Y.B. Int'l. Law 3 [E. McWhinney, "Canadian Federalism and the Foreign Affairs and Treaty Power: The Impact of Québec's Quiet Revolution"]; Ronald G. Atkey, "The Role of the Provinces in International Affairs" (1970) 26 Int.J. 249; André Dufour, "Fédéralisme canadien et droit international" in Ronald St. John MacDonald, Gerald L. Morris and Douglas M. Johnston, eds., *Canadian Perspectives on International Law and Organization* (Toronto: University of Toronto Press, 1974) 72; Ronald St. John MacDonald, "The Relationship between International Law and Domestic Law in Canada" in Ronald St. John MacDonald, Gerald L. Morris and Douglas M. Johnston, eds., *Canadian Perspectives on International Law and Organization* (Toronto: University of Toronto Press, 1974) 88 [R. St. John MacDonald, "The Relationship between International Law and Domestic Law in Canada"]; Gerald L. Morris, "Canadian Federalism and International Law" in Ronald St. John MacDonald, Gerald L. Morris and Douglas M. Johnston, eds., *Canadian Perspectives on International Law and Organization* (Toronto: University of Toronto Press, 1974) 55; Covey T. Oliver, "The Enforcement of Treaties by a Federal State" (1974) 14 Can.Y.B. Int'l. Law 331; Ronald St. John MacDonald, "International Treaty Law and the Domestic Law of Canada" (1975) 2 Dal. L.J. 307 [R. St. John MacDonald, "International Treaty Law and the Domestic Law of Canada"]; Anne-Marie Jacomy-Millette, "L'État fédéré dans les relations internationales contemporaines: le cas du Canada" (1976) 14 Can. Y.B. Int'l L 20; Thomas A. Levy, "Provincial International Status Revisited" (1976-77) 3 Dal. L.J. 70; Brian M. Mazer, "Sovereignty and Canada: An Examination of Canadian Sovereignty from a Legal Perspective" (1977-78) 42 Sask. L.R. 1; Claude C. Emmanuelli and Stanislas Slosar, "L'application et l'interprétation des traités internationaux par le juge canadien" (1978) 13 R.J.T. 69; Anne-Marie Jacomy-Millette, "Le rôle des provinces dans les relations internationales" (1979) 10 Études internationales 285; Francis Rigaldies and Jose Woehrling, "Le juge interne canadien et le droit international" (1980) 21 C. de D. 293 [F. Rigaldies and J. Woehrling, "Le juge interne canadien et le droit international"]; John Claydon, "The Application of International Human Rights Law by Canadian Courts" (1981) 30 Buff. L. R. 727 [J. Claydon, "The Application of International Human Rights Law by Canadian Courts"]; Alice Desjardins, "La mise en oeuvre au Canada des traités relatifs aux droits de la personne" (1981) 12 R.G.D. 359; Maxwell Cohen and Anne

Bayefsky, "The Canadian Charter of Rights and Freedoms and International Law" (1983) 61 Can. Bar Rev. 265 [M. Cohen and A. Bayefsky, "The Canadian Charter of Rights and Freedoms and International Law"]; Jacques-Yvan Morin, "La personnalité internationale du Québec" (1984) 1 R.Q.D.I. 163 [J.-Y. Morin, "La personnalité internationale du Québec"]; Daniel Turp, "Le recours en droit international aux fins de l'interprétation de la Charte canadienne des droits et libertés: un bilan jurisprudentiel" (1984) 18 R.J.T. 353; John Humphrey, "The Canadian Charter of Rights and Freedoms and International Law" (1985-86) 50 Sask. L. Rev. 13; Michel Lebel, "L'interprétation de la Charte canadienne des droits et libertés au regard du droit international des droits de la personne – Critique de la démarche suivie par la Cour suprême du Canada" (1988) 48 R. du B. 743; Armand L.C. De Mestral, "Le Québec et les relations internationales" in Pierre Patenaude, ed., *Québec – Communauté française de Belgique*, (Montréal: Wilson & Lafleur, 1991) 209 [A.L.C. de Mestral, "Le Québec et les relations internationales"]; Anne Bayefsky, "International Human Rights Law in Canadian Courts" in Irwin Cotler and Pearl Éliadis, eds., *International Human Rights Law – Theory and Practice* (Montréal: CHRF, 1992) 115 [A. Bayefsky, "International Human Rights Law in Canadian Courts"]; Douglas Sanders, "The Canadian Charter and the Protection of International Human Rights" (1993) 4 Crim. L.F. 413; Irit Weiser, "Effect in Domestic Law of International Human Rights Treaties Ratified without Implementing Legislation" (1998) 27 Can. Council Int'l L. Proc. 132; Karen Knop, "Here and There: International Law in Domestic Courts" (2000) 32 N.Y.U.J. Int'l Law & Pol. 501 [K. Knop, "Here and There: International Law in Domestic Courts"]; Hugh Kindred, "Canadians as Citizens of the International Community: Asserting Unimplemented Treaty Rights in the Courts" in Stephen G. Coughlan and Dawn Russell, eds., *Citoyenneté et participation à l'administration de la justice / Citizenship and Citizen Participation in the Administration of Justice* (Montréal: Thémis, 2001) 265 [H. Kindred, "Canadians as Citizens of the International Community: Asserting Unimplemented Treaty Rights in the Courts"]; Stephen J. Toope, "Inside and Out: The Stories of International Law and Domestic Law" (2001) 50 U.N.B L.J. 11; Stephen J. Toope, "The Uses of Metaphor: International Law and the Supreme Court of Canada" (2001) 80 Can. Bar Rev. 534, reprinted in Stephen G. Coughlan and Dawn Russell, eds., *Citoyenneté et participation à l'administration de la justice / Citizenship and Citizen Participation in the Administration of Justice* (Montréal: Thémis, 2001) 289 (also available at <http://www.themis.umontreal.ca/ pdf/icaj_citoyennete/full_icaj_citoyennete.pdf>) [S.J. "The Uses of Metaphor: International Law and the Supreme Court of Canada" with reference to the version published in Stephen G. Coughlan and Dawn Russell, eds., *Citoyenneté et participation à l'administration de la justice / Citizenship and Citizen Participation in the Administration of Justice* (Montréal: Thémis, 2001)]; France Houle, "L'arrêt Baker: Le rôle des règles administratives dans la réception du droit international des droits de la personne en droit interne" (2002) 27 Queen's L.J. 511 [F. Houle, "L'arrêt Baker"]; Louis LeBel and Gloria Chao, "The Rise of International Law in Canadian Constitutional Litigation: Fugue or Fusion? Recent Developments and Challenges in Internalizing International Law" (2002) 16 Sup. Ct. L. Rev. (2nd) 23 [L. LeBel and G. Chao, "The Rise of International Law in Canadian Constitutional Litigation: Fugue or Fusion? Recent Developments and Challenges in Internalizing International Law"]; Stéphane Beaulac, "Recent Developments on the Role of International Law in Canadian Statutory Interpretation" (2004) 25 Stat. L. Rev. 19; Stéphane Beaulac, "National Application of International Law: The Statutory Interpretation Perspective" (2004) Can. Y.B. of Int'l L. 225; France Houle, "La légitimité constitutionnelle de la réception directe des normes du droit international des droits de la personne en droit interne canadien" (2004) 45 C. de D. 295 [F. Houle, "La légitimité constitutionnelle de la réception

never accepted the "Gérin-Lajoie doctrine". They all claimed that the federal authorities were the ones who could speak for Canada and that provinces may, with the consent of federal authorities, play certain limited roles in Canada's foreign relations. But sovereignty was the prism through which political desires were read. And, according to this mindset, because a sovereign state ought not only to enjoy the powers to make treaties but should also enjoy the domestic powers to implement

---

directe des normes du droit international des droits de la personne en droit interne canadien"] (edited version of France Houle, "La réception du droit international des droits de la personne en droit interne canadien: de la théorie de la séparation des pouvoirs vers une approche fondée sur les droits fondamentaux" in Patricia Hughes and Patrick Molinari, eds., *Justice et participation dans un monde global: la nouvelle règle de droit? / Participatory Justice in a Global Economy: The New Rule of Law? Proceedings of the Canadian Institute for the Administration of Justice Conference, Banff, 2003* (Montréal: Thémis, 2004)) 173); Stéphane Beaulac, "The Canadian Federal Constitutional Framework and the Implementation of the Kyoto Protocol" (2005) 5 R.J.P. 125; Joanna Harrington, "Redressing the Democratic Deficit in Treaty Law Making" (2005) 50 McGill L.J. 465 [J. Harrington, "Redressing the Democratic Deficit in Treaty Law Making"]; Joanna Harrington, "Scrutiny and Approval: The Role for Westminster-style Parliaments in Treaty-Making" (2006) 55 I.C.L.Q. 121 [J. Harrington, "Scrutiny and Approval: The Role for Westminster-style Parliaments in Treaty-Making"]; Joanna Harrington, "The Role for Parliament in Treaty-Making" in Oonagh Fitzgerald *et al.*, eds., *The Globalized Rule of Law: Relationships between International and Domestic Law* (Toronto: Irwin Law, 2006) 159.

Books have also been written about the treaties and Canadian domestic law. See among others: James M. Hendry, *Treaties and Federal Constitutions* (Washington: Public Affairs Press, 1955); Jacques Brossard, André Patry and Elisabeth Weiser, eds., *Les pouvoirs extérieurs du Québec* (Montréal: Presses Universitaires de l'Université de Montréal, 1967); Allan E. Gotlieb, *Canadian Treaty Making* (Toronto: Butterworths, 1968); Canada, Department of Foreign Affairs, *Federalism and International Relations* by Paul Martin, Sr. (Ottawa: Queen's Printer, 1968) [P. Martin, Sr., *Federalism and International Relations*]; Anne-Marie Jacomy-Millette, *Treaty Law in Canada*, trans. by Thomas V. Helwig (Ottawa: University of Ottawa Press, 1975) [Anne-Marie Jacomy-Millette, *Treaty Law in Canada*]; William Schabas, *International Human Rights Law and the Canadian Charter*, 2nd ed. (Toronto: Carswell, 1996); Gibran van Ert, *Using International Law in Canadian Courts* (New York: Kluwer Law International, 2002) [G. van Ert, *Using International Law in Canadian Courts*]; Oonagh E. Fitzgerald, ed., *The Globalized Rule of Law: Relationship Between Domestic and International Law* (Toronto: Irwin Law, 2006); William Schabas and Stéphane Beaulac, *International Human Rights and Canadian Law — Legal Commitment, Implementation and the Charter* (Toronto: Thomson Carswell, 2007).

As for general constitutional doctrine, one can refer to the following classic references: Kenneth C. Wheare, *Federal Government*, 3rd ed. (London: Oxford University Press, 1953) at 178ff.; Frederick P. Varcoe, *The Constitution of Canada* (Toronto: Carswell, 1965) at 178ff.; Bora Laskin, *Canadian Constitutional Law*, 4th ed. by Albert S. Abel and John I. Laskin (Toronto: Carswell, Toronto, 1975) at 202ff.; François Chevrette and Herbert Marx, *Droit constitutionnel: notes et jurisprudence* (Montréal: Presses de l'Université de Montréal, 1982) at 1181ff. [F. Chevrette and H. Marx, *Droit constitutionnel*].

them, many authors favourable to Ottawa's position have, over the years, called for a reversal of the famous *Labour Conventions* decision.

The issue of provincial treaty powers was never entirely resolved. However, Québec did not wait for approval to engage more deeply in international affairs. In effect, the *Ministère des Relations internationales* claims that Québec is currently engaged in "prospecting and promotion" activities,[42] "intergovernmental cooperation" and development of international norms.[43] These actions are made possible not only by an important bureaucratic apparatus in Québec city but also by six "general delegations" covering all sectors of provincial jurisdiction,[44] four delegations with a more limited mandate,[45] nine government bureaux offering limited service to a single sector,[46] six trade branches headed by a resident of the host country and offering services in limited sectors[47] and three business agents.[48]

---

[42] The *Ministère des Relations internationales* explains these two terms in the following way:

> Prospecting consists in recruiting investors and immigrants, exploring export markets, targeting groups of potential tourists and encouraging organizers to hold their conventions and cultural events in Québec. The deployment of these functions is greatly facilitated by Québec's permanent presence abroad. In the case of recruiting and selecting immigration candidates, this foreign presence is essential.

> Efforts by Québec to promote its attractions, socioeconomic characteristics and culture are distinct from but closely related to prospecting activities, as they contribute to enhancing international awareness of Québec. This objective is achieved through lectures, Web sites, articles, advertising, and participation in trade shows, symposiums and exhibitions.

See Québec, *Ministère des Relations internationales, Activities – Prospecting and Promotion*, online: *Ministère des Relations internationales* <http://www.mri.gouv.qc. ca/en/politique_internationale/activites/prospection_promotion.asp> [Québec, *Activites – Prospecting and Promotion*] .

[43] See Québec, *Ministère des Relations internationales, Types of Activities*, online: *Ministère des Relations internationales* <http://www.mri.gouv.qc.ca/en/politique _internationale/activites/activites.asp>. The English version of the Ministère's text refers to "shared general standards" but the French version is more precise and uses the expression "normes internationales".

[44] They are in Brussels, London, Mexico City, New York City, Paris and Tokyo.

[45] They are in Boston, Buenos Aires, Chicago and Los Angeles.

[46] They are in Barcelona, Beijing, Damascus (Immigration Office), Hong Kong (Immigration Office), Miami, Munich, Shanghai, Vienna (Immigration Office) and Washington (Tourism Office).

[47] They are in Atlanta, Berlin, Rome, Santiago, Seoul and Taipei.

[48] They are in Lima, Hanoi and Milan. All this information is found at Québec, *Ministère des Relations internationales, Québec Offices Abroad*, online: *Ministère des Relations internationales* <http://www.mri.gouv.qc.ca/en/action_internationale/ representations_etranger/representations_etranger.asp>.

It is of particular interest to us here what the government of Québec does in terms of "intergovernmental cooperation" and development of international norms. Of the first type of action, the Ministère writes:

> For purposes of mutual support, economy and efficiency, governments often decide to pool their resources and expertise. The Government of Québec has thus developed official relations with a number of American states, particularly border states, over the years. It has also forged links with states and regions on other continents, based mainly on cultural affinities and economic complementarity. The framework for this type of cooperation is generally specified in an intergovernmental agreement.[49]

As for the second type of actions, the one about the development of international norms, the Ministère explains that "[t]he Government of Québec is affected in a number of ways by international standards,[50] particularly in areas under its jurisdiction such as labour, health, civil law, education and justice administration."[51] The Ministère states that certain norms "are negotiated bilaterally by individual governments – e.g., standards negotiated by Québec with respect to recognition of driver's licences, international adoption and judicial cooperation." Since 1964, Québec has entered into at least 550 international agreements with international bodies and foreign governments on a wide range of issues (e.g. agriculture, education, energy, transportation, telecommunications, environment, etc.).[52]

Regarding the complex issue of international norms that are elaborated by international organisations or adopted at international conferences, the Ministère writes:

> In most cases, Québec is not a member of the international organization in question. It nevertheless contributes to the organization's efforts by assigning experts to organizational task forces and cooperating with the federal government prior to input by the latter as a member of the organization. In some cases, Québec participates in organizational decision-making as part of the Canadian delegation. In the case of the Organisation internationale de la francophonie ("La Francophonie") and its agencies, the Government of Québec participates directly as a full-fledged member.

---

[49] Québec, *Ministère des Relations internationales, Activities – Intergovernmental Cooperation*, online: *Ministère des Relations internationales* <http://www.mri.gouv. qc.ca/en/politique_internationale/activites/cooperation.asp>.

[50] Again, the French version uses the expression "norme".

[51] Québec, *Ministère des Relations internationales, Activities – Development of Shared General Standards*, online: *Ministère des Relations internationales* <http://www. mri.gouv.qc.ca/en/politique_internationale/activites/normes.asp> [Québec, *Activities – Development of Shared General Standards*].

[52] Québec, *Ministère des Relations internationales, International Commitments*, online: *Ministère des Relations internationales* <http://www.mri.gouv.qc.ca/en/action_ internationale/ententes/index.asp>.

The Government of Québec also participates directly in negotiations aimed at harmonizing certain legislation of federal component states in various countries.

In some cases, thanks to its experience and the expertise available in Québec, the Government of Québec plays a highly influential international role. In 1999, for instance, Québec was responsible for the original initiative aimed at promoting and developing an international legal instrument in the area of cultural diversity.[53]

All the while Québec and other provinces are actively involved internationally, the federal government refuses to recognize that provinces possess a limited *jus tractatus*. However, in the last few years, probably as a result of the increasing impacts of globalisation and the creation of transnational legal regimes, the issue of managing treaty powers has resurfaced with vigour in Canada, as it has in other federations.[54] The

---

[53] See Québec, *Activities – Development of Shared General Standards, supra* note 51. The *Ministère* refers to the *Convention on the Protection and Promotion of the Diversity of Cultural Expressions* approved at the General Conference of the United Nations Educational, Scientific and Cultural Organization (UNESCO) on 20 October, 2005 (UNESCO, *Convention on the Protection and Promotion of the Diversity of Cultural Expressions*, 20 October, 2005 online: UNESCO <http://unesdoc.unesco.org/images/0014/001429/142919e.pdf>). On 10 November, 2005, the *Assemblée nationale* unanimously adopted the following resolution: "... conformément à l'article 22.3 de la *Loi sur le ministère des Relations internationales*, l'Assemblée nationale approuve l'entente internationale concernant la Convention sur la protection et la promotion de la diversité des expressions culturelles." (Québec, National Assembly, *Journal of Debates*, 37th Leg. 1st sess., Vol. 38 No. 182 (10 November 2005).

[54] For example, the debates about federalism and international law in the United States have regained a lot of vigour in the last few years. See for example: Jack L. Goldsmith, "Federal Courts, Foreign Affairs, and Federalism" (1997) 83 Va. L. Rev. 1617; Gerald L. Neuman, "The Global Dimension of RFRA" (1997) 14 Const. Commentary 33; Gavin R. Villareal, "One Leg to Stand On: The Treaty Power and Congressional Authority for the Endangered Species Act After United States v. Lopez", Note, (1998) 76 Tex. L. Rev. 1125; James A. Deeken, "A New Miranda For Foreign Nationals? The Impact of Federalism on International Treaties that Place Affirmative Obligations on State Governments in the Wake of Printz v. United States", Note, (1998) 31 Vand. J. Transnat'l L. 997; Thomas Healy, "Is Missouri v. Holland Still Good Law? Federalism and the Treaty Power", Note, (1998) 98 Colum. L. Rev. 1726; G. Edward White, "The Transformation of the Constitutional Regime of Foreign Relations" (1999) 85 Va. L. Rev. 1; Michael D. Ramsey, "The Power of the States in Foreign Affairs: The Original Understanding of Foreign Policy Federalism" (1999) 75 Notre Dame L. Rev. 341; Curtis A. Bradley, "The Treaty Power and American Federalism" (1998) 97 Mich. L. Rev. 390; Curtis A. Bradley, "The Treaty Power and American Federalism II" (2000) 99 Mich. L. Rev. 98; David M. Golove, "Treaty-Making and the Nation: The Historical Foundations of the Nationalist Conception of the Treaty Power" (2000) 98 Mich. L. Rev. 1075; Omar N. White, "The Endangered Species Act's Precarious Perch: A Constitutional Analysis Under the Commerce Clause and the Treaty Power", Comment, (2000) 27 Ecology L.Q. 215; Edward T. Swaine, "Negotiating Federalism: State Bargaining and the Dormant Treaty Power" (2000) 49 Duke L.J. 1127; Janet R.

tensions between centralism and provincial self-government as well as the need felt for an effective presence at the international level have fuelled intense political debates.[55] It is time to review the state of Cana-

---

Carter, "Commandeering Under the Treaty Power", Note, (2001) 76 N.Y.U.L. Rev. 598; Robert Anderson IV, "'Ascertained in a Different Way': The Treaty Power at the Crossroads of Contract, Compact, and Constitution" (2001) 69 Geo. Wash. L. Rev. 189; Robert Knowles, "Starbucks and the New Federalism: The Court's Answer to Globalization", Note, (2001) 95 Nw. U.L. Rev. 735; James J. Pascoe, "Time for a New Approach? Federalism and Foreign Affairs after Crosby v. National Foreign Trade Council" (2002) 35 Vand. J. Transnat'l L. 291; Edward T. Swain, "Does Federalism Constrain the Treaty Power?" (2003) 103 Colum. L. Rev. 403; Ana Maria Merico-Stephens, "Of Federalism, Human Rights, and the Holland Caveat: Congressional Power to Implement Treaties" (2004) 25 Mich. J. Int'l L. 265; Katrina L. Fischer, "Harnessing the Treaty Power in Support of Environmental Regulation of Activities that Don't 'Substantially Affect Interstate Commerce': Recognizing the Realities of the New Federalism" (2004) 22 Va. Envtl. L.J. 167; Nicholas Quinn Rosenkrantz, "Executing the Treaty Powers" (2005) 118 Harv. L. Rev. 1867; Ryan Patton, "Federal Preemption in an Age of Globalization", Note, (2005) 37 Case W. Res. J. Int'l L. 111. See also the articles published in the three following Symposia: *Foreign Affairs Law at the End of the Century*, (1999) 70 U. Colo. L. Rev. 1089; *New Voices on the New Federalism*, (2001) 46 Vill. L. Rev. 907; *Federal Courts and Foreign Affairs*, (2002) 42 Va. J. Int'l L. 365.

[55] Here is a sample of the newspaper articles published on the issue between October 2004 and October 2005: Gilles Toupin, "Martin reçoit l'aval de Chirac pour son G20" *La Presse* (15 October 2004) A21; Serge Joyal, "La fin du Canada ? D'une asymétrie à l'autre, il risque de rester bien peu de la fédération" *La Presse* (22 October 2004) A19; Lysiane Gagnon, "Howard Dean à Montréal" *La Presse* (28 October 2004) A21; Mario Cloutier, "Rencontre Charest-Fox" *La Presse* (29 October 2004) A8; Louise Beaudouin, "Remettre le Québec à sa place" *La Presse* (19 November 2004) A14; Mario Cloutier, "Mission au Mexique" *La Presse* (20 November 2004) A19; Joël-Denis Bellavance, "Harper promet de laisser le Québec s'exprimer sur la scène internationale" *La Presse* (28 November 2005) A3; Benoît Pelletier, "Un rôle accru" *La Presse* (1 December 2004) A21; Gilles Normand, "Conseil de la fédération" *La Presse* (27 December 2004) A16; Éric Clément, "Le Québec et la France main dans la main" *La Presse* (8 January 2005) A6; Jocelyne Richer, "Québec veut contribuer au succès des élections en Haïti" *La Presse* (5 February 2005) A8; Isabelle Hachey, "Le début d'un temps nouveau" *La Presse* (6 February 2005) PLUS 5; Constant Brand, "Charest réclame un plus grand rôle international pour le Québec" *La Presse* (5 March 2005) A14; Jocelyne Richer, "Jean Charest souhaite rencontrer Hillary Clinton à Washington" *La Presse* (12 March 2005) A18; Tommy Chouinard and Joël-Denis Bellavance, "Conseil de la fédération" *La Presse* (10 August 2005) A9; Isabelle Rodrigue, "Pettigrew tient son bout face à Charest" *La Presse* (9 September 2005) A11; Isabelle Rodrigue, "Pettigrew et Pelletier bientôt face à face" *La Presse* (13 September 2005) A23; Tommy Chouinard, "Relations internationales" *La Presse* (15 September 2005) A10; Michel Gauthier, "Le parti libéral n'a pas de leçon à donner à personne" *La Presse* (16 September 2005) A21; Marie-Claude Lemieux, "Boisclair veut faire mieux que René Lévesque" *La Presse* (19 September 2005) A1; André Pratte, "Deux doctrines" *La Presse* (19 September 2005) A16; Gilles Toupet, "Rejet du projet de loi sur la consultation des provinces" *La Presse* (30 September 2005) A7; Presse Canadienne, "Line Beauchamp parlera pour le Canada" *La Presse* (4 October 2005) A7; Sylvain Larocque, "Désaccord sur le rôle du Québec sur la scène interna-

tionale" (5 October 2005) A5; Réginald Harvey, "Concertation et coopération" *Le Devoir* (9 octobre 2004) G3; Antoine Robitaille, "La goutte d'eau de trop dans le vase asymétrique" *Le Devoir* (16 October 2004) B4; Michel David, "La doctrine Charest" *Le Devoir* (23 November 2004) A3; Alec Castonguay, "Paul Martin envoie des renforts à Sgro et Frulla" *Le Devoir* (3 December 2004) A3; Jean-Guillaume Dumont, "Faute de leadership, le Québec stagne" *Le Devoir* (5 February 2005) G5; Christian Rioux, "Québec veut participer aux négociations avec l'Europe" *Le Devoir* (4 March 2005) A2; Normand Thériault, "Au cœur des nations" *Le Devoir* (9 March 2005) C1; Claude Morin, "L'obstacle oublié" *Le Devoir* (9 March 2005) C6; Mylène Tremblay, "Retour sur la doctrine Gérin-Lajoie" *Le Devoir* (9 March 2005) C7; Stéphane Paquin, "Une réforme indispensable" *Le Devoir* (9 March 2005) C6; Jean-Guillaume Dumont, "Le gouvernement doit agir pour préserver l'identité québécoise" *Le Devoir* (9 March 2005) C5; Robert Aird, "Signé André Patry" *Le Devoir* (9 March 2005) C4; Michel David, "Les slogans creux" *Le Devoir* (19 March 2005) B3; Éric Desrosiers, "Se mêler de ses affaires" *Le Devoir* (19 March 2005) C3; Michel David, "Le prix de la mollesse" *Le Devoir* (30 June 2005) A3; Robert Dutrisac, "Ottawa se crispe, Québec s'alarme" *Le Devoir* (2 July 2005) A1; Jocelyne Richer, "Québec veut s'avancer sur la scène internationale" *Le Devoir* (9 August 2005) A3; Louise Harel and Gilles Duceppe, "Le Québec n'est plus libre de ses choix" *Le Devoir* (18 August 2005) A7; Danic Parenteau and Ian Parenteau, "La question de l'identité québécoise à l'heure de l'altermondialisme" *Le Devoir* (22 August 2005) A6; Lucie Lamarche, "La place du Québec sur la scène internationale: qu'en est-il des droits de la personne?" *Le Devoir* (24 August 2005) A7; Daniel Turp, "Je ne suis pas candidat et j'appuie André Boisclair" *Le Devoir* (26 August 2005) A9; Monique Gagnon-Tremblay, "L'action internationale du Québec et les droits de la personne: des efforts réels" *Le Devoir* (31 August 2005) A7; Robert Dutrisac, "Le Canada doit parler d'une seule voix" *Le Devoir* (2 September 2005) A1; Robert Dutrisac, "Québec entend renforcer la doctrine Gérin-Lajoie" *Le Devoir* (3 September 2005) A5; Bernard Descôteaux, "Le corset de M. Pettigrew" *Le Devoir* (6 September 2005) A6; Stéphane Paquin, "La réforme proposée par le gouvernement du Québec est plus nécessaire que jamais" *Le Devoir* (9 September 2005) A9; Robert Aird, "La magie canadienne" *Le Devoir* (9 September 2005) A9; Louise Beaudouin, "Mensonges et reculs" *Le Devoir* (9 September 2005) A9; Isabelle Rodrigue, "Pettigrew craint une récupération par les 'fanatiques de l'indépendance'" *Le Devoir* (9 September 2005) A1; Benoit Pelletier and Monique Gagnon-Tremblay, "La doctrine Gérin-Lajoie: un cadre de référence toujours d'actualité" *Le Devoir* (10 September 2005) B5; Bernard Descôteaux, "Les sophismes de Pettigrew" *Le Devoir* (10 September 2005) B4; Presse Canadienne and Le Devoir, "Québec hausse le ton" (10 September 2005) A1; Chantal Hébert, "Pettigrew Kamikaze" *Le Devoir* (12 September 2005) A3; Presse Canadienne, "Pettigrew et Pelletier se parleront" *Le Devoir* (13 September 2005) A3; Robert Dutrisac, "Québec fera sa place dans le monde après entente avec Ottawa" *Le Devoir* (15 September 2005) A3; Hélène Buzzetti, "La bonne vieille méthode" *Le Devoir* (21 September 2005) A3; Monique Gagnon-Tremblay, "C'est la meilleure entente qui soit" *Le Devoir* (23 September 2005) A8; Tomy Menninger, "Les États fédérés et la scène internationale" *Le Devoir* (28 September 2005) A6; Antoine Robitaille, "C'est à Ottawa de parler de droits de l'homme, dit l'entourage de Charest" *Le Devoir* (30 September 2005) A4; Sylvain Larocque, "Pettigrew fait baisser les attentes" *Le Devoir* (3 October 2005) A3; Alec Castonguay, "Diversité culturelle: dernière ligne droite à l'UNESCO" *Le Devoir* (3 October 2005) A1; Antoine Robitaille, "Le débat sur la place du Québec continue de faire rage" *Le Devoir* (5 October 2005) A2; The Gazette, "Ex-MNA Christos Sirros named as Quebec's man in Brussels" The Gazette (7 October 2004) A16; Mike de Souza, "Harper touts Belgium as a Federal model" The Gazette

dian constitutional law in relation to treaty-making powers and to reas-

(16 October 2004) A13; Anne Dawson, "Harper backs ADQ program" The Gazette (19 October 2004) A12; The Gazette, "Who wants a more complicated Canada" The Gazette (20 October 2004) A30; Anne Dawson, "Belgium" plan might be tough sell in Ontario" The Gazette (22 October 2004) A14; Mike de Souza, "Charest as little to say on anti-missile shield" The Gazette (1 December 2004) A12; Kevin Dougherty, "Our man in London" The Gazette (5 December 2004) D.1.BRE; Mike de Souza, "Ex-ambassador challenges Quebec's international role" The Gazette (18 February 2005) A9; Mike de Souza, "Canada should play bigger international role: Pettigrew" The Gazette (19 February 2005) A11; Elizabeth Thompson, "Feds set to work with Quebec" The Gazette (6 March 2005) A6; Irwin Block and Mike de Souza, "Pelletier makes pitch for greater Quebec role" The Gazette (18 March 2005) A8; Kevin Dougherty, "Vietnam orphans caught in war of words: Accord scuttled Ottawa, Quebec in jurisdiction fight" The Gazette (2 July 2005) A12; Kevin Dougherty, "Feds, province end Vietnam adoption spat" The Gazette (13 September 2005) A17; Don Macdonald, "Charest outlines goals of trip to China" The Gazette (14 September 2005) B1; Kevin Dougherty, "Wider role sought on world stage: Provincial minister takes hard line with Pettigrew" The Gazette (15 September 2005) A11; Josée Legault, "Pettigrew makes me pine for the Stephane Dion days" The Gazette (16 September 2005) A21; Kevin Dougherty, "Deal signed in Quebec to resume Vietnamese adoptions" The Gazette (16 September 2005) A9; Don Macpherson, "Quebec, Ottawa spar over foreign affairs" The Gazette (17 September 2005) A31; The Gazette "Canada must speak in one united voice" The Gazette (19 September 2005) A22; Monique Gagnon-Tremblay, "Quebec needs place at table" The Gazette (3 September 2005) A21; Elizabeth Thompson, "Province, feds jockey over roles in world: Quebec minister to read part of UNESCO speech" The Gazette (4 October 2005) A10; Anne Dawson, "Harper's Canada: Belgium: Calls for devolved powers, backs Dumont's Quebec plan" National Post (19 October 2004) A1; National Post, "Firewall folly, take two" National Post (20 October 2004) A23; Robert Fife, "PM threatens 'one Canada', Liberal says: Asymmetrical federalism" National Post (21 October 2004) A4; Stephen Harper, "My plan for 'open' federalism" National Post (27 October 27 2004) A19; Graeme Hamilton, "'Country' of Quebec" National Post (15 November 2004) A6; Mike de Souza, "Quebec bids to improve international presence" National Post (18 February 2005) A8; Monique Gagnon-Tremblay, "Quebec and America" National Post (14 March 2005) A17; Robert Sauvé, "Americans' view of Quebecers" National Post (15 March. 2005) A17; Jack Aubry, "Ottawa set to discuss Quebec's world role: Seeks increased profile" National Post (1 September 2005) A9; Lorne Gunter, "Who may speak for Canada?" National Post (12 September 2005) A11; The Globe and mail, "France and Quebec plan joint mission" The Globe and Mail (14 October 2004) A1; Jeffrey Simpson, "Ottawa, please stop trying to please" The Globe and Mail (15 October 2004) A23; Jeffrey Brooke *et al.*, "With the Liberal Party holding a policy convention this weekend, the Globe and Mail asked a sampling of members for their views on three issues" The Globe and Mail (5 March 2005) A4; Alan Freeman, "Premiers raise fear over border plans. Charest, McGuinty talk to US official" The Globe and Mail (19 April 2005) A18; The Globe and Mail, "Martin chats with Globe's editorial board. Sweeping conversation covers successes, economy, NDP, Darfur and Gomery probe" The Globe and Mail (26 April 2005) A6; Shawn McCarthy, "Chretien defends handling of ad scandal" The Globe and Mail (30 April 2005) A19; Konrad Yakabuski, "Big dreams in Canada's city that never sleeps. The mayor is working overtime to help Montreal get its groove back" The Globe and Mail (16 July 2005) A3; Rhéal Séguin, "Quebec will work with Ottawa in representing Canada abroad" The Globe and Mail (15 September 2005) A4.

sess the assumptions that have lain behind the different positions in order to better imagine ways to go forward in the new world order that we are now facing.

The Canadian federation is deeply involved in the web of relations with other states and non-state actors that form our current world order. However, despite the fact that the federal and provincial governments are actively engaged in establishing and maintaining such relations, the exact operational boundaries of each player are the subject of disagreement among them. As we have seen, this is partly due to the fact that the written Constitution of Canada does not expressly attribute the powers to make and implement international agreements binding on Canada or the provinces. A second factor that helps explain the lack of express resolution of the operational boundaries between the federal government and the provinces in relation to international agreements flows from a mistaken association between two questions: the recognition of the international capacity to make treaties and the international recognition of an independent state. Again, as I have said, fearing that any recognition of provincial powers over treaties could feed the Québec sovereignist theses, the federal government has, over the second-half of the last century, tended systematically to downplay the federalist nature of the treaty powers in favour of a centralisation of such powers in Ottawa.

However, it appears that there is more than enough constitutional material to construct an appropriate and rather precise set of operational rules defining the respective roles of the federal and provincial authorities. Furthermore, it is entirely possible to solve the longstanding conflict between Ottawa and Québec on this issue without having any impact – positive or negative – on the strength of a potential provincial bid to obtain international recognition after having declared secession from the rest of Canada. In the next section, I will briefly flesh out the constitutional traditions that inform the way in which I will go about uncovering the set of constitutional imperatives that govern treaty powers in Canada.

The Voluntarist and the Organic Constitutional Perspectives

The reader might wonder why the *Constitution Act, 1867*[56] does not expressly allocate either to the federal or provincial authorities the powers to engage in international relations. Why is there such an obvious gap? While many states have clear constitutional provisions dealing with international relations and the incorporation of international law

---

[56] *Constitution Act, 1867, supra* note 39.

within their domestic sphere,[57] Canada did not have at the time of Gérin-Lajoie's address – and still, to this day, does not have – any active constitutional provision expressly referring to those subjects. Section 132 of the *Constitution Act, 1867* might seem relevant at first glance since it states that the Parliament and Government of Canada "shall have all Powers necessary or proper for performing the Obligations of Canada or of any Province thereof, as Part of the British Empire, towards Foreign Countries, arising under Treaties between the Empire and such Foreign Countries".[58] However, as Gérin-Lajoie rightly pointed out, this provision has become obsolete since Canada gained her international autonomy from Great Britain. Canada can no longer be bound by Imperial treaties adopted since then[59] and s. 132 is simply not applicable to treaties that Canada ratifies.[60] It must be remembered that the *Constitu-*

---

[57] For example, Article VI, § 2 of the *Constitution of the United States of America* declares that:

> This Constitution, and the Laws of the United States which shall be made in Pursuance thereof; and all Treaties made, or which shall be made, under the Authority of the United States, shall be the supreme Law of the Land; and the Judges in every State shall be bound thereby, any Thing in the Constitution or Laws of any State to the Contrary notwithstanding.

The Constitution of the United States declares at art. II, § 2, cl. 2 that the President "shall have power, by and with the advice and consent of the Senate, to make treaties, provided two thirds of the Senators present concur ..." and at art. I, § 10, cls. 1 and 3 that "[n]o state shall enter into any treaty, alliance, or confederation" and "[n]o state shall, without the consent of Congress ... enter into any agreement or compact with another state, or with a foreign power, or engage in war, unless actually invaded, or in such imminent danger as will not admit of delay".

[58] *Constitution Act, 1867, supra* note 39.

[59] Of course, Imperial treaties formed prior to Canada's international autonomy can still bind Canada according to the regular rules of state succession. However, s. 132 can no longer be used to justify implementation measures by the federal Parliament or Government of those treaties since those treaties no longer impose obligations on "Canada or of any Province thereof, *as Part of the British Empire*" (*Constitution Act, 1867, ibid.*, s. 132 (emphasis added)). *Contra R. v. Sikeya*, [1964] 2 C.C.C. 325, 43 C.R. 83, aff'd. [1965] 2 C.C.C. 129, 44 C.R. 266.

[60] *Labour Conventions* case, *supra* note 19 at 350 ("While it is true, as was pointed out in the *Radio* case, [1932] A.C. 304, that it was not contemplated in 1867 that the Dominion would possess treaty-making powers, it is impossible to strain the section [132] so as to cover the uncontemplated event."). This position is fully accepted by the federal government. In a letter dated February 1, 1985 (reproduced in Edward G. Lee, "Canadian Practice in International Law at the Department of External Affairs / La pratique canadienne en droit international en 1985 au ministère des Affaires extérieures" (1986) 24 Can. Y.B. Int. L. 386 at 397 in 1985 [Canada, Letter from the Legal Bureau of the Department of External Affairs to the Council of Europe (1 February 1985)]), the Legal Bureau of the Department of External Affairs replied to a Council of Europe questionnaire on treaty making practices that: "The Canadian Constitution contains no provisions regarding treaty-making apart from Section 132 of the

tion Act, 1867 was a colonial constitution and that the British Parliament did not expect, at the time of its enactment, that Canada and the provinces would engage in international relations on par with "sovereign states" and independently from London's Foreign Office.[61] This would not mean, however, that provincial governments, for example, could not engage in some activities abroad such as the recruitment of immigrants.[62] It simply means that, when the *Constitution Act, 1867* was adopted, treaty powers were not attributed to the federal government nor to the provinces but remained an Imperial prerogative.

The issue concerning the division of powers between federal authorities and the provinces in relation to international affairs thus emerged only as Canada gained her autonomy from the British Empire. Canada's autonomy from Great Britain was gained gradually. In the British tradition of flexible constitutionalism, changes were brought slowly and pragmatically through a series of statutes, administrative instruments, executive decisions and judicial opinions. Thus, in 1871, Canadian representatives participated in negotiations leading to an imperial treaty affecting Canada (*Treaty of Washington*, 1871[63]). Canada then signed such international agreements as a member of the Empire (*Treaty of Versailles*, 1919[64]) and finally signed such agreements on her own behalf (*Halibut Fisheries Treaty*, 1923[65]). At the 1926 Imperial Conference, the general principle to the effect that no autonomous Dominion

---

Constitution Act, 1867 [*supra* note 39], which has fallen into disuse because it has no relevance to present day conditions."

[61] It is to be noted, however, that the Federal Parliament has power over "Militia, Military and Naval Service, and Defence." See *Constitution Act, 1867, ibid.* s. 91 (7). However, this allocation of legislative jurisdiction did not mean that the Federal government was free to develop its own defence policies independently from London. S. 15 of the *Constitution Act, 1867, ibid.* clearly states that the Queen is the Commander-in-Chief of the militia, military and naval service and at the time, the Crown was still a pretty unified concept. For the gradual division of the Crown in the Empire, see section II.A.1.ii.

[62] *Constitution Act, 1867, ibid.*, s. 95 provides for concurrent federal and provincial power over immigration. For a brief overview of official representations made abroad by the province of Québec (starting in 1871 with the dispatch of immigration agents to the European continent, the British islands and to New England and with the opening of permanent offices in 1872 in Ireland and Scotland), see Québec, *Ministère des Relations internationales, History*, online: *Ministère des Relations internationales* <www.mri.gouv.qc.ca/en/politique_internationale/historique/historique.asp>.

[63] *Treaty between the United Kingdom and the United States for the Amicable Settlement of All Causes of Differences Between the Two Countries*, 8 May 1871, 17 U.S. Stat. 863, 143 Consol. T.S. 145 [*Treaty of Washington*].

[64] *Treaty of Peace between the Allied and Associated Powers and Germany*, 28 June 1919, 225 Cons. T.S. 188, 2 Bevans 43 (entered into force 28 June 1919) [*Treaty of Versailles*].

[65] *Halibut Fisheries Convention 1923*, 1923, 32 L.N.T.S. No. 93.

could be bound by commitments incurred by the Imperial Government except with the consent of the Dominion concerned was confirmed. The *Balfour Declaration* stated that "They (Great Britain and the Dominions) are autonomous communities within the British Empire, equal in status, in no way subordinate one to another in any aspect of their domestic or external affairs, though united by a common allegiance to the Crown, and freely associated as members of the British commonwealth of Nations".[66] The *Statute of Westminster* gave, in large parts, legal effect to that declaration in 1931.[67] The process leading to independence seems to have been mainly achieved by the end of the 1930s, when Canada entered World War II with a formal declaration of war issued separately from the United Kingdom's declaration of war. But the independence process was not completely over. Canada had gained her

---

[66] U.K., Inter-Imperial Relations Committee, *Proceedings and Memoranda (Balfour Declaration)*, E (I.R./26) Series, p. 2 [*Balfour Declaration*]. See also Maurice Olliver, ed., *The Colonial and Imperial Conferences from 1887 to 1937*, Vol. 3. (Ottawa: Queen's Printer, 1954) at 146.

[67] S. 4 of the *Statute of Westminster, 1931*, (U.K.), 22 & 23 Geo. V, c. 4 [*Statute of Westminster*] proclaimed that "No Act of Parliament of the United Kingdom passed after the commencement of this Act shall extend or be deemed to extend, to a Dominion as part of the law of that Dominion, unless it is expressly declared in that Act that that Dominion has requested, and consented to, the enactment thereof." However, s. 7 provided that:

> 7. (1) Nothing in this Act shall be deemed to apply to the repeal, amendment or alteration of the British North America Acts, 1867 to 1930, or any order, rule or regulation made thereunder.
>
> (2) The provisions of section two of this Act shall extend to laws made by any of the Provinces of Canada and to the powers of the legislatures of such Provinces.
>
> (3) The powers conferred by this Act upon the Parliament of Canada or upon the legislatures of the Provinces shall be restricted to the enactment of laws in relation to matters within the competence of the Parliament of Canada or of any of the legislatures of the Provinces respectively.

The Supreme Court of Canada claimed, in 1967 that:

> [t]here can be no doubt now that Canada has become a sovereign state. Its sovereignty was acquired in the period between its separate signature of the *Treaty of Versailles* in 1919 and the *Statute of Westminster*. Section 3 of the *Statute of Westminster*, provides in an absolutely clear manner and without any restrictions that the Parliament of a Dominion has full power to make laws having extra-territorial operation.

(*Re Ownership of Offshore Mineral Rights*, [1967] S.C.R. 792, 816 [*Re Ownership of Offshore Mineral Rights*]). S. 3 of the *Statute of Westminster* also provided that "the Parliament of a Dominion has full power to make laws having extra-territorial operation." However, as I will show later in section II.A.1.iv., (a) gaining international status does not necessarily mean gaining full formal independence and (b) the reference *Re Ownership of Offshore Mineral Rights* does not stand for the proposition that the federal government has inherited of the entire international powers of the federation.

international status, her international autonomy, but she had not yet completely gained her formal independence from the United Kingdom. In 1947, the King issued new Letters Patent to the Governor General devolving his remaining executive powers in relation to "Canada" to him:

> II. And We do hereby authorize and empower Our Governor General, with the advice of Our Privy Council for Canada or of any members thereof or individually, as the case requires, to exercise all powers and authorities lawfully belonging to Us in respect of Canada, and for greater certainty but not so as to restrict the generality of the foregoing to do and execute, in the manner aforesaid, all things that may belong to his office and to the trust We have reposed in him according to the several powers and authorities granted or appointed him by virtue of the Constitution Acts, 1867 to 1940 and the powers and authorities hereinafter conferred in these Letters Patent and in such Commission as may be issued to him under Our Great Seal of Canada and under such laws as are or may hereinafter be in force in Canada.[68]

In 1949, the possibility of appeal to the Privy Council was terminated. Canada had to wait until 1982 for the "patriation" of the Canadian constitution.[69] But the *Constitution Act, 1982*[70] was not the formal result of the Canadian Parliament and provincial legislatures but an annex to a British statute!

Because the independence of Canada from the United Kingdom was acquired over time through a continuous transformation of their mutual relationship, there is simply no clear demarcation line between the dependence and the independence periods. Thus, trying to identify the exact moment of their separation is akin to trying to identify the moment at which a man has lost enough hair to be considered bald...

Understanding that Canada's independence was achieved over time and not at a specific moment helps us understand two important things for the purpose of making sense of the evolution of treaty powers in Canada. First, it helps understand *why* Canada's "birth" as an independent country did not cause – nor was it the result of – an entirely new

---

[68] *Letters Patent Constituting the Office of the Governor General of Canada*, reproduced at R.S.C. 1985, Appendix II, No. 31 [*Letters Patent Constituting the Office of the Governor General of Canada*].

[69] The appeals to the judicial committee of the Privy Council were completely abolished by *An Act Amending the Supreme Court Act*, S.C. 1949, c.37, s. 3.

For various political reasons, including the fact that the federal government and the provinces could not agree on (1) a proper constitutional amending formula and on (2) an appropriate redistribution of powers between the center and the provinces, the core of the Canadian constitution could be amended only by London even after 1931.

[70] *Constitution Act, 1982*, being Schedule B to the *Canada Act 1982* (U.K.), 1982, c. 11 [*Constitution Act, 1982*].

constitutional order but happened through a continuous process of constitutional transformations. Second, because Canadian constitutionalism is not exclusively the product of constitutional enactments at specific points in time, the ways in which constitutional changes are conceived in Canada differ in very important ways from the ways those changes are conceived in a constitutionalism primarily based on narratives of popular will. Canadian constitutional law relating to international relations is much more a product of immanent progressive growth than an instant act of will. Let me say more about this.

Constitutional regimes that portray themselves as products of popular revolutions (such as the United States or France) have clearer narratives about their founding moments. I will call "Voluntarists" those revolutionary traditions and the traditions of others who mainly emphasise Will as the source of constitutional legitimacy. The narratives of those traditions are often constructed around the idea that the constitution is the product of the will of "the People",[71] a will that expressed itself through a rejection of past authorities. These traditions imagine "Peoples" as constitution-makers that intervene intermittently to set up structures of government after having made *tabula rasa* of their previous settings. Thus, revolutionary constitutionalism advocates both the destruction of a past and the construction of new institutional arrangements.[72] And because Peoples are conceived as capable of creating *ex nihilo* their new forms of government, they are constrained only by their own wills and desires. However, because the individuals who form Peoples would not be ready to submit themselves to arbitrary decisions (the alleged arbitrariness of authorities being often a motive invoked for revolutions), the constitutions that Peoples set up are imagined to be not only the result of their will, but also the expression of Reason. In fact, not being constrained by the remnants of the previous regimes, Peoples

---

[71] The famous preamble of the *Constitution of the United States of America, supra* note 57, declares: "We the People of the United States, in order to form a more perfect union, establish justice, insure domestic tranquility, provide for the common defense, promote the general welfare, and secure the blessings of liberty to ourselves and our posterity, do ordain and establish this Constitution for the United States of America." The "We the People" appeared as a collective agent earlier with the American Declaration of Independence. Jacques Derrida highlighted the *aporia* in the production of that Declaration: the People whose representatives signed the document was simultaneously constituted as a People by this Declaration. In other words, the Declaration was simultaneously a "declarative" and "performative" act. See Jacques Derrida, *"Déclarations d'indépendance"*, dans *Otobiographies: L'enseignement de Nietzsche et la politique du nom propre* (Paris: Galilée, 1984) at 13ff., translated in English at "Declarations of Independence" (1986) 15 New Political Science 7.

[72] For an interesting discussion of the tensions between law and revolution, see Paul W. Kahn, *The Reign Of Law: Marbury v. Madison and the Construction of America* (New Haven: Yale University Press, 1997).

imagine themselves trying to put in place the most "rational" system. They imagine themselves starting from scratch and putting in place an overall plan. The new constitutional imperatives are taken to be the will of the People which, hopefully, corresponds to reason institutionally incarnated.[73] The work of those who then follow the "founders" is to implement the founders' Will, to fill the gaps left in the masterwork of the founders and to protect the founders' achievements – at least until "the People" wakes up again after discovering that it had made a mistake earlier on[74] or that its will has changed.[75] This leads the Voluntarist

---

[73] Paul W. Kahn has demonstrated how Will and Reason have been perceived as separate and often conflicting sources of legitimacy in the American constitutional tradition (Paul W. Kahn, *Legitimacy and History: Self-Government in American Constitutional Theory* (New Haven: Yale University Press, 1992) [P.W. Kahn, *Legitimacy and History*]. Legitimacy, in the dominant American constitutional narratives, depends on the idea that (1) self-government has been established by the will of the People and continues to be exercised as the expression of that continuous will and (2) the Constitution is the embodiment of Reason. By Reason, I mean here a theorized form of practical reason that presents itself either in an achieved form or as a work in progress. Thus, Reason embodied in the Constitution is perceived as a limit on the unreflective moments of the People and as the result of its finer instants. A democratic polity might hope that the Will of the People will coincide with what is perceived as the requirements of Reason but it might not always be the case. When the two do not coincide, the polity has the gut-wrenching task of privileging one over the other. There is no necessary conflict here but there is always a potential one.

[74] There are at least two possible senses of "mistake" from the point of view of the Voluntarist. The first one refers to mistakes in the implementation of the initial Will of the People. Such mistakes can be corrected by the agents responsible for the implementation of the constitution. For example, courts might come to the conclusion that this or that constitutional doctrine that they have applied for some time is in fact not in conformity with the People's Will as expressed in the constitution. They will then go on to correct it without awakening the sleeping giant that is the People in order to do so. Such modification, at least in its rhetoric, is a restoration of the true meaning of the constitutional norm and does not require the intervention of the Constituent power. The second type of "mistake" is one that would require the intervention of the Constituent power to correct and that is a mistake in the constitutional imperative itself. In other words, that mistake would consist in the adoption of a wrong constitutional imperative or omission to adopt a proper constitutional imperative. Such mistake would require the intervention of the Constituent power since it means modifying the Will of the People.

Obviously, unless one has views as to how it is possible to determine with any precision the content of the Will of the collective agent that is "the People", the frontier between those two types of mistakes is not always easy to identify in practice. Understanding this helps to explain why so much attention has been brought in American constitutional scholarship to the proper interpretative methods to be used by judges when they are engaged in judicial review of state action. In effect, from the Voluntarist perspective, if one cannot distinguish between the two types of mistakes, one has a hard time justifying judicial review unless one finds a way for unelected judges to be conceived as not merely repeating what the People has said, repeating the voice of the Constituent power, but directly speaking in its name. One can read two of the most influential American constitutional theories of the 20th century as attempts to do

to allow for both dramatic changes in constitutional setting and very conservative attitudes once he believes that the constitutional imperatives in place are the institutionalised eternal truths of theoretical reason.

A purely Voluntarist perspective does not adequately fit Canadian constitutionalism. Although constitutional enactments account for large parts of Canada's governmental skeleton, the Will that is behind them is not clearly the one of "*the* People". Rather, the main Canadian constitutional narratives describe those constitutional enactments as the products of the will of a series of collective agents. For example, the *Constitution Act, 1867* was described recently by the Supreme Court as being the result of (a) the "initiative of elected representatives of the people then living in the colonies scattered across part of what is now Canada", (b) the approval of the "local Parliaments" and (c) a formal enactment

---

just that. See Alexander Bickel, *The Least Dangerous Branch: The Supreme Court at the Bar of Politics* (Indianapolis: Bobbs-Merrill, 1962) who, when the exercise of "passive virtues" was not sufficient, imagined Courts as trying to anticipate the future will of the People (but see Bickel's important qualifications in *Supreme Court and the Idea of Progress* (New York: Harper and Row, 1970) at 173-181) and John Hart Ely, *Democracy and Distrust: A Theory of Judicial Review* (Cambridge: Harvard University Press, 1980) who imagined courts as guardians of the accessibility of the political process rather than enforcers of substantive views. However, for Ely, when the process has been deficient, courts have a representation-reinforcement role that entails that they may substitute for an actual result the putative outcome that would have resulted from the political process had it been kept sufficiently open. On the other hand, the difficulty of identifying judicial review with the "voice of the People" and the need to heed the Will of the latter has led Robert Bork to suggest a constitutional amendment so that the current People could be able to override through legislative means every decision of the Supreme Court. See Robert Bork, *Slouching Toward Gomorrah: Modern Liberalism And American Decline* (New York: Regan Books, 1996) at 117-19. For an exploration of some other difficulties associated with the idea of constitutionality as the "voice of the People", see Jed Rubenfeld, *Freedom And Time: A Theory Of Self-Government* (New Haven: Yale University Press, 2001).

[75] On how the succeeding generations of American constitutionalists imagined their roles in relation to the American Constitution from its adoption until the 1990s, see the enlightening account of P.W. Kahn, *Legitimacy and History*, *supra* note 73.

Because American constitutionalism relies heavily on the "We the People" both as a source of legitimacy for the Constitution and as a source of legitimacy for everyday political decisions made by legislatures and the executive, it has to offer an account as to why these latter decisions ought to be constrained by the Constitution. In other words, if "the People" modifies the Constitution and the same "People" speaks through its elected officials in the legislatures, why are legislatures bound by constitutional norms? Would not it be an implicit indication that the People have changed their mind over certain constitutional issues when they adopt laws incompatible with the Constitution? Many constitutionalists have tried to solve that problem by distinguishing between the People acting as the "Constituent power" and the People acting in the course of "normal politics". For a version of such a "democratic dualism" theory, see Bruce Ackerman, *We The People: Foundations* (Cambridge: Harvard University Press, 1991), esp. c. 1, 9, 10 and 11.

by the Imperial Parliament in London.[76] And because Canada gradually became independent from the United Kingdom, that independence did not result in a momentous reconstruction of the Canadian constitutional order. As we have seen, independence was not the product of, nor did it result in, a complete reformulation of Canadian constitutional texts that would mark clearly the transition from dependence. In other words, the bulk of the *Constitution Act, 1867* has remained intact and the *Constitution Act, 1867* still dictates the division of powers between the federal government and the provinces according to the same terms. Even when the *Constitution Act, 1982* was adopted, seventeen years after Gérin-Lajoie's speech, changes made to the division of powers established by the *Constitution Act, 1867* between the center and the provinces were limited to the adoption of new constitutional amending formulas,[77] express provisions dealing with "equalization payments" between provinces[78] and provincial jurisdiction in relation to natural resources.[79] In other words, the "People" of Canada seems to have acquired their independence *in absentia*. It was not the occasion of a new start trumpeted by the People but rather the gradual transformation of power structure within organic wholes.

Although the *Constitution Act, 1982* broke the last constitutional ties to the British Parliament by providing for an entirely Canadian amending formula,[80] formal constitutional changes did not deal with the attribution of the authorities to form and implement treaties nor did they deal with the issue of who can intervene in international forums and maintain external relations.[81] From a Voluntarist perspective, it would

---

[76] See *Reference Re Secession of Québec*, [1998] 2 S.C.R. 217 at paras. 35-47 [*Reference Re Secession of Québec*].

[77] See *Constitution Act, 1982, supra* note 70, ss. 38-49.

[78] S. 36 (2) of the *Constitution Act, 1982, ibid.* provides that "Parliament and the government of Canada are committed to the principle of making equalization payments to ensure that provincial governments have sufficient revenues to provide reasonably comparable levels of public services at reasonably comparable levels of taxation."

[79] *Constitution Act, 1867, supra* note 39, s. 92A.

[80] In light of the uncertainties about the effects of devolutions on the so-called sovereignty of Parliament, one could possibly argue that the British Parliament still has the legal capacity to repeal the *Canada Act* of 1982. However, even if that repeal were to be valid for the purposes of the British legal system, the Canadian legal system would simply ignore it. To borrow a phrase from autopoiesis, the independence of the Canadian legal system means that it is now "operatively closed" to the British system.

[81] In fact, the *Constitution Act, 1982, supra* note 70, only mentions international law in the *Canadian Charter of Rights and Freedoms*, Part I of the *Constitution Act, 1982*, being Schedule B to the *Canada Act 1982* (U.K.), 1982, c.11 [*Canadian Charter of Rights and Freedoms*] once, guaranteeing that:

11. Any person charged with an   11. Tout inculpé a le droit:
offence has the right

appear utterly strange – if not a complete sign of weakness of will – that a state acquiring its independence does not have a comprehensive constitutional text that provides for at least all the essential aspects of its new autonomous life. And treaty powers seem quite important for a state that hopes to develop fruitful relations with other members of the international community. But the Canadian constitution is made of much more than simply Voluntarist constitutional enactments. The fact that the written constitutional texts are not taken to be exhaustive of the Constitution helps to understand why the Voluntarist perspective may sound partly foreign to Canadians. In fact, like its British counterpart, Canadian constitutionalism also relies greatly on an "Organic" constitutional narrative.[82]

The British Organic tradition[83] is one of slow, careful, pragmatic and

---

...	...
(g) not to be found guilty on account of any act or omission unless, at the time of the act or omission, it constituted an offence under Canadian or	g) de ne pas être déclaré coupable en raison d'une action ou d'une omission qui, au moment où elle est survenue, ne constituait pas une infraction d'après le
tional law or was criminal according to the general principles of law recognized by the community of nations; ...	droit interne du Canada ou le droit international et n'avait pas de caractère criminel d'après les principes généraux de droit reconnus par l'ensemble des nations; ...

This section, at best, recognizes implicitly through the word "or" placed between "Canadian" and "international law" that international law is distinct from Canadian law and that the former is not automatically incorporated into the latter – otherwise the word "Canadian" would be redundant.

[82] Lord Sankey famously wrote that the Canadian constitution was like a "living tree capable of growth and expansion within its natural limits" (*Edwards v. Canada (A.G.)*, [1930] A.C. 124 (P.C.) at 136 [*Edwards*]).

[83] The British Organic tradition is made up of many strands of thought that emphasize different purported similarities between law and biology. One of the major strands uses the organic metaphor to describe the nature of the polity by comparing it to an organic entity. A classic example of such use of the organic metaphor is to be found in John of Salisbury's *Policraticus* (John of Salisbury, *Policraticus (1159)*, transl. and ed. by Cary J. Nederman (Cambridge: Cambridge University Press, 1990) at 66-69) where Salisbury analogized the polity to a person to highlight both the mutual dependency of each member of the polity and to justify a certain structure of authority where each "member" and "organ" has a specific function in the maintenance of the general body. For a stimulating history of the idea of the "body politic" and the "corpus mysticum" in the Middle Age, see Ernst Kantorowicz, *The Kings Two Bodies: A Study in Mediaeval Political Theology* (Princeton: Princeton University Press, 1957) [Kantorowicz, *The Kings Two Bodies*]. See also: David George Hale, *The Body Politic: A Political Metaphor in Renaissance English Literature* (The Hague-Paris, Mouton, 1971).

It is important to note, however, that the organic perspective does *not* have to be committed to the "human body" metaphor. For example, in the context of understanding the place of Aboriginal rights in Canada, Brian Slattery argues that an organic

continuous jurisprudential developments through *analogical* reasoning from case to case.[84] But what characterises the Organic perspective is not only the fact of gradual growth but also the imperative that each decision be harmoniously integrated within an already dense web of earlier decisions. The Organic perspective is biased towards incremental changes that have to fit within an already well-developed structure. From an Organic perspective, order is conceived as the preservation of a dense fabric of assumptions and expectations.[85] Past decisions are

---

conception of the Constitution ought to be viewed as an appropriate alternative to what he conceived as the inappropriate "Imperial model" of constitutionalism that emphasises monism and sovereignty as the power to command obedience (see Brian Slattery, "The Organic Constitution: Aboriginal Peoples and the Evolution of Canada" (1996) 34 Osgoode Hall L.J. 101). Thus, Slattery argues that Canada is a "multinational federation" (*ibid.* at 107) with a Constitution that "is the product of slow and continuing growth" (*ibid.* at 108). And that Constitution is "not limited to such enactments as the Constitution Acts of 1867 and 1982" and "[t]hese enactments depend for their legitimacy on a more fundamental body of law, which may be called the common law of the Constitution" (*ibid.* at 109). Slattery's organic model, "subscribes to a pluralist conception of the sources of law and authority, viewing the Crown as the constitutional trustee of coordinate spheres of jurisdiction rather than their exclusive source" and "it portrays the law as immanent in our collective practices and traditions" (*ibid.* at 111). Jean Leclair proposes a similar organic model as the foundation of his "federal constitutionalism" (see Jean Leclair, "Federal Constitutionalism and Aboriginal Difference" (2006) 31 Queen's L. J. 521). Thus, according to this organic model, law is not mainly the product of the command expressed by the "Head" to the other "members" of the "body politic" but is rather the result of the immanent growth of the different parts within the body itself. This leads to another strand of the Organic tradition (legal development as organic growth) that will be presented in more detail in what follows.

84 Earl of Halsbury L.C. wrote in *Quinn v. Leathem*, [1901] A.C. 495 (H.L.), at p. 506 [*Quinn*]) that:

there are two observations of a general character which I wish to make, and one is to repeat what I have very often said before, that every judgment must be read as applicable to the particular facts proved, or assumed to be proved, since the generality of the expressions which may be found there are not intended to be expositions of the whole law, but governed and qualified by the particular facts of the case in which such expressions are to be found. The other is that a case is only an authority for what it actually decides.

Albert V. Dicey also agreed with these two principles. See Albert V. Dicey, *An Introduction to the Study of the Constitution*, 10th ed. with an introduction of Emlyn C.S. Wade (London: MacMillan, 1967) [Dicey, *An Introduction to the Study of the Constitution*] at 291.

85 The House of Lords, at a time when it did not claim the power to overrule itself, displayed an extreme cautiousness in treating very narrowly the rule of precedents (see *Quinn, ibid.*) Recently, the Supreme Court of Canada recognized that it was no longer necessary to hold on to such a narrow view of precedents (see *Henry v. R*, [2005] 3 S.C.R. 609, 2005 SCC 76 [*Henry*] at para. 53 (Binnie J. for a unanimous panel of 9 judges)). This was particularly true in light of the fact that "much of the Court's work (particularly under the *Charter*) required the development of a general

perceived as worthy for having withstood the test of time.[86] However, for that very reason, past wisdom is not venerated as eternal truth, it is rather taken to be right so long as it is adapted to its time.[87] From the Organic perspective, the rightness of institutional forms and legal imperatives is not determined by "theoretical reason" but rather by "practi-

---

analytical framework which necessarily went beyond what was essential for the disposition of the particular case" and that "the Court nevertheless intended that effect be given to the broader analysis" ((*ibid.*): Nonetheless, the Court maintained that (*ibid.* at para. 57):

> The issue in each case, to return to the Halsbury question, is what did the case decide? Beyond the ratio decidendi which, as the Earl of Halsbury L.C. pointed out, is generally rooted in the facts, the legal point decided by this Court may be as narrow as the jury instruction at issue in Sellars or as broad as the Oakes test. All obiter do not have, and are not intended to have, the same weight. The weight decreases as one moves from the dispositive ratio decidendi to a wider circle of analysis which is obviously intended for guidance and which should be accepted as authoritative. Beyond that, there will be commentary, examples or exposition that are intended to be helpful and may be found to be persuasive, but are certainly not "binding" in the sense the Sellars principle in its most exaggerated form would have it. The objective of the exercise is to promote certainty in the law, not to stifle its growth and creativity. The notion that each phrase in a judgment of this Court should be treated as if enacted in a statute is not supported by the cases and is inconsistent with the basic fundamental principle that the common law develops by experience.

[86] For a fascinating study of the origins of the common law doctrine of the "Ancient Constitution", see John G.A. Pocock, *The Ancient Constitution and the Feudal Law: A Study of English Historical Thought in the Seventeenth Century* (Cambridge: Cambridge University Press, 1957), chap. II, VII and IX and Pocock's further developments on the issue at John G.A. Pocock, "Burke and the Ancient Constitution: A Problem in the History of Ideas" in John G.A. Pocock, *Politics, Language & Time: Essays on Political Thought and History* (Chicago: University of Chicago Press, 1989) at 202.

[87] There is, however, a strong presumption that past decisions are right. In *Henry, supra* note 85, for example, the Supreme Court of Canada stated that:

> The Court's practice, of course, is against departing from its precedents unless there are compelling reasons to do so: *R. v. Salituro*, [1991] 3 S.C.R. 654; *R. v. Chaulk*, [1990] 3 S.C.R. 1303; *R. v. B. (K.G.)*, [1993] 1 S.C.R. 740, at pp. 777-83; and *R. v. Robinson*, [1996] 1 S.C.R. 683, at paras. 16-46. Nevertheless, while rare, departures do occur. In *Clark v. Canadian National Railway Co.*, [1988] 2 S.C.R. 680, it was said that "[t]his Court has made it clear that constitutional decisions are not immutable, even in the absence of constitutional amendment" (p. 704), and in the *Charter* context the Court in *United States v. Burns*, [2001] 1 S.C.R. 283, 2001 SCC 7, effectively overturned the result (if not the reasoning) in *Kindler v. Canada (Minister of Justice)*, [1991] 2 S.C.R. 779, and *Reference re Ng Extradition (Can.)*, [1991] 2 S.C.R. 858. In the area of human rights, important reappraisals were made in *Central Alberta Dairy Pool v. Alberta (Human Rights Commission)*, [1990] 2 S.C.R. 489 (overturning the reasoning in *Bhinder v. Canadian National Railway Co.*, [1985] 2 S.C.R. 561), and *Brooks v. Canada Safeway Ltd.*, [1989] 1 S.C.R. 1219 (overturning *Bliss v. Attorney General of Canada*, [1979] 1 S.C.R. 183). The Court should be particularly careful before reversing a precedent where the effect is to diminish *Charter* protection.

cal reason" (*phronesis*).[88] This means that institutional forms and legal imperatives are not cast in stone, but that changes ought to be brought smoothly and incrementally through gradual adaptation to particular circumstances. As Daniel J. Boorstin once noted, in Great Britain, "constitutional theory has taken for granted the *gradual* formulation of a theory of society."[89] He therefore added: "No sensible Briton would say that his history is the unfolding of the truths implicit in Magna Carta and the Bill of Rights. Such documents are seen as only single steps in a continuing process of definition"[90] Moreover, changes are brought piecemeal because jurists are aware that a small change in one part of the web of constitutional law might require many constitutional adaptations elsewhere.

While the Organic perspective is open to constant reforms or, to be more precise, "development",[91] it is generally biased, for pragmatic reasons, against massive systemic modifications. In effect, wiping out significant parts of a web of imperatives would leave agents with little guidance as to how to resolve particular issues until a new experience pool has been developed. The need for heuristic devices might help to explain why, despite self-proclaimed revolutionary changes, people often continue to rely on older categories and habits. Thus, while the

---

[88] Practical reason is always situated and, at common law, this means practical reason takes into consideration a web of past decisions. The fact that the exercise of practical reason at common law requires a deep knowledge of past practices can be illustrated by the very important opinion given by Sir Edward Coke to King James I as to why the latter did not enjoy the privilege of personally deciding cases at law. Coke reports the exchange between him and King James I in the following terms:

> Then the King said, that he thought the law was founded upon reason, and that he and others had reason, as well as the Judges: to which it was answered by me, true it was, that God had endowed his Majesty with excellent Science, and great endowments of nature; but his Majesty was not learned in the laws of his realm of England, and causes which concern the life, or inheritance, or goods, or fortunes of his subjects, are not to be decided by natural reason, but by the artificial reason and judgment of law, which law is an act which requires long study and experience before that a man can attain to the cognizance of it ...

(Emphasis added. *Prohibitions del Roy*, [1607] 12 Co. Rep. 63, 64-65, 77 Eng. Rep. 1342, 1342-43).

[89] Daniel J. Boorstin, *The Genius of American Politics* (Chicago: University of Chicago Press, 1953) at 15 [*The Genius of American Politics*].

[90] *Ibid.*

[91] An organic conception of constitutionalism does not have to distinguish between "mistakes of constitutional implementation" and "mistakes in constitutional norms" since constitutional imperatives are not conceived as determinate pre-existing rules to which situations must "conform". Rather, constitutional imperatives are indicators of the elements that must necessarily be integrated in our practical reasoning process on particular issues. In other words, the constitutional imperative is not necessarily the solution to a particular problem but the way to arrive at it.

Organic perspective might at first sight appear more conservative than the Voluntary perspective, it is not necessarily the case. In effect, because the actual is known to be simply an approximation of the good, it leaves plenty of space to the Organicist for the quest for a better arrangement. While contentment might be the attitude resulting from the Voluntary perspective,[92] prudent hope might be what animates the Organic perspective.

To better highlight the differences between these two ways of looking at constitutionalism, let me use another metaphor. The Voluntarist imagines "the People" as an architect who attempts to design a perfect house. To succeed, the architect must have at least a general knowledge of the future dwellers and of their needs, she must be aware of the properties of the materials available and of the land upon which the house will be erected and she must have a sufficient understanding of building techniques to ensure that her plans will be able to be concretely put in place. According to the Organic perspective, the presumed architect necessary lacks the experience to design the perfect house on her first attempt. To the extent that it is ready to think of the "People" as a "person" that inhabits a constitutional house, the Organic perspective would rather imagine that the People has inherited her constitutional house from past times. The house might not be perfect, it might have parts that were suited for past needs and that no longer serve any useful or meaningful purposes, but the general structure has withstood the test of time. It then belongs to the current inhabitants to maintain and renovate the building to suit their needs while being aware that they are also holding it in trust for future generations. Having lived in that house, its current inhabitants have had time to acquire the skills and expertise to renovate the house and have been able to experience its concrete shortcomings. Renovations may require that an entire part of the house be demolished and rebuilt – or that the house be divided to be transformed into a condominium building – but the Organic view does not start from nothing. In effect, the new construction will not be possible until the old one is taken out of the way and the new building will necessarily be built in opposition to certain key features of the old one; otherwise, it would have been wiser to simply renovate it. While the Voluntarist perspective imagines the Constitution as the rational product of a bril-

---

[92] Daniel Boorstin made a similar point about the American Voluntarist perspective when he wrote in *The Genius of American Politics, supra* note 89, that:

Our theory of society is thus conceived as a kind of exoskeleton, like the shell of a lobster. We think of ourselves as growing *into* our skeleton, filling it out with the experience and resources of recent ages. But we always suppose that the outlines were rigidly drawn in the beginning. Our mission, then, is simply to demonstrate the truth – or rather the workability – of the original theory.

liant architect, the Organic perspective sees it more as the well-maintained house of a particularly dextrous handyman.

Canadian constitutional law, despite being partly made of explicit constitutional enactments, remains shot through with this Organic perspective.[93] In effect, the Supreme Court of Canada recently stated that "our constitutional history demonstrates that our governing institutions have adapted and changed to reflect changing social and political values. This has generally been accomplished by methods that have ensured continuity, stability and legal order."[94] These are not the words of a post-revolutionary court.

Therefore, Canada's constitution, from both a Voluntarist and an Organic perspective, is a strange beast. It is partly made of Voluntarist elements in the form of constitutional enactments of the Imperial Parliament, the federal Parliament and provincial legislatures. However, these are not the works of a *single* collective author. Thus, the Will expressed in those enactments does not necessarily emerge from a single entity; Canada is a complex multinational state that is the result of a pact between different political communities, a pact sanctioned by an impe-

---

[93] While American Constitutionalism seems to be strongly animated by the Volontarist perspective, the Organic perspective is not totally absent. For example, Woodrow Wilson, wrote that "government is not a machine, but a living thing. It falls, not under the theory of the universe, but under the theory of organic life. It is accountable to Darwin, not to Newton." (Woodrow Wilson, *Constitutional Government in the United States* (New York: Columbia University Press, 1908) at 56-57.). On the historic use of the organic metaphor in American constitutionalism, see P.W. Kahn, *Legitimacy and History*, *supra* note 73, chap. 2; Thomas H. Peebles, "A Call To High Debate: The Organic Constitution in its Formative Era, 1890-1920" (1980-1981) 52 U. Colo. L. Rev. 49 and Anonymous, "Organic and Mechanical Metaphors in Late Eighteenth-Century American Political Thought" (1996-1997) 110 Harv. L. Rev. 1832.

A contemporary return to a form of organic perspective has been heralded in the United States by David A. Strauss under the expression "common law constitutionalism". See, in particular, David A. Strauss, "Common Law Constitutional Interpretation" (1996) 63 U. Chi. L. Rev. 877; David A. Strauss, "Tragedies Under the Common Law Constitution" in William Eskridge and Sanford Levinson, eds. *Constitutional Stupidities, Constitutional Tragedies* (New York: New York University Press, 1998); David A. Strauss, "Constitutions, Written and Otherwise" (2000) 19 *Law and Philosophy* 451; David A. Strauss, "The Irrelevance of Constitutional Amendments" (2001) 114 Harv. L. Rev. 1457; David A. Strauss, "Common Law, Common Ground, and Jefferson's Principle" (2003) 112 Yale L.J. 1717.

This form of "common law constitutionalism" ought not to be confused with its British homonym criticised by Thomas Poole. See: Thomas Poole, "Dogmatic Liberalism? T.R.S. Allan and Common Law Constitutionalism" (2002) 65 Modern L. Rev. 463; Thomas Poole, "Back to the Future? Unearthing the Theory of Common Law Constitutionalism" (2003) 23 O.J.L.S. 435; Thomas Poole, "Questioning Common Law Constitutionalism" (2005) 25 L.S. 142.

[94] *Reference Re Secession of Québec*, *supra* note 76 at para. 33.

rial power.[95] Nonetheless, these are expressions of Will and the Organic perspective must try to make sense of the existence of such expressions.

---

[95] Although the majority of the Supreme Court of Canada declared in *Re Resolution to Amend the Constitution (Manitoba (Attorney General) v. Canada (Attorney General)*, [1981] 1 S.C.R. 753, 803 [*Patriation Reference*] that the Compact Theory was merely a political doctrine and does not "engage the law", the majority nonetheless recognized that it "might have some peripheral relevance to actual provisions of the British North America Act and its interpretation and application". Despite this modest role recognized by the Supreme Court, the Compact Theory nonetheless still plays an important role in Canadian foundational narratives. In effect, in an age when democracy and self-government are taken to lie at the heart of political legitimacy, there are immense pressures to find ways to justify constitutions on the basis of popular will. Because Canada was not the result of a revolutionary movement that united "the People", the Compact theory plays a similar role. However, while this Voluntarist narrative provides legitimacy to constitutional enactments, it also logically imposes constraints. In effect, to the extent that a constitutional enactment is considered a pact, it means that it cannot be changed without the prior approval of the representatives of the collective agents that formed it or – depending on the interpretation given to the meaning of the pact – the new collective agents that they have agreed to form.

That being said, the Canadian Compact Theory comes in different versions. In effect, there are at least three important narratives concerning the identity of the relevant collective agents who took part in the pact to form a new political entity. These narratives are in tension with one another. The first one sees the *Constitution Act, 1867, supra* note 39, as a pact between the (French-)*Canadiens* and the British Crown (and Her English-speaking subjects). A similar narrative has taken hold among many Aboriginal Peoples who see the treaties signed with the British Crown and "recognized and affirmed" by the *Constitution Act*, 1982, *supra* note 70, s. 35, as a pact between themselves and the British Crown. The second narrative is one about a pact between self-governing *colonial legislatures* on the one hand, and the British Parliament, on the other, to form a local federation or confederation that would be a subpart of the larger Imperial system. Thus, the first type of narratives identify collective agents through "pre-political" attributes – that is, attributes not entirely produced by existing state institutions – while the second type starts from the perspective that existing state institutions already incarnate the relevant collective agents. See Paul Romney, "Provincial Equality, Special Status and the Compact Theory of Canadian Confederation" (1999) 32 Canadian Journal of Political Science/Revue canadienne de science politique 21. I wish to suggest that a third narrative, a complementary variant of the first two, also exists. That variant sees territorially defined "regions" (Ontario, Québec, the Maritime, Western provinces) as the relevant collective agents. Equal representation of regions in the Senate would be an outcome of that sensibility. At any rate, those narratives have often been seen by commentators as colliding with one another because they all assume the equality of incompletely overlapping collective identities. However, those narratives can be reconciled if one imagines that provinces deserve equal respect *among themselves* but a specific province might have the particular duty to protect and promote the existence of the Francophones in light of the fact that it is the only province in which the French-*Canadiens* are a majority. In light of that special duty, that province might need to enjoy particular powers to fulfil her mission without having a higher status than other provinces. An alternative way to overcome this tension would be to clearly create a third level of government that would incarnate the linguistic communities and that would be responsible for their protection and promotion – as it has been done in Belgium.

One way in which it tries to do so is simply to integrate such expressions into the larger web of constitutional imperatives; to make those rules examples of larger patterns or instantiations of more general principles.[96] That way, acts of will are presented as increments in the development of the whole.[97]

However, fully harmonizing those two perspectives is not simple because one bases legitimacy on the *identity of the rule-maker* – and, incidentally, on the ultimate truth of the rules – while the other perspective bases legitimacy on the *virtues of practical reasons* and because both perspectives affirm that their claim to legitimacy must be paramount to the other. But that problem should not, in principle, arise in the current context since the constitutional imperatives relative to treaty powers in Canada are entirely the product of the Organic growth of the Canadian constitution.

---

[96] A similar strategy is at play in *Reference Re Secession of Québec, supra* note 76, when the Court declared that: "Our Constitution is primarily a written one, the product of 131 years of evolution. Behind the written word is an historical lineage stretching back through the ages, which aids in the consideration of the underlying constitutional principles. These principles inform and sustain the constitutional text: *they are the vital unstated assumptions upon which the text is based*" (at para. 49, emphasis added). Thus, particular constitutional rules are taken to make sense only when viewed from the perspective of the whole system; they are not merely acts of Will, they are instantiations of a larger constitutional principle.

[97] One might be tempted to think that the Organic perspective will necessarily have a harder time competing against the Voluntarist narrative when formal constitutional enactments have been adopted precisely to repudiate past constitutional imperatives. In such cases, the image of natural growth might tend to lose to the image of the victorious Will, the image of horizontal or diagonal legal developments being displaced by one of vertical authority. However, when the organic narrative succeeds in dominating the general constitutional culture, constitutional amendments are not necessarily interpreted in a narrow originalist way but, rather, they may be taken as contextual indications about the directions towards which further progressive interpretations must be heading. The *Reference* re Employment Insurance Act (Can.), *ss. 22 and 23*, [2005] 2 S.C.R. 669 [*Reference* re Employment Insurance Act] illustrates this quite well. Justice Deschamps writes (at para. 40):

> While the views of the framers are not conclusive where constitutional interpretation is concerned, the context in which the amendment was made is nonetheless relevant. If the objectives of the framers are taken as a starting point, it will be easier to determine the scope of the jurisdiction that was transferred, and then to determine how it may be adapted to contemporary realities.

In light of the changes in the labour market, a 1940 constitutional amendment transferring from provinces to the federal Parliament legislative powers over "Unemployment insurance" (s. 91 (2A)) was interpreted as allowing the federal Parliament to legislate in order to establish "a public insurance program the purpose of which is to preserve workers' economic security and ensure their re-entry into the labour market by paying income replacement benefits in the event of an interruption of employment" (at para. 68) in the form of maternity and parental benefits.

In effect, in Canada, the issue of treaty powers is entirely governed by the large web of rules, principles and other legal heuristics flowing from judicial decisions that have developed in harmony with other constitutional doctrines. Thus, while Canada and the provinces cut their colonial ties to the British Parliament, their connections with the external world were left to be defined by the natural growth of pre-existing constitutional sources rather than through an explicit new constitutional text.

At the center of the constitutional web is the *Labour Conventions* case. In that case, the Privy Council fleshed out the consequences of the Canadian federal structure and concluded, in short, that the implementation of treaty obligations was not an independent matter that belonged to the federal Parliament but, rather, that the authority to implement such obligations was divided according to the subject-matter of the obligations. Therefore, if a treaty dealt with matters belonging to the provincial jurisdiction, it was up to the provincial legislatures to adopt the proper laws to implement the obligations flowing from the treaty.

However, despite the fact that Organic growth has been in conformity with the expressed will of different provinces over time, there has been a counter will expressed mainly by the representatives of the federal government. The federal representatives and the scholars who support them have claimed that the division of responsibilities between the federal Parliament and the provincial legislatures is not appropriate. They usually claim that it would be more efficient if the powers to implement treaty obligations were centralised at the federal level. They claim that the current division of powers might weaken Canada's ability to negotiate with her international partners because Canada is not in a position to assure those partners that she will be capable of respecting her obligations. I have not seen any credible evidence yet that substantiates those claims. At any rate, one of the main problems for those who oppose the result of the natural growth of the Canadian doctrine is that they cannot rely on any solid constitutional foundations to make their point; their position is simply foreign to the actual web of constitutional doctrines. To reverse the current position would not simply mean adjusting a few constitutional strings here and there; it would mean a radical redrawing of the Canadian federation.

In effect, this is a great example of how a seemingly little change in the constitutional web of doctrines can actually mean the total unfolding of the web. While this might not be apparent at first sight, I will argue in this essay that rules dealing with treaty powers are now at the very heart of Canadian federalism. It is important to have this fact clearly in mind if we are going to think about reforming those rules. In the next section,

I will briefly outline the spirit in which I intend to propose organic reforms.

An Exercise in Conceptual Maintenance

In order to adapt the legal framework of the Canadian federation for the purpose of meeting the needs of international relations in the 21st century, we need to do some conceptual work. We have to sift through our current stocks of constitutional conceptions, keep the ones that continue to resonate with our reality, refurbish the ones that are dated but that can still be salvaged, parsimoniously delete the ones that have outlived their usefulness or that are just plain detrimental – and propose alternative conceptions when necessary.

This exercise in conceptual maintenance is always an important, but difficult part of law reform. It is an important task to accomplish lest we develop legal doctrines that assume the existence of a world that either no longer exists or that has never existed. For example, developing legal doctrines based on the conception that Canada is a *Dominion* in the British Empire[98] would be nonsensical since the status of "Dominion" no longer signifies anything in the current world order.

Conceptual maintenance is a difficult task for at least two reasons. First, it is difficult because we often grow so comfortable using age-old conceptions that we do not think about questioning their contemporary relevance. The conventional use of conceptions is often taken as sufficient proof of their appropriateness. A legitimate fear that we might lose an important knot in our web of meanings also reinforces this tendency: we are afraid that by discarding or transforming a conception in use we might adversely affect the other ideas that depend on it. However, when conceptions remain unquestioned despite significant changes in the cultural, material, and political conditions that made them possible, there is always the risk that such conceptions will prove ill-structured to grasp our current reality. Luckily, this is not the case here with the idea of "Dominion" or the idea that Canada is a member of the "British Empire". We therefore do not have to disentangle this obsolete conceptual web to solve our problem since this has already been done in the last century by our predecessors.

Second, the exercise in conceptual maintenance is a difficult task because finding viable alternatives to legal conceptions that we have either trashed or that we want to reform is quite complex. Oftentimes, adapting

---

[98] *Constitution Act, 1867, supra* note 39, Preamble, where reference is made to the fact that the "Provinces of Canada, Nova Scotia, and New Brunswick have expressed their Desire to be federally united into One Dominion" and that "such a Union would conduce to the Welfare of the Provinces and promote the Interests of the British Empire".

the meaning of existing legal vocabularies will do. The classic example here is the famous *Edwards* case in which the Privy Council decided that the term "person" in the *Constitution Act, 1867* had now to be read as applying both to men and women despite the fact that the term might have been originally taken to be applicable only to men.[99] The trick here is to come up with an interpretation that is different from the original and yet, is consistent with the developing narratives in which other parts of the Constitution are embedded.

Sometimes, however, no such vocabulary is available in the relevant constitutional texts because the older conceptions precluded the development of such a vocabulary in the first place. When this happens, we can either modify the Constitution through formal amendments or it can be adapted through changes in constitutional conventions or in the conceptual web that forms the background assumptions that render the constitutional texts intelligible. Either way, the challenge is to pick a conceptual apparatus fit for the job, an assemblage of conceptions that will easily be inscribed in political narratives and capable of future development and adjustments.

One of the risks that we have to avoid when selecting the proper conceptual apparatus is laziness: instead of coming up with an appropriate framework designed for our conditions, we might be tempted to simply borrow inadequate conceptual frameworks developed by other polities despite their structural differences and despite the fact that they may already be obsolete for the polities that had developed them. This risk reflects one of the ironies of decolonisation: too often, former colonies gained their independence simply to return to their colonial habit of mimicking the ways of the colonialist. Former colonies often brought in state structures as they were being abandoned by the colonial powers for being obsolete in a globalisation era. One of the conceptual frameworks that we should avoid buying from Europe's flea-market of political thoughts is "sovereignty".

That concept was constructed around the need to justify the autonomy of the Princes, the Emperor of the Holy Roman Empire and the Pope from each other's claims of supremacy. At the same time it was used to justify the monopolisation of powers within each realm. Thus, the concept was meant to protect each realm from any *de jure* and *de facto* intrusion by external authorities (what has been called "external"[100]

---

[99] *Edwards, supra* note 82.

[100] Daniel Philpot, *Revolutions in Sovereignty: How Ideas Shaped Modern International Relations* (Princeton: Princeton University Press, 2001) at 18 [Daniel Philpot, *Revolutions in Sovereignty*].

or "negative sovereignty"[101]) and to ensure that the monopoly of *de jure* authority would be concentrated within one institution within that realm (what has been called "internal sovereignty"[102] or "positive sovereignty"[103]). This system was believed to ensure the stability of the world order; if each state remains within its jurisdiction, peace would ensue.

Thus, according to this conception of sovereignty, international law – or to be more accurate, "inter-state" law – is mainly oriented towards protecting each state's conditions of existence through the principle of non-intervention. Hurting another Monarch's subject meant hurting his possession and his claim to exclusive power over his possessions, thus, it meant hurting that other Monarch's dignity. Treaties were originally conceived as the personal obligations of the Monarch and, as states were abstracting themselves from the person of the King, they kept the older conceptual framework. According to this dated view of the world order, treaties are inter-state agreements that correspond roughly to the liberal conception of contracts between individuals. But this theory was developed with a view of the world order that no longer corresponds to today's reality. In effect, while certain aspects of that theory remain valid today – for example, states enjoy a high degree of autonomy to make laws within their realm and external military intervention is only exceptionally permitted – we no longer live in that world.

There has been a paradigm shift in international relations.[104] As UN Secretary General Kofi Annan has pointed out: "States are now widely understood to be instruments at the service of their peoples, and not vice versa."[105] This shift has two very important consequences. First, to the

---

[101] Paul W. Kahn, "The Question of Sovereignty" (2004) 40 Stan. J. Int'l L. 259, 260 [Paul W. Kahn, "The Question of Sovereignty"].

[102] Daniel Philpot, *Revolutions in Sovereignty, supra* note 100 at 18.

[103] Paul W. Kahn, *supra* note 101 at 260.

[104] For different perspectives on these changes, see for example: Louis Henkin, "International Law: Politics, Values, Functions" (1990) 216 Rec. des Cours 13, 24-25; John H. Jackson, "The Great 1994 Sovereignty Debate: United States Acceptance and Implementation of the Uruguay Round Results" (1997) 36 Colum. J. Transnat'l L. 157; John O. McGinnis, "The Decline of the Western Nation State and the Rise of the Regime of International Federalism" (1996) 18 Cardozo L. Rev. 903; Oscar Schachter, "The Decline of the Nation-State and its Implications for International Law" (1997) 36 Colum. J. Transnat'l L. 7; Christoph Schreuer, "The Waning of the Sovereign State: Toward a New Paradigm of International Law?" (1993) 4 E.J.I.L. 447 [C. Schreuer, "The Waning of the Sovereign State: Toward a New Paradigm of International Law?"].

[105] Kofi A. Annan, "Two Concepts of Sovereignty" *The Economist* 352 (18 September 1999) 49, at 49. See also Kofi Annan, *Annual Report of the UN Secretary-General to the 54ᵗʰ General Assembly session,* UN Press Release, SG/SM 7136, GA/9596 (20 September 1999). Léon Duguit predicted this transformation much earlier. See: Léon

extent that states are to be understood as service providers, it means that we can evaluate them in instrumental terms. And if states are our instruments, they can be shaped to optimise the interests of those to whom they belong. Second, because states are no longer merely the embodiment of an "existential community"[106] but rather serve certain functions, states can serve more than one existential community at the same time. In other words, the state seen as an instrument may serve more than one nation. It does not mean that a state can no longer be the embodiment of an existential community, it simply means that this may or may not be the primary way in which every member of that state relates to it.

With the rise of the welfare and regulatory state and with the increasing worldwide mobility and economic integration made possible by technological advances, our models for securing peace, order and good governance have changed.[107] State powers are divided both functionally (between the different branches of the government and within those branches according to the specialized expertise of different departments) and territorially. States are no longer the only actors in our world order; our world's ontology now includes international organisations, non-governmental organisations, transnational corporations, individuals, etc.[108] As domestic law is no longer dominated by the criminal law model of prohibitions and sanctions but by distributive, enabling and coordinating legal rules, the ordinary life of international law is no longer primarily occupied with boundary protection but with transnational cooperation, harmonization and integration. Thus, while international law was mainly preoccupied by inter-state affairs, it is now mainly occupied with what was previously seen as "domestic" affairs:

Duguit, *Les transformations du droit public* (Paris: Librairie Armand Colin, 1913) at 32-72.

[106] I will describe later in this essay "existential communities" as "communities through which individual selfhood is constituted by a deep sense of 'love', loyalty and identity to the other members of the group. In other words, an existential community is what makes it possible for the self to transcend the individual." See II.A.2.iv..

[107] One of the things that is often eclipsed in the story about the shift from the old world of Monarchs to our world is the transformation of what was merely a technique to guarantee one State against another State's intrusion into an organising principle of the new world order: mutual pledges. While Monarchs often sent their children to be married to the sons and daughters of other regents for the purpose of creating new alliances, they served as "guarantee deposits" to ensure the peace. To the extent that the parents had affection for the child that they had sent to a foreign land, they were cautious in their conduct with the receiving family. On the other hand, to the extent that the receiving family cared about their son's or daughter's well-being with his or her husband or wife, they had an interest in not hurting their in-laws. In the post-industrial age, corporations, non-governmental organisations and the mobile citizenry have replaced the sons and daughters of monarchs.

[108] See section II.A.1.iv.

"private" law (family law, law of persons, property law, contracts, etc.), education, individual and collective rights, economic development, etc. We have moved from an opaque inter-state model to a multi-layered transnational governance model where different governing institutions coordinate their actions or compete with one another in their many roles.

Also, we increasingly recognize that individuals are members of a multitude of often overlapping existential communities. Because we recognize that nation-states are not the only political model available, we can now imagine multinational states where individuals are members of more than one political community. If we can already imagine that individuals may be citizens of more than one state – dual citizenship is accepted in Canada –, we certainly can imagine that individuals might have different forms of attachment to the different parts of the state: one individual might see herself primarily as Canadian while another might see himself primarily as *Québécois*, while they both feel that they belong to the two communities. The state apparatus ought to be able to accommodate these different senses of belonging. Thus, our challenge is to imagine the state without using the centralising idea of sovereignty. We ought to imagine a state that will be both the incarnation of different existential communities and will provide us with the necessary apparatuses of functional regimes.

I hope to demonstrate in this essay that once actual Canadian constitutional rules are freed from the artificial cast of the "sovereignty" frame in which a plethora of scholars have decided to put them and once we start taking seriously Canadian constitutional law sources, we will discover that the Canadian constitution is far more adapted to that new global reality than what many might have thought. In effect, the federalism principle entrenched in the Canadian constitution[109] is far more adapted to today's reality than the "sovereignty" model that certain scholars are trying to impose on the Constitution. As William Paul Maclure Kennedy had already written in 1922: the "evolution of Canadian government has constituted a decisive challenge to the absolute Austinian doctrine of sovereignty."[110]

I will demonstrate that it is often the views of those centralist scholars who cry that the modern world requires treaty powers to be held exclusively in the hands of the federal authorities that are not attuned with the reality of our current world order. We will see that their com-

---

[109] *Reference Re Secession of Québec, supra* note 76 at paras. 32, 47, 49, 55-60, 66, 76, 88, 90-92, 148, 149, 151.

[110] William P. M. Kennedy, *The Constitution of Canada: An Introduction to Its Development and Law* (London U.K.: Oxford University Press, 1922) at vii. I am indebted to David Schneiderman, "Harold Laski, Viscount Haldane, and the Law of the Canadian Constitution in the Early Twentieth Century", *supra* note 5, for this quote.

plaints often stem from the fact that our actual constitutional rules do not sufficiently accord with their obsolete "sovereignist" views. Thus, I will propose here a very orthodox reading of the Constitution, one that takes seriously the traditional sources of constitutional law and examines them with all the diligence they deserve. The picture that will emerge from this analysis is a truly federalist one where federal and provincial authorities have the means to fulfil their respective constitutional missions, including making binding international agreements to ensure the cooperation of foreign jurisdictions.

To advance my argument, I will proceed in the following way: Since most of the terms of the modern debate between the federal government and the provinces about treaty powers can be found in the famous 1930s *Labour Conventions* case,[111] it is worth reviewing at length that case. Therefore, chapter I will be dedicated to that review. This thorough review is quite important because the case has been commented upon by so many scholars[112] over the years that one might legitimately be afraid that the comments have taken a life of their own, killing the original and substituting themselves for the wise words of the Privy Council! Therefore, I will try to stay clear from impersonation charges by letting the Privy Council speak for itself and by limiting myself to paraphrasing it, or by making it clear when I am adding my own comments. Also, to get a better understanding of the debate, I will reconstruct the federal and

---

[111] *Labour Conventions* case, *supra* note 19.

[112] See for example: C.W. Jenks, "The Present Status of the Bennett Ratifications of International Labour Conventions", *supra* note 41; W.I. Jennings, "Dominion Legislation and Treaties", *supra* note 41; Vincent C. MacDonald, "The Canadian Constitution Seventy Years Later" (1937) 15 Can. Bar Rev. 401 [V.C. MacDonald, "The Canadian Constitution Seventy Years Later"]; Arthur B. Keith, "The Privy Council Decisions: A Comment from Great Britain" (1937) 15 Can. Bar Rev. 428 [A.B. Keith, "The Privy Council Decisions: A Comment from Great Britain"]; Frederick C. Cronkite, "The Social Legislation References" (1937) Can. Bar Rev. 495; William P.M. Kennedy, "The British North America Act: Past and Future" (1937) 15 Can. Bar Rev. 393; Frank R. Scott, "The Consequences of the Privy Council Decisions" (1937) 15 Can. Bar Rev. 485 [F.R. Scott, "The Consequences of the Privy Council Decisions"]; Frank R. Scott, "Centralization and Decentralization in Canadian Federalism" (1951) 29 Can. Bar Rev. 1095; Lord Wright of Durley, *Commentaire*, (1955) 33 Can. Bar Rev. 1123; Frank R. Scott, "Labour Conventions Case: Lord Wright's Undisclosed Dissent" (1956) 35 Can. Bar Rev. 114; Gerald V. La Forest, "The Labour Conventions Case Revisited" (1974) 12 Can. Y.B. Int'l L. 137 [G.V. La Forest, "Labour Conventions Case Revisited"]; Jean-Charles Bonenfant, "L'étanchéité de l'A.A.N.B. est-elle menacée ?" (1977) C. de D. 383; Pierre Patenaude, "L'érosion graduelle de la règle d'étanchéité: une nouvelle menace à l'autonomie du Québec" (1977) 20 C. de D. 229; Armand L.C. de Mestral, "L'évolution des rapports entre le droit canadien et le droit international un demi-siècle après l'affaire des conventions internationales de travail" (1987) 25 Can. Y.B. Int'l L. 301 [A.L.C. de Mestral, "L'évolution des rapports entre le droit canadien et le droit international un demi-siècle après l'affaire des conventions internationales de travail"].

provincial arguments from the notes taken by the court reporter in a way that highlights their respective vision of the post-independence Canadian polity. This reconstruction will be useful in re-discovering the initial claims of the participants in the debate but, mostly, it will help in presenting different institutional options and their likely constitutional consequences. Thus, I will focus on technical details of the arguments to the extent that they tell us something about political visions and constitutional arrangements. Finally, I will contextualise the varying claims made by the actors by giving some background information on the constitutional cases upon which they rely.

Chapter II will examine the state of the current constitutional law of treaty-*making* powers. When we carefully examine all the arguments invoked in favour of recognizing plenary treaty-making powers to the federal government – be it the Letters Patent of 1947, the prerogatives of the Crown, constitutional conventions, constitutional usage or international Law –, none of these is able to withstand a strict constitutional scrutiny; if federal authorities possess treaty-making powers in relation to provincial subject-matters, it is only as the result of a form of implied consent by provinces. I will also argue that there are very strong policy arguments in our current context in favour of not recognizing a federal exclusive plenary treaty-making power to federal authorities.

I will then examine the case for provincial treaty-making powers. I will first offer an overview of the extensive practices that the different Canadian provinces (and territories) are engaged in at the international level. I will then examine the legality of provincial treaty-making powers in light of both Canadian constitutional law and at international law. When considering international law, I will not limit myself to examining arguments based on orthodox international law. Rather, taking cues from game theory and from constructivism, I will show why the weak centralised sanction mechanisms of international law create incentives to recognize federated states at the international level.

The third chapter will be concerned with treaty *implementation* and, more precisely, with examining the arguments often invoked in favour of reversing the *Labour Conventions* case. I will review the basis upon which arguments often invoked in favour of reversing the *Labour Conventions* case are built (i.e. the possibility of reviving s. 132 of the *Constitution Act, 1867* (3.a), the possibility of using the "Peace, Order and Good Government" clause[113] (3.b.) and the possibility of invoking the allegedly "extra-territorial" character of treaty implementation (3.c.)), and I will demonstrate that all those arguments are based on fundamentally flawed assumptions about Canadian constitutional law.

---

[113] See *Constitution Act, 1867, supra* note 39, s. 91.

Those who want to reverse the *Labour Conventions* case do not seem to realize that reversing that fundamental case as they wish to do would ring the death knell of federalism: Canada would become akin to a unitary state. None of the powers invoked by those who would want the *Labour Conventions* case reversed are *exclusive* federal powers. Finally, I will show that the current amending procedures actually advocates *against* judicially overruling the *Labour Conventions* case.

PART I

STEPPING OUT OF THE FOOTSTEPS OF THE EMPIRE

CHAPTER I

The *Labour Conventions* Case

This chapter will serve as the entry point into the diverse parts of the Canadian constitutional web that are involved in the issue of treaty-making powers. I will not limit myself to analysing the particular outcome of the *Labour Conventions* case but I will be attentive to the immediate consequences of the alternative solutions proposed by the different actors and to the consequences that those proposals would have had on this constitutional web.

Thus, the first section (I.A.) will present the general factual and legal context in which the *Labour Conventions* case was heard and decided. The next sections will present the federal (I.B.) and provincial (I.C.) arguments presented to the Privy Council. And finally, section 1.d. will present a detailed analysis of the decision rendered in the *Labour Conventions* case by the Privy Council.

A. The Factual and Legal Context of the *Labour Conventions* Case

Let's start with the often-forgotten context of the case.[114] When World War I ended, a Treaty of Peace was made at Versailles on June 28, 1919[115] between the Allied and Associated Powers and a defeated Germany. The "British Empire" was described as one of the Allied and Associated Powers with His Majesty the King as one of the High Contracting Parties. The King was represented generally by English Ministers and for the Dominion of Canada by two Canadian Ministers. Canada was thus present as a member of the Empire and not as a High Contracting Party.

In Part I of the Treaty, the High Contracting Parties convened to set up the League of Nations and agreed that all signatories named in the annex to the covenant were to be the original members of the League. Canada, by being a signatory, became a member of the League. Part

---

[114] The next two paragraphs, giving an account of the factual context, are a paraphrased version of the Privy Council's own version of the facts in the *Labour Conventions* case, *supra* note 19 at 343-44.

[115] *Treaty of Versailles*, *supra* note 64.

XIII of the Treaty, entitled "Labour", provided that the High Contracting Parties agree to the establishment of the International Labour Organisation (I.L.O.) for the promotion of social justice and improved labour conditions throughout the world. The Treaty provided that the members of the League of Nations shall be the members of this organisation. The organisation was to consist, among other things, of a general conference of representatives of the members. Art. 405 (2) provided that a draft convention could be adopted with two-thirds of the votes cast by the delegates present at one such conferences. According to Art. 405 (5), once a draft convention was adopted each of the members had no more than eighteen months after the closing of the session of the conference to "bring the ... draft convention before the authority or authorities within whose competence the matter lies, for the enactment of legislation or other action."[116] Also, it provided that "if it obtains the consent of the authority or authorities within whose competence the matter lies, [the member will] communicate the formal ratification of the convention to the Secretary-General and will take such action as may be necessary to make effective the provisions of such convention."[117]

The current case arose out of three such conventions adopted by I.L.O. conferences between 1919 and 1928.[118] In the mid-1930s, the federal Parliament decided to adopt statutes to implement the three above-mentioned conventions, which it had claimed to have ratified in 1935.[119] The Governor-General in Council then referred the question of the validity of the statutes to the Supreme Court of Canada. Upon receiving the divided opinion of the Supreme Court, the federal government then appealed it to the Privy Council.

But why did the case only arise in the mid-1930s? Why not earlier since the delay to "bring the ... draft convention before the authority or authorities within whose competence the matter lies, for the enactment

---

[116] *Ibid.*, Art. 405 (5).

[117] *Ibid.*, Art. 405 (7).

[118] *ILO Convention Limiting the Hours of Work in Industrial Undertakings to Eight in the Day and Fourty-Eight in the Week*, 3 November 1919, 38 U.N.T.S. 17 [*ILO Convention Limiting the Hours of Work in Industrial Undertakings*]; *ILO Convention Concerning the Application of the Weekly Rest in Industrial Undertakings*, 17 November 1921, 38 U.N.T.S. 187 [*ILO Convention Concerning the Application of the Weekly Rest*]; *ILO Convention Concerning the Creation of Minimum Wage-Fixing Machinery*, 16 June 1928, 39 U.N.T.S. 3 [*ILO Convention Concerning the Creation of Minimum Wage-Fixing Machinery*].

[119] Resolutions of the Senate and House of Commons of Canada approving the conventions were adopted and an order of the Governor-General in Council approved the ratification. That order was then recorded in an instrument of ratification by the Secretary of State for External Affairs for Canada and communicated to the Secretary-General of the League of Nations. *Labour Conventions* case, *supra* note 19 at 346.

of legislation or other action" was of only eighteen months after the closing of the session of the conference and the first draft convention dated 1919? The Privy Council offers a striking explanation that seems to have been largely forgotten:

> In 1925 the Governor-General in Council referred to the Supreme Court questions as to the obligations of Canada under the provisions of Part XIII. of the *Treaty of Versailles*, and as to whether the Legislatures of the Provinces were the authorities within whose competence the subject-matter of the conventions lay. The answers to the reference, which are to be found in *In re Legislative Jurisdiction over Hours of Labour*, [1925] Can. S.C.R. 505, were that the Legislatures of the Provinces were the competent authorities to deal with the subject-matter, save in respect of Dominion servants, and the parts of Canada not within the boundaries of any Province: and that the obligation of Canada was to bring the convention before the Lieutenant-Governor of each Province to enable him to bring the appropriate subject-matter before the Legislature of his Province, and to bring the matter before the Dominion Parliament in respect of so much of the convention as was within their competence. This advice appears to have been accepted, and no further steps were taken until those which took place as stated above in 1935.[120]

In fact, the *unanimous* position of the Supreme Court in the 1925 reference simply confirmed the views earlier expressed in a report by the then federal Minister of Justice and embodied in an Order in Council taken on November 6, 1920.[121] The then Minister of Justice of the Dominion was of the view that the provisions of the conventions

> involve legislation which is competent to Parliament in as far as Dominion works and undertakings are affected, but which the provincial legislatures have otherwise the power to enact and apply generally and comprehensively.[122]

As the Privy Council would later state, the legislation "is not within the enumerated classes of subjects in s. 91: and it appears to be expressly excluded from the general powers given by the first words of the section."[123] But why then was there a sudden change in attitude by the federal government in 1935? Why, if the Supreme Court had decided in 1925 in relation to two out of three of the conventions at issue here[124]

---

[120] *Labour Conventions* case, *supra* note 19 at 347.

[121] *Reference re Legislative Jurisdiction over Hours of Labour*, [1925] S.C.R. 505 [*Reference re Legislative Jurisdiction over Hours of Labour*].

[122] *Ibid.* at 508.

[123] *Labour Conventions* case , *supra* note 19 at 350.

[124] *ILO Convention Limiting the Hours of Work in Industrial Undertakings*, *supra* note 118 and *ILO Convention Concerning the Application of the Weekly Rest*, *supra* note 118.

that this type of labour legislation came within the class of subjects assigned exclusively to the provinces by virtue of s. 92 (13) *Constitution Act, 1867*, did the federal government think fit to again refer the issue ten years later to the same Court?

The reason is that in the intervening years, the federal government came to have reasons to believe that it had the exclusive powers to implement any treaty binding on Canada and the provinces on the basis of the opening words of s. 91 *Constitution Act, 1867* (the power to adopt laws for "Peace, Order and Good Government"). That impression was first created by the *Aeronautics Reference* [125] in which the Judicial Committee of the Privy Council, after examining an aviation treaty characterised as a s. 132 treaty, stated that:

> [t]here may also be cases where the Dominion is entitled to speak for the whole, and this not because of any judicial interpretation of ss. 91 and 92, but by reason of the plain terms of s. 132, *where Canada as a whole*, having undertaken an obligation, is given the power necessary and proper for performing such obligation. [126]

It then concluded that:

> To sum up, having regard (a) to the terms of s. 132; (b) to the terms of the Convention which covers almost every conceivable matter relating to aerial navigation; and (c) to the fact that further legislative powers in relation to aerial navigation reside in the Parliament of Canada by virtue of s. 91(2) (5) and (7), it would appear that substantially the whole field of legislation in regard to aerial navigation belongs to the Dominion. There may be a small portion of the field which is not by virtue of specific words in the B.N.A. Act vested in the Dominion; but neither is it vested by specific words in the Provinces. As to such small portion it appears to the Board that it must necessarily belong to the Dominion under its power to make laws for the peace, order and good government of Canada. Further their Lordships are influenced by the facts that the subject of aerial navigation and the fulfilment of Canadian obligations under s. 132 are matters of national interest and importance; and that aerial navigation is a class of subject which has attained such dimensions as to affect the body politic of the Dominion. [127]

Although it talked of obligation undertaken by "Canada as a whole", that case was, in the end, simply hinting at a general power over treaties to be found in s. 91. That is because the case was in fact one of s. 132 application:

---

[125] *In re Regulation and Control of Aeronautics in Canada (The Aeronautics Reference)*, [1932] A.C. 54 [*Aeronautics Reference*].

[126] *Ibid.* at 73 (emphasis added).

[127] *Ibid.* at 77.

With regard to some of them, no doubt, it would appear to be clear that the Dominion has power to legislate, for example, under s. 91(2), for the regulation of Trade and Commerce, and under (5) for the Postal Services, but it is not necessary for the Dominion to piece together its powers under s. 91 in an endeavour to render them co-extensive with its duty under the Convention when s. 132 confers upon it full power to do all that is legislatively necessary for the purpose.[128]

One point must be added here. This case was very much anchored in the colonial mindset in the sense that s. 132 was not only granting powers to the Dominion but it was also *imposing obligations* for the protection of the Empire. In effect, the Privy Council, after stating that the Dominion had powers to adopt the statute in question, wrote "and we think that the Dominion Parliament not only has the right, *but also the obligation*, to provide by statute and by regulation that the terms of the Convention shall be duly carried out."[129]

What truly gave the federal Parliament the impression that it had exclusive powers to legislatively implement treaties was to come a few months later. In effect, in the *Radio Reference* of 1932, the Judicial Committee appeared to have decided that the power to legislate for the purpose of performing treaty obligations resides *exclusively* in the Parliament of Canada:

> This idea of Canada as a Dominion being bound by a convention equivalent to a treaty with foreign powers was quite unthought-of in 1867. It is the outcome of the gradual development of the position of Canada vis-a-vis to the mother country Great Britain, which is found in these later days expressed in the Statute of Westminster (1931 (Can.), p. v.). It is not therefore to be expected that such a matter should be dealt with in explicit words in either s. 91 or s. 92. The only class or treaty which would bind Canada was thought of as a treaty by Great Britain, and that was provided for by s. 132. Being therefore not mentioned explicitly in either s. 91 or s. 92, such legislation falls within the general words at the opening of s. 91 which assign to the Government of the Dominion the power to make laws "for the Peace, Order and good Government of Canada, in relation to all Matters not coming within the Classes of Subjects by this Act assigned exclusively to the Legislatures of the Provinces." [130]

Being under the impression that it was now in charge of international relations for Canada, the Dominion wanted to assert its newfound powers by adopting the three statutes referred above. However, to make sure that the Dominion's interpretation of its newfound powers was

---

[128] *Ibid.*

[129] *Ibid.* (emphasis added).

[130] *In re Regulation and Control of Radio Communication in Canada*, [1932] A.C. 304 at 312 [*Radio Reference*].

right, it wanted the opinion of the Supreme Court. In particular, there could have been uncertainties as to the real *ratio* of the *Radio Reference*: was that opinion truly based on a "treaty power" found in s. 91 or was it simply the result of a conclusion that radio communications in itself fell within s. 91?[131] After all, the Privy Council had left the door open to the latter interpretation by writing that "the question does not end with the consideration of the convention"[132] and had stated that radio broadcasting could fit under the exception to the provincial powers granted to Parliament at 92 (10) (a).[133] The federal government thus needed a clear finding on the issue. To get such a finding, Ottawa needed a case in which the subject-matter would clearly fall within s. 92 before any consideration related to the issue of treaty implementation. The implementation of the Labour Conventions raised exactly that question.[134] Hence the reference to the Supreme Court.[135] Unhappy with a tie (three to three) in the Supreme Court on the validity of the legislation, the federal government appealed to the Judicial Committee of the Privy Council in London to get a clear answer to its question. That was particularly important in light of the fact that many provinces were clearly opposed to the federal views on treaty powers.

---

[131] There might also have been uncertainties as to the correctness of the *Radio Reference, ibid.* For example, Vincent C. MacDonald, "Canada's Power to Perform Treaty Obligations" (1933) 11 Can. Bar Rev. 581 [V.C. MacDonald, "Canada's Power to Perform Treaty Obligations"] at 581 argued that the Privy Council was mistaken to read any treaty powers in s. 91. According to him, s. 132 was the only section applicable:

> It is the submission of the writer that this section [s. 132] properly construed is the sufficient and sole source of Canada's power to perform any and all treaties and that the Privy Council has not only placed an erroneous construction upon it, whereby it reached the result that some treaties fall within it and others fall within the 'peace, order and good government' clause of sec. 91 of the BNA Act, but, further, that it reached this unsatisfactory result by a method of approach to the Act which is both wrong and dangerous.

[132] *Radio Reference, ibid.* at 314.

[133] *Ibid.*. The *Constitution Act, 1867*, s. 92 (10) grants power to Legislatures in relation to "Local Works and Undertakings *other than* such as are of the following Classes: (a) Lines of Steam or other Ships, Railways, Canals, Telegraphs, and other Works and Undertakings connecting the Province with any other or others of the Provinces, or extending beyond the Limits of the Province ..." (emphasis added).

[134] It is true that the Attorney General initially submitted to the Privy Council that the *Reference re Legislative Jurisdiction over Hours of Labour, supra* note 121, "was wrongly decided" (*Labour Conventions* case, *supra* note 19 at 329) but in the end, "[i]t was admitted at the bar that each statute affects property and civil rights within each Province; and that it was for the Dominion to establish that nevertheless the statute was validly enacted under the legislative powers given to the Dominion Parliament by the British North America Act, 1867" (*Labour Conventions* case, *supra* note 19 at 342).

[135] *Reference Re: Weekly Rest in Industrial Undertakings Act (Canada)*, [1936] S.C.R. 461 [*Labour Conventions* case – *SCC*].

In effect, two very different conceptions of the nature of the Canadian state opposed each other. While the federal government tended to imagine itself as the sole heir to the Empire, the provinces saw in the newly autonomous Canadian state a true federation. Those opposing conceptions were reflected in their respective interpretations of the legal consequences of Canada's recently gained autonomy from the Empire. And it is these visions that underlie the arguments that the federal government and the provinces presented to the Privy Council. Let's examine them in turn.

B. "There is Only One Heir to the Mother Country": The Federal Government's Sovereignist Arguments

As we have seen, Canada's new international status was the result of *de facto* changes, developing conventions, official policy statements and then, *de jure* recognition.[136] The *Statute of Westminster* did not speak of treaties but allowed the Dominions to adopt extraterritorial laws.[137] As a result of Canada's new autonomy, the Attorney General for Canada argued that the Dominion's Ministers had been vested with the right to advise His Majesty in relation to international obligations affecting Canada, thus inheriting the effective exercise of the Imperial foreign affairs prerogatives to make treaties for Canada.[138] But the Dominion also claimed to be alone in having inherited these prerogatives; provinces would have no such powers.[139] Once the Dominion had claimed the prerogative to make treaties, she further claimed that she necessarily had the powers to implement them. In other words, she claimed that Canada's new international status brought to the federal government the capacity to conclude treaties and, consequently, the capacity to implement them legislatively.

---

[136] The 1923 and 1926 Imperial conferences recognized that Dominion governments had powers to conclude treaties and set up rules of practice between members of the Empire. See in particular the *Balfour Declaration, supra* note 66.

[137] *Statute of Westminster, supra* note 67, s. 3.

[138] *Labour Conventions* case , *supra* note 19 at 330-31:

By the constitutional developments, particularly since the Treaty of Versailles, the constitutional right to advise His Majesty in respect of international obligations affecting Canada has become vested in his Canadian Ministers. That is sometimes expressed by saying that the right to exercise the prerogative in respect of Canadian affairs has been transferred to the Canadian executive.

And later, at 341:

Canada has the right to enter into international obligations so far as Canada is concerned. With regard to the growth and development of the treaty-making power, Canada has a duty to make treaties; nobody else can make them for her ...

[139] *Ibid.* at 341 ("The Provinces have no status to enter into international obligations of any kind. They have only Provincial jurisdiction legislatively.")

Thus, despite the fact that the federal government recognized that the subject-matter of the statutes in question here would ordinarily come within provincial powers under s. 92 (13), it claimed that those questions had been taken out of provinces' jurisdiction. This was to be the result of the new international status of Canada. The Dominion presented two arguments in favour of her position.

The Dominion first argued that the issue pertained to s. 132. She generally argued that the Dominion had the duty under the *Treaty of Versailles* to adopt the impugned legislation and that she had the power to do so by virtue of s. 132. She argued that while s. 132 "speaks of obligations as part of the British Empire towards foreign countries", the expression "Empire" ought to be read to mean "His Majesty".[140] In other words, s. 132 would have had to be read to apply to treaties entered into by the Dominion as if she were the immediate successor of the Empire. However, she did not put too much emphasis on those arguments. In fact, it seems, from the Privy Council's report of the federal government's arguments, that the Attorney General for Canada did not even make reference to the *Aeronautics Reference*. This may indicate that the federal government was really looking for a decision that would free Parliament from the colonial structure of s. 132.

Thus, the Dominion argued that if the issue here was not one flowing from s. 132 – and despite the absence of any formal change in the text of the Constitution – then the power to implement international agreements in Canada had been *exclusively* bestowed on her by reason of the "residuary clause" of s. 91 of the *Constitution Act, 1867*, which grants Parliament the power "… to make Laws for the Peace, Order, and good Government of Canada, in relation to all Matters not coming within the Classes of Subjects by this Act assigned exclusively to the Legislatures of the Provinces …"

Here, the Dominion did not simply argue for an overriding federal power but for what I would call a *preemption doctrine*:

> … where Canada has properly incurred an international obligation with respect to any matter whatsoever, that within whatever classes in ss. 91 and 92 it may be described as coming under other circumstances, once the matter has assumed the aspect of an international bargain *it is no longer to be treated as belonging to any one of the enumerated classes.*"[141]

In this, the Dominion was seeking a confirmation of her reading of the *Radio Reference.*[142]

---

[140] *Ibid.* at 332.

[141] *Ibid.* at 330 (emphasis added).

[142] *Supra* note 130.

The Attorney General also argued that "[a] matter which may be local and Provincial in its nature may assume another aspect once the country becomes committed as a whole to some other country under a treaty." At first, this may sound like what we now know as the "double aspect" doctrine. In 1883, the Privy Council had announced in *Hodge v. R.* that "subjects which in one aspect and for one purpose fall within s. 92, may in another aspect and for another purpose fall within s. 91".[143] In such cases, legislatures and Parliament can validly adopt statutes on the *same object* and *at the same time* so long as they deal with different *aspects* of that object. But on a closer look, we discover that the Attorney General did not mean to argue for the application of the double aspect doctrine. In fact, from the court's report, the Attorney General for Canada does not seem to have argued *Hodge v. R.* at all.[144]

Instead, he argued two other cases in support of his claim. The first case upon which the Attorney General for Canada relied had established a non-exclusive yet overriding federal power to fix prices during times of national emergencies, such as war.[145] The distinct "federal aspect" is hard to discern in that case. Nonetheless, the Privy Council recognized a federal power to intervene in what would otherwise be considered as falling within the provincial jurisdiction over "property and civil rights". This power was to be limited to the time of the emergency. In all fairness, this case is probably better seen as one of those "wartime jurisprudence" where anxiety took over juridical orthodoxy and expediency replaced legality.[146] Of course, it is always hazardous to rely on wartime

---

[143] *Hodge v. R.*, *supra* note 14 at 130.

[144] *Hodge v. R.*, *ibid.* is not cited once in either the Privy Council opinion or the Supreme Court decision.

[145] *Fort Frances Pulp & Power Co. v. Manitoba Free Press Co.*, [1923] A.C. 695 [*Fort Frances Pulp & Power Co.*].

[146] See for example, *Fort Frances Pulp & Power Co.*, *ibid.* at 706 where the Privy Council exceptionally allowed the federal executive to effectively suspend the division of powers rules during a wartime crisis and, unless "very clear evidence that the crisis had wholly passed away" was provided to the judiciary, the Privy Council left it to the statesmanship of the federal executive to decide when the suspension of the normal rules of federalism was no longer necessary:

> The question of the extent to which provision for circumstances such as these may have to be maintained is one on which a Court of law is loathe to enter. No authority other than the central government is in a position to deal with a problem which is essentially one of statesmanship. It may be that it has become clear that the crisis which arose is wholly at an end and that there is no justification for the continued exercise of an exceptional interference which becomes ultra vires when it is no longer called for. In such a case the law as laid down for distribution of powers in the ruling instrument would have to be invoked. But very clear evidence that the crisis had wholly passed away would be required to justify the judiciary, even when the question raised was one of ultra vires which it had to decide, in over-ruling the decision of the Government that exceptional measures were still requisite.

jurisprudence to discern longstanding principles.[147] But at any rate, it could be used to suggest that there might be, at least temporarily, concurrent jurisdiction on an issue based on a state of national emergency; something that might otherwise be "local" could be temporarily said to be affecting "Canada as a whole".[148]

The second precedent upon which the Dominion relied was more directly connected to the issue here: *British Columbia (Attorney General) v. Canada (Attorney General)*.[149] That case involved the validity of a British Columbia statute that provided that in contracts, licences and leases made by the government, a provision should be made that no Chinese or Japanese person should be employed in connection therewith. That provincial statute ran against a federal legislation that had been adopted to implement an imperial treaty with Japan that provided, among other things, that the subjects of each of the High Contracting Parties should be treated equally in relation to their industries to the subjects or citizens of the most favoured nation. The Privy Council recognized federal powers to adopt laws to implement s. 132 treaties and to deal with "naturalization and aliens" (91 (25)) that would override provincial laws on "property and civil rights".

> This comes close to Carl Schmitt's conception of the role of the executive in deciding of the "exception", that is, of the suspension of the Constitution (see Carl Schmitt, *Political Theology: Four Chapters on the Concept of Sovereignty*, trans. by George Schwab (London: MIT Press, 1985.) [C. Schmitt, *Political Theology*]

[147] The Privy Council itself stated that it was bending the normal rules in light of exceptional circumstances (*Fort Frances Pulp & Power Co.*, *ibid.* at 703):

> It is clear that in normal circumstances the Dominion Parliament could not have so legislated as to set up the machinery of control over the paper manufacturers which is now in question. The recent decision of the Judicial Committee in the Board of Commerce Case (1) [*Canada (A.G.) v. Alberta (A.G.)*, [1922] 1 A.C. 191, 60 D.L.R. 513], as well as earlier decisions, shew that as the Dominion Parliament cannot ordinarily legislate so as to interfere with property and civil rights in the Provinces, it could not have done what the two statutes under consideration purport to do had the situation been normal. But it does not follow that in a very different case, such as that of sudden danger to social order arising from the outbreak of a great war, the Parliament of the Dominion cannot act under other powers which may well be implied in the constitution.

[148] See *Fort Frances Pulp & Power Co.*, *ibid.* at 704:

> The general control of property and civil rights for normal purposes remains with the Provincial Legislatures. But questions may arise by reason of the special circumstances of the national emergency which concern nothing short of the peace, order and good government of Canada as a whole. The over-riding powers enumerated in sec. 91, as well as the general words at the commencement of the section, may then become applicable to new and special aspects which they cover of subjects assigned otherwise exclusively to the Provinces.

[149] *British Columbia (A.G.) v. Canada (A.G.)*, [1924] A.C. 203.

At first glance, this case might suggest more clearly the idea of the double aspect doctrine that we know today. But the Attorney General for Canada saw something else in that case; he believed that it stood for the proposition that Parliament "is the *only* competent authority to pass the legislation where a convention has been entered into" and that "[t]he legislation could not be enacted by the provinces afterwards".[150] From this last statement, it is hard to see how we could characterise the Dominion's position as one supporting the "double aspect" doctrine. At best, one could say that the Dominion contented that there were *two temporal aspects*: (a) when, in the absence of a treaty binding Canada on a subject-matter, the province would have full jurisdiction over that subject-matter, and (b) when, after Canada being bound by a treaty, the Parliament would have full and exclusive jurisdiction over the subject-matter of the treaty. This is incompatible with the *simultaneous* nature of statutes validated by the double aspect doctrine.

To summarize, the federal government claimed to act on the international stage as the successor of the Imperial government for Canada, that Imperial powers related to maintaining and developing international relations were transferred to Ottawa through a transfer of the Imperial prerogatives[151] and that the Parliament had exclusive jurisdiction over any matter that was related to an international obligation incurred by treaty. In short, the federal government claimed to incarnate the new sovereign for Canada, that newly emancipated daughter of the "the mother country, Great Britain."[152]

C. "But We Are Equally Sisters": The Provinces' Federalist Arguments

Ontario, New Brunswick and British Columbia contradicted those pretensions by claiming that no such powers were devolved to the

---

[150] *Labour Conventions* case, *supra* note 19 at 331 (emphasis added).

[151] *Ibid.* at 330-31:

> By the constitutional developments, particularly since the Treaty of Versailles, the constitutional right to advise His Majesty in respect of international obligations affecting Canada has become vested in his Canadian Ministers. That is sometimes expressed by saying that the right to exercise the prerogative in respect of Canadian affairs has been transferred to the Canadian executive.

[152] The expression is taken from the *Radio Reference*, *supra* note 130 at 312 ("This idea of Canada as a Dominion being bound by a convention equivalent to a treaty with foreign powers was quite unthought-of in 1867. It is the outcome of the gradual development of the position of Canada vis-a-vis to the mother country, Great Britain.")

federal government and that, in essence, the Constitution Act, 1867 established a federation and not a unitary state.[153]

1. Ontario

Ontario's general constitutional arguments relied in large part on the assumption that what was at play here was a federal claim to be acting under s. 132 powers. However, because the arguments relied on the general structure of the Canadian constitution, they were also largely applicable to cases falling outside the purview of s. 132.

Ontario first argued for the *equal* constitutional status and *parallel powers* of the provinces and the Dominion. She argued that the only "authority competent to sign a treaty creating obligations is the King or some authority specially delegated to do so by the King. ..."[154] and that "[t]here are no grounds whatever for saying that the parties to advise His Majesty in matters relating to the jurisdiction of the provinces have in some way come to be the Dominion Ministers."[155] After all, "[t]here is nothing in the British North America Act which suggests that foreign affairs as affecting Provincial jurisdiction have been committed to the Dominion Government."[156] Therefore, when a s. 132 treaty affecting a matter within the provincial legislative competence is contemplated, Ontario argued that the King should give his assent on the advice of his provincial advisers as opposed to his federal advisers.[157] Doing otherwise would mean that s. 132 would defeat the purposes of the main provisions of the Constitution (i.e. ss. 91 and 92).[158]

And since "[t]he Province is as *equally sovereign* as the Dominion in its own sphere",[159] the consequence of the recognition of the equal status of the executive and legislative authority of the provinces and the Dominion was the claim that "Ontario has a right to enter into an agree-

---

[153] Arguments presented by the provinces are reconstructed from the reporter's notes presented with the decision of the Judicial Committee: *Labour Conventions* case, *supra* note 19 at 327-41. Alberta, Saskatchewan, Manitoba and Québec had presented arguments when the reference was heard by the Supreme Court of Canada (see *Labour Conventions* case – *SCC*], *supra* note 135) but did not participate in the appeal to the Privy Council.

[154] *Labour Conventions* case, *ibid.* at 333.

[155] *Ibid.*

[156] *Ibid.* at 340.

[157] *Ibid.* at 333 and 340.

[158] *Ibid.* at 334 ("It is not to be considered that those who drafted the Canadian constitution intended to write a constitution which was subject to defeat in its main provisions by competing jurisdictions. The concentration of power in the hands of the Dominion is fatal to Canada as it has been known in the past.")

[159] *Ibid.* at 340 (emphasis added).

ment with another part of the British Empire or *with a foreign State*."[160] Thus, Ontario considered herself to be bound directly – not through the Dominion – by the *Treaty of Versailles* as a member of the British Empire.[161]

In other words, neither the Dominion nor the provinces were superior to the other, they were simply responsible for different issues: the "division of powers" was also meant to be a "division of labour" among equals. Neither of them could speak for the other.

Ontario argued that the powers given to the Parliament and the federal government by virtue of s. 132 became effective only once binding obligations flowing from an Imperial treaty was in force. Also, once those powers were activated, they were not to be exclusive but simply overriding. This meant that once an Imperial treaty was imposing obligations related to provincial matters – property law, for example – provinces did not lose jurisdiction over that subject-matter. It simply meant that the Parliament could adopt implementing legislation that would override a conflicting provincial statute. In other words, s. 132 would merely be a remedial provision for when provinces would renege on their international promises in ways that would affect the responsibility of the Empire as a whole.

Then, after making the general constitutional argument on the status of provinces in the federation, Ontario made a series of arguments specific to the case at hand: (1) the only thing that could amount to a s. 132 obligation in the *Treaty of Versailles* might be Art. 405 (5) duty to "bring the ... draft convention before the authority or authorities within whose competence the matter lies, for the enactment of legislation or other action"[162] and that duty was fulfilled when the said conventions were brought to the attention of provinces; (2) the Parliament could not have gained legislative competence over the subject-matter of the conventions by virtue of s. 132 because no Imperial obligation binding on the Dominion or the provinces could have been created by the alleged Dominion's ratification of the conventions; such ratification was not in accordance with the dates set by the *Treaty of Versailles*; (3) moreover, the alleged Dominion's ratification could not be said to amount to an independent agreement between countries but merely to an offer.

Turning to a pure division of legislative powers issue, Ontario also distinguished this case from the *Radio Reference*[163] and the *Aeronautics*

---

[160] *Ibid.* at 333 (emphasis added).

[161] *Ibid.* at 333-34.

[162] See notes 116 and 117 and accompanying text.

[163] *Supra* note 130.

Reference[164] by arguing that those cases dealt with subject-matters that fell within s. 91 and not s. 92. That is, the real *ratio* of those cases was not about treaty implementation powers but rather about powers over radio communications (and the infrastructures that made them possible[165]) and aeronautics as such. Respective legislative powers had to be kept separate because "[t]he concentration of power in the hands of the Dominion is fatal to Canada as it has been known in the past."[166]

However, quite surprisingly, after having so strongly defended the autonomy of provinces, and after having argued that "[i]t is not to be considered that those who drafted the Canadian constitution intended to write a constitution which was subject to defeat in its main provisions by competing jurisdictions",[167] Ontario accepted that the statute might be valid on the basis of an extended version of what has come to be known to us as the "national concern" doctrine under s. 91 of the *Constitution Act, 1867*:

> ... present matters were of such national importance, of such wide import as to affect the body politic of the Dominion in the overriding way that was

---

[164] *Supra* note 125.

[165] Crocket J. had read the *Radio Reference, supra* note 130 in a similar way (*Labour Conventions* case – *SCC, supra* note 135 at 534-35):

Their Lordships held that broadcasting fell within the excepted matters as being an undertaking connecting one province with another, and extending beyond the limits of the province and therefore came within enumerated head 29 of s. 91. ... Their Lordships, moreover, held that broadcasting fell within the description of "telegraphs," which subject is excepted from "local works and undertakings," specified in s. 92(10), and therefore takes its place in 91(29). ... It appears, therefore, to me that, while one of the grounds of the decision in the *Radio* case [[1932] A.C. 304] was the form and nature of the convention itself, was the basis of the decision, as put in the judgment itself, "the pre-eminent claims of s. 91," which, I take it to refer to the fact that the subject matter of that convention fell under one of the enumerated heads of s. 91, viz: no. 29. For that reason the authority of Parliament in relation to the subject matter of the convention and of the legislation would override the legislative authority of the provinces in relation thereto, not because of the residuary clause in the introduction of that section, but in virtue of the declaration that,

> *notwithstanding anything in this Act*, the exclusive legislative authority of the Parliament of Canada extends to all matters coming within the classes of subjects

set forth in the 29 enumerated heads of that section, and the closing words of s. 91 as well that,

> Any matter coming within any of the classes of subjects enumerated in this section shall not be deemed to come within the class of matters of a local or private nature comprised in the enumeration of the classes of subjects by this Act assigned exclusively to the Legislatures of the Provinces.

This, as I read the judgment, is the fundamental basis of the decision.

[166] *Labour Conventions* case, *supra* note 19 at 334.

[167] *Ibid.*

found in *Russell v. The Queen*, ...,[168] if they were taken out of the specific heads of s. 92, then Ontario is satisfied to see his legislation supported. ... The Acts are of national importance, and the subject has attained such proportions as to affect the body politic."[169]

This concession confirmed that Ontario still demanded that the Parliament have jurisdiction over the subject-matter by virtue of s. 91 to be able to implement the Convention but, at the same time, it was gutting provincial powers by taking subject-matters completely out of the provinces' purview. Ultimately, after having argued for multi-layered political communities, she seemed to have reverted to the image of Canada as a single "body politic". New Brunswick and British Columbia would not retreat down that path.

---

[168] *Russell v. R*, (1882) 7 A.C. 829 [*Russell v. R.*].

[169] *Labour Conventions* case, *supra* note 19 at 334-35. One must note that the authority of the *Russell v. R.* decision to which the Attorney General for Ontario was referring had been significantly gutted by the *Local Prohibition* case (*Ontario (A.G.) v. Canada (A.G.)*, [1896] A.C. 348). That decision basically restricted *Russell v. R.* to the specific facts of the case. It therefore recognized that provinces could adopt statutes prohibiting alcohol. On what would later be interpreted as part of the "national concern" doctrine, Lord Watson wrote (*Local Prohibition* case, *ibid.* at p. 361):

> If it were once conceded that the Parliament of Canada has authority to make laws applicable to the whole Dominion, in relation to matters which in each province are substantially of local or private interest, upon the assumption that these matters also concern the peace, order and good government of the Dominion, *there is hardly a subject enumerated in section 92 upon which it might not legislate, to the exclusion of the provincial legislature.*
>
> ...
>
> Their Lordships do not doubt that some matters, in their origin local and provincial, might attain such dimensions as to affect the body politic of the Dominion, and to justify the Canadian Parliament in passing laws for their regulation or abolition in the interest of the Dominion. But great caution must be observed in distinguishing between that which is local or provincial, and therefore within the jurisdiction of the provincial legislatures, and that which has ceased to be merely local or provincial, and has become matter of national concern, in such sense as to bring it within the jurisdiction of the Parliament of Canada. (Emphasis added.)

Russell v. R., then largely discredited, gained a second lease on life in 1946 when it was reaffirmed by the Privy Council in *Ontario (A.G.) v. Canada (A.G.)*, [1946] A.C. 193 [*Reference re Canada Temperance Act*]. The "national concern" doctrine will be discussed in more details at notes 242-260 and accompanying text. On this so-called "national concern" or "national interest", see also Hugo Cyr, "L'interprétation constitutionnelle, un exemple de postpluralisme" (1998) 43 McGill L.J. 565, 575-76 [H. Cyr, "L'interprétation constitutionnelle, un exemple de postpluralisme"]; Jean Leclair, "The Elusive Quest for the Quintessential 'National Interest'" (2005) 38 U.B.C. L. Rev. 353 and Kenneth Lysyk, "The Constitutional Reform and the Introductory Clause of Section 91: Residual and Emergency Law-Making Authority" (1979) 57 Can. Bar Rev. 531.

2. New Brunswick

New Brunswick first argued that no s. 132 obligations were involved here and that therefore, to succeed, the Attorney General for Canada had to demonstrate "two propositions or principles: (1.) That the Dominion has the capacity to create treaty obligations binding on the Provinces; and (2.) that the Parliament of Canada has power to perform such obligations."[170] New Brunswick argued that the Dominion failed on both counts.

New Brunswick based her arguments on a vision of Canada as being an aggregate of self-governing entities that took part in a second layer of aggregation that corresponded to the Commonwealth of Nations that had replaced the Empire. Thus, before arguing on those two propositions, New Brunswick made one important preliminary point. It briefly reviewed the historical changes in the treaty powers in the Empire over the last centuries to show that despite the fact that "[o]riginally in Great Britain the treaty-making power and the treaty-performing power were vested in the same person", that situation had changed greatly due to a number of changes in British constitutionalism: gone were the days when "the King was sovereign in fact as in name".[171] As a result of those changes, treaty-making and treaty-performing were powers that now rested on *separate* entities. Among the changes highlighted by New Brunswick were "(a) the growth of representative institutions; (b) parliamentary sovereignty; (c) responsible government; (d) colonial self-government; (e) the federal system of government in Canada; and (f) the growth of the British Commonwealth of nations".[172] Thus, New Brunswick's historical contextualisation tells the tale of the fragmentation of the Imperial Crown along the lines of the self-governing political communities: the Empire was transformed into a Commonwealth made of equal and autonomous members and those Commonwealth members were sometimes further fragmented into federal governments and "provinces" (e.g. Canada) or "states" (e.g. Australia) to better allow overlapping political communities to govern themselves. This helps to explain New Brunswick's reluctance to see in s. 132 and in the doctrine of national emergency powers[173] anything but non-exclusive, yet overriding, legislative powers.[174]

---

[170] *Labour Conventions* case, *supra* note 19 at 335.

[171] *Ibid.* at 336.

[172] *Ibid.*

[173] *Ibid.* On the "national emergency" doctrine, see *supra* note 146 and accompanying text.

[174] *Ibid.*

From this historical narrative, New Brunswick moved to the first question. After reviewing different possible sources for the Dominion's alleged power to enter into treaties binding upon provinces, she concluded that no such sources granted that power. "[T]he Dominion can only enter into agreements with other states in respect of matters which fall within her legislative competence."[175] And since labour issues were admittedly provincial issues falling under s. 92 (13) ("Property and Civil Rights in the Province"), that meant that the federal government did not have the power to ratify such conventions.

On the second question, she refused the analogy between treaties and contracts that was used by the Dominion to suggest that the power to conclude an agreement presupposes a capacity to perform it. New Brunswick argued that a new international status for Canada did not result in granting legislative supremacy to Parliament. This new status simply changed the constitutional relation between Canada and the government of Great Britain and nothing more: "If by virtue of a new status Canada is to have the right by treaties to change the law of the Provinces it should be by constitutional amendment."[176]

As to the *Radio Reference*, New Brunswick contended, as Ontario and Crocket J. did,[177] that it did not establish a general power to implement treaties but that it simply stated that radio communications did not fall within s. 92 and that they either fell in one of the subsections of s. 91 or within the federal residuary powers. New Brunswick further supported her argument by suggesting that to decide otherwise would mean the destruction of the "principle enunciated by this Board about the object of the *British North America Act* in numerous cases".[178] In particular, New Brunswick referred to *Liquidators of the Maritime Bank of Canada*.[179] In that important case, the Privy Council stated that the object of the *British North America Act* was:

> ... neither to weld the provinces into one, nor to subordinate provincial governments to a central authority, but to create a federal government in which they should all be represented, entrusted with the exclusive administration of affairs in which they had a common interest, each province retaining its independence and autonomy. That object was accomplished by distributing, between the Dominion and the provinces, all powers executive and legislative, and all public property and revenues which had previously belonged to the provinces; so that the Dominion Government should be vested with such of these powers, property, and revenues as were necessary for the due per-

---

[175] *Ibid.* at 337.

[176] *Ibid.*

[177] See *supra* note 165 and accompanying text.

[178] *Labour Conventions* case, *supra* note 19 at 338.

[179] *Supra* note 23.

formance of its constitutional functions, and that the remainder should be retained by the provinces for the purposes of provincial government. But, in so far as regards those matters which, by sect. 92, are specially reserved for provincial legislation, the legislation of each province continues to be free from the control of the Dominion, and as supreme as it was before the passing of the Act.[180]

The Privy Council had also written that "a Lieutenant-Governor, when appointed, is as much a representative of Her Majesty, for all purposes of Provincial government as the Governor-General himself is for all purposes of Dominion government".[181] New Brunswick thus pushed forcefully on the idea that provinces and the Dominion were equal within their own spheres.

Finally, New Brunswick opposed Ontario's position that the statute should be validated on grounds of expediency. Canada was a federation and, therefore, what was good for one part might not necessarily be good for all parts.

3. British Columbia

British Columbia also highlighted the federal nature of the Constitution by making reference to a version of the "compact theory": "*The British North America Act, 1867*, has been said to be in the nature of a treaty by which the Provinces surrendered certain of their rights and preserved others."[182]

From that starting point, British Columbia viewed with alarm the arguments made on behalf of the Dominion and the concession that Ontario had made. She argued that if the impugned bills were to be validated on the basis of s. 91 powers to make laws for the "Peace, Order and Good Government", "it w[ould] be even more fatal, even more of an invasion of Provincial rights, than if it [were] upheld under treaty-making powers".[183] In effect, it would mean that issues specifically attributed to provinces by s. 92 – and upon which legislatures have validly legislated – would be taken out of provinces' powers and given to Parliament merely on the basis of "what is termed a change in recognition of conditions".[184] One can sense that British Columbia, here, was not only worried that this doctrine would endanger validly adopted provincial laws, but that the arbitrariness in the "recognition" of

---

[180] *Ibid.* at 441-42.

[181] *Ibid.* at 443.

[182] *Labour Conventions* case, *supra* note 19 at 339.

[183] *Ibid.* at 338.

[184] *Ibid.*

"changes in condition" was really going to transform the initial constitutional bargain.

She then argued that there is constitutional precedent for legislation by "subordinate powers" to fulfil the international obligations of the supreme authority. Having established that principle, she argued that provinces have all the legislative powers necessary to implement the conventions.[185] This highlights something important here: complying with treaty obligations can take multiple forms. As I will show later, even the executive can implement certain treaty obligations without the participation of any legislative body[186]; just think, for example, of military orders commanding a ceasefire or a withdrawal of troops following an armistice treaty.

British Columbia followed New Brunswick in arguing that Canada's new international status only changed her relation to foreign states; it did not change in anyway the distribution of powers provided by ss. 91 and 92 of the *Constitution Act, 1867*. Thus, it was to be "the nature of the subject-matter itself which determines the class into which it falls".[187] Here, the subject-matter of the legislation fell squarely within the exclusive jurisdiction of provinces. In support of that argument, reference was made to the *Aeronautics Reference* [188] and the *Radio Reference*.[189] This probably indicates that British Columbia accepted the interpretation that Ontario and New Brunswick made of that decision: radio communication in itself must fall within s. 91.

After setting up those general arguments, the report is rather vague on the further claims made by British Columbia. She apparently made

---

[185] *Ibid.* at 339. Here, the Privy Council's report of the argument is somewhat ambiguous. It is unclear whether British Columbia considered provinces' powers to implement the conventions as an application of the principle that subordinated powers can take part in treaty implementation or whether it was an *a fortiori* argument to the effect that if subordinated powers can do so, provinces, which are not subordinated, must necessarily be capable too. Because it is not clear what British Columbia considered a "subordinate power", it is hard to tell. Would, for example, British Columbia have considered the Dominion a "subordinated power" in relation to the Imperial power? If "subordinate" means a "delegation", then that would be wrong (see *Hodge v. R.*, *supra* note 14). However, if it means "non-autonomous", then it would be right. And then s. 132 would be a good example of such precedent since it reflects an explicit recognition that Imperial treaties could be implemented by "subordinate powers". However, the arguments presented by New Brunswick, in particular, the absence of changes in the nature of relations between the federal and the provinces after Canada's change of international status suggests that British Columbia may have intended her argument to be one *a fortiori*.

[186] See *infra* notes 219-221 and accompanying text.

[187] *Labour Conventions* case, *supra* note 19 at 339.

[188] *Supra* note 125.

[189] *Supra* note 130.

two claims that must have been alternative propositions. It was first claimed that Art. 405, paras. 5 and 7 of the *Treaty of Versailles* had not been respected because the draft conventions had not been presented to the relevant authorities for the purpose of obtaining their consent. This argument seems to point to the absence of a binding international obligation due to a failure in respecting the procedure set-up by Art. 405 of the *Treaty of Versailles*. The second claim seems to assume that valid s. 132 obligations might have been created. In that context, New Brunswick argued that when the subject-matters of a s. 132 treaty falls clearly within s. 92, it would not be proper for Parliament to intervene when provinces have enacted or had not yet the chance to enact appropriate legislation. In other words, s. 132 was interpreted as a remedial provision. British Columbia then argued that provinces were not given the opportunity, after ratification, to confirm whether or not they were ready to conform to their obligations.

D. "Canada is a Federation": The Judicial Committee of the Privy Council

The assumption behind the Privy Council's decision is that Canada is a federation and that was the only way to bring together her distinct parts. A legislative union, although possibly more efficient, was simply not possible. The members of the Privy Council, if they were not already aware of that political fact before hearing the appeal, had the chance to read in Cannon J.'s opinion accounts of the negotiations given by many key players at the time.[190]

Here is a brief taste of what the Law Lords were able to read from Cannon J.'s opinion. Sir John A. Macdonald, then Attorney General for Upper Canada, had been in favour of the idea of creating one single unified political unit in Canada. However, he stated, before the Canadian Parliament in 1865, that he had retreated from his position:

> The third and only means of solution for our difficulties was the junction of the provinces either in a Federal or a Legislative Union. Now, as regards the comparative advantages of a Legislative and a Federal Union, I have never hesitated to state my own opinions. I have again and again stated in the House, that, if practicable, I thought a Legislative Union would be preferable. I have always contended that if we could agree to have one government and one parliament, legislating for the whole of these peoples, it would be the best, the cheapest, the most vigorous, and the strongest system of government we could adopt. But, on looking at the subject in the Conference, and discussing the matter as we did most unreservedly, and with a desire to arrive at a satisfactory conclusion, we found that such a system was

---

[190] *Labour Conventions* case – *SCC, supra* note 135 at 514-18.

impracticable. ... So that those who were, like myself, in favour of a Legislative Union, were obliged to modify their views and accept the project of a Federal Union as the only scheme practicable, even for the Maritime Provinces.[191]

Macdonald concluded that the constitutional scheme that was agreed upon was the result of multiple concessions and that "we must consider this scheme in the light of a treaty."[192] Lord Carnavon said, on the second reading of the *British North America Act* in the House of Lords, that "[a] legislative union is under existing circumstances impracticable."[193] Chief Justice Dorion, who had participated in the Confederation Debates when he was a member of the legislature wrote: "There is no difference between the powers of the local and Dominion legislatures within their own sphere. That is the powers of the local legislature within its own sphere are co-extensive with the powers of the Dominion government within its own sphere. The one is not inferior to the other."[194]

In that spirit, the Privy Council wrote that "[n]o one can doubt that this distribution is one of the most essential conditions, probably the most essential condition, in the inter-provincial compact to which the *British North America Act* gives effect."[195] It then went on to specify why such system was necessary for the different parts of the federation.[196] The Privy Council thus wrote its decision with the awareness that Canada was the result of a political compromise that required the utmost respect for the autonomy of provinces. That is one of the reasons why,

---

[191] *Ibid.* at 514-15.

[192] *Ibid.* at 515.

[193] *Ibid.* at 517. Lord Carnavon further added (*ibid.*):

> The Maritime Provinces are ill-disposed to surrender their separate life, and to merge their individuality in the political organization of the general body. It is in their case, impossible, even if it were desirable, by a stroke of the pen to bring about a complete assimilation of their institutions to those of their neighbours. Lower Canada, too, is jealous, as she is deservedly proud, of their ancestral customs and traditions; she is wedded to her peculiar institutions, and will enter this Union only upon the distinct understanding she retains them.

[194] *Ibid.*

[195] *Labour Conventions* case, *supra* note 19 at 351.

[196] *Ibid*:

> If the position of Lower Canada, now Quebec, alone were considered, the existence of her separate jurisprudence as to both property and civil rights might be said to depend upon loyal adherence to her constitutional right to the exclusive competence of her own Legislature in these matters. Nor is it of less importance for the other Provinces, though their law may be based on English jurisprudence, to preserve their own right to legislate for themselves in respect of local conditions which may vary by as great a distance as separate[s] the Atlantic from the Pacific.

to put it shortly, the Privy Council concluded that "no further legislative competence is obtained by the Dominion from its accession to international status".[197]

Let's examine in detail the opinion of the Privy Council.

1. Distinguishing Between Making and Implementing Treaties

The Judicial Committee of the Privy Council first responded that "[w]ithin the British Empire there is a well-established rule that the making of a treaty is an executive act, while the performance of its obligations, if they entail alteration of the existing domestic law, requires legislative action."[198] So it is important to distinguish between the two first stages in the life of a treaty-based norm: (1) the period during which the treaty is concluded – whereby the international obligation is formed[199] – and (2) the period during which the treaty is implemented – or, in the words of the Judicial Committee, whereby the obligation is "performed".[200] Thus, the signature and ratification of treaties are traditionally the prerogative of the Crown and, as such, fall to the executive branch.[201]

The Privy Council noted that it is wise for the executive to obtain an expression of approval from the legislature that would later be called to implement legislatively the international obligations in question. How-

---

[197] *Ibid.* at 352.

[198] *Ibid.* at 347.

[199] Depending on the type of agreement, different formalities will be applicable. In modern day usage, "Heads of States" treaties (i.e. treaties upon which the Head of the State him or herself puts his or her seal on the documents) have been abandoned for intergovernmental treaties (i.e. treaties concluded by a representative of each government). In Canada, the degree of formality of modern (written) treaties vary from more formal treaties where the agreements are first signed by governments' negotiators and later ratified by decisions of the government to simple exchanges on notes between governments.

[200] *Labour Conventions* case, *supra* note 19 at 347.

[201] The fact that the federal executive now ratifies without necessarily seeking the approval from the Parliament has been criticised for the lack of transparency and the undemocratic character of the process. See J. Harrington, "Redressing the Democratic Deficit in Treaty Law Making: (Re-)Establishing a Role for Parliament", *supra* note 41. On ratification, see among others: Claude Emanuelli, *Droit International Public*, Vol. 1 (Montréal: Wilson & Lafleur, 1990) at 64; J.-Y. Morin, "La conclusion d'accords internationaux par les provinces canadiennes", *supra* note 4; J.-Y. Morin, "La personnalité internationale du Québec" *supra* note 41; A.L.C. de Mestral, "Le Québec et les relations internationales", *supra* note 41 at 209; Thomas A. Levy, "Provincial International Status Revisited" (1976-77) 3 Dal. L.J. 70; R. St. John MacDonald, "The Relationship Between International Law and Domestic Law in Canada", *supra* note 41; Edward McWhinney, "The Constitutional Competence Within Federal Systems as to International Agreements", *supra* note 41.

ever, such an expression of approval does not "operat[e] as law"[202] and does not preclude current and future legislatures from declining to implement the treaty obligations incurred.[203]

2. *Making Treaties on Provincial Matters: A Silent Overruling*

Contrary to what commentators sometimes assume,[204] after distinguishing between "forming" and "performing" international obligations, the Privy Council *refused* to rule on the issue of whether or not the federal executive had powers to ratify the conventions; it was unnecessary to take position on that point since the case could be decided by simply examining the question of legislative competence.[205] It is true that when Lord Atkin wanted to highlight the complexity of the relations between the executive and the legislative concerning treaties in the context of federal states he wrote: "The obligations imposed by treaty may have to be performed, if at all, by several Legislatures; and the executive have the task of obtaining the legislative assent not of the one Parliament to whom they may be responsible, but possibly of several Parliaments to whom they stand in no direct relation".[206] But in the end, the Privy Council could hardly be clearer:

> Reverting again to the original analysis of the contentions of the parties, it will be seen that the Provincial contention 1.(b) ["[t]hat the Canadian Government had no executive authority to make any such treaty as was alleged."[207]] relates only to the formation of the treaty obligation, while 1.(c)

---

[202] *Labour Conventions* case, *supra* note 19 at 348.

[203] *Ibid.*

[204] See for example, Donald M. McRae and John H. Currie who, forgetting Ontario's, New Brunswick's and Rinfret J.'s position (*supra* notes 154-161 and 175 and accompanying text) in the case, wrote in "Treaty-Making and Treaty Implementation: The Kyoto Protocol" (2003) 29:2 Canadian Council on International Law Bulletin that

> [i]t has never been seriously doubted that treaty-making authority rests exclusively with the federal executive branch. No legislative concurrence, either by Parliament or the provincial legislatures, has ever been legally required prior to ratification of treaties by the federal government. That position was confirmed as early as 1936 by the Supreme Court in the *Labour Conventions* case, and has not been seriously doubted since.

McRae and Currie, while discussing the respective roles of the executive and the legislative powers take for granted that the federal executive has undivided powers to make treaties. However, Gérald-A. Beaudoin, *Le fédéralisme au Canada* (Montréal: Wilson & Lafleur, 2000) at 877 and Henri Brun and Guy Tremblay, *Droit constitutionnel*, 4th ed. (Cowansville (Qc): Yvon Blais, 2002) at 66 [Henri Brun and Guy Tremblay, *Droit constitutionnel*] note correctly that the Privy Council never recognized such jurisdiction to the federal executive.

[205] *Labour Conventions* case, *supra* note 19 at 349.

[206] *Ibid.* at 348.

[207] *Ibid.* at 342.

has reference to the alleged limitation of both executive and legislative action by the express terms of the treaty. *If, however, the Dominion Parliament was never vested with legislative authority to perform the obligation
these questions do not arise. And, as their Lordships have come to the conclusion that the reference can be decided upon the question of legislative
competence alone, in accordance with their usual practice in constitutional
matters they refrain from expressing any opinion upon the questions raised
by the contentions 1.(b) and (c), which in that event become immaterial.*[208]

Therefore, the extent of the federal power to negotiate, sign and ratify
treaties dealing *with matters falling in the provincial sphere of legislative competence was explicitly left undecided.*[209]

Nonetheless, some might want to argue that it seems that Lord Atkin
later intuited, in an *obiter*, that the federal executive may now have the
power to conclude treaties with other states on subject-matter relating to
s. 92 when he wrote:

It is true, as pointed out in the judgment of the Chief Justice, that *as the executive is now clothed with the powers of making treaties* so the Parliament
of Canada, to which the executive is responsible, has imposed upon it responsibilities in connection with such treaties, for if it were to disapprove of
them they would either not be made or the Ministers would meet their constitutional fate. But this is true of all executive functions in their relation to
Parliament. *There is no existing constitutional ground for stretching the
competence of the Dominion Parliament so that it becomes enlarged to keep
pace with enlarged functions of the Dominion executive. If the new functions
affect the classes of subjects enumerated in s. 92 legislation to support the
new functions is in the competence of the Provincial Legislatures only.* If
they do not, the competence of the Dominion Legislature is declared by s.
91 and existed ab origine. *In other words, the Dominion cannot, merely by
making promises to foreign countries*, clothe itself with legislative authority
inconsistent with the constitution which gave it birth.[210]

However, this statement in no way explains the legal basis for this
federal power. In fact, this excerpt can equally support two readings:
(a) the federal executive possesses a constitutional power to make
treaties that is independent of the Parliament's sphere of competence
and that has an autonomous constitutional source, or (b) the federal
executive has the power to make treaties outside of the Parliament's

---

[208] *Ibid.* at 348-49 (emphasis added).

[209] V.C. MacDonald, "The Canadian Constitution Seventy Years Later", *supra* note 112
at 418, fn 32, is of the same opinion: "The point taken by the provinces and expressly
left open by the Judicial Committee awaits determination, *viz.*, whether the Dominion
Executive is competent to *make* any treaty as to subject-matters falling within provincial legislative competence."

[210] *Labour Conventions* case, *supra* note 19 at 352 (emphasis added).

jurisdiction through a delegation of powers from the provinces. Thus, I will examine the possible constitutional basis of both hypotheses to decide which one fits better within our constitutional web. This will be done in Chapter II.

Before going any further, it is necessary to correct another assumption. Many think that the majority of the Supreme Court (four out of six) has set a binding precedent in favour of an exclusive federal power to make treaties and, not having been overruled by the Privy Council, this ruling still stands. The argument goes: out of the six judges who took part in the Supreme Court's reference, three (Duff C.J., and Davis and Kerwin JJ.) thought that the Dominion had plenary powers to conclude and implement treaties and one (Crocket J.) believed that the Dominion could conclude such treaties but that implementation had to follow the normal division of legislative powers. However, once we examine the opinions closely, we find that the reference cannot ultimately stand as a precedent for the proposition that the federal executive has an exclusive plenary power to make treaties.

The position of the three judges who claimed that the federal government had such plenary powers to conclude and implement treaties was quite undermined after the Privy Council's decision. First, the trio took the view that the Dominion Parliament has the authority to adopt the impugned statutes on the basis that it is implementing a s. 132 treaty obligation.[211] This would mean that their position on the Dominion executive plenary powers over treaties outside of s. 132 situations would simply be an *obiter dictum*. The trio was later overruled on the applicability of s. 132 by the Privy Council. Second, the trio relied on the idea that it is the Parliament that has plenary authority over foreign affairs and treaty implementation to derive the conclusion that the federal government has plenary powers to conclude treaties – not the other way around. In effect, the treaty-making power, in the trio's opinion, depends on Parliament's legislative powers.[212] Thus, the Dominion's

---

[211] *Labour Conventions* case – *SCC, supra* note 135 at 500:

> It follows from what has been said that this treaty obligation is an obligation within section 132 and, consequently, that the authority to make the convention effective exclusively rests in the Parliament and Government of Canada and, therefore, that the Parliament of Canada is, at least, one of the authorities before which the convention must be brought under the terms of article 405.

[212] *Ibid.* at 488-89 and 492:

> The Canadian executive, again, constitutionally acts under responsibility to the Parliament of Canada and it is that Parliament alone which can constitutionally control its conduct of external affairs. ...

> The judgments of the Judicial Committee of the Privy Council in the *Aeronautics* case [[1932] A.C. 54] and the *Radio* case [[1932] A.C. 304] constrain us to hold that jurisdiction to legislate for the purpose of performing the obligation – for

executive powers were supposed to be hanging from the Dominion legislative hook, but once the Privy Council said – as we will soon see – that no such plenary power existed, the Dominion executive lost its attach to provincial legislative matters. In other words, the Privy Council might not have commented on the capacity of the Dominion to form treaties on subject-matters normally falling in the provincial legislative ambit, but it destroyed the basis upon which the trio of the Supreme Court had constructed such power. It was an indirect overruling. In those circumstances, the precedential value of the trio's position is nil.

If we turn to the fourth judge, Crocket J., who disagreed with Duff C.J, Davis J. and Kerwin J. on the result but agreed with the Chief Justice that the federal executive had the power to conclude treaties dealing with provincial subject-matters, again, we see that his position on treaty-making powers was an *obiter*.[213] After all, if he believed the statutes to be invalid on division of legislative powers ground, it was clearly unnecessary to say whether or not the Dominion had powers to make treaties dealing with provincial legislative subject-matters. In any case, he said nothing of the possible role of provinces in the ratification process.

Rinfret J., contrary to the four previously mentioned judges, based his entire opinion on the issue of the Dominion's treaty-making powers. Rinfret J., whose *ratio decidendi* rested on that question, found that the Dominion *could not* create international obligations dealing with subject-matters that would otherwise fall within the exclusive jurisdiction of provinces without their consent.[214] Rinfret believed that precedents

---

bringing the law of the Canadian provinces into harmony with the provisions of the convention, for example – resides exclusively in the Parliament of Canada; and, by parity of reasoning, if not, indeed, as an obvious logical consequence of that proposition, jurisdiction resides, in so far as executive action is required, exclusively in the Government of Canada.

[213] *Ibid.* at 535:

While I agree with the learned Chief Justice that the Government of Canada must now be held to be the proper medium for the formal conclusion of international conventions, whether they affect the Dominion as a whole or any of the provinces separately, I do not think that this fact can be relied on as altering in any way the provisions of the B.N.A. Act as regards the distribution of legislative power as between the Dominion Parliament and the provincial legislatures or as necessarily giving to any matter, which may be made the subject of legislation in Canada, any other meaning or aspect than that which bears in our original constitution. Whether such a matter is one which falls under the terms of either s. 91 or of s. 92 or of s. 132, must depend upon the real intendment of the B.N.A. Act itself, as gathered from the terms of those sections and the Act as a whole.

[214] *Ibid.* at 511:

If the effect of the undertaking is that a subject of legislation within the exclusive jurisdiction of the province will thereby be transferred from that jurisdiction to the

established that once a valid treaty was formed, legislative powers to implement such treaty were transferred to the Parliament. However, if a proposed treaty was related to a provincial subject-matter, it had to be consented to by provinces before being validly formed. Here, since Rinfret believed that no such consent was given and no treaty obligation was duly created, the impugned statutes were deemed *ultra vires* because there was no transfer of legislative powers from the provinces to the Parliament on issues that fell squarely in the ambit of provincial legislative jurisdiction.

Cannon J., took the position that the statutes fell within the exclusive jurisdiction of the provinces and that the division of legislative powers could not be affected by the mere adoption of international obligations. However, Cannon J. also added that before the Dominion could ratify a treaty "*affecting* the provinces", there must be "*consultations* between the federal and provincial self-governing parts of our Confederation".[215]

---

jurisdiction of the Dominion Parliament, I consider it to be within the clear spirit of the British North America Act that the obligation should not be created or entered into before the provinces have given their consent thereto. In the particular case that we are now considering, it is my humble view that such was the effect of the judgment of this Court in the matter of the Reference of 1925 [[1925] S.C.R. 505]. ...

A civil right does not change its nature just because it becomes the subject-matter of a convention with foreign States. It continues to be the same civil right. When once the convention has been properly adopted and ratified, it is, no doubt, transferred to the federal field for the enactment of laws necessary or proper for performing the obligations arising under the convention. That is, as I understand it, the effect of the decisions of the Privy Council on the *Aeronautics* [[1932] A.C. 54] and *Radio* [[1932] A.C. 304] References. But before the international obligation has been properly and competently created, the civil right under the jurisdiction of the provinces is always the same civil right, and I cannot see where the Dominion Parliament in the *British North America Act* finds the power to appropriate it for the purpose of dealing with it internationally without having previously secured the consent of the provinces.

[215] *Ibid.* at 518-19:

The procedure recommended by the Imperial Conferences in 1926 and 1930 regarding legislation or international agreements by one of the self-governing parts of the Empire which may affect the interests of other self-governing parts, i.e. previous consultation between His Majesty's ministers in the several parts concerned, should be applied by the central and provincial governments specially before ratifying any international agreement – not falling under Section 132 of the B.N.A. Act. The only direct legislative authority expressly given to the Parliament and Government of Canada concerning foreign affairs is found in this section and is limited to the performance of the obligations of Canada or any province thereof arising under treaties between the Empire as a whole and a foreign country. The Imperial Parliament saw to it that Imperial interests would be protected by federal legislation. *But to pass legislation – affecting the provinces – to ratify a treaty or agreement by Canada alone – under an evolution which came to pass since Confederation – with a foreign power, previous consultations between the federal and provincial self-governing parts of our Confederation seem to me logical and the only way to pre-*

In this, he was in line with the rules adopted at the 1923 Imperial Conference and in the 1926 *Balfour Declaration*:

> It was agreed in 1923 that any of the Governments of the Empire contemplating the negotiation of a treaty should give due consideration to its possible effect upon other Governments and should take steps to inform Governments likely to be interested of its intention.
>
> This rule should be understood as applying to any negotiations which any Government intends to conduct, so as to leave it to the other Governments to say whether they are likely to be interested.
>
> When a Government has received information of the intention of any other Government to conduct negotiations, it is incumbent upon it to indicate its attitude with reasonable promptitude.
>
> So long as the initiating Government receives no adverse comments and so long as its policy involves no active obligations on the part of the other Governments, it may proceed on the assumption that its policy is generally acceptable. It must, however, before taking any steps which might involve the other Governments in any active obligations, obtain their definite assent.[216]

This statement helps to see why Cannon and Rinfret JJ. do not necessarily hold different opinions on the level of involvement required by provinces in the conclusion of treaties. In effect, their positions can be reconciled. There is a distinction to be drawn between "laws *relative* to X" and "laws *affecting* X" in Canadian constitutional law. In the first category, X refers to the dominant feature of the law, its "pith and substance". In the second type of laws, X is a secondary feature of the law. So, for example, a province can validly adopt a statute *relative* to "direct taxation" (s. 92 (2)) that would *affect* banking (s. 91 (15)).[217] However, if the "pith and substance" of the provincial statute were not "direct taxation" but banking, then the statute would be invalid.[218] Thus,

---

> serve peace, order and good government in Canada and save the very roots of the tree to which our constitution has been compared. In order to grow, if it be a growing instrument, it must keep contact with its native soil – and draw from the constituting provinces new force and efficiency. (Emphasis added).

[216] *Balfour Declaration*, *supra* note 66, 6-7. The term "government" is not defined and could possibly be interpreted as applying to provincial governments. Remember that in 1923, the idea that the Dominion could conclude treaties on its own was no less a novelty than imagining provinces doing so.

[217] *Bank of Toronto v. Lambe*, (1887) 12 A.C. 575. On this point, see Peter Hogg, *Constitutional Law of Canada: Student Edition 2002* (Toronto: Carswell, 2002) at §15.5 (a) [P. Hogg, *Constitutional Law of Canada*, 2002] and Chevrette and Marx, *Droit constitutionnel*, *supra* note 41 at 303-05.

[218] *Alberta (A.G.) v. Canada (A.G.)*, [1939] A.C. 117 [*Alberta Bank Taxation* case]. The Supreme Court of Canada recently restated the distinction between "laws relative to X" and "laws affecting X" in *Canadian Western Bank v. Alberta*, [2007] 2 S.C.R. 3, 2007 SCC 22 [*Canadian Western Bank*] in these terms:

per Rinfret J., a treaty *relative to* a subject-matter falling in the exclusive legislative jurisdiction of provinces could only be ratified by the federal government after receiving the *consent* of the provinces and, *per* Cannon J., a treaty *affecting* such provincial jurisdiction could only be ratified by Ottawa after *consultations.* This was exactly the policy developed for the relations in the Commonwealth.

From all this, it is hard to see how one can be confident in asserting that the Supreme Court set a precedent recognizing the exclusive role of the federal executive in treaty-making. In fact, it seems quite the contrary. What remains after the destruction by the Privy Council of the basis of the *obiter* of Duff C.J., and Davis and Kerwin JJ. seems to be (1) the *ratio decidendi* of Rinfret J. requiring consent of the provinces when the federal government intends to ratify a treaty *relative to* a provincial subject-matter, (2) an *obiter* by Cannon J. requiring consultations with the provinces before the ratification by the federal executive of a treaty *affecting* a provincial subject-matter and, finally, (3) an *obiter* by Crocket J. approving of Duff C.J. dictum that the federal government has the power to conclude treaties.

3. *Executive Roles in Implementing Treaties*

The Privy Council stated that "performance of [the state's] obligations, if they entail alteration of the existing domestic law, requires legislative action".[219] I would note here that with respect to the implementation stage, the executive branch can fulfill treaty obligations of the

---

The fundamental corollary to this approach to constitutional analysis is that legislation whose pith and substance falls within the jurisdiction of the legislature that enacted it may, at least to a certain extent, affect matters beyond the legislature's jurisdiction without necessarily being unconstitutional. At this stage of the analysis of constitutionality, the "dominant purpose" of the legislation is still decisive. Its secondary objectives and effects have no impact on its constitutionality: "merely incidental effects will not disturb the constitutionality of an otherwise *intra vires* law" (*Global Securities Corp. v. British Columbia (Securities Commission)*, [2000] 1 S.C.R. 494, 2000 SCC 21, at para. 23). By "incidental" is meant effects that may be of significant practical importance but are collateral and secondary to the mandate of the enacting legislature: see *British Columbia v. Imperial Tobacco Canada Ltd.*, [2005] 2 S.C.R. 473, 2005 SCC 49, at para. 28.

It has to be said that a law may be *valid* according to the rules governing the division of legislative powers but it may nonetheless be *inapplicable* in particular circumstances. While "the Court does not favour an intensive reliance on [that] doctrine" (*Canadian Western Bank, ibid.* at para. 47), a statute may be deemed inapplicable "when the adverse impact of a law adopted by one level of government increases in severity from "affecting" to "impairing" (without necessarily "sterilizing" or "paralyzing") ... the "core" competence of the other level of government (or the vital or essential part of an undertaking it duly constitutes) ... (*Canadian Western Bank, ibid.* at para. 48.).

[219] *Labour Conventions* case, *supra* note 19 at 347.

state in such matters as national defence and diplomatic relations without legislative action if fulfilling its obligations does not require a modification of domestic law.[220] However, legislative implementation of the treaty is necessary when (a) the treaty affects private rights of individuals; (b) involves a modification of the common or statute law;[221] (c) requires the vesting of additional powers in the Crown; (d) imposes additional financial obligations upon the government; or (e) involves a

---

[220] F. Rigaldies and J. Woehrling, "Le juge interne canadien et le droit international", *supra* note 41 at 314 reported that around 1980, 296 treaties ratified by Canada did not require any legislative action for their implementation. For a list of treaties falling within the exclusive jurisdiction of the executive branch, see *Francis v. R.*, [1956] S.C.R. 618 at 625ff [*Francis v. R.*].

[221] *Labour Conventions* case, *supra* note 19 at 347. See also: *Re Arrow and Tributaries Slide & Boom Co.*, [1932] S.C.R. 495 at 510-11; *Francis v. R., ibid.* at 621 and 626; *Capital Cities Communications v. Canada (Canadian Radio-television and Telecommunications Commission)*, [1978] 2 S.C.R. 141 at 173 [*Capital Cities Communications v. C.R.T.C.*] and *Operation Dismantle v. Canada*, [1985] 1 S.C.R. 455 at 484.

Joseph G. Starke, *Introduction to International Law*, 9th ed. (London: Butterworths, 1984) at 79, notes that there are under British law at least three exceptions to the rule that a treaty affecting individuals' rights or involving a modification of the common or statute law must be legislatively implemented. The first exception to the rule covers an agreement to admit a foreign armed force and to concede certain immunities from the local jurisdiction to its members (see *Chow Hung Ching v. R.*, [1949] 77 C.L.R. 449). The second exception is a treaty between Great Britain and a foreign government for the recognition of that government. The third exception is that a peace treaty to which Great Britain is a party will put an end to the situation under which persons carrying on business or voluntarily resident in enemy territory are treated as enemy aliens who are not entitled to bring proceedings in the courts without the permission of the Crown (see *Porter v. Freudenberg*, [1915] 1 K.B. 857 (U.K.)).

Under Canadian law, some decisions have dealt with the effect of a peace treaty, but they were not quite conclusive. In *Canada (Secretary of State) v. United States (Alien Property Custodian)*, [1931] S.C.R. 168 at 198 [*Canada (Secretary of State) v. United States (Alien Property Custodian)*], Duff J. writes this *obiter*: "The treaty it is to be observed, being a Treaty of Peace, had the effect of law quite independently of legislation". This proposition was referred to by Angers J. in *obiter* in *Ritcher v. R.*, [1943] 3 D.L.R. 540 (Ex. Ct.) at 545. However, the Exchequer Court wrote another *obiter* in *Bitter v. Canada (Secretary of State)*, [1943] 3 D.L.R. 482 [*Bitter v. Canada*], stating that Duff J. was wrong in *Canada (Secretary of State) v. United States (Alien Property Custodian), ibid.* and that as any other treaty, a peace treaty cannot affect individuals' rights without legislation; its only effect would be to end hostilities. R. St. John Mac-Donald, "The Relationship Between International Law and Domestic Law in Canada", *supra* note 41 at 119-121, submits that the *Bitter v. Canada, ibid.*, decision should be the leading authority and that the peace treaty signed by the Crown can only end the hostilities and allow certain land cessions (a power within the prerogative of the Crown). A middle ground solution seems desirable: even if the content of the treaty is not directly incorporated into domestic law, some of its effects must be recognized in the domestic legal order such as the change of status of the belligerent State that ratifies the peace treaty. The peace treaty would thus have an impact on the domestic law in that it is a *fact* that modifies legal characterizations.

land cession. Of course, all this is apart from the need for the government to secure from Parliament the necessary funds to fulfil its obligations.

4. Section 132 Constitution Act, 1867,
Only Applies to Imperial Treaty Obligations

The Privy Council refused to apply s. 132 to the conventions at hand.
In plain terms, it concluded that the obligations in question were simply
"not obligations of Canada as part of the British Empire, but of Canada,
by virtue of her new status as an international person, and do not arise
under a treaty between the British Empire and foreign countries."[222] In
saying so, it confirmed the *Radio Reference*[223] ruling that s. 132 did not
apply to all international obligations that Canada or the provinces might
have; the text of s. 132 limits its applicability to obligations incurred "as
part of the Empire" and "arising under Treaties between the Empire and
such Foreign Countries". Indeed, the Privy Council concludes that "it is
impossible to strain the section so as to cover the uncontemplated event
[that the Dominion would possess treaty-making powers]."[224]

The Privy Council also rejected the view that the *Treaty of Versailles*
– to which s. 132 could be applicable – required the conventions to be
implemented. No such obligation to legislate arose until the Canadian
executive decided to bind itself independently from the *Treaty of Versailles*.

5. No Treaty Powers in Section 91
of the Constitution Act, 1867

Since s. 132 could not be counted on to justify the federal bill at issue, the Privy Council reverted to the general division of powers regime
provided at ss. 91 and 92 of the *Constitution Act, 1867*. Lord Atkin
noted right away that the impugned legislation would normally fall
"within the classes of subjects by s. 92 assigned exclusively to the
Legislatures of the Provinces" and that "it appears to be expressly
excluded from the general powers given by the first words" of s. 91.[225]
He then referred to the 1925 Supreme Court decision mentioned earlier
and claimed that, but for the opinion of Chief Justice Duff that the
Aeronautics Reference[226] and the *Radio Reference*[227] gave exclusive

---

[222] *Labour Conventions* case, *supra* note 19 at 349.

[223] *Supra* note 130.

[224] *Labour Conventions* case, *supra* note 19 at 350.

[225] *Ibid.*

[226] *Supra* note 125.

[227] *Radio Reference*, *supra* note 130.

jurisdiction to the Parliament of Canada to legislate for the purpose of performing the obligation of a treaty, the Court would not have departed from its precedent.

Because the *Aeronautics Reference* [228] was governed by s. 132, the case was not a relevant authority here. The crux of the decision thus resided in the interpretation that the Privy Council would give to the *Radio Reference.* [229]

The Privy Council read that latter case as one essentially based on the ordinary rules of the division of powers. Radio communications did not come generally within the enumeration of provincial powers in ss. 92 and 91, except for the express exclusion of s. 92 (10) (a) for interprovincial telegraphs. Radio communications were thus to be regulated by the Parliament based on s. 92 (10) (a) and the residuary powers of s. 91. The Privy Council then not only stated that "neither case affords a warrant for holding that legislation to perform a Canadian treaty is exclusively within the Dominion legislative power"[230] but also that "[f]or the purposes of ss. 91 and 92, i.e., the distribution of legislative powers between the Dominion and the Provinces, *there is no such thing as treaty legislation as such.*"[231] For the purpose of the division of powers, there is no difference between legislation performing treaty obligations and legislation adopted for any other reason; the ordinary rules governing the attribution of powers apply.

To better understand the Privy Council's decision, I would suggest that, taken as a merely exegetic task, it was not easy to choose between the two alternative readings of the *Radio Reference.* [232] What was the *ratio*? What was the *obiter*? The Privy Council's hermeneutic choice is illuminated when one looks at two additional arguments it advanced upon considering the consequences of reading the *Radio Reference* as recognizing plenary treaty-performing powers.

The first argument is implicitly based on a combination of two deep-rooted principles of constitutional law: first, a legal entity can have no greater power than its constitutive rules provide for[233] and, second, one

---

[228] *Supra* note 125.

[229] *Radio Reference, supra* note 130.

[230] *Labour Conventions* case, *supra* note 19 at 351.

[231] *Ibid.* (emphasis added).

[232] *Radio Reference, supra* note 130.

[233] See for example *In re The Initiative and Referendum Act*, [1919] A.C. 935 [*In re The Initiative and Referendum Act*] where the Privy Council decided that, although provincial legislatures had the power to amend "from time to time, notwithstanding anything in this Act, ... the constitution of the Province, except as regards the office of Lieutenant-Governor" under the old s. 92 (1), they could not amend their provincial

is not allowed to do indirectly what one is prohibited from doing directly. Thus, the Privy Council wrote that "the Dominion cannot, merely by making promises to foreign countries, clothe itself with legislative authority inconsistent with the constitution which gave it birth."[234]

The second argument is related to this first one but it emphasises more the practical consequences that such interpretation would have over the general economy of the Constitution. When Lord Atkin had questioned the Dominion on the constitutional consequences of her position on the provinces, the Attorney General had made the improbable claim that "[b]y the transference of the treaty-making power to the Dominion executive, and correlative power to legislate to carry out the obligations, nothing is taken from the Provinces."[235] Lord Atkin, during the hearing of the case, had already seen that the plausible consequences of that doctrine, if it were upheld, would have been quite radical.[236] In effect, federal powers derived from the residuary clause are deemed *exclusive*.[237] Basically, this doctrine would mean that Ottawa could

---

constitutions to transform their legislatures by excluding the Lieutenant-Governor. The Privy Council added (at 945):

> Sect. 92 of the Act of 1867 entrusts the legislative power in a Province to its Legislature, and to that Legislature only. No doubt a body, with a power of legislation on the subjects entrusted to it so ample as that enjoyed by a Provincial Legislature in Canada, could, while preserving its own capacity intact, seek the assistance of subordinate agencies ... but it does not follow that it can create and endow with its own capacity a new legislative power not created by the Act to which it owes its own existence.

The Privy Council did not make explicit reference to that case in its decision. However, as the Privy Council reports, the Attorney General for Ontario had referred to the case in the course of his argument. This argument was later used and elaborated upon by the Supreme Court of Canada's opinion in the *Reference Re Legislative Authority of the Parliament of Canada in Relation to the Upper House*, [1980] 1 S.C.R. 54 [*Reference Re Senate Reform*].

[234] *Labour Conventions* case, *supra* note 19 at 352.

[235] *Ibid.* at 329-30.

[236] Lord Atkin is reported as stating that the Dominion's argument was "... a very far-reaching doctrine: it means that Canada could make an agreement with any State which would seriously affect Provincial rights" (*ibid.* at 330).

[237] Duff C.J., Davis and Kerwin JJ. were quite clear about this point when they wrote in *Labour Conventions* case – *SCC*, *supra* note 135 at 489:

> As the subject of agreements with foreign countries is not one of the subjects embraced within section 92, or within any of the enumerated heads of section 91, it follows that the authority must rest upon the residuary clause from which Parliament derives its power to make laws for the peace, order and good government of Canada; and it follows from what has already been said that this power is plenary. It is for the Parliament of Canada to determine the conditions upon which such agreements shall be entered into *as well as the manner in which they shall be performed and this may be done by antecedent legislation or by legislation taking ef-*

simply ignore the division of powers provided by ss. 91 and 92 of the *Constitution Act, 1867* by concluding treaties on anything with any other state – and nowadays, even with non-state actors[238] – and thus could completely *oust* provincial legislatures from their otherwise *exclusive* provincial sphere of competence.

The Attorney General for Canada replied that "[t]his matter must not be looked at as though Canada is going to look about the world to find some one with whom to make an agreement for the purpose of robbing the Provinces of their constitutional rights."[239] Obviously, the Attorney General for Canada had to concede that "... logically, it must be admitted that whatever Canada and such other country agree to do can be effected by Canada."[240] However, one did not have to "look about the world to find some one with whom to make an agreement" on issues related to provincial matters. As the Labour conventions exemplified, the nature of international agreements had been changing and many more of them dealt with what was traditionally seen as "domestic matters". That is surely one of the reasons why the Privy Council decided that the federal executive could not extend Parliament's legislative powers simply by agreeing with a foreign country to enact certain legislation. If it were otherwise, "[s]uch a result would appear to undermine the constitutional safeguards of Provincial constitutional autonomy."[241] As I will show in Part II of this essay, this was prescient considering the later developments in international law.

6. The Irrelevancy of the "National Concern" Doctrine

The Privy Council finally concluded that the impugned statutes could not be saved by the "national concern" doctrine. The Law Lords were of the view that when Lord Watson, in the *Local Prohibition* case,[242] wrote his famous passage about the possibility that "matters, in their origin local and provincial, might attain such dimensions as to affect the body politic of the Dominion, and to justify the Canadian Parliament in passing laws for their regulation or abolition in the interest of the Do-

---

    fect ex post facto. These propositions are, indeed, corollaries of the proposition that the power is plenary. (Emphasis added).

[238] See *Vienna Convention on the Law of Treaties between States and International Organizations or between International Organizations*, 21 March 1986, 25 ILM 543 [*Vienna Convention on the Law of Treaties between States and International Organizations or between International Organizations*].

[239] *Labour Conventions* case, *supra* note 19 at 330.

[240] *Ibid.* at 330.

[241] *Ibid.* at 352.

[242] *Local Prohibition* case, *supra* note 169.

minion",[243] he never intended to establish any principle of constitutional law. For the Privy Council, these were only "cautious words intended to safeguard [against] possible eventualities which no one at the time had any interest or desire to define."[244]

The Privy Council further declared that it considered the law settled on the issue in the cases cited by the Chief Justice Duff and the principles that the latter declared in the *Reference Re Natural Products Marketing Act*.[245] There, the Chief Justice declared that it is not enough for a matter to have attained such proportions "as to affect the body politic of Canada" to "constitute a sufficient basis for the exercise of jurisdiction by the Dominion Parliament".[246] The presence of a general evil, present throughout Canada that "seriously prejudiced the well being of the people of Canada as a whole" and that would be important to suppress was not considered enough of a reason to allow for a provincial matter to acquire a federal aspect sufficient to permit Parliament to legislate.[247] In this, the Chief Justice had cited and followed the principles laid down in *Re the Board of Commerce Act, 1919, and the Combines and Fair Prices Act, 1919*[248] and *Toronto Electric Commissioners v. Snider*.[249] In fact, Duff C.J. notes that Lord Watson's statement had been used only once[250] to suggest that a matter which was *prima facie* of provincial jurisdiction had acquired by exceptional circumstances aspects bringing it within the ambit of the introductory words of s. 91.[251] In fact, the Privy Council, citing previous cases, referred to the different expressions used to suggest when such power could be justified: "abnormal circum-

---

[243] *Ibid.* at 361:

> Their Lordships do not doubt that some matters, in their origin local and provincial, might attain such dimensions as to affect the body politic of the Dominion, and to justify the Canadian Parliament in passing laws for their regulation or abolition in the interest of the Dominion. But great caution must be observed in distinguishing between that which is local and provincial, and therefore within the jurisdiction of the provincial legislatures, and that which has ceased to be merely local or provincial, and has become matter of national concern, in such sense as to bring it within the jurisdiction of the Parliament of Canada.

[244] *Labour Conventions* case, *supra* note 19 at 353.

[245] *Reference Re Natural Products Marketing Act*, [1936] S.C.R. 398 at 414ff [*Reference Re Natural Products Marketing Act*].

[246] *Ibid.* at 423.

[247] *Ibid.* at 422-23.

[248] *Re the Board of Commerce Act, 1919, and the Combines and Fair Prices Act, 1919*, [1922] 1 A.C. 191 [*Re the Board of Commerce Act, 1919, and the Combines and Fair Prices Act, 1919*].

[249] *Toronto Electric Commissioners v. Snider*, [1925] A.C. 396 [*Toronto Electric Commissioners v. Snider*].

[250] *Fort Frances Pulp & Power Co.*, *supra* note 145.

[251] *Reference Re Natural Products Marketing Act*, *supra* note 245 at 422.

stances",[252] "exceptional conditions",[253] "standard of necessity",[254] "some extraordinary peril to the national life of Canada"[255] and "highly exceptional".[256] Examples of such possible situations are "war",[257] "famine",[258] or an "epidemic of pestilence".[259] As the Privy Council notes, "[t]he Chief Justice [Duff], naturally from his point of view, excepted legislation to fulfil treaties."[260]

7. *Cooperative Federalism and "Watertight Compartments"*

To conclude, the Privy Council noted that Canada, as a whole, possessed all the necessary powers to legislate in performance of treaty obligations. However, such powers were not held simply in one institution, they were distributed along the general division of legislative powers. Thus, the famous image invoked by the Privy Council: "[w]hile the ship of state now sails on larger ventures and into foreign waters she still retains the watertight compartments which are an essential part of her original structure."[261] Because each level of government is responsible for certain issues and not others, all levels must cooperate.

I would add here that this cooperation is not only necessary for efficiency reasons, it is necessary because it makes it possible for the country to stay together. After all, federalism is a middle ground between two possible sovereignties: that of a central Canadian state and that of the provinces. Respect for each jurisdiction is the necessary condition for making the arrangement acceptable to all.

I will now turn to assessing a set of new approaches to understanding treaty powers in the contemporary Canadian federation. Two main

---

[252] *Re the Board of Commerce Act, 1919, and the Combines and Fair Prices Act, 1919, supra* note 248 at 200 ("This is a principle which, although recognized in earlier decisions, such as that of *Russell* v. *The Queen* ..., both here and in the Courts of Canada, has always been applied with reluctance, and its recognition as relevant can be justified only after scrutiny sufficient to render it clear that the *circumstances are abnormal.*" (Emphasis added)).

[253] *Ibid.* ("It has already been observed that circumstances are conceivable, such as those of war or famine, when the peace, order and good Government of the Dominion might be imperiled under *conditions so exceptional* that they require legislation of a character in reality beyond anything provided for by the enumerated heads in either s. 92 or s. 91 itself." (Emphasis added)).

[254] *Ibid.*

[255] *Toronto Electric Commissioners v. Snider, supra* note 249 at 412.

[256] *Ibid.*

[257] *Fort Frances Pulp & Power Co., supra* note 145 (World War I).

[258] *Toronto Electric Commissioners v. Snider, supra* note 249 at 414.

[259] *Ibid.* at 412.

[260] *Labour Conventions* case, *supra* note 19 at 353.

[261] *Ibid.* at 354.

principles will guide this discussion. The first one is methodological: my analysis will mostly focus on what is possible within the bounds defined by current constitutional norms and their possible organic extension. Thus, I will spend very little time on issues that would require formal constitutional amendments. The second principle is substantive: this essay will develop treaty powers from a *federalist* perspective. And by "federalist", I do not mean a form of "Canadian sovereignism" whereby the federal government is deemed to be supreme over the provinces and deemed to speak for all Canadians in all circumstances. To the contrary, I will take up the federalist idea that the federal and the provincial governments are equally legitimate governments within their respective spheres of power because they incarnate two equally legitimate and overlapping political communities. In this respect, I will examine what it means for treaty powers genuinely to respect the Supreme Court's statement in the *Reference Re Secession of Québec* about the relation between the two entrenched constitutional principles of "democracy" and "federalism":

> It is, of course, true that democracy expresses the sovereign will of the people. Yet this expression, too, must be taken in the context of the other institutional values we have identified as pertinent to this Reference. The relationship between democracy and federalism means, for example, that in Canada there may be different and equally legitimate majorities in different provinces and territories and at the federal level. No one majority is more or less "legitimate" than the others as an expression of democratic opinion, although, of course, the consequences will vary with the subject matter. A federal system of government enables different provinces to pursue policies responsive to the particular concerns and interests of people in that province. At the same time, Canada as a whole is also a democratic community in which citizens construct and achieve goals on a national scale through a federal government acting within the limits of its jurisdiction. The function of federalism is to enable citizens to participate concurrently in different collectivities and to pursue goals at both a provincial and a federal level.[262]

I will thus start by re-examining the treaty-*making* powers. I will demonstrate that there are no valid constitutional justifications for the proposition that the federal executive has exclusive and plenary powers over treaty-making. I will also develop proposals to increase democratic accountability in treaty-making, to ensure respect of the federal principle enshrined in the Constitution and to maintain both the flexibility and efficiency required in today's international environment.

---

[262] *Reference Re Secession of Québec*, *supra* note 76 at para. 66.

PART II

TRYING TO FIND OUR OWN PATH
BEYOND THE *LABOUR CONVENTIONS* CASE

CHAPTER II

Treaty-Making in the Canadian Federation

The federal government has been claiming for a long time that it has *plenary* and *exclusive* treaty-making powers.[263] But as we have seen earlier, neither the Privy Council nor the Supreme Court of Canada can be said to have established in the *Labour Conventions* case[264] that the federal government has either plenary or exclusive jurisdiction over treaty-making. To my knowledge, the Supreme Court of Canada has not, in any subsequent case, explicitly established those principles either.

Perhaps there is, however, one curious and contradictory *obiter dictum* in a concurring opinion by Justice L'Heureux-Dubé and McLachlin J. (as she then was) in *Thomson v. Thomson*[265] that might be seen as siding with the federal government's claims. In that opinion, Justice L'Heureux-Dubé starts by contradicting the Privy Council's decision in the *Labour Conventions* case (and every court and scholar ever since) by stating that the "[f]ederal treaty-making power is found in s. 132 of the *Constitution Act, 1867* ..."[266] She then goes on to write that "[a]lthough this provision makes it clear that the treaty-making power lies within federal jurisdiction, it has, nevertheless, been suggested that a concurrent provincial jurisdiction for treaty-making may exist for matters within provincial control."[267] She nevertheless dismisses the provincial claim by quoting Peter Hogg, who had written that "it suffices to say that the provincial claim has never been accepted by the federal government, and the federal government does in fact exercise exclusive treaty-making powers."[268] This is, quite bluntly, an untenable argument

---

[263] See for example: P. Martin, Sr., *Federalism and International Relations, supra* note 41 at 11-16 and the letter dated February 1, 1985 from the Legal Bureau of the then Department of External Affairs responding to a Council of Europe questionnaire (Canada, Legal Bureau of the Department of External Affairs, Letter February 1, 1985, *supra* note 60).

[264] See *Labour Conventions* case – *SCC, supra* note 135 and *Labour Conventions* case, *supra* note 19.

[265] *Thomson v. Thomson*, [1994] 3 S.C.R. 551 at paras. 112-114 [*Thomson v. Thomson*].

[266] *Ibid.* at para. 112.

[267] *Ibid.*

[268] *Ibid.* quoting Peter Hogg, *Constitutional Law of Canada*, 3rd ed., Carswell, Scarborough, 1992 at 283 [P. Hogg, *Constitutional Law of Canada*, 1992].

for rejecting the provincial position. First, since when does the federal government have monopoly over deciding what is constitutional and what it is not? If the federal government had such power, there would be no need anymore for constitutional judicial review… Second, it was one of the main points of the Supreme Court of Canada in the *Reference Re Secession of Québec* that *facts* – effectivity – is not enough to make something constitutionally valid in Canada:

> A distinction must be drawn between the right of a people to act, and their power to do so. They are not identical. A right is recognized in law: mere physical ability is not necessarily given status as a right. The fact that an individual or group can act in a certain way says nothing at all about the legal status or consequences of the act. A power may be exercised even in the absence of a right to do so, but if it is, then it is exercised without legal foundation. Our Constitution does not address powers in this sense. On the contrary, the Constitution is concerned only with the rights and obligations of individuals, groups and governments, and the structure of our institutions.

> In our view, the alleged principle of effectivity has no constitutional or legal status in the sense that it does not provide an *ex ante* explanation or justification for an act. In essence, acceptance of a principle of effectivity would be tantamount to accepting that the National Assembly, legislature or government of Quebec may act without regard to the law, simply because it asserts the power to do so.[269]

Thus, to accept Justice L'Heureux-Dubé's argument that it would suffice to say "that the federal government does in fact exercise exclusive treaty-making powers"[270] in order to establish that the federal government indeed has that exclusive constitutional power would amount to suggesting that Québec would indeed have the *right* to secede unilaterally if it did so in fact! There is little doubt as to whether the federal government would agree with this argument…

At any rate, Justice L'Heureux-Dubé goes on to write the ambiguous statement that "[r]egardless of this exclusive jurisdiction, federal treaty-making power is, nonetheless, limited by the constitutional division of powers"[271] and then hopes to support her statement by adding that

> As has long been set out in the *Labour Conventions* case …:

> But in a State where the Legislature does not possess absolute authority, in a federal State where legislative authority is limited by a constitutional document, or is divided up between different Legislatures in accordance with the classes of subject-matter submitted for legislation, the problem is

---

[269] *Reference Re Secession of Québec, supra* note 76 at paras. 106-107.

[270] Which, as we will see later, is not true.

[271] *Thomson v. Thomson, supra* note 265 at para. 113.

complex. The obligations imposed by treaty may have to be performed, if at all, by several Legislatures; and the executive have the task of obtaining the legislative assent not of the one Parliament to whom they may be responsible, but possibly of several Parliaments to whom they stand in no direct relation.[272]

L'Heureux-Dubé's statement has the dubious quality of being contradictory in each of its two possible meanings. On a first reading, it makes the claim that the federal treaty-making power is exclusive but yet limited to the division of powers. Because she later claims that the particular treaty under consideration is relative to a provincial matter and that the federal government nonetheless has concluded it validly, she appears to contradict her statement that the treaty-making power is "limited by the constitutional division of powers". On a second reading, however, she could rather be meaning that treaty-*making* is an exclusive power of the federal government but that legislative *implementation* would be subject to the division of powers. In other words, she would simply be conflating treaty-making and treaty-implementing in her statement. That second reading is supported by her later statement that "although the federal government had the necessary jurisdiction to sign the Convention, it remains within the jurisdiction of the individual provinces to implement the Convention."[273] However, if that were the case, L'Heureux-Dubé J. would then be contradicting her earlier claim that treaty powers flow from s. 132 because that section explicitly gave Parliament the power to implement treaty obligations that it covered![274] In fact, the *Labour Conventions* case quote that she uses was precisely written by the Privy Council because s. 132 was *not* available to Parliament! Although she does well to support the *Labour Conventions* case ruling on treaty implementation, the opinion is so confused on treaty-*making* that it would have been better had this *obiter* been omitted from L'Heureux-Dubé's opinion.

At any rate, if the Supreme Court ever intends to establish that the federal government has plenary and exclusive treaty-making powers, it would have a very hard time justifying it under current constitutional law. In effect, once past superficial appearances, there is very little to support the federal government's claims that (a) it inherited *plenary* powers to negotiate, sign and ratify treaties (i.e. treaty-making powers over matters falling not only within its own legislative sphere but also

---

[272] *Ibid.*

[273] *Ibid.*, at para. 114.

[274] *Constitution Act, 1867, supra* note 39, s. 132 reads: "The Parliament and Government of Canada shall have all Powers necessary or proper for performing the Obligations of Canada or of any Province thereof, as Part of the British Empire, towards Foreign Countries, arising under Treaties between the Empire and such Foreign Countries."

on matters related to provincial jurisdiction), and that (b) such powers are *exclusive* (i.e. that only the federal government has treaty-making powers and not its provincial counterparts). In the first section of this chapter (II.A.), I propose to focus the discussion on the claim that the federal government inherited plenary treaty-making powers. To do so, I will first examine the severe weaknesses of the legal arguments presented in favour of the federal claim (II.A.1.) and then present some policy arguments against the federal government's position (II.A.2.). The second claim – that of exclusivity – will be examined in the following section (II.B.). There, I will show that the provinces are actively and openly involved in international relations (II.B.1.) and that they do so in full respect of the law (II.B.2.). Finally, about the legal soundness of the traditional federal government's claim regarding treaty-making powers in the federation, I will present in a short section (II.B.3.) a way to understand the true source of the federal power to make treaties related to provincial subject-matters.

A. Rebutting the Case for Plenary Federal Treaty-Making Powers

1. The Evanescent Legal Arguments in Favour of Federal Plenary Treaty-Making Powers

Those who argue that the federal government possesses a general power to make treaties on any substantive matter usually try to support their position with a series of legal arguments uncritically received from past generations. Unfortunately for their claim, none of these is able to sustain serious scrutiny in light of the current state of Canadian constitutional law. I propose to examine the strength of each one of these arguments in turn.

i. The Letters Patent of 1947

Defenders of the traditional federal position on general treaty-making power first rely on the "Letters Patent constituting the office of the Governor General",[275] issued by the King in 1947.[276] Clause II of those Letters Patent authorizes the Governor General to "exercise all

---

[275] *Letters Patent Constituting the Office of the Governor General of Canada, supra* note 68.

[276] See for example B. Laskin, "The Provinces and International Agreements", *supra* note 40 at 108 and P. Hogg, *Constitutional Law of Canada*, 1992, *supra* note 268 at 282-83 §11.2. As G. van Ert reminds us (G. van Ert, *Using International Law in Canadian Courts, supra* note 41 at 75), this was also the interpretation given by the then Prime Minister, Louis St-Laurent, of the meaning of the Letters (Canada, Hansard, *House of Commons Debates* (12 February 1948) at 126 (Louis St-Laurent)).

powers and authorities lawfully belonging to Us [the King] in respect of Canada."[277] On the surface, this might seem to support the idea that the federal government, through the powers recognized to the Governor General, inherited the general prerogative related to treaty-making. There is, however, a series of legal arguments that have struck fatal blows to that seemingly transparent interpretation.

Gibran van Ert has highlighted that the Letters refer to powers and authorities belonging to the King or Queen *"in respect of Canada"*.[278] Canadian constitutional law does not simply use the expression "Canada" to refer to the entire country (federal and provincial levels included); it also uses it when it refers exclusively to the federal entity. For example, when s. 101 of the *Constitution Act, 1867* grants Parliament the power to establish "any additional courts for the better administration *of the laws of Canada"*,[279] it is well-established that it only refers to *federal laws* as opposed to provincial laws.[280] Or when the now repealed s. 91 (1) of the *Constitution Act, 1867*[281] gave Parliament the power over "the amendment from time to time *of the Constitution of Canada"*[282] (except for certain expressly mentioned matters), the Supreme Court wrote in the *Reference Re Senate Reform* that

> the word "Canada" as used in s. 91(1) does not refer to Canada as a geographical unit but refers to the juristic federal unit. "Constitution of Canada" does not mean the whole of the *British North America Act*, but means the constitution of the federal government, as distinct from the provincial governments.[283]

Thus, the mere use of the word "Canada" in the Letters is far from determinative as to whether the document was meant to transfer all powers and authorities to the Governor General in respect of Canada as a whole or simply those powers and authorities with respect to the federal government.

---

[277] *Letters Patent Constituting the Office of the Governor General of Canada, supra* note 68 § 2.

[278] G. van Ert, *Using International Law in Canadian Courts, supra* note 41 at 76.

[279] *Constitution Act, 1867, supra* note 39 (emphasis added).

[280] See for example *Quebec North Shore Paper Co. v. Canadian Pacific*, [1977] 2 S.C.R. 1054 at 1065-66; *McNamara Construction (Western) Ltd. v. The Queen*, [1977] 2 S.C.R. 654 [*McNamara Construction (Western) Ltd.*]; *Reference Re Secession of Québec, supra* note 76 at para. 7.

[281] That section was added to the then *British North America Act* in 1949 by *British North America (No. 2) Act, 1949* (U.K.), 13 Geo. VI, c. 81. That subsection was repealed by the schedule to the *Constitution Act, 1982*, item 1 and replaced by s. 4 (2) and by provisions found in Part V of the *Constitution Act, 1982, supra* note 70.

[282] *Constitution Act, 1867, supra* note 39 (emphasis added).

[283] *Reference Re Senate Reform, supra* note 233 at 69-70.

As we have known since at least 1882, Crown prerogatives have been vested in both the federal government and the provinces.[284] No one seriously argues that the Letters Patent were meant to transfer any powers and authorities from the Lieutenant Governor to the Governor General. It would indeed appear far-fetched to claim that the Governor General inherited all the provincial prerogatives by virtue of the Letters, simply because those prerogatives were the King's to start with. Thus, as van Ert argues, "in respect of Canada" must be read "to exclude those powers and authorities lawfully belonging to the sovereign *in respect of the provinces*".[285]

This has two consequences: first, insofar as provinces have acquired by any means powers to make international agreements, the Letters Patent did not affect such powers in any way. This would go against the federal exclusivity claim, to which I will turn in the next section. But the second consequence here is that, if the words "in respect of Canada" have to be read as "in respect of the federal government", then the Letters Patent add nothing to the argument. In effect, thus read, it simply says that the King transferred his authorities and powers in respect to the federal government to the Governor General, but it does not establish that such powers and authorities include the plenary powers to make treaties. In other words, this sends us back to the initial problem that the Letters were supposed to help us solve: we still have to find what those powers, as opposed to those of the provinces, really are.

Besides, Canada started making treaties on her own well before 1947. If it were the Letters Patent that had granted the federal government the power to make treaties, then we could not justify the validity of those treaties concluded by the Canadian government (without ratification by King Edward VIII or Georges VI) prior to 1947. This would mean, for example, that Canada would not have validly ratified the *Charter of the United Nations!*[286] If such treaties are constitutionally valid – in spite of not having been concluded formally by the Monarch of the day – it means that the authority to make them did not come from the Letters Patent. One has to find another source for the federal government's treaty-making power. Thus, the Letters are not instructive in any way for the purpose of deciding whether the federal government has plenary power to make treaties.

---

[284] *Liquidators of the Maritime Bank, supra* note 23. See also *Canada (A.G.) v. Ontario (A.G.)*, [1894] 23 S.C.R. 458 [*Canada v. Ontario (power of pardon)*] (prerogative of power of pardon divided between the federal and the provincial governments).

[285] G. van Ert, *Using International Law in Canadian Courts, supra* note 41 at 76.

[286] *Charter of the United Nations*, 26 June 1945, Can. T.S. 1945 No. 7 (ratified 9 November 1945).

What has been said so far must not be read as suggesting that the Letters Patent were simply declaratory with regards to treaty-making in all its aspects. There is one thing over which we could imagine that the Letters Patent operated a real transfer of power in relation to treaty-making, and that is in relation to what we call "Head of State" treaties. "Head of State" treaties are highly formal treaties that are concluded by the Monarch him or herself: they are treaties upon which the Head of the state him or herself puts his or her seal. Peace agreements are characteristic of such treaties. This form of treaty was developed at a time when treaties were assumed to create personal obligations between monarchs. As personal obligations of monarchs were progressively replaced by obligations of states in a modernizing world, the formality involved with "Head of State" treaties became largely unnecessary, if not burdensome, in the modern regulatory state. After all, treaties in the modern world are not simply concerned with "inter-state" matters but are part of the general tools of domestic governance. Thus, "Head of State" treaties were gradually replaced by "intergovernmental treaties". The latter treaties are much less formal in character and are concluded by members of governments following a general or specific delegation of powers. That being said, before the Letters Patent, a good argument could have been made that the Governor General did not possess the capacity to conclude "Head of State" treaties because the Governor General lacked the necessary prerogative to truly act as the Head of the state. However, we must note that this type of treaty has become so rare at international law that it apparently has not been used once by Canada since the Letters Patent were given to the Governor General.[287] What this discussion shows as a general point is that, under Canadian constitutional law, the representative of the Crown, even without the full attributes of the Head of the state, can authorise the government to conclude treaties with foreign powers.[288] More importantly, what it further demonstrates is that any transfer of powers in the Letters Patent did not affect provincial matters; it was simply a vertical transfer of powers from the King (or Queen) to the Governor General with respect to federal matters.

---

[287] P. Hogg, *Constitutional Law of Canada*, 1992, *supra* note 268 at 283 § 11.3.

[288] See for example the *Labour Conventions* case – *SCC*, *supra* note 135 at 476, where Duff C.J. writes:

> The Conference of 1926 categorically recognizes treaties in the form of agreements between governments in which *His Majesty does not formally appear, and in respect of which there has been no Royal intervention.* It is the practice of the Dominion to conclude with foreign countries agreements in such form, and agreements even of a still more informal character – merely by an exchange of notes. (Emphasis added).

ii. *The Prerogatives of the Crown*

If the treaty-making powers of the federal government do not have a textual basis in the Constitution nor do they come from the Letters Patent of 1947, it seems that they could only flow, as in the United Kingdom, from the Crown's prerogatives.[289]

Crown prerogatives can only be understood when seen in light of the historical development of state powers in the United Kingdom. The theory behind prerogatives is that the King possesses all powers, privileges and immunities except those that the "King in Parliament" has devolved to others. Therefore, since at least Albert Venn Dicey, royal prerogatives are understood to be "the residue of discretionary or arbitrary authority, which at any given time is left in the hands of the Crown".[290] So the logic is one of Crown diminishment of powers rather than one of Crown *acquisition* of powers. In other words, the concept of Crown prerogative is antithetical with the idea that the Crown could *acquire* prerogatives: either the Crown possesses a particular prerogative as it always has, or else it has lost it by devolution.

This poses, at first sight, a hurdle in our understanding of the federal government gradually *acquiring* treaty-making powers. In effect, how could the federal government have *acquired* treaty-making power through *gradually acquiring* prerogative powers if such powers are not subject to acquisition? It is one thing to say that the Crown possessed the prerogative of first creditor,[291] as of the moment when it was established, and it is another to claim that it *acquired* that prerogative at some later point in time. And here, no one claims that the federal government possessed plenary treaty-making powers right from the start.

The answer to this problem is to be found in the fact that while prerogatives cannot be created or acquired, the nature of the Crown itself changed over time.[292] While the Crown was initially understood to be

---

[289] We will explain in the next argument why those powers cannot flow from "constitutional usage" or "constitutional conventions".

[290] Dicey, *An Introduction to the Study of the Constitution, supra* note 84 at 424. See *Reference re Effect of Exercise of Royal Prerogative of Mercy Upon Deportation Proceedings*, [1933] S.C.R. 269 at 272-73; *Vancouver Island Peace Society* v. *Canada*, [1994] 1 F.C. 102, 64 F.T.R. 127 (T.D.), aff'd (1995), 16 C.E.L.R. (N.S.) 24, 179 N.R. 106 (F.C.A.) and *United Kingdom (A.-G.)* v. *DeKeyser's Royal Hotel*, [1920] A.C. 508 [*United Kingdom (A.-G.)* v. *DeKeyser's Royal Hotel*] at 526.

[291] See *Liquidators of the Maritime Bank, supra* note 23.

[292] In writing this part about the transformation of the institution of the Crown, I benefited greatly from Professor Andrew Heard's research presented in a 1990 text entitled "Canada's Independence" that can be found on his website at the Simon Fraser University at: http://www.sfu.ca/~aheard/324/Independence.html.

"one and indivisible",[293] this constitutional doctrine was slowly trans-formed. This was made necessary by several constitutional develop-ments that came with the Empire. We can discern two general stages in the transformation of the unitary principle of the Crown. The first transformation involved the idea that while the Crown might be one, it might have multiple instantiations. This transformation was made necessary to make sense of litigations between two or more colonial governments caused, for example, by the federal structures of Canada and Australia.[294] At that stage, each avatar of the Crown possessed both a distinct legal personality and the Crown prerogatives necessary for their functioning[295] (the Imperial prerogatives not being among those). This is much like the idea of the Holy Trinity according to which there is "One God in Three Persons"[296]: the Crown is one but it is composed of many persons, each with their competences. The second type of transformation built on the first one and consisted in the gradual thin-ning of the Imperial Crown in favour of the colonial Crowns. This happened when the different Imperial prerogatives gradually started to be exercised by the colonial Crowns and when the remaining Imperial Crown started acting only on the advice of the governments concerned by such prerogatives.[297] These two types of transformations resulted in

---

[293] See for example Augustus H.F. Lefroy, *A Short Treatise on Canadian Constitutional Law* (Toronto: Carswell, 1918) at 59-60: "The Crown is to be considered as one and indivisible throughout the Empire; and cannot be severed into as many kingships as there are Dominions, and self-governing colonies."

[294] See William H.P. Clement, *The Law of the Canadian Constitution*, 3rd ed. (Toronto: Carswell, 1916) at 14-15.

[295] See for example *Liquidators of the Maritime Bank, supra* 23 (prerogative of first creditor possessed by both the Crown in right of Canada and the Crown in right of the province); *R. v. Gauthier*, [1918] 56 S.C.R. 176 (provincial legislation can only bind the federal Crown "by express terms or necessary intendment"); *Quebec (A.-G.) v. Canada (A.-G.)*, [1932] A.C. 524, (*sub nom. In re Silver Bros. Ltd.*) at 524 (revenues and properties of the Crown in right of the Dominion and the Crown in right of the province are separate: "There are two purses.").

[296] As Carl Schmitt highlighted, many of our legal and political concepts have their roots in theological concepts. He wrote, for example (Carl Schmitt, *Political Theology*, *supra* note 146 at 36):

All significant concepts of the modern theory of the state are secularized theologi-cal concepts not only because of their historical development – in which they were transferred from theology to the theory of the state, whereby, for example, the om-nipotent God became the omnipotent lawgiver – but also because of their systema-tic structure, the recognition of which is necessary for a sociological consideration of these concepts.

[297] The Report of the 1926 Imperial Conference stated that Dominions "are autonomous Communities within the British Empire, equal in status, in no way subordinate one to another in any aspect of their domestic or external affairs, though united by a common allegiance to the Crown, and freely associated as members of the British Common-wealth of Nations" (*Balfour Declaration, supra* note 66.) That conference also laid

the fact that the Imperial Crown was stretched so thin that it was effectively divided among the different governments.[298] Thus, in this story,

---

down the basis for the convention according to which the Crown seeks the authorization of the Dominion before the Parliament can authorize the changes to the Royal Style and Titles. That convention would later be recognized in the second paragraph of the preamble of the *Statute of Westminster, supra* note 67. Following that Imperial Conference, the principle of equality of status was pushed further to establish that only the Dominions had the right to advise the Crown on matters related to themselves.

[298] The abdication of King Edward VIII in 1936 further gave the opportunity to illustrate the divisible nature of the Crown, at least in respect of the Irish Free State and South Africa. Both the Irish Free State and South Africa adopted acts declaring that the abdication took effect on different dates than the one stated in the British Parliament's act. When the British government, in 1937, informed the Dominion governments that it intended to introduce in Parliament a bill to provide for a regent in case of the monarch's incapacity, Dominions took the same position as they did during a 1935 conference: they did not feel the need for it since they already had Governor Generals whom they thought could perform royal tasks during the incapacitation of the monarch (see A. Berriedale Keith, "Notes on Imperial Constitutional Law" (1937) 19 J.C.L. & I.L 264 at 265 and James R. Mallory, *The Structure of Canadian Government*, 2nd ed. (Toronto: Gage, 1984) at 36-37.) Thus, the Dominions were not included in the bills adopted by the British Parliament over the issue in 1937, 1943 and 1953 and, therefore, according to s. 4 of the *Statute of Westminster, supra* note 67, they were not affected by such legislation (see William P.M. Kennedy, "The Regency Acts, 1837-53" (1953-54) 10 U.T.L.J. 248). In 1952, at a meeting of Commonwealth governments, it was decided that "it would be in accord with established constitutional position that each member country should use for its own purposes a form of title which suits its own particular circumstances but retains a substantial element which is common to all" (Canada, Office of the Prime Minister, Press Release, (12 December, 1952), online: Canada, Foreign Affairs and International Trade Canada, *Documents on Canadian International Relations*, Vol. 18, c. 1, part 2, doc. 4 <http://www.dfait-maeci.gc.ca/department/history/dcer/details-en.asp?intRefid=3500>. Also cited in Kenneth C. Wheare, "The Nature and Structure of the Commonwealth" (1953) 47 American Political Science Review 1016 at 1021). In the following months, the federal Parliament adopted *An Act Respecting The Royal Style and Titles*, S.C. 1952-53, c.9 in which it used the following formulation to refer to the Monarch: "Elizabeth the Second, by the Grace of God of the United Kingdom, Canada and Her other Realms and Territories Queen, Head of the Commonwealth, Defender of the Faith." (See William P.M. Kennedy, "The Royal Style and Titles" (1953-54) 10 U.T.L.J. 83. The current statute is entitled the *Royal Style and Titles Act*, R.S.C. 1985, c. R-12). The historian Nicholas Mansergh noted in 1953 that with the "several – to be exact seven – Royal Titles describing in formal language the relationship to the Crown of the seven member nations of the Commonwealth which are monarchies", "[t]he once heretical doctrine of the divisibility of the Crown was thus embedded in the new orthodoxy". (Nicholas Mansergh, "The Commonwealth at the Queen's Accession" (1953) 29 International Affairs 277 at 280). However, it must be noted that Mr. Saint-Laurent, then Prime Minister, stated during the debate over the adoption of the Canadian *Act Respecting Royal Style and Titles* that

Her Majesty is now the Queen of Canada but she is the Queen of Canada because she is Queen of the United Kingdom and because the people of Canada are happy to recognize as their sovereign the person who is the sovereign of the United King-the prerogatives are not gradually devolved to colonial governments, it is the Crown itself that was gradually dislocated and with the dislocation of the Crown came the dislocation of the Crown's prerogatives.

Those who argue that the federal Crown inherited the entire treaty-making prerogatives only focus on the second type of Crown transformation, while forgetting about the initial transformation that laid down the conditions of possibility for the second one to occur. Thus, we have to examine how the prerogatives were to be divided within federations to see if it is possible that the federal Crown might have inherited plenary treaty-making powers.

It is well established that in Canada, at least since the Privy Council's decision in 1892 in *Liquidators of the Maritime Bank of Canada*, Crown prerogatives parallel legislative powers and are determined by the latter.[299] For example, the Privy Council, referring to the new distri-

---

dom. It is not a separate office. ... [I]t is the sovereign who is recognized as the sovereign of the United Kingdom who is our sovereign. ... (*House of Commons Debates*, No. 95 (3 February 1953) at 1566)

In 1973, Australia chose to withdraw any reference to the United Kingdom in her change of the formulation of the monarch for Australia and adopted the following one: "Elizabeth the Second, by the Grace of God Queen of Australia and Her other Realms and Territories, Head of the Commonwealth" (*Royal Style and Titles Act 1973* (Cth.), Sch.). If there were any remaining doubts about the complete separation of the Canadian Crown from the British one in 1953, the separation was completed before the patriation of the Canadian constitution. In *R. v. Secretary of State for Foreign and Commonwealth Affairs, ex parte Indian Association of Alberta et al.*, [1982] All E.R. 118 at 127-28 (C.A.) (leave to appeal refused by the House of Lords (*R. v. Secretary of State for Foreign and Commonwealth Affairs, ex parte Indian Association of Alberta et al.*, [1982] 2 All E.R. 140 (H.L.)) for reasons that confirm the rightness of the substantive decision of the Court of Appeal), Lord Denning even wrote that:

The Crown became separate and divisible, according to the particular territory in which it was sovereign. This was recognised by the Imperial Conference of 1926. ... henceforth the Crown was no longer single and indivisible. It was separate and divisible for each self-governing Dominion or province or territory.

Based on this opinion, he denied that the British Crown was responsible to Aboriginals for duties owed to them by the Crown; the Canadian Crown did. It might be noted, however, that because of s. 41 (a) of the *Constitution Act, 1982, supra* note 70, the federal Parliament might not be able to take the expression "United Kingdom" out of the Royal Style and Titles of the Canadian monarch without unanimous consent of the provinces.

[299] *Liquidators of the Maritime Bank, supra* note 23 (prerogative of preferred creditor and of appropriation, more generally). See also *Canada v. Ontario (power of pardon), supra* note 284 (prerogative power of pardon for provincial offences); *Bonanza Creek Gold Mining Co., supra* note 23 at 580 (power of incorporation) ("The distribution under the new grant of executive authority in substance follows the distribution under the new grant of legislative powers. In relation, for example, to the incorporation of companies in Ontario with provincial objects, the powers of incorporation which the Governor-General or Lieutenant-Governor possessed before the Union must be taken to have passed to the Lieutenant-Governor of Ontario, so far as concerns companies

bution of powers that came with the *Constitution Act, 1867*, wrote in 1916 in *Bonanza Creek Gold Mining Co.* that "[t]he distribution under the new grant of executive authority in substance follows the distribution under the new grant of legislative powers."[300] In 1962, Justice Kerwin, writing for the majority of the Court in *British Columbia Power Corporation v. British Columbia Electric Company* stated that

> [i]n a federal system, *where legislative authority is divided, as are also the prerogatives of the Crown, as between the Dominion and the Provinces*, it is my view that it is not open to the Crown, either in right of Canada or of a Province, to claim a Crown immunity based upon an interest in certain property, where its very interest in that property depends completely and solely on the validity of the legislation which it has itself passed, if there is a reasonable doubt as to whether such legislation is constitutionally valid.[301]

This *dictum* was later cited with approval in three unanimous Supreme Court decisions: in *Amax Potash Ltd. v. Saskatchewan*[302] in 1977, in *Canada (A.-G.) v. Law Society of British Columbia*[303] in 1982 and in *Air Canada v. British Columbia (A.-G.)*[304] in 1986. Chief Justice Laskin, together with Martland, Judson, Ritchie, Pigeon, Dickson and Beetz JJ. recognized in 1978 in *Alberta v. Canada (Transport Commission)* that "[t]he Constitution of Canada distributes legislative power between a central Parliament and provincial Legislatures and prerogative or executive power (which is formally vested in the Queen) *is similarly distributed to accord with the distribution of legislative power*, thus pointing to different, executive authorities."[305] Chief Justice Dickson also wrote, in a concurring opinion in 1990 in *Mitchell v. Peguis Indian Band*, that "[d]ivisibility of the Crown recognizes the fact of a division of legisla-

---

with this class of objects"); *Reference re Adoption Act (Ontario)*, [1938] S.C.R. 398 (provincial prerogative to appoint judges, magistrates and justices of the peace); *Canada v. Carroll*, [1948] S.C.R. 126 [*Canada v. Carroll*] (the Lieutenant-Governor incarnates the Government of the province for which s/he is appointed and it is not an office of the Governor General in Council). The issue of Crown property and appropriation is a complex one in the Canadian federation. See in general F. Chevrette and H. Marx, *Droit constitutionnel*, *supra* note 41 at 1105-21 and François Chevrette, "*Dominium* et *imperium*: l'État propriétaire et l'État puissance publique en droit constitutionnel canadien" in Benoît Moore, ed., *Mélanges Jean Pineau* (Montréal, Éditions Thémis, 2003) 665.

[300] *Ibid.* at 580.

[301] *British Columbia Power Corporation v. British Columbia Electric Company*, [1962] S.C.R. 642 at 644 (emphasis added).

[302] *Amax Potash v. Saskatchewan*, [1977] 2 S.C.R. 576.

[303] *Canada (A.-G.) v. Law Society of British Columbia*, [1982] 2 S.C.R. 307.

[304] *Air Canada v. British Columbia (A.-G.)*, [1986] 2 S.C.R. 539.

[305] *Alberta v. Canada (Transport Commission)*, [1978] 1 S.C.R. 61 at 71 (emphasis added).

tive power and a parallel division of executive power. If a principle so basic needed the confirmation of high judicial authority, it can be found as far back as the Privy Council decision in *Maritime Bank of Canada (Liquidators of) v. Receiver-General of New Brunswick*, [1892] A.C. 437 ..."[306] More recently, in the *Reference Re Secession of Québec*,[307] a unanimous Supreme Court referred with approval to the section of the *Liquidators of the Maritime Bank* decision that established that Crown prerogatives follow legislative powers.[308]

This rule is not only supported by well-established authorities, it also relies on a clear constitutional rationale. It is settled law that "the King hath no prerogative, but that which the law of the land allows him"[309] and that the principle of parliamentary supremacy means that legislatures can limit or abolish any prerogative.[310] Put otherwise, Crown prerogatives exist so long as they have been recognized by courts and *have not yet* been abolished, limited or displaced by legislation. This is what Dicey meant when, as we have seen earlier, he wrote that Crown prerogatives are "the residue of discretionary or arbitrary authority, which at any given time *is left* in the hands of the Crown".[311] The principle of parliamentary supremacy means that no executive power can remain unchecked or immune from parliament's control. It is thus logical that this "residue" follows the legislature that exercises its authority over its maintenance, displacement, limitation or abolition. Therefore, it is the legislative capacity to limit, abolish or displace Crown prerogatives that drives their locations and not the other way around.

However, one might be tempted to argue that Crown prerogatives would not be immune from modification if we considered the dislocation of the Crown to imply also the transfer of the relevant legislative powers to modifying such Crown prerogatives. But in the absence of any constitutional text to that effect, why should we infer that Parliament or the legislatures have received through the process of Crown dislocation new legislative powers that go against the existing division of powers simply in order to modify the "the residue of discretionary or arbitrary authority, which at any given time is left in the hands of the Crown"?[312] This bizarre legislative power would moreover have had the odd characteristic of being diminished by the very fact of being used. In

---

[306] *Mitchell v. Peguis Indian Band*, [1990] 2 S.C.R. 85 at para. 23.

[307] *Reference Re Secession of Québec, supra* note 76 at para. 56.

[308] The principles of *Liquidators of the Maritime Bank, supra* note 23, have also been unanimously approved in *Patriation Reference, supra* note 95 (majority and dissent).

[309] *Case of Proclamations* (1611) 12 Co. Rep. 74, 77 E.R. 1352 (K.B.).

[310] See for example *United Kingdom (A.-G.) v. DeKeyser's Royal Hotel, supra* note290.

[311] *Supra* note 84 (emphasis added).

[312] *Ibid.*

effect, every statute displacing or abolishing a Crown prerogative would by the same token have caused the disappearance of a chunk of legislative powers: no more prerogative, no more legislative power... The very exercise of legislative power to abolish or displace a prerogative would cut the constitutional limb upon which it is seated. That would have the very undesirable effect that once a prerogative had been displaced or abolished by statute, the legislature that had adopted the statute would not have had the powers to subsequently modify that same statute. For such legislative powers to survive the disappearance of the Crown prerogatives, they have to be grounded in something else. That is why they must be grounded in one or more of the legislative powers distributed by the Constitution between the federal and the provincial legislatures. These are some of the reasons why the legislative powers necessarily come first and the prerogatives follow.

At any rate, the divisibility of prerogative powers along the same lines as the legislative powers was well accepted by provinces that were arguing against the validity of the Labour Conventions statutes *as well as* by Duff C.J., Davis and Kerwin JJ. who thought that the impugned statutes were valid in their Supreme Court decision.[313] This is also the argument that the Québec government has put forward since the mid-1960s.[314]

The notion of divisibility of prerogative powers means here that so long as no plenary legislative power to implement treaties is recognized to Parliament, the federal Crown can have no equivalent plenary prerogative to make treaties. As *Bonanza Creek Gold Mining Co.* taught us, it is the executive prerogatives that flow from the legislative powers and not the other way around.[315] This is important to keep in mind in order to spot the circularity of certain types of arguments in favour of federal plenary treaty-making powers. When the issue is that of who possesses treaty-making powers, proponents of the federal government thesis often rely on an argument which is based in turn on their own views of the division of legislative powers. However, when the issue comes up as to the extent of the federal powers to legislatively implement treaties,

---

[313] See *supra* note 155ff. and accompanying text.

[314] See *supra* note 23 and accompanying text. See also Anne-Marie Jacomy-Millette, *L'introduction et l'application des traités internationaux au Canada* (Paris: Librairie générale de droit et de jurisprudence, 1971). An English version of that book also exists: Anne-Marie Jacomy-Millette, *Treaty Law in Canada*, *supra* note 41.

[315] See also *supra* note 23 and accompanying text. That is why Gerald Morris (G.R. Morris, "The Treaty-Making Power: A Canadian Dilemma", *supra* note 22 at 490) and Ivan C. Rand (I.C. Rand, "Some Aspects of Canadian Constitutionalism", *supra* note 41) were wrong when they argued that if the power of implementation logically involves the power to negotiate treaties, as Gérin-Lajoie claimed, then the reverse proposition would be equally true.

proponents of the federal thesis will often argue that since the Canadian government now possesses the power to make treaties with foreign countries, it would follow that it should also have the power to enforce these treaties by appropriate legislation![316]

I will examine in detail in Chapter III why Parliament *does not* and *should not* have general powers to implement treaties in relation to what is now provinces' exclusive legislative jurisdiction. However, it is worth making a few general remarks right away on this issue.

First, it has been argued against the *Labour Conventions* case that the "present interpretation of the Canadian constitution restricts the powers of the Federation far more narrowly than they were ever restricted in the contemplation of Sir John Macdonald and the other fathers of the federation".[317] This argument should be moved out of our way quickly by simply pointing out that, as many others have mentioned before, the "Fathers" did not contemplate either that Canada would, one day, make treaties on her own. This goes to show that whatever the "Fathers" had in mind in relation to the division of powers, the current rules dealing with Canadian treaty-making cannot contradict their non-existing views on that issue.

The second point that I want to make here is related to the arguments sometimes advanced that since treaties are, by nature, "international", they cannot be about matters that are "local or private",[318] thus, they cannot be provincial matters. If they cannot be provincial, they must then be federal.[319] Again, more will be said about extraterritoriality and legislative powers later but it is worth making a few comments on executive powers here. Vincent C. Macdonald, for example, thought that it was "absurd to say that a matter which has become the subject of international agreement can yet be considered a matter of a 'private and

---

[316] See A.B. Keith, "The Privy Council Decisions: A Comment from Great Britain", *supra* note 112 at 430.

[317] *Ibid.* at 429.

[318] *Constitution Act, 1867, supra* note 39, s. 92 (16) grants legislative powers to provinces over "[G]enerally all Matters of a merely local or private Nature in the Province." Many heads of provincial legislative powers refer to intraprovincial matters. For example, s. 92 (13) provides for provincial legislative powers over "Property and Civil Rights *in the Province*".

[319] See V.C. MacDonald, "The Canadian Constitution Seventy Years Later", *supra* note 112 at 419; B. Laskin, "The Provinces and International Agreements", *supra* note 40 at 106-108; R. J. Delisle, "Treaty-Making Power in Canada" in Ontario, Ontario Advisory Committee on Confederation, *Background Papers and Reports*, Vol. 1 (Toronto: Queen's Printer, 1967) 115 at 132 [R. J. Delisle, "Treaty-Making Power in Canada"]; G.R. Morris, "The Treaty-Making Power: A Canadian Dilemma", *supra* note 22 at 485.

local nature.'"[320] But it is certainly mistaken, as van Ert points out, "to assume that the content of treaty obligations cannot be local or private. States today conclude treaties that have as much to do with their own internal affairs as they do with international affairs."[321] Also, as Lorne Giroux suggested, extraterritoriality refers to the power of Parliament to make laws in relation to a matter or a person outside Canada's borders: "It is different in the case of an international treaty or agreement, because what is involved is an act of will that does not imply any extension of the executive power outside the borders, since it produces its effects on the very territory of the signatory party."[322]

Before moving on to the next section, we need to address a few cases that might have sowed doubts in our mind about the correctness of this approach to the division of the prerogatives according to the division of legislative powers. Professor Henri Brun and Professor Guy Tremblay have suggested[323] that the Supreme Court took the view that only the federal government has "external sovereignty" and that, therefore, provinces have no international legal status in *Re Ownership of Offshore Mineral Rights*[324] and in *Reference re Newfoundland Continental Shelf* [325] and the *Patriation Reference*.[326] While we will examine in more depth the issue of international legal personality from the perspective of public international law in section II.A.1.iv., we will now examine that question from the perspective of Canadian constitutional law.

Professor Brun and Professor Tremblay write:

Le modèle classique veut que, sur le plan interne, la souveraineté canadienne s'exprime à deux niveaux (fédéral et provincial), mais que sur le plan

---

[320] V.C. MacDonald, "The Canadian Constitution Seventy Years Later", *ibid.* at 419. Similar arguments were presented by B. Laskin, "The Provinces and International Agreements", *ibid.* at 106; R. J. Delisle, "Treaty-Making Power in Canada", *ibid.* at 132 and G.R. Morris, "The Treaty-Making Power: A Canadian Dilemma", *ibid.* at 485.

[321] Gibran van Ert, "The legal character of provincial agreements with foreign governments" (2001) 24 C. de D. 1093 at 1108 [G. van Ert, "The legal character of provincial agreements with foreign governments"]. It is interesting to note that V.C. Mac-Donald, "The Canadian Constitution Seventy Years Later", *ibid.* at 418, had also recognized in 1937 that "[i]t is precisely in relation to matters within provincial competence ... that treaties have been and will be particularly desirable, *e.g.*, social security and industrial control legislation."

[322] My translation. L. Giroux, "La capacité internationale des provinces en droit constitutionnel canadien", *supra* note 23 at 266.

[323] Henri Brun and Guy Tremblay, *Droit constitutionnel, supra* note 204 at 64.

[324] *Supra* note 67.

[325] *Reference re Newfoundland Continental Shelf*, [1984] 1 S.C.R. 86 [*Reference re Newfoundland Continental Shelf*].

[326] *Supra* note 95.

extérieur, elle s'exprime par l'intermédiaire du seul Gouvernement fédéral. Pour cette raison, le mot "Canada" est souvent utilisé dans deux sens radicalement différents. Il peut désigner l'ordre de gouvernement central (le fédéral) mais dans sa capacité limitée sur le plan intérieur par le partage des compétences entre les provinces et lui ... Ou il peut désigner le même ordre de gouvernement, le Gouvernement fédéral, comme représentant tout le Canada au plan international: voir l'*Avis sur les droits miniers sous-marins*, [1967] R.C.S. 792 et le *Renvoi relatif au plateau continental de Terre-Neuve*, [1984] 1 R.C.S. 86. Dans ce dernier renvoi, la Cour écrit que "Sa Majesté du chef du Canada", c'est-à-dire le gouvernement d'Ottawa, est la seule entité au Canada qui possède la souveraineté extérieure" (p.116). On trouve aussi des *dicta* suggérant que les provinces n'ont pas de statut international dans le *Renvoi: résolution pour modifier la Constitution*, [1981] 1 R.C.S. 753, 799, 802, 806 et 872.

These Supreme Court opinions are not enough, in my view, to support the propositions that (a) there is only one international legal personality in Canada and (b) the federal government is its representative. Let's examine in turn those opinions.

First, it is true that in *Re Ownership of Offshore Mineral Rights*[327] the Court concluded that

> There are two reasons why British Columbia lacks the right to explore and exploit and lacks legislative jurisdiction:
>
> (1) The continental shelf is outside the boundaries of British Columbia, and
>
> (2) Canada is the sovereign state which will be recognized by international law as having the rights stated in the Convention of 1958, and it is Canada, not the Province of British Columbia, that will have to answer the claims of other members of the international community for breach of the obligations and responsibilities imposed by the Convention. Canada is the sovereign state which will be recognized by international law as having the rights stated in the [*Geneva*] *Convention* [*on the Territorial Sea and the Contiguous Zone*] of 1958, and it is Canada, not the Province of British Columbia, that will have to answer the claims of other members of the international community for breach of the obligations and responsibilities imposed by the Convention.[328]

That might be entirely true without denying that provinces may have an international legal personality. In fact, the Court did not claim here that provinces do not have an international legal personality, it merely stated that it is Canada and not the provinces that is responsible at international law for the rights and obligations contained in the *Geneva Convention on the Territorial Sea and the Contiguous Zone* of 1958. In effect, the

---

[327] *Supra* note 67.
[328] *Ibid.* at 821.

first reason given by the Court was enough to answer the question asked. What the Court presents as the second reason might also be seen as a *consequence* of the first reason. In effect, once the Court concluded that (a) British Columbia had no property rights in the disputed territory when she was a colony, nor had such rights when she entered the federation[329], that (b) the disputed territorial sea was never within the limits of the province of British Columbia[330], that (c) she did not acquire the property rights of the disputed territorial sea and resources either by alienation or otherwise since then, and (d) she did not acquire jurisdiction over that territory by an extension of her boundaries in conformity with the appropriate constitutional amending formula[331], the case was pretty much settled. One might disagree with the Court about whether or not British Columbia might have possessed such rights at the time of entering the federation, but once she was within it, changes to the provincial boundaries are entirely dictated by the text of the Constitution. Without a proper constitutional amendment, the province could not extend her territorial jurisdiction. And because the lands and resources disputed were found *outside* of the provincial territory, British Columbia has no power to legislate over them since the province's legislative powers are limited to matters "in the Province" according to s. 92 of the *Constitution Act, 1867*.[332] In such circumstances, without any property rights or legislative jurisdiction over the disputed resources, whether or not British Columbia had international legal personality, it makes sense to say that she could not act in relation to such resources. The territorial seas outside the provinces' boundaries are thus similar to the land of the Northwest Territories; they are not owned by any of the provinces and they are under the legislative jurisdiction of the Parliament.[333] This has nothing to do with whether or not provinces may or may not have a legal personality at Canadian constitutional law or international law.

---

[329] *Ibid.* at 808:

> We have already said that, in our opinion, in 1871 the Province of British Columbia did not have ownership or property in the territorial sea and that the province has not, since entering into Confederation, acquired such ownership or property. We are not disputing the proposition that while British Columbia was a Crown Colony the British Crown might have conferred upon the Governor or Legislature of the colony rights to which the British Crown was entitled under international law but the historical record of the colony does not disclose any such action.

[330] See *Constitution Act, 1867, supra* note 39, s.109. For a case where the Court found that a specific portion of the offshore was included within British Columbia's boundaries, see *Re Strait of Georgia*, [1984] 1 S.C.R. 388.

[331] See *Constitution Act, 1871* (U.K.), 34 & 35 Vic., c. 28, s. 3 [*Constitution Act, 1871*].

[332] The issue of the territorial limitations to provincial legislation will be examined in more depth in section III.C.

[333] See *Constitution Act, 1871, supra* note 331, s. 4.

In *Reference re Newfoundland Continental Shelf*[334], the question asked was quite similar to those asked in the *Re Ownership of Offshore Mineral Rights* with the difference that what was in dispute was not the territorial sea but the rights to explore and exploit the *continental shelf*.[335] The Court was thus asked to clarify who had jurisdiction over an area *outside* the boundaries of both Newfoundland and Canada, or as the Court put it, who was the beneficiary of the "extraterritorial rights" in the continental shelf recognised under international law. Newfoundland argued that her situation was different from British Columbia because of her distinct constitutional history, in particular, her late admission into the federation in 1949. Newfoundland thus claimed (1) that international law recognised the limited "rights to explore and exploit" the continental shelf prior to her admission in the federation – and prior to their codification in the 1958 *Geneva Convention on the Continental Shelf*[336], (2) that "the Crown in right of Newfoundland must have been in a position to acquire these rights"[337], and (3) that the Crown in right of Newfoundland did not lose those rights under the Terms of Union with Canada.[338] After stating that Newfoundland must be able to demonstrate each of these three points in order to win, the Court wrote something very significant: "The first point concerns matters of international law; *the latter two raise questions of constitutional law*".[339] Thus, whether or not Newfoundland could have been in a position to acquire the rights in question was not considered by the Court as a question of international law but as question of constitutional law.[340] The only question of international law that had to be answered was whether or not the limited rights to explore and exploit the continental shelf prior to Newfoundland's admission in the federation were recognized by international law at the relevant period. Whatever the Court said about the two other questions has to be seen as an interpretation of Canadian constitutional law and not an interpretation of international law.

---

[334] *Reference re Newfoundland Continental Shelf, supra* note 325.

[335] *Supra* note 67.

[336] *Convention on the Continental Shelf*, 29 April 1958, 499 U.N.T.S. 311 (entered into force10 June 1964. Accession by Canada 08 March 1970).

[337] *Reference re Newfoundland Continental Shelf , supra* note 325 at 98.

[338] *Ibid.*

[339] *Ibid.* (emphasis added).

[340] The Court added, *ibid.* at 99:

> We do not think it is necessary to determine whether, in the eyes of international law, Newfoundland ever became an independent State. In the days of Empire, international law had nothing to say about whether international rights accorded to the Empire accrued to the Crown in right of the colony or in right of the Imperial Crown. That is a matter for determination under Imperial constitutional law.

The Court was of the view that the limited rights to explore and exploit the continental shelf were not recognised at international law at the relevant period. Because the three conditions identified by the Court for Newfoundland to win were cumulative, any statement about whether or not Newfoundland could have been in a position (a) to acquire such rights prior to her admission in the federation or (b) to keep them when she entered the federation has to be considered an *obiter dictum*.

The question as to whether or not Newfoundland could have acquired such rights prior to the union with Canada was more a matter of Imperial constitutional law than one of Canadian constitutional law. In effect, because of Newfoundland's tumultuous constitutional history between 1934 and 1949 – a period in which she went from being a Dominion with all the independence from the United Kingdom that this status entailed[341] to be reduced to having a "Government by Commission" that was appointed and controlled by the government in London – the question as to whether or not Newfoundland would have been able to acquire the disputed rights really was one about her internal status within the Empire. The Court concluded on that point

> that the suspension of self-government necessarily suspended the external sovereignty of Newfoundland recognized in the *Balfour Declaration*. Any continental shelf rights available at international law between 1934 and 1949 therefore accrued to the Crown in right of the United Kingdom, not the Crown in right of Newfoundland.[342]

Therefore, that question was irrelevant for our purposes.

The last question was perhaps more interesting for us. Because the Court thought that "[c]ontinental shelf rights are in pith and substance incidents of external sovereignty"[343] and not proprietary rights to be divided according to Term 37 of the Terms of Union, the issue that had to be resolved, then, was which government had the capacity to acquire and manage those rights. Without so much as an argument, the Court then declared:

> Assuming, *arguendo*, that a right to explore and exploit the continental shelf was recognized by international law in 1949, we conclude that on Union it would have had to devolve as an incident of external sovereignty, whether from the Crown in right of Newfoundland or, as we think, from the Crown in right of the United Kingdom, to the only entity within Canada possessing external sovereignty – the Crown in right of Canada. Even if – contrary to our opinion – Newfoundland did have the external sovereignty necessary to

---

[341] See the *Balfour Declaration, supra* note 66 and accompanying text and the *Statute of Westminster, supra* note 67 and accompanying text.

[342] *Reference re Newfoundland Continental Shelf, supra* note 325 at 110.

[343] *Ibid.* at 115-116.

acquire continental shelf rights prior to joining Canada, the effect of the Terms of Union would be that Canada, not Newfoundland would have the right to explore and exploit the continental shelf.[344]

Despite the fact that the Court claimed that this precise question was one of Canadian constitutional law rather than one of international law, "external sovereignty" is not a term of art in Canadian constitutional law. To what was the Supreme Court precisely referring to when it used that expression? The answer appears to be found in the following paragraph:

> In the 1967 *Offshore Reference* this Court noted that sometime between 1919 and 1931 the Canadian federal government acquired external sovereignty. The Canadian Parliament's extraterritorial legislative competence was recognized in the *Statute of Westminster* ... The first nine Canadian provinces, by contrast, never gained extraterritorial legislative competence: *Interprovincial Co-Operatives Ltd. v. Dryden Chemicals Ltd.*, [1976] 1 S.C.R. 477 at p. 512. They have never acquired external sovereignty. They are thus incapable of acquiring continental shelf rights.[345]

The Court thus establishes a clear connection between what it calls "external sovereignty" for the purpose of acquiring continental shelf rights and extraterritorial legislative competence. The idea being that since those rights are "extraterritorial" by nature – they are related to the management of resources found entirely outside the territory of the state – the appropriate level of government for dealing with those rights must have the legislative power to do so. Only the federal Parliament has power to adopt legislation for the primary purpose of dealing with extraterritorial rights[346] and thus, only the federal government could claim to have the necessary powers to manage such resources.

When the Court ascribed "external sovereignty" – an unknown expression in Canadian constitutional law – to the federal government, it was merely restating that only the federal Parliament has full extraterritorial legislative power and that, according to the principles of Canadian constitutional law, the prerogatives follow the legislative powers. In other words, only the federal government has the appropriate prerogatives to acquire *public* [347] rights to explore and exploit the continental shelf outside its territory. In that context, the utility of using new

---

[344] *Ibid.* at 116.

[345] *Ibid.* at 103.

[346] See a detailed analysis of the territorial limits to provincial legislative powers at section III.C.

[347] Acquisition of *private* property rights is not truly a prerogative power. Provinces can thus acquire property rights in commercial projects situated outside of their boundaries without constitutional problem.

expressions such as "external sovereignty" that are unknown to the constitutional tradition is quite dubious. In effect, the concept of "external sovereignty" does *absolutely no* work in the explanation of the Court's reasoning; it only adds confusion in an already difficult area of the law.

In effect, the introduction of such an expression into the constitutional discourse was most unwise. Political thoughts in the Euro-American world has been so much dominated in the last centuries by the idea of "sovereignty" that it is has been one of the chief challenges, if not the ultimate stumbling block, for any theorist of federalism to explain how the idea of sovereignty being one and indivisible by definition could be reconciled with the idea of a federation composed of two or more levels of government of equal status. To attempt to reconcile the idea of sovereignty with the Canadian federal system, the Privy Council and the Supreme Court of Canada have had recourse to the oxymoronic idea of a "divided sovereignty": both the federal government and the provinces are said to be "sovereign" in their own respective field of legislative competence. Clearly, in Canada, state powers are divided among different institutions responsible to different – and partly over-lapping – constituencies. However, any attempt at explaining how these divided powers nonetheless fit within the conceptual apparatus of "sovereignty" is doomed to fail. This is because, as the most astute and courageous observers have simply acknowledged and accepted, sovereignty and federalism are simply antinomic. Any successful theory of federalism must necessarily be decoupled from any theory of sovereignty.[348] When the facts don't fit the explanations, we have to change the explanations, not the facts... This is especially true when the explanation was developed to understand a phenomenon different from the one that we are observing. The concept of "sovereignty" is simply not appropriate to describe the divided nature of powers within the Canadian federation. Introducing a further distinction between "internal" and "external sovereignty" into the mix was thus most inconvenient. How could Canadian sovereignty be, by definition, one and indivisible, and yet be divided along the federal/provincial and the internal/external lines?

This contradiction in terms, this internal inconsistency, explains why the concept of sovereignty does not help solving any of the constitutional problems to which it is called to solve in a federation. In effect, sovereignty is always called to help when one seeks to identify which jurisdiction has power over one matter or another. In those circum-

---

[348] For a similar view and for a clear synthesis of the scholarship on the issue, see Olivier Beaud, *Théorie de la fédération* (Paris: Presses universitaires de France, 2007) at 39-65.

stances, how could the concept of "sovereignty" help us decide between two or more equal political institutions which one has jurisdiction over a specific issue when the very concept of sovereignty denies the very possibility of a division of jurisdictions among equal powers. This is not to say that we do not need a way to express the normative supremacy of an institution over others within a jurisdiction. However, once we acknowledge the equality of status between the different levels of government, the only idea that we need in place of "sovereignty" is the idea of autonomous jurisdictional spheres of powers. This will not answer all our questions but it will at least point us towards the right place in which to find them: the actual division of powers set out in the Constitution. It will be more useful to examine those distinct powers directly rather than following the lead of an inconsistent theory that brings us nowhere but quite literally into a state of confusion.

Be that as it may, whatever the normative source upon which the Court based its opinion that the federal government was the only one that possessed the type of international legal personality necessary for acquiring the "rights to explore and exploit", this is not enough to conclude that the provinces lack *all* international capacities. Jumping to that conclusion would make us victims of the fallacy known as "denying the antecedent": if A (X has "the type of international legal personality necessary for acquiring rights to explore and exploit the continental shelf"), then B (X has an "international legal personality"). Not A (X does not have "the type of international legal personality necessary for acquiring rights to explore and exploit the continental shelf"), then not B (X does not have an "international legal personality"). Because different rights and obligations may be attached to different types of international personalities, the fact that provinces do not have the type of international legal personality entitling them to acquire "rights to explore and exploit" the continental shelf says nothing of their other possible international rights and duties.

The third and last authority to which Professor Brun and Professor Tremblay turn is the majority's opinion in the *Patriation Reference* [349] on the issue of the legality of a federal request to the Parliament of the United Kingdom, without the consent of the provinces, to modify the Canadian Constitution in order to, *inter alia*, transfer all the powers to amend the Canadian Constitution from the British Parliament to local institutions. S. 4 of the *Statute of Westminster* reads:

---

[349] *Supra* note 95. The Court examined separately two issues: (a) the legality of a federal unilateral request for patriation of the Constitution, and (b) the conformity of such a request to Canadian constitutional conventions. The composition of the respective majorities on those two issues was not the same.

> No Act of Parliament of the United Kingdom passed after the commencement of this Act shall extend, or be deemed to extend, to a Dominion as part of the law of that Dominion, unless it is expressly declared in that Act that that Dominion has requested, and consented to the enactment thereof.[350]

At best, because of the doctrine of parliamentary supremacy, this clause only imposed on the British Parliament the obligation to "expressly declare" that a Dominion to which it wants to apply one of its laws has "requested" and "consented" to that enactment. The fact that such Dominion actually requested the said enactment was technically irrelevant because what mattered was simply the use of the "magic phrase" in the statute in question. That being said, because the Parliament of the United Kingdom was committed to respecting the autonomy of the Dominions and because it was bound by a firm convention to that effect, it did not enact such statutes extending to the Dominions unless proper requests were made and appropriate consent was given to the statutes in question and systematically did enact such legislations when it was requested. The questions, then, were whether or not the two Houses of the federal Parliament had the authority to adopt a resolution requesting a modification to the then *British North America Act* and to send such resolution to Her Majesty the Queen, without the consent of the provinces, where provincial powers and federal-provincial relationships would thereby be affected. The federal government argued that the Resolution was not a law and that it was not therefore amenable to judicial analysis, that the two Houses of the federal Parliament can adopt whatever resolution they wish to. The provinces argued, among other things, that the texts of the then *British North America Act* and of the *Statute of Westminster* did not allow the federal Parliament to accomplish the changes it sought in the Canadian Constitution. Therefore, the provinces argued that if the federal Parliament could not do directly what it wanted to do, the two Houses of the federal Parliament could not *indirectly* achieve that result either through a Resolution addressed to the Parliament of the United Kingdom. They also claimed that the basic structure of Canadian federalism prohibited the two Houses of the federal Parliament to address the disputed Resolution to Her Majesty the Queen without first obtaining their consent. Such address would violate the federalism principle that underlies the structure of the Canadian Constitution. The provinces supported their argument with a series of complex textual, historical and institutional arguments that is unnecessary to review here. The provinces claimed that if the federal government could go ahead with its project without the consent of the provinces, on the basis of the same reasoning, the federal government could

---

[350] *Supra* note 67.

also go ahead and destroy the federal system by addressing a Resolution to the Parliament of the United Kingdom requesting the abolition of the division of powers. The federal government even recognised that this was one of the possible consequences of its arguments.

Upon reading the majority opinion, it appears rather evident that the dissenting opinion was first produced and then, the majority opinion was written as a reaction. This makes for a very messy and confused majority opinion; instead of being built upon its own line of reasoning, it more or less shadows the line of reasoning adopted by the dissenting judges. Often, in that majority opinion, apodictic statements are offered in *lieu* of arguments as if the perceived burden of the author of that opinion was simply to oppose the conclusions arrived at by the other opinion's reasoning. This is most unfortunate since it only leaves behind partial conclusions based on very little reasoning. On its way to such conclusions, the majority dropped a few unarticulated statements, including a decisive one about the uselessness of constitutional principles in constitutional adjudication:

> What is put forward by the provinces which oppose the forwarding of the address without provincial consent is that external relations with Great Britain in this respect must take account of the nature and character of Canadian federalism. It is contended that a legal underpinning of their position is to be found in the Canadian federal system as reflected in historical antecedents, in the pronouncements of leading political figures and in the preamble to the *British North America Act.*
>
> ...
>
> History cannot alter the fact that in law there is a British statute to construe and apply in relation to a matter, fundamental as it is, that is not provided for by the statute. Practices which took account of evolving Canadian independence, did, of course, develop. They had both intra-Canadian and extra-Canadian aspects in relation to British legislative authority. The former have already been canvassed, both in the reasons on Question 2 and Question B and, to a degree, in these reasons. Theories, whether of a full compact theory (which, even factually, cannot be sustained, having regard to federal power to create new provinces out of federal territories, which was exercised in the creation of Alberta and Saskatchewan) or of a modified compact theory, as urged by some of the provinces, operate in the political realm, in political science studies. They do not engage the law, save as they might have some peripheral relevance to actual provisions of the *British North America Act* and its interpretation and application.
>
> ...

> In short, ... there is nothing in the reference to theories of federalism reflected in some case law that goes beyond their use as an aid to a justiciable question raised apart from them.[351]

Two important comments must be made here. First, when the majority on the issue of the "legality" of the federal Resolution writes that the "intra-Canadian" practices "have *already* been canvassed" [my emphasis] in the reasons on Question 2 and Question B, this is an editorial mistake that is quite telling of what might have been a previous division of opinions in the Court. Question 2 and Question B, which relate to the issue as to whether or not a unilateral federal request to London to have the Canadian Constitution modified would violate constitutional conventions, are only dealt with in the second part of the decision. More significantly, while Chief Justice Laskin and Estey and McIntyre JJ. are part of the majority on the issue of the "legality" of the Resolution, they find themselves to be the three dissenters on the constitutional conventions issue. The four other judges who were part of the majority on the "legality" issue join, on the question of the constitutional conventions, Martland and Ritchie JJ. who had dissented on the "legality" question. This leads me to my second comment. In both their majority opinion on the legality of the Resolution and their dissenting opinion as to whether or not a unilateral federal request to amend the Canadian Constitution would violate Canadian constitutional conventions, Chief Justice Laskin and Estey and McIntyre JJ. denied the role of constitutional principles in constitutional adjudication. The contrary is true of the dissenting view on the issue of legality and the majority view on the requirements of Canadian constitutional conventions. In other words, it is highly likely that the four judges who ended up forming a majority with the Chief Justice Laskin and Estey and McIntyre JJ. initially were forming a majority with Martland and Ritchie JJ. That would explain the inconsistency between the positions taken by those four judges on the issue of the use of the principles of federalism in constitutional adjudication. Why would Dickson, Beetz, Chouinard and Lamer JJ. jump ship? We can only speculate. But our informed guess is that, on the one hand, they feared that declaring that the federal government could not go ahead without the unanimous approval of the provinces would have put the process of constitutional amendment in a bind. On the other hand, if they had sided with the dissent that stated that it was not necessary to answer the question asked in the reference to specify the degree of provincial agreement legally required to pass the disputed amendment, they would only invite further constitutional litigation over a potentially very divisive national issue that would probably force them either to (a)

---

[351] *Ibid.* at 803-04.

recognise the necessity of unanimity among provinces or (b) develop a constitutional rule that would not appear arbitrary yet would not include all the provinces.

Fortunately, the position held by the majority on the legality of the federal Resolution has since been corrected by a series of very important Supreme Court opinions, including the *Reference Re Manitoba Language Rights*,[352] *Reference re Remuneration of Judges of the Provincial Court (P.E.I.)*,[353] and, especially, the *Reference Re Secession of Québec*.[354] In the latter reference, a unanimous Supreme Court not only affirmed in clear terms the importance of constitutional principles in constitutional adjudication, but also, in more subtle terms, took side with the dissenting view on the issue of the legality of the federal Resolution against the majority opinion in the *Patriation Reference*[355] in declaring:

> Underlying constitutional principles may in certain circumstances give rise to substantive legal obligations (have "full legal force", as we described it in the *Patriation Reference, supra*, at p. 845 [The Supreme Court quotes here the dissenting opinion]), which constitute substantive limitations upon government action. ... The principles are not merely descriptive, but are also invested with a powerful normative force, and are binding upon both courts and governments. "In other words", as this Court confirmed in the *Manitoba Language Rights Reference, supra*, at p. 752, "in the process of Constitutional adjudication, the Court may have regard to unwritten postulates which form the very foundation of the Constitution of Canada". ...
>
> (b) *Federalism*
>
> ...
>
> In interpreting our Constitution, the courts have always been concerned with the federalism principle, inherent in the structure of our constitutional arrangements, which has from the beginning been the lodestar by which the courts have been guided.
>
> This underlying principle of federalism, then, has exercised a role of considerable importance in the interpretation of the written provisions of our Constitution. In the *Patriation Reference, supra*, at pp. 905-9, we confirmed that the principle of federalism runs through the political and legal systems of Canada. Indeed, Martland and Ritchie JJ., dissenting in the *Patriation Reference*, at p. 821, considered federalism to be "the dominant principle of Canadian constitutional *law*". With the enactment of the *Charter*, that proposition may have less force than it once did, but there can be little doubt

---

[352] *Reference Re Manitoba Language Rights*, [1985] 1 S.C.R. 721.

[353] *Reference re Remuneration of Judges of the Provincial Court (P.E.I.)*, [1998] 1 S.C.R. 3.

[354] *Supra* note 76.

[355] *Supra* note 95.

that the principle of federalism remains a central organizational theme of our Constitution. [356]

Thus, federalism is a dominant principle of constitutional *law*. When the unanimous Supreme Court opinion in the *Reference Re Secession of Québec*[357] says that "[i]n the *Patriation Reference, supra,* at pp. 905-9, we confirmed that the principle of federalism runs through the political and legal systems of Canada", the Court is referring, among other things to the following views expressed by the majority views in the *Patriation Reference* in the section dealing with constitutional conventions:

> ... Canada is a federal union. The preamble of the *B.N.A. Act* states that
>
> ... the Provinces of Canada, Nova Scotia, and New Brunswick have expressed their Desire to be federally united ...
>
> The federal character of the Canadian Constitution was recognized in innumerable judicial pronouncements. We will quote only one, that of Lord Watson in *Liquidators of the Maritime Bank of Canada v. Receiver-General of New Brunswick, supra,* at pp. 441-42:
>
> > The object of the Act was neither to weld the provinces into one, nor to subordinate provincial governments to a central authority, but to create a federal government in which they should all be represented, entrusted with the exclusive administration of affairs in which they had a common interest, each province retaining its independence and autonomy.
>
> The federal principle cannot be reconciled with a state of affairs where the modification of provincial legislative powers could be obtained by the unilateral action of the federal authorities. It would indeed offend the federal principle that "a radical change to ... [the] constitution [be] taken at the request of a bare majority of the members of the Canadian House of Commons and Senate" (Report of Dominion Provincial Conference, 1931, at p. 3).
>
> This is an essential requirement of the federal principle which was clearly recognized by the Dominion-Provincial Conference of 1931.[358]

The dissenting opinion on the issue of legality, applying to the question at hand "the dominant principle of Canadian constitutional law" that is federalism – the very principle approved by the Court in the *Reference Re Secession of Québec* [359] – wrote:

> The *Statute of Westminster, 1931* gave statutory recognition to the independent sovereign status of Canada as a nation. However, while Canada, as a nation, was recognized as being sovereign, the government of the nation remained federal in character and the federal Parliament did not acquire sole

---

[356] *Supra* note 76 at para 57 (emphasis added).

[357] *Ibid.*

[358] *Supra* note 95 at 905-06.

[359] *Supra* note 76.

control of the exercise of that sovereignty. Section 2 of the *Statute of Westminster, 1931* standing alone, could be construed as giving that control to the federal Parliament, but the enactment of s. 7, at the instance of the provinces, was intended to preclude that exercise of power by the federal Parliament. Section 7(3) in particular gave explicit recognition to the continuation of the division of powers created by the *B.N.A. Act*. The powers conferred on the Parliament of Canada by the *Statute of Westminster, 1931* were restricted to the enactment of laws in relation to matters within the competence of the Parliament of Canada.[360]

And later:

> The contention of the Attorney General of Canada in the present proceedings is that only the federal Parliament can speak for Canada as a sovereign state. ...

> In our opinion the accession of Canada to sovereign international status did not enable the federal Parliament, whose legislative authority is limited to the matters defined in s. 91 of the *B.N.A. Act*, unilaterally by means of a resolution of its two Houses, to effect an amendment to the *B.N.A. Act* which would offend against the basic principle of the division of powers created by that Act. The assertion of such a right, which has never before been attempted, is not only contrary to the federal system created by the *B.N.A. Act*, but also runs counter to the objective sought to be achieved by s. 7 of the *Statute of Westminster, 1931.*[361]

Thus, to the extent that the majority opinion in the *Patriation Reference*[362] is based on its wilful ignorance of the constitutional principle of federalism, its precedential value is null. The majority decision completely ignored the federal character of the Canadian Constitution and then relied partly on a very weak formalist analysis of the relevant texts and partly on a series of bootstrapping assertions to the effect that because Canada was now sovereign, only the federal government could communicate with Her Majesty the Queen to request a constitutional amendment from London and had to consent to such an amendment. The latter assertions have a circular character because they basically argue that Canada is "sovereign" because it expresses itself through the mouth of the federal government and it expresses itself through the mouth of the federal government because it is "sovereign"![363] Whatever the Court might have said about the respective roles of the federal government and the provinces in relation to external relations, it is fatally tainted by serious constitutional and analytical mistakes. Thus,

---

[360] *Patriation Reference, supra* note 95 at 835.

[361] *Ibid.* at 845-46.

[362] *Ibid.*

[363] *Patriation Reference, supra* note 95 at 802.

the majority opinion on the legality of the federal Resolution is now read only for its historical value.

In the end, it is clear that the well-established constitutional rule that Crown prerogatives are divided according the division of legislative powers precludes the federal government from having plenary and exclusive powers to make treaties.

iii. Constitutional Conventions and Constitutional Usage

When faced with the fact that constitutional *law* does not support convincingly Ottawa's argument, some thought that they could find support for their position in constitutional *usages* or *conventions*. Duff C.J., for example, in the *Labour Conventions* case – *SCC* claimed that:

> As a rule, the crystallization of constitutional usage into a rule of constitu-
> tional law to which the Courts will give effect is a slow process extending
> over a long period of time; but the Great War accelerated the pace of devel-
> opment in the region with which we are concerned, and it would seem that
> the usages to which I have referred, the practice, that is to say, under which
> Great Britain and the Dominions enter into agreements with foreign coun-
> tries in the form of agreements between governments and of a still more in-
> formal character, must be recognized by the Courts as having the force of
> law.[364]

Or, to take another example, Gerald Morris argued that

> ... [i]t is perhaps appropriate to attach less importance to any debate over
> the precise source of the federal treaty-making power than to the fact that
> the exclusive federal power to sign and ratify treaties has gone virtually
> without serious challenge, either domestically or internationally, from the
> time Canada assumed substantial treaty-making power until the past several
> years.[365]

However, this statement by Morris is not true. As we have seen in the *Labour Conventions* case,[366] Ontario and New Brunswick explicitly challenged the federal government's claim. Québec has also long pro-tested this situation. As Minister Paul Gérin-Lajoie said in his address pronounced on April 12, 1965 in Montréal, before the Consular Corps:

> Il fut un temps où l'exercice exclusif par Ottawa des compétences interna-
> tionales n'était guère préjudiciable aux intérêts des États fédérés puisque le
> domaine des relations internationales était assez bien délimité ... Mais de

---

[364] *Labour Conventions* case – *SCC, supra* note 135 at 477.

[365] G.R. Morris, "The Treaty-Making Power: A Canadian Dilemma", *supra* note 22 at 484.

[366] *Supra* note 19.

nos jours, il n'en est plus ainsi. Les rapports interétatiques concernent tous les aspects de la vie sociale.[367]

Québec thus opposed the federal claim from at least the 1960s on. Despite recognizing Québec's persistent objection,[368] Gibran van Ert, wrote:

> As a matter of pure constitutional law, the Quebec argument seems a winner. Yet the question of provincial treaty-making is not one of pure constitutional law, for it also involves constitutional practice and international recognition. It is here that the Quebec position breaks down. Canadian practice in treaty-making points clearly towards an undivided federal treaty power, in spite of Quebec's persistent objections.[369]

The author then goes on to try to find a possible power source in the "crystallization of constitutional *usage*" for a general and exclusive federal treaty-making power because:

> Only the 'crystallization of constitutional usage' argument offers any means of reconciling Quebec's seemingly sound statement of the law, founded on *Maritime Bank*, with the blunt reality that the federal claim is accepted by most provinces and recognized by international practice.[370]

However, in an apparent reversal of position, van Ert ends up concluding that in his view "Quebec's persistent objection has the effect of precluding the development of any unwritten constitutional law in favour of exclusively federal treaty-making power".[371] Thus, "the blunt reality that the federal claim is accepted by most provinces and recognized by international practice" would cut no ice at Canadian constitutional law. Even if he ends up rejecting it, I propose to examine more closely the "crystallization" argument presented by Gibran van Ert. The reason for doing so is that there are much stronger arguments to oppose the "crystallization" argument than those found in van Ert's analysis.

As we know, constitutional conventions are rules – written or not – that: (a) govern the functioning of political institutions; (b) are perceived as mandatory (by actors involved in the institutions) because of their *raison d'être*, their pertinence or their antiquity; (c) serve to complete (or sometimes contradict) the formal legal constitution; and (d) may be determined to exist by the Courts but will never be enforced by the latter. Gibran does well to remind his readers that the first objection to

---

[367] Paul Gérin-Lajoie, *Discours de Paul Gérin-Lajoie devant le corps consulaire de Montréal, supra* note 6.

[368] G. van Ert, *Using International Law in Canadian Courts, supra* note 41 at 79.

[369] *Ibid.* at 87.

[370] *Ibid.* at 88. We will come back to the issue of the international practice in the next argument.

[371] *Ibid.* at 92.

the "crystallization" argument is that the theory of the crystallization of a constitutional convention into constitutional law has been clearly *rejected* by the Supreme Court in the *Patriation Reference*.[372] In the *Patriation Reference*, the majority of the Court writes in very clear terms:

> No instance of an explicit recognition of a convention as having matured into a rule of law was produced. The very nature of a convention, as political in inception and as depending on a consistent course of political recognition by those for whose benefit and to whose detriment (if any) the convention developed over a considerable period of time is inconsistent with its legal enforcement.

> The attempted assimilation of the growth of a convention to the growth of the common law is misconceived. The latter is the product of judicial effort, based on justiciable issues which have attained legal formulation and are subject to modification and even reversal by the courts which gave them birth when acting within their role in the state in obedience to statutes or constitutional directives. No such parental role is played by the courts with respect to conventions.[373]

Moreover, in that case the Court considered specifically the statement by Duff C.J. reproduced above[374] and concluded that, at best, what that statement could refer to was the "… evolution which is characteristic of customary international law"[375] but that it could not describe the domestic constitution-making process. The Court writes: "There is nothing in the other judgments delivered in the *Labour Conventions* case, either in the Supreme Court or in the Privy Council that takes the matter there beyond its international law setting or lends credence to the crystallization proposition urged by counsel for the Attorney General of Manitoba …"[376]

More importantly, I must add that even if the "crystallization of convention" argument had been accepted, the argument would still fail because for crystallization to happen, a convention must first exist. Referring to the majority's views in *Patriation Reference*,[377] a unanimous Supreme Court wrote in the *Québec Veto Reference*[378] that "the majority opinion held that *precedents and usage* did not suffice to establish a convention, that they had to be normative and be founded on

---

[372] *Patriation Reference, supra* note 95.

[373] *Ibid.* at 774-75.

[374] See note 364 and accompanying text.

[375] *Patriation Reference, supra* note 95 at 778.

[376] *Ibid.* at 779.

[377] *Ibid.* at 888.

[378] *Reference re Objection by Québec to a Resolution to Amend the Constitution*, [1982] 2 S.C.R. 793 [*Québec Veto Reference*].

acceptance by the actors in the precedents."[379] In the *Québec Veto Reference* this meant that while the Supreme Court recognized that precedents clearly pointed in the direction of unanimity for any amendment affecting provinces' legislative competence, no such convention had developed because, as the majority had said in the *Patriation Reference*, "it does not appear that *all the actors* in the precedents have accepted the unanimity rule as a binding one."[380] Concerning the issue of treaty-making powers, therefore, it would be clear that Québec's persistent objection is sufficient to declare that no constitutional convention recognizing a federal plenary treaty-making power exists.

The argument developed by van Ert, however, relies on the distinction between "constitutional conventions" and "constitutional usage". He is certainly right in pointing out that a constitutional usage "is one which is constitutional in nature (meaning that it concerns the basic operation of government) but which lacks the obligatoriness that renders its breach 'unconstitutional in the conventional sense'".[381] But then, however, he believes that while the Supreme Court rejected the crystallization argument for conventions, it did not necessarily do so for constitutional usage.[382] This is unconvincing. In general terms, if the Supreme Court rejected the crystallization argument for conventions, it must *a fortiori* have rejected the argument for usages.

More concretely, what van Ert seems to forget to mention is that a constitutional *usage* is just that, a usage, a regularity of practice and not a *rule*.[383] When a usage begins to be perceived by those who are involved as no longer being a mere regularity, it may turn into a constitutional convention if the practice becomes internalised by the actors as

---

[379] *Ibid.* at 807 (emphasis added).

[380] *Patriation Reference, supra* note 95 at 904 (emphasis added) cited by a unanimous Court in the *Québec Veto Reference, supra* note 378 at 808. The Supreme Court also cites in *Québec Veto Reference, ibid.*, the *Patriation Reference, ibid.* at 894 and 901: "Indeed, if the precedents stood alone, it might be argued that unanimity is required." and "It seems clear that while the precedents taken alone point at unanimity, the unanimity principle cannot be said to have been accepted by all the actors in the precedents". The unanimous Supreme Court then concludes (*Québec Veto Reference, ibid.*): "It necessarily follows that, in the opinion of the majority, one essential requirement for establishing a conventional rule of unanimity was missing. This requirement was acceptance by all the actors in the precedents." (Emphasis added).

[381] G. van Ert, *Using International Law in Canadian Courts, supra* note 41 at 90.

[382] *Ibid.* at 89-92.

[383] See for example P. Hogg, *Constitutional Law of Canada*, 1992, *supra* note 268 at § 1.10(c): "Conventions are often distinguished from "usages": a convention is a rule which is regarded as obligatory by the officials to whom it applies; a *usage is not a rule*, but merely a governmental practice which is ordinarily followed, although is not regarded as obligatory" (emphasis added).

being obligatory.[384] It would therefore appear most surprising that a convention – which has an obligatory nature – cannot crystallize into a constitutional law, whereas a mere usage – with no obligatory nature whatsoever – could crystallize into something that would not only have an obligatory nature but also a legal constitutional value. If the step from constitutional convention to law was a long one, it is even longer from usage to law.

It seems that the reason why van Ert makes a wrong turn at this point of the argument is because he closely associates constitutional usage with unwritten constitutional law.[385] He states that

> [s]ome examples of unwritten laws of the constitution include: the rule that the Crown is not the source of law; the doctrine of implied repeal; the rule that customary international law is incorporated by the common law of Canada; the requirement that treaties be implement [ed] by legislation to have domestic effects (a version of the prohibition on Crown legislation); and the law of parliamentary privilege.[386]

He then goes on to write that "[i]n short, unwritten constitutional laws have no single author, no standard form, and no common pedigree. The most that can be said about them as a general proposition is that they arise from constitutional practice and are given imprimatur of law by the judges".[387] But, contrary to what van Ert asserts, this is not the "most that can be said" about those unwritten constitutional laws. For one, the Supreme Court explained at length the origins of unwritten constitutional principles in the *Reference Re Secession of Québec*.[388] Among other things, the Court stated that:

> In order to endure over time, a constitution must contain a comprehensive set of rules and principles which are capable of providing an exhaustive legal framework for our system of government. Such principles and rules emerge from an understanding of the constitutional text itself, the historical context, and previous judicial interpretations of constitutional meaning.[389]

---

[384] Herbert L.A. Hart famously distinguished between the mere regularity of behaviour and the rule-guided behaviour in Herbert L.A. Hart, *The Concept of Law*, 2nd ed. with postscript by Jospeh Raz and Penelope A. Bulloch (Oxford: Oxford University Press, 1994) [H.L.A. Hart, *The Concept of Law*] at 9-11 and 55-60.

[385] G. van Ert, *Using International Law in Canadian Courts*, supra note 41 at 90-92.

[386] *Ibid.* at 91 (footnotes omitted).

[387] *Ibid.* at 92.

[388] *Reference Re Secession of Québec*, supra note 76.

[389] *Ibid.* at para. 32.

In line with this statement, all the examples van Ert gives (except maybe one[390]), are in fact common law rules that have been developed over time by courts, like the rest of the common law. But, as argued above, it is not possible to point to anything that resembles a slow and gradual development of the common law rules recognizing a federal plenary treaty-making power. This is precisely the reason why some commentators have tried to have recourse to other sources. Moreover, in light of the federal principle found by the Supreme Court to be underlying the Constitution in the *Reference Re Secession of Québec*,[391] it would appear surprising that such a rule could develop out of thin air.

Gibran van Ert eventually concludes that there is "quite simply, no legal answer" to the question of the impact of Québec's persistent

---

[390] The law of Parliamentary privileges is a complex case that has developed as a result of legislation, the *common law*, the *lex parliamentis*, the *Constitution Act, 1867, supra* note 39, and the *Constitution Act, 1982, supra* note 70. But it cannot be said to have evolved around practices that simply received the "imprimatur of courts"; the whole idea of *parliamentary privileges* was the refusal of the Parliament to be subjected to the Courts' powers... On parliamentary privileges in Canada, see *New Brunswick Broadcasting Co. v. Nova Scotia*, [1993] 1 S.C.R. 319; Joseph P. Maingot, *Parliamentary Privilege in Canada* (Toronto: Butterworths, 1982) (the French translation includes also a chapter on Québec's National Assembly: Joseph P. Maingot, *Le privilège parlementaire au Canada* (Cowansville: Yvon Blais, 1987); John G. Bourinot, *Parliamentary Procedure and Practice*, 4th ed. by Thomas B. Flint (Toronto: Canada Law Book Co., 1916); William F. Dawson, "Parliamentary Privilege in the Canadian House of Commons"(1959) 25 R.C.E.S.P. 462; William F. Dawson, "Privilege in the Senate of Canada" (1967) P.L. 212; John Mark Keyes and Anita Mekkunnel, "Traffic Problems at the Intersection of Parliamentary Procedure and Constitutional Law" (2001) 46 McGill L.J. 1037; Samuel J. Watson, *The Powers of Canadian Parliaments* (Toronto: Carswell, 1880); N. Ward, "Called to the Bar of the House of Commons" (1957) 35 Can. Bar Rev. 529. For British sources, see John Hatsell, *Precedents of Proceedings in the House Commons*, 3rd ed., Vol. 1 (London: T. Payne, 1796); William Mackay *et al.*, *Erskine May's Treatise on the Law, Privileges, Proceedings and Usage of Parliament*, 23th rev. ed. (London (U.K.): Butterworths Law, 2004); Charles H. McIlwain, *The High Court of Parliament and its Supremacy: an Historical Essay on the Boundaries Between Legislation and Adjudication in England* (New Haven: Yale University Press, 1910); Joseph Redlich, *The Procedure of the House of Commons* (London: Archibald Constable & Co., 1903).

[391] *Reference Re Secession of Québec, supra* note 76 at para. 56:

> In a federal system of government such as ours, political power is shared by two orders of government: the federal government on the one hand, and the provinces on the other. Each is assigned respective spheres of jurisdiction by the *Constitution Act, 1867*. See, e.g., *Liquidators of the Maritime Bank of Canada v. Receiver-General of New Brunswick*, [1892] A.C. 437 (P.C.), at pp. 441-42. It is up to the courts "to control the limits of the respective sovereignties": *Northern Telecom Canada Ltd. v. Communication Workers of Canada*, [1983] 1 S.C.R. 733, at p. 741. In interpreting our Constitution, the courts have always been concerned with the federalism principle, inherent in the structure of our constitutional arrangements, which has from the beginning been the lodestar by which the courts have been guided.

objection to the development of an unwritten constitutional rule recognizing an undivided federal power over treaty-making.[392] However, he
believes that "it is unfathomable to [him] that Quebec's long and continuing opposition to the existence of an undivided federal treaty power
could have no effect whatever on the purported development of an
unwritten constitutional law."[393] Although I do agree with him on this
last point, I would say that there are sufficient *legal arguments* to deny
that any unwritten constitutional norm granting undivided treaty power
to the federal government exists. Therefore, once all this has been said, I
do not think that we have to go to the political principle of consent to
reject, as van Ert does, the "crystallization" argument.

iv. *International Law and International Legal Personality*

Now that we have seen that nothing in Canadian constitutional law
supports the federal claim, some people have suggested that international law could offer a last alternative argument. In general terms, it has
to be mentioned at the outset that, whatever that argument might have
been worth fifty years ago, it is certainly not worth much today. But in
any case, the argument which needs to be answered on its own terms
generally goes along these lines[394]: (1) Canada is now a "sovereign
state"; (2) "sovereign states" have one undivided international personality; (3) only that personality is allowed to make treaties at international
law; (4) since the federal government is the one habilitated to speak for
Canada, it is the one only allowed to make treaties; (5) the constitution
must necessarily follow those international rules. While I agree with (1),
to the extent that "sovereignty" means anything today, I would dispute
segments (2) and (5) as simply wrong, and would further suggest that
segments (3) and (4) beg the question that they are supposed to answer.
Since segment (4) is, on its face, question begging, I will skip it and will
deal first with (5) and then examine briefly (2) and (3) to show how this
argument is yet another losing one for Ottawa's claim.

The first segment of the argument relates to the assumption that the
Canadian constitution must necessarily – from a constitutional point of
view – follow international law. While one might wish that it would be
so – from the point of view of international law – it is simply not the
case at Canadian constitutional law. To see why, I will examine briefly
how international law is incorporated into Canadian law.

---

[392] G. van Ert, *Using International Law in Canadian Courts, supra* note 41 at 92.

[393] *Ibid.*

[394] See for example B. Laskin, "The Provinces and International Agreements", *supra*
note 40 at 108; J.-Y. Grenon, "De la conclusion des traités et de leur mise en œuvre au
Canada", *supra* note 40 and G.R. Morris, "The Treaty-Making Power: A Canadian
Dilemma", *supra* note 22.

Canadian authors generally claim that Anglo-Canadian jurisprudence on the reception of customary law[395] (as opposed to conventional law)[396] adheres to the theory of *adoption*. The theory of adoption claims that customary international law is automatically adopted in domestic law without having to be "transformed" into a domestic norm through legislative approval. Doubts had recently been expressed by Professor Stephen J. Toope that Canada had effectively adopted the British ap-

---

[395] A. Bayefsky, "International Human Rights Law in Canadian Courts", *supra* note 41 at 118; M. Cohen and A. Bayefsky, "The Canadian Charter of Rights and Freedoms and International Law", *supra* note 41 at 275; J. Claydon, "The Application of International Human Rights Law by Canadian Courts", *supra* note 41 at 730; F. Rigaldies and J. Woehrling, "Le juge interne canadien et le droit international", *supra* note 41 at 304; R. St. John MacDonald, "The Relationship Between International Law and Domestic Law in Canada", *supra* note 41 at 88ff.; D.C. Vanek, "Is International Law Part of the Law of Canada?", *supra* note 41 at 263.

[396] The cases most often cited are as follows: *Buvot v. Barbuit*, (1736) 3 Burr. 1481; *Triquet v. Bath*, (1774) 3 Burr. 1478; *R. v. Chung Chi Cheung*, [1939] A.C. 160 [*Chung Chi Cheung*] (interpreted as adhering to an adoptionist approach by D.C. Vanek, "Is International Law Part of the Law of Canada?", *ibid. Contra:* James Crawford, (1976-77) 48 Brit. Y.B. Int. L. 357); *Dunbar v. Sullivan*, (1907) 11 Ex. C.R. 179 at 188; *Trendtex Trading Corporation Ltd v. Central Bank of Nigeria*, [1977] 1 All E.R. 881 at 903 (leave to appeal to the House of Lords granted, but the case was settled out of court) [*Trendtex*]; *I. Congreso del Partido*, [1978] 1 Q.B. 500 (A.C. U.K.); *The Ship "North" v. The King*, (1906) 37 S.C.R. 385 at p. 394 (Davies J. for the majority of the Court) [*The Ship "North" v. The King*]; *In the Matter Of a Reference As To The Powers Of The Corporation Of The City Of Ottawa And The Corporation Of The Village Of Rockliffe Park To Levy Rates On Foreign Legations And High Commissioners' Residences*, [1943] S.C.R. 208 [*Foreign Legations case*] (M. Cohen and A. Bayefsky noted in "The Canadian Charter of Rights and Freedoms and International Law", *ibid.* at 277 that despite some ambiguities, this case tends to be considered by the doctrine as accepting the adoptionist theory: see R. St. John MacDonald, "The Relationship Between International Law and Domestic Law in Canada", *ibid.* at 101-102; D.C. Vanek, "Is International Law Part of the Law of Canada?", *ibid.* at 277-79; F. Rigaldies and J. Woehrling, "Le juge interne canadien et le droit international", *ibid.* at 303. See also: William A. Schabas, *International Human Rights Law and the Canadian Charter – A Manual for the Practitioner*, 1ˢᵗ ed. (Toronto: Carswell, 1991) at 19 [Schabas (1ˢᵗ ed.)]); *Reference Re Exemption of U.S. Forces from Canadian Criminal Law*, [1943] S.C.R. 483, [1943] 4 D.L.R. 11 at 41 (Taschereau J.) (despite some ambiguities, this decision is also considered by authors as favouring the adoptionist theory: see M. Cohen and A. Bayefsky, "The Canadian Charter of Rights and Freedoms and International Law", *ibid.* at 278; R. St. John MacDonald, "The Relationship Between International Law and Domestic Law in Canada", *ibid.*; D.C. Vanek, "Is International Law Part of the Law of Canada?", *ibid.* at 285; and J. Claydon, "The Application of International Human Rights Law by Canadian Courts", *ibid.* at 730.); *Municipality of Saint John v. Fraser-Brace Overseas Corp.*, [1958] S.C.R. 263; *Bouzari v. Islamic Republic of Iran* (2004), 71 O.R. (3d) 675 (C.A. Ont.) (leave to appeal to the Supreme Court refused, [2005] 1 S.C.R. vi); *Re Alberta Union of Provincial Employees v. R.*, (1981) 120 D.L.R. (3ʳᵈ) 590 (Q.B. Alta) (leave to appeal to the Supreme Court refused: Dec.7, 1981) [*Re A.U.P.E.*].

proach on the subject. [397] Since Toope published his article, the majority of the Supreme Court has expressly taken a stand in favour of the adoptionist doctrine in the common law context.[398] It seems unnecessary to draw a distinction between the *ius commune* of Québec (as found in the *Civil Code of Québec (C.C.Q.)*) and the common law in that regard; a similar position was taken by French law even before civil law was re-established in Québec.[399]

In general, Canadian scholars maintain that the adoption is automatic. However, Professors Rigaldies and Woehrling[400] have claimed that, strictly speaking, there is no real *automatic* adoption since judges must proceed to the incorporation of the international rule in domestic law. One might be tempted to think that this is simply an academic issue, but the issue of whether *the judge recognizes the customary international rule* or rather *actively incorporates it in the domestic legal order* is arguably an important one. Professors Rigaldies and Woehrling's position risks defeating the very purpose of adoption. In effect, to accept that the act of recognition of the customary rule by the judge is what "creates" the parallel rule within our common law system runs the risk, depending on the strength that we are willing to give to the

---

[397] Stephen Toope bases his doubts on three cases. See S.J. Toope, "The Uses of Metaphor: International Law and The Supreme Court of Canada", *supra* note 41. He first cites and comments at 292: "*La République Démocratique du Congo v. Venne*, [1971] S.C.R. 997 (where changes in customary law did not operate to affect Canadian domestic law); and *Reference Re Mineral and Other Natural Resources of the Continental Shelf*, (1983) 145 D.L.R. (3d) 9 (Nfld. C.A.) (implicitly requiring transformation of customary law into domestic law)." He then adds "In the recent *Québec Secession Reference*, the Court offered an at best enigmatic aside that it could not apply "pure" international law directly. If the Court believed that customary international law could condition domestic law, then such an application would be in no way precluded." (Citation omitted.)

[398] *R. v. Hape*, 2007 SCC 26 at para. 39 (LeBel J. (McLachlin C.J. and Deschamps, Fish and Charron JJ. concurring)) [*R. v. Hape*]:

In my view, following the common law tradition, it appears that the doctrine of adoption operates in Canada such that prohibitive rules of customary international law should be incorporated into domestic law in the absence of conflicting legislation. The automatic incorporation of such rules is justified on the basis that international custom, as the law of nations, is also the law of Canada unless, in a valid exercise of its sovereignty, Canada declares that its law is to the contrary. Parliamentary sovereignty dictates that a legislature may violate international law, but that it must do so expressly. Absent an express derogation, the courts may look to prohibitive rules of customary international law to aid in the interpretation of Canadian law and the development of the common law.

[399] Pierre Lardy, La force obligatoire du droit international en droit interne – Étude de droit constitutionnel comparé (Paris: Librairie générale de droit et de jurisprudence, 1966) at 97ff. The author refers to French decisions dating back to the relevant period.

[400] F. Rigaldies and J. Woehrling, "Le juge interne canadien et le droit international", *supra* note 41 at 304-05.

principles of *stare decisis* and precedents, of freezing the customary rule in the domestic legal order,[401] thus defeating the very objective of the theory of adoption which is to allow the domestic rule to espouse the international rule.[402] In fact, Professors Rigaldies and Woehrling have recognized that this seems to be the point of the practice of adoption: "une fois la coutume adoptée et introduite dans l'ordre juridique du Canada, les juges se comportent généralement par la suite comme si, à leurs yeux, cette norme conservait sa nature propre".[403]

Professors Rigaldies and Woehrling seem to have made the same mistake as the one made by some versions of American Legal Realism which considered "*no* statute to be law until it is actually applied by a court".[404] H.L.A Hart replied to those Legal Realists that "[t]here is a difference, crucial for our understanding of law, between the truth that if a statute is to be law, the courts must accept the rule that certain legislative operations make law, and the misleading theory that nothing is law till it is applied in a particular case in court."[405] Similarly, Professors Rigaldies and Woehrling are right when they suggest that the courts must accept the rule that customary international law makes common law, but they are wrong when they suggest that customary international law is not part of common law till it is applied by courts. This mistake rests on a confusion between the *validity of a norm* (i.e. its membership in a specific legal system), on the one hand, and the *official application of the norm*, on the other. As Hart has taught us, in a legal system, there are different types of "second order rules", that is, rules about other rules. One of them is the "rule of recognition",[406] which specifies what norms may count as members of the system, while another set of secondary rules are the "rules of adjudication",[407] which specify who should adjudicate disputes and what procedures they ought to follow. In a legal system, it may be true that a norm may not validly exist if those charged with the application of the law by the legal system's "rules of adjudication" do not recognize it. But the basis for the norm's existence within

---

[401] It is interesting to note that the *stare decisis* rule is not recognized by the International Court of Justice. Article 59 of its enabling statute (*Statute of the International Court of Justice annexed to UN Charter*, Jun. 26, 1945, 59 Stat. 1055, T.S. No. 993) provides that the decision of the Court has no binding force except between the parties in a particular case.

[402] See for example Lord Denning's opinion in *Trendtex, supra* note 396 at 889-890.

[403] F. Rigaldies and J. Woehrling, "Le juge interne canadien et le droit international", *supra* note 41 at 306. [Transl.: "once adopted or introduced into the Canadian legal system, judges then generally behave as if the custom kept its own nature."]

[404] H.L.A. Hart, *The Concept of Law, supra* note 384 at 65.

[405] *Ibid.*

[406] *Ibid.* at 94-95.

[407] *Ibid.* at 97.

the system is the "rule of recognition" that is applied by the adjudicators, and not the adjudicators' decision *per se*. Therefore, it is sufficient for a norm to exist within a legal system that it be validated by the system's "rule of recognition". While the rule of recognition may mandate it, there are no reasons why, in principle, the rule of recognition could not validate within the domestic legal system a norm that is identical to the customary international norm, without first having this norm accepted by the courts. If it were otherwise, we would be forced to conclude that the normative content of customary international law would always be applied retroactively to the cases presented in court. In the end, the theory of truly automatic incorporation seems to be more in line with general principles of the common law – and its dominant Blackstonian "declaratory" narrative[408] – while corresponding to actual judicial behaviour.[409]

However, in order to maintain "parliamentary sovereignty"[410] and the separation of powers as between Parliament and the judiciary, the customary rule must yield to a clear statutory provision.[411] Similarly, a well-established common law rule will override the customary international rule if they are in conflict.[412] Custom thus can serve as a subsidi-

---

[408] See William Blackstone, *Commentaries on the Laws of England* (1765), Vol. 1 (Buffalo (N.Y.): William S. Hein & Co, 1992) at 69-70. The doctrine has been updated and adapted to make sense of prospective overruling (see *In re Spectrum Plus Ltd. (in liquidation)*, [2005] 2 A.C. 680, [2005] UHKL 41 (H.L.) and (in the Canadian context) of prospective constitutional remedies (*Canada (A.-G.) v. Hislop*, 2007 SCC 10 at paras. 81-108).

[409] That being said, courts nevertheless retain a certain degree of flexibility to define the customary norm that they apply in a given case.

[410] This is a hyperbole that plays the role of a regulative idea in countries of the British Commonwealth. It basically claims that Parliament is legally superior to courts and to the Monarch (although She is a constituent part of the Parliament) and thus can adopt any law it wishes to. Of course, in countries like Canada, these legislative powers are limited by a series of constitutional constraints entrenched in their constitutions (e.g. division of powers between the Parliament and provincial legislatures, Charter of Rights and Freedoms, amending formulas, etc.). On the history of the idea, see Jeffrey Goldsworthy, *The Sovereignty of Parliament: History and Philosophy* (Oxford: Oxford University Press, 2001).

[411] *R. v. Hape*, *supra* note 398 at para. 53 ("Parliamentary sovereignty requires courts to give effect to a statute that demonstrates an unequivocal legislative intent to default on an international obligation."). See also: *Mortensen v. Peters*, (1906) 14 Scots L.T.R. 227; *British Columbia Electric Ry v. R.*, [1946] A.C. 527; *Reference re Japanese Canadians*, [1947] A.C. 87 at 104; *Gordon v. R*, [1980] 5 W.W.R. 668 at 671 (B.C.S.C.), (1980) 22 B.C.L.R. 17 (B.C. C.A.) (appeal dismissed on another issue); *GreCon Dimter inc. v. J.R. Normand inc.*, [2005] 2 S.C.R. 401 at para. 39 [*GreCon Dimter v. J.R. Normand*].

[412] *Chung Chi Cheung*, *supra* note 396 at 168; M. Cohen and A. Bayefsky, "The Canadian Charter of Rights and Freedoms and International Law", *supra* note 41 at 276;

ary, yet binding, source in the absence of a clear statutory provision or an established common law rule.

A customary rule can also serve as an interpretative tool. Indeed, there is a presumption under which Parliament and the legislatures do not wish to legislate contrary to a customary law or a treaty law rule.[413] Recently, a majority of the Supreme Court reaffirmed the existence of such a presumption in unequivocal terms:

> It is a well-established principle of statutory interpretation that legislation will be presumed to conform to international law. The presumption of conformity is based on the rule of judicial policy that, as a matter of law, courts will strive to avoid constructions of domestic law pursuant to which the state would be in violation of its international obligations, unless the wording of the statute clearly compels that result. R. Sullivan, *Sullivan and Driedger on the Construction of Statutes* (4th ed. 2002), at p. 422, explains that the presumption has two aspects. First, the legislature is presumed to act in compliance with Canada's obligations as a signatory of international treaties and as

---

F. Rigaldies and J. Woehrling, "Le juge interne canadien et le droit international", *supra* note 41 at 304.

[413] See for example: *Foreign Legations case, supra* note 396; *The Ship "North" v. The King, supra* note 396; *Daniels v. R.*, [1968] S.C.R. 517; *Society of Composers Authors and Publishers Association of Canada Ltd. v. CTV Television Network Ltd.*, [1968] S.C.R. 676; *R. v. Keegstra*, [1990] 3 S.C.R. 697; *National Corn Growers Association v. Canada (Import Tribunal)*, [1990] 2 S.C.R. 1324 at 1371-1372 (per Gonthier J.) [*National Corn Growers Association*]; *Pushpanathan v. Canada (Minister of Citizenship and Immigration)*, [1998] 1 S.C.R. 982 at 1019-1022 (per Bastarache J.) [*Pushpanathan*]; *Schreiber v. Canada (Attorney General)*, [2002] 3 S.C.R. 269, 2002 SCC 62, at para. 50 [*Schreiber v. Canada*]; *Salomon v. Commissioners of Customs and Excise*, [1967] 2 Q.B. 116 at 141-143 (U.K.) (Lord Diplock); *Bloxam v. Favre*, (1883) 8 P.D. 101.

The same presumption applies to the *Civil Code of Québec* (*GreCon Dimter v. J.R. Normand, supra* note 411).

Of particular interest is *Baker v. Canada (Minister of Citizenship and Immigration)*, [1999] 2 S.C.R. 817 at paras. 69-71 [*Baker*] where a majority of the Supreme Court held that even when dealing with *unimplemented* treaties, the "values reflected in international human rights law may help inform the contextual approach to statutory interpretation and judicial review."

See also F. Rigaldies and J. Woehrling, "Le juge interne canadien et le droit international", *supra* note 41 at 308; M. Cohen and A. Bayefsky, "The Canadian Charter of Rights and Freedoms and International Law", *ibid.* at 280-281; A. Bayefsky, "International Human Rights Law in Canadian Courts", *supra* note 41 at 120; Samuel G.G. Edgar, ed., *Craies On Statute Law*, 6th ed. (London (U.K.): Sweet and Maxwell, 1963) at 461ff.; Peter St. J. Langan, ed., *Maxwell on the Interpretation of Statutes*, 12th ed. (London (U.K.), Sweet and Maxwell, 1969) at 152ff.; P.-A. Côté, *The Interpretation of Legislation in Canada*, 3rd ed., (Scarborough: Carswell, 2000) at pp. 367-68; H. Kindred, "Canadians as Citizens of the International Community: Asserting Unimplemented Treaty Rights in the Courts", *supra* note 41 at 269; S.J. Toope, "The Uses of Metaphor: International Law and The Supreme Court of Canada", *supra* note 41 at 294. More will be said about this presumption in the concluding remarks of this essay.

a member of the international community. In deciding between possible interpretations, courts will avoid a construction that would place Canada in breach of those obligations. The second aspect is that the legislature is presumed to comply with the values and principles of customary and conventional international law. Those values and principles form part of the context in which statutes are enacted, and courts will therefore prefer a construction that reflects them. The presumption is rebuttable, however. ... The presumption applies equally to customary international law and treaty obligations.[414]

For example, in the *Foreign Legations* case,[415] the Supreme Court "read down"[416] an Ontario municipal tax by-law to exclude embassies from its purview in order to comply with the customary rule concerning diplomatic immunity.

This presumption against violation of international law implies that powers delegated by Parliament or legislatures do not allow for the infringement of an international customary or treaty norm unless this power is expressly specified.[417] In effect, if Parliament is presumed not to want to violate international law, *a fortiori* it must be presumed that it does not delegate powers to do so. We can therefore say that international law generally takes precedence over delegated legislation (i.e. regulations) in that Parliament rarely provides for, implicitly or expressly, the possibility of violating international law. Obviously, this could be a powerful tool to implement international law in the era of the regulatory state.

In any event, the foregoing points serve as the basis on which some authors have claimed that the Canadian Parliament and the provincial legislatures were bound by international law. Vanek,[418] for example, was of the view that neither Canada nor the provinces could legislate in violation of international law, given the presumption that a power

---

[414] *R. v. Hape, supra* note 398 at paras. 53-54. In *Baker, supra* note 413 at para. 70, the majority of the Court, quoting with approval a previous edition of Ruth Sullivan, ed., *Driedger on the Construction of Statutes.* 3rd ed. (Toronto: Butterworths, 1994) at 330, went further than it did in *R. v. Hape* with regard to the role of "the values and principles enshrined in international law, both customary and conventional" by suggesting that *"In so far as possible, therefore, interpretations that reflect these values and principles are preferred."* (emphasis added by the Supreme Court).

[415] *Supra* note 396.

[416] Despite no apparent sign of such intention in the provincial statute and the municipal by-law, the Supreme Court interpreted the texts in question as implicitly excluding embassies from their reach.

[417] See for example: D.C. Vanek, "Is International Law Part of the Law of Canada?", *supra* note 41; G.V. La Forest, "May the Provinces Legislate in Violation of International Law?", *supra* note 41; F. Rigaldies and J. Woehrling, "Le juge interne canadien et le droit international", *supra* note 41 at 308.

[418] D.C. Vanek, "Is International Law Part of the Law of Canada?", *ibid.* at 263.

delegated by the Parliament in London does not, unless expressly stated, empower to legislate contrary to international law. Since the *Constitution Act, 1867*, does not contain any such mention, it would follow that legislation cannot be introduced in Canada in violation of international law. This argument seems difficult to defend in light of Canada's independence and the *Statute of Westminster* and it ignores the fact that legislative powers possessed by Canada and the provinces are not the result of "delegations", strictly speaking, as determined by the Judicial Committee of the Privy Council in *Hodge v. R.*[419] It must be noted here that even if Vanek's arguments were to be accepted, they could only go to *limit* federal or provincial powers but not to *grant* such powers. Therefore, a further argument would have to be developed as to the possible power-granting force of international law.

In any case, after having been systematically rejected by legal scholars, Vanek's arguments were in turn rejected by the Supreme Court. For example, in *Ordon Estate* v. *Grail*, the Court wrote:

> *Although international law is not binding upon Parliament or the provincial legislatures*, a court must presume that legislation is intended to comply

---

[419] *Hodge v. R., supra* note 14. The Privy Council in *Queen v. Burah*, (1878) 3 A.C. 889 (P.C.) at 904-05, had previously stated about the "subordinated" legislatures created by the Imperial Parliament that:

> The Indian legislature has powers expressly limited by the Act of the Imperial Parliament which created it, and it can, of course, do nothing beyond the limits which circumscribe these powers. But, when acting within those limits, *it is not in any sense an agent or delegate of the Imperial Parliament, but has, and was intended to have, plenary powers of legislation, as large, and of the same nature, as those of Parliament itself.* (Emphasis added).

This latter statement was cited with approval by a unanimous Supreme Court in *Reference Re: Saskatchewan Natural Resources*, [1931] S.C.R. 263.

While he was Dean, Rand J. also claimed that provinces could not legislate contrary to international law based on the argument that the jurisdiction on foreign affairs fell entirely upon the Dominion (I.C. Rand, "Some Aspects of Canadian Constitutionnalism", *supra* note 41 at 143-44). It is hard to reconcile this proposition with the decision rendered in the *Labour Conventions* case *supra* note 19 as to legislative powers. Also, while he was professor, La Forest J. also defended the thesis that provinces could not legislate in violation of international law by invoking the constitutional doctrine of extra-territoriality and, alternatively, for the reason advanced by Vanek (G.V. La Forest, "May the Provinces Legislate in Violation of International Law?", *supra* note 41 at 81-87). The doctrine of extra-territoriality is not of great assistance here because, as La Forest put it, it "was developed to prevent violations of international law by the colonies" which could attract the liability of the metropolitan State. It cannot be said that provinces are "colonies or dependencies" of the federal government. Other arguments related to extraterritoriality will be examined in depth in section III.C.

with Canada's obligations under international instruments and as a member of the international community.[420]

While Vanek's arguments did not work, they invite us to question the relevance of using the general rules for the incorporation of international law in the context of *constitutional law*. Here, the rules differ. The general Canadian rule regulating the interplay between international law and the Canadian constitution has been set in Chief Justice Dickson's famous statements in the *Reference Re Public Service Employee Relations Act (Alta.)*:

> The various sources of international human rights law – declarations, covenants, conventions, judicial and quasi-judicial decisions of international tribunals, customary norms – must, in my opinion, *be relevant and persuasive sources* for interpretation of the *[Canadian] Charter [of Rights and Freedoms]*'s provisions. ...

> The general principles of constitutional interpretation require that these international obligations be a *relevant and persuasive* factor in *[Canadian] Charter [of Rights and Freedoms]* interpretation. ...

> In short, though *I do not believe the judiciary is bound by the norms of international law in interpreting the [Canadian] Charter [of Rights and Freedoms], these norms provide a relevant and persuasive source for interpretation of the provisions of the Charter*, especially when they arise out of Canada's international obligations under human rights conventions.[421]

---

[420] *Ordon Estate* v. *Grail*, [1998] 3 S.C.R. 437 at para. 137 (per Iacobucci and Major JJ for the Court) (emphasis added) [*Ordon Estate*].

[421] *Reference Re Public Service Employee Relations Act (Alta.)*, [1987] 1 S.C.R. 313 at 348-350 [*P.S.A.C.*] (Dickson C.J. and Wilson J.) (dissenting on the result but not on this point) (emphasis added). That statement has been quoted with approval by Gonthier, Cory and Iacobucci JJ. (dissenting on another point) in *R. v. Zundel*, [1992] 2 S.C.R. 731 at para. 160 [*R. v. Zundel*] and by retired Justice L'Heureux-Dubé (Claire L'Heureux-Dubé, "From Many Different Stones: A House of Justice" (2003) 41 Alta. L. Rev. 659). The use of international law merely as a "persuasive authority" to interpret the Constitution has been discussed by many authors. See for example: Ken Norman, "Practising What We Preach in Human Rights: A Challenge in Rethinking for Canadian Courts" (1991) 55 Sask. L. Rev. 289; Anne Bayefsky, *International Human Rights Law, Use in Canadian Charter of Rights and Freedom Litigation*, Toronto, Butterworths, 1992 [A. Bayefsky, *International Human Rights Law., Use in Canadian Charter of Rights and Freedom Litigation*]; William A. Schabas, *International Human Rights Law and the Canadian Charter*, 2nd ed. (Toronto, Carswell, 1996); Daniela Bassan, "The Canadian Charter and Public International Law: Redefining the State's Power to Deport Aliens" (1996) 34 Osgoode Hall L.J. 583; William Schabas, "Twenty-Five Years of Public International Law at the Supreme Court of Canada" (2000) 79 Can. Bar Rev. 174; Karen Knop, "Here and There: International Law in Domestic Courts", *supra* note 41; G. van Ert, *Using International Law in Canadian Courts*, *supra* note 41 at 91; Gaile McGregor, "The International Covenant on Social, Economic, and Cultural Rights: Will It Get Its Day in Court?" (2002) 28 Man. L.J. 321; Anne W. La Forest, "Domestic Application of International Law in Charter

In other words, whatever the rules for the interpretation of statutes or the common law, international law in constitutional interpretation is merely a "relevant and pertinent source". This means that it is *not a binding subsidiary source*. Thus, it does not automatically remedy textual lacunae that may exist in the Constitution, as it might do with infra-constitutional common law.

Recently, however, the Supreme Court has picked up on another statement found in Chief Justice Dickson's opinion to strengthen the role of international law in the context of *Canadian Charter of Rights and Freedoms*[422] interpretation. In a statement difficult to square with his main position, Chief Justice Dickson had written that he "believe[d] that the *Charter* should generally be presumed to provide protection at least as great as that afforded by similar provisions in international human rights documents which Canada has ratified."[423] A majority of the Court turned the late Chief Justice's belief into law by stating that "the *Charter* should be presumed to provide at least as great a level of protection as is found in the international human rights documents that Canada has ratified."[424] And this presumption was turned into an injunction to the Courts: "in interpreting the scope of application of the *Charter*, the courts should seek to ensure compliance with Canada's binding obligations under international law *where the express words are capable of supporting such a construction*".[425] *R. v. Milne*[426] is probably one such case where the language of the provision did not allow for the application of the presumption. In that case, the Court concluded that even if s. 11 (i) of the *Canadian Charter of Rights and Freedoms*[427] clearly guarantees less rights than Art. 15 of the *International Covenant on Civil and Political Rights*[428] (to which Canada agreed to be bound), the latter international norm is not pertinent to interpret the clear prescription of the Constitution.

Cases: Are We There Yet?" (2004) 37 U.B.C. L. Rev. 157; Irit Weiser, "Undressing The Window: Treating International Human Rights Law Meaningfully in the Canadian Commonwealth System" (2004) 37 U.B.C. L. Rev. 113.

[422] *Supra* note 81.

[423] *P.S.A.C.*, *supra* note 421 at para. 59.

[424] *Health Services and Support — Facilities Subsector Bargaining Assn. v. British Columbia*, 2007 SCC 27 at para. 70. See also para. 79.

[425] *R. v. Hape*, *supra* note 398 at para. 56 (emphasis added).

[426] *R. v. Milne*, [1987] 2 S.C.R. 512 at 527.

[427] *Supra* note 81.

[428] *International Covenant on Civil and Political Rights*, 19 December 1966, 999 U.N.T.S. 171, Can. T.S. 1976 No. 47, 6 I.L.M. 368 (entered into force 23 March 1976, accession by Canada 19 May 1976) [*I.C.C.P.R.*].

If the presumption discussed in the previous paragraph is to remain within Canadian constitutional law, it ought to be viewed as a special exception to the general rule and ought to be restricted to the *Canadian Charter of Rights and Freedoms*.[429] In effect, whatever the case may be for infra-constitutional norms, there are very strong constitutional policy reasons to maintain the original Supreme Court's position on the role of international law with regards to the Constitution. First, by limiting international law to being simply a "relevant and pertinent" source rather than being a binding source of constitutional law, this rule ensures that the executive branch will not be able to indirectly circumvent the stringent amending formulas provided at Part V of the *Constitution Act, 1982*. A second reason is that it avoids the possibility that constitutional changes could be caused by modifications in international customary norms without Canadians' approval. In other words, it avoids granting outsiders the power to amend the Canadian constitution. In effect, whatever we might think of the validity of the "persistent objector" doctrine at international law,[430] the fact remains that once a customary rule would have entered the Canadian constitution, it would be very hard for Canadians to modify the new constitutional rule because it would be subject to the same amending formulas as any others.

At any rate, even if we were to apply the infra-constitutional standard of incorporation of international law to remedy a textual lacuna, international law could not be used to displace clear and well-established common law rules. Thus, it could not displace the common law rule recognizing that the executive's prerogatives parallel legislative competence.

Thus, the analysis could, and actually should, stop here.

However, for the sake of the argument, I will address segments (2) (""sovereign states" have one undivided international personality") and (3) ("only that personality is allowed to make treaties at international

---

[429] *Supra* note 81.

[430] The "persistent objector" doctrine is to the effect that a state is not bound by a customary rule of international law if that state consistently objected to that rule before it became firmly established as a rule of customary international law. See *Fisheries Case (United Kingdom v Norway)*, 1951 ICJ 116 at 139; Ted L. Stein, "The Approach of a Different Drummer: The Principle of the Persistent Objector in International Law" (1985) 26 Harv. Int'l L.J. 457 and Ian Brownlie, *Principles of Public International Law*, 5th ed. (Oxford: Oxford University Press, 1998) at 10. But see Anthony A. D'Amato, *The Concept of Custom in International Law* (Ithaca (N.Y.): Cornell University Press, 1971) at 233-63; Jonathan Charney, "The Persistent Objector Rule and the Development of Customary International Law" (1986) 56 Brit. Y.B. Int'l L. 1 and Jonathan Charney, "Universal International Law" (1993) 87 Am J Intl L 529 at 538-42.

law") of the international law argument, to show that they could not be used to support the federal government's exclusivist claim.

Segment (2) relies on a confusion that was common among earlier publicists,[431] which consisted in erroneously equating "state sovereignty" with "international personality".[432] This mistake is based on a "sovereignty bias", i.e. the idea that at international law, only "sovereign states" have an international personality. This is wrong. Having a "legal personality" means having the capacity to be a bearer of rights and obligations. International law is made of all sorts of legal entities having all sorts of different rights, powers and obligations.[433] The International Court of Justice recognised explicitly this phenomenon when it wrote in 1948:

> The subjects of law in any legal system are not necessarily identical in their nature or in the extent of their rights, and their nature depends upon the needs of the community. Throughout its history, the development of international law has been influenced by the requirements of international life, and the progressive increase in the collective activities of States has already given rise to instances of action upon the international plane by certain entities which are not States.[434]

Thus, this is not a new phenomenon.[435] For example, the League of

---

[431] See for example B. Laskin, "The Provinces and International Agreements", *supra* note 40 at 108 and J.-Y. Grenon, "De la conclusion des traités et de leur mise en œuvre au Canada", *supra* note 40.

[432] See A.L.C. de Mestral, "Le Québec et les relations internationales", *supra* note 41 at 220, discussing the confusion between "state sovereignty" and "legal personality".

[433] Louis Henkin, *International Law: Politics and Values* (Dordrecht: Martinus Nijhoff, 1995) at 16-17, writes: "It has often been said that only states are subjects of international law. It is not clear what such statements mean, but whatever they mean, they are misleading if not mistaken." (cited in Thomas D. Grant, "Defining Statehood: The Montevideo Convention and Its Discontents" (1999) 37 Colum. J. Transnat'l L. 403 at 405 [T.D. Grant, "Defining Statehood: The Montevideo Convention and Its Discontents"].)

[434] *Reparation for Injuries Suffered in the Service of the United Nations*, Advisory Opinion, [1949] I.C. J. Rep. 174 at 178.

[435] T.D. Grant, "Defining Statehood: The Montevideo Convention and Its Discontents", *supra* note 433 at 405, for example, refers to Daniel Patrick O'Connell, *International Law*, 2nd ed. (London (U.K.): Stevens, 1970) [D.P. O'Connell, *International Law*] where the latter writes (at 80): "A half century ago the international lawyers could content themselves with the proposition that "States only are subjects of international law"". Grant also refers to Ignaz Seidl-Hohenveldern, *Corporations in and Under International Law* (Cambridge (U.K.): Grotius Publications, 1987) writing (at 5): "The idea that public international law addressed itself only to States and that therefore only States could be persons and subjects under public international law was not abandoned until the end of the nineteenth century." and to the famous Hans Kelsen who had already acknowledged that states were not the only subjects of international law in the reformulation of his *General Theory of Law and State*, trans. by Anders

Nations itself had a legal personality, so did "A" mandates[436] imposed on parts of the former Ottoman Empire. The simple fact is that international law does not limit itself to "sovereign states" even though those legal entities have been regarded in the Euro-American international legal tradition – at least since the demise of the Holy German Empire – as having the widest array of legal powers. But individuals, universities, municipalities, non-governmental organisations, multinational corporations, intergovernmental organisations, etc.[437] all benefit from having restricted forms of international status. Therefore, it is not surprising to read in standard international law books like *Oppenheim's International Law* that there is "no justification for the view that [member states of federations] are necessarily deprived of any status whatsoever within the international community: while they are not full subjects of international law, they may be international persons for some purposes."[438] We can similarly read in Shaw's *International Law* that federated states may be regarded as having a "degree of international personality".[439] In fact,

---

Wedberg (Cambridge (MA): Harvard University Press, 1949) at 342-48. While these authors debate about when international started being populated by more than simply "sovereign states", one can question whether international law was *ever* only populated by such subjects except in the mind of certain jurists who simply dismissed many other entities as being mere "exceptions" or "aberrations".

[436] Quincy Wright, "Sovereignty of the Mandates" (1923) 17 Am. J. Int'l L. 691 at 696. This article is also quite instructive as to the difficulties then encountered in trying to locate "sovereignty" in the mandate system.

[437] See for example T.D. Grant, "Defining Statehood: The Montevideo Convention and Its Discontents", *supra* note 433 at 405-406 wrote that "it does appear that modern developments have increased the relative legal status of such actors. Strengthening the role of the individual in international law is critical in this regard. Intermediate between states and natural persons, corporations, political or religious parties or movements, organized interest groups, transnational ethnic communities, and other non-governmental organizations (NGOs) have proliferated and assumed a role in international society, and this development, too, has required writers to reassess what can constitute a person under international law." In footnotes, he refers, among other sources, to the *European Convention on the Recognition of the Legal Personality of International Non-governmental Organizations*, 24 April 1986, Europ. T.S. No. 124; Barry E. Carter and Philip R. Trimble, *International Law* (Boston: Little, Brown, 1991) at 411 ("States, international organizations, individuals, corporations, and other entities have varying legal status under international law"); Jonathan I. Charney, "Transnational Corporations and Developing International Law" (1983) 1983 Duke L.J. 748; P.K. Menon, "The International Personality of Individuals in International Law: A Broadening of the Traditional Doctrine" (1992) 1 J. Transnat'l L. & Pol'y 151; David J. Ettinger, "The Legal Status of the International Olympic Committee" (1992) 4 Pace Y.B. Int'l L. 97.

[438] Sir Robert Jennings and Sir Arthur Watts, eds., *Oppenheim's International Law*, 9th ed., Vol. 1 (Harlow (U.K.): Longman, 1992) at 249.

[439] Malcolm N. Shaw, *International Law*, 5th ed. (Cambridge: Cambridge University Press, 1997) at 197.

let's remember that Byelorussia and Ukraine were admitted to the United Nations in 1945, while they were federated states within the Soviet Union.[440] Thus, although international law recognizes that Canada has a legal personality, this in itself is not sufficient to demonstrate that it is the only entity to do so within the territory of Canada. As we have seen earlier, to make such an argument is to fall prey to the fallacy known as "denying the antecedent".[441] In other words, Canada's international status does not in itself preclude provinces from also having a form of international legal personality. That being the case, international law does not preclude federations from being composed of multiple overlapping legal personalities.[442] Therefore, even if the Canadian constitution was bound to respect international law, in no way does international law force federations to have only one single international personality for all possible purposes.

Moreover, even if international law required any federation to have only one legal personality for all possible international purposes, one would have to make the additional hopeless demonstration that international law (a) dictates through which domestic organs this legal personality will express itself and, (b) dictates that it is only through the federal executive that this could be done.[443] One can simply point at the Belgian case – where certain federal treaties can be negotiated and concluded by the federated parts in the name of the whole federation – to show that any attempt at such demonstration would be fruitless. This is not surprising because states are so diverse in their internal power structures that international law has not developed standard rules as to which institutions can conclude treaties binding on their states.[444]

---

[440] *Ibid.* at 196.

[441] See accompanying text between notes 348 and 349.

[442] It is true that the *Montevideo Convention on the Rights and Duties of States*, 26 December 1933, 165 L.N.T.S. 19 [*Montevideo Convention*], to which Canada is *not* a party, states that (Art. 2): "[t]he federal state shall constitute a sole person in the eyes of international law". While other parts of the convention might embody customary law, Art. 2 does not necessarily reflect the contemporary practice of recognizing the multiplicity of international legal personalities both at the "supranational" and "infranational" levels in Europe. This should not come as a surprise since the ideas of the "state" and of the "government" have changed tremendously in the global regulatory age.

[443] For a similar argument, see L. Giroux, "La capacité internationale des provinces en droit constitutionnel canadien", *supra* note 23 at 264.

[444] It is, however, important to note that diverse international jurisdictional bodies have recently been ready to open up the proverbial "black box" of the state and have directed their orders not to the federal authorities but rather directly to the institutions deemed to be in breach of international obligations. Ward Ferdinandusse, "Out of the Black-Box? The International Obligations of State Organs" (2003) 29 Brook. J. Int'l L. 53 at 80 writes that the "ICJ is not alone in its efforts to speak directly to relevant

Again, these arguments on segment (2) are enough to put to rest the federal government's claim to a general treaty-making power based on the "international law argument". Nonetheless, to conclude on this line of argumentative defence, I would like to address its segment (3) (i.e. only fully sovereign states have the required international personality to make treaties at international law).

In its more extreme form, this segment can be illustrated by Bora Laskin's opinion according to which, "if a province presently purported on its own initiative to make an enforceable agreement with a foreign state on a matter otherwise within provincial competence, it would either have no international validity, or, if the foreign state chose to recognize it, would amount to a declaration of independence …"![445] This helps to highlight the mistaken belief, held by certain commentators, that treaty-making is necessarily associated with "state sovereignty". This is however far from being the case. After all, no one would claim that international organizations are "sovereign". Nonetheless, they clearly have the international capacity to make treaties.[446]

---

actors within the State. In fact, it is only taking the first cautious steps on a path where other international courts have made considerable progress." Ferdinandusse discusses, among others, the cases of *LaGrand (Germany* v. *United States of America)*, Order of 3 May 1999, [2002] I.C.J. Rep. 9 at para. 28 where the International Court stated that "the Governor of Arizona is under the obligation to act in conformity with the international undertakings of the United States" and the advisory opinion in *Difference Relating to Immunity from Legal Process of a Special Rapporteur of the Commission on Human Rights*, Advisory Opinion, [1999] I.C.J. Rep. 62 at 89-90 where the International Court quite clearly held that the international obligations were not only those of the state of Malaysia but also those of the state organs, namely those of the Malaysian *courts*. Ferdinandusse also discusses cases from the European Court of Justice, the Inter-American Court of Human Rights, the International Criminal Tribunal for the former Yugoslavia.

While it is far from clear if and how the federal government may bind directly the provincial governments at international law, the current movement towards "piercing the state's veil" might help to understand the otherwise enigmatic assertions by Justice Lebel for the Court to the effect that "Quebec is a party to the *Convention on the Recognition and Enforcement of Foreign Arbitral Awards*, 330 U.N.T.S. 3, of June 10, 1958 (*"New York Convention"*), as a result of Canada's belated accession to the Convention …" and that "As a result of the requirement that art. 3148, para. 2 *C.C.Q.* be interpreted in a manner consistent with Quebec's international commitments, arbitration clauses are binding despite the existence of procedural provisions such as art. 3139 *C.C.Q.*" (*GreCon Dimter v. J.R. Normand*, *supra* note 411 at paras. 40 and 45 (emphasis added)).

[445] B. Laskin, "The Provinces and International Agreements", *supra* note 40 at 111.

[446] See the *Vienna Convention on the Law of Treaties between States and International Organizations or between International Organizations*, *supra* note 238.

The *Vienna Convention on the Law of Treaties*[447] provides at its Art. 6 that every *state* possesses the capacity to conclude treaties. However, it must be noted that the *Vienna Convention* is not meant to establish exhaustive rules about treaties: Art. 6 must be read as indicative of the type of entities covered by the Treaty rather than as indicative of the only entities capable of concluding treaties at international law. In effect, Art. 3 a) specifies that the *Convention* does not affect the legal validity of any other international agreement concluded between a state and any "other subject of international law".[448]

So if entities "less than sovereign" can make treaties, how about federated states? Before answering this question, I need to add a few words on the notion of "state" for treaty-making purposes at international law.

The *Vienna Convention on the Law of Treaties* does not specify what a "state" is for the purpose of the *Convention*. One must thus have recourse to other sources of international law to identify what a "state" is for the treaty. "Textbook traditionalists" often refer to Art. 1 of the 1933 *Montevideo Convention*,[449] to which Canada is not a party, as if it stated the strict criteria of statehood in current international law. That provision states that "[t]he state as a person of international law should possess the following qualifications: a) a permanent population; b) a defined territory; c) government; and d) capacity to enter into relations with the other states." But the usefulness of such criteria to distinguish between states and other international entities is widely in doubt and it represents, at best, "soft law" for those who did not ratify the convention.[450] Nguyen Quoc Dinh, Patrick Daillier and Alain Pellet criticized the *Montevideo Convention* for merely representing necessary but not sufficient conditions for statehood.[451] In general terms, even to call those criteria "necessary" is probably excessive. Highly eminent international

---

[447] *Vienna Convention on the Law of Treaties*, 23 May 1969, [1980] Can.T.S No. 37 [*Vienna Convention on the Law of Treaties*].

[448] *Ibid.*, Art. 3 a) reads:

International agreements not within the scope of the present Convention

The fact that the present Convention does not apply to international agreements concluded between States and other subjects of international law or between such other subjects of international law, or to international agreements not in written form, shall not affect:

(a) the legal force of such agreements;

[449] *Montevideo Convention, supra* note 442.

[450] See, in general, on this and the other questions related to "statehood" T.D. Grant, "Defining Statehood: The Montevideo Convention and Its Discontents", *supra* note 433.

[451] On the general uselessness of the *Montevideo Convention, supra* note 442, to distinguish states from other international subjects, see Nguyen Quoc Dinh, Patrick Daillier, Alain Pellet, *Droit International Public*, 3rd ed. (Paris: Librairie générale de droit et de jurisprudence, 1994) at 398-99.

law publicists such as Joseph G. Starke and James Crawford have, for example, demonstrated that territory[452] and effectiveness[453] of control are not even necessary, if we take into consideration the factor of recognition of statehood. It is also noteworthy here that the last criteria (the "capacity to enter into relations with the other states") has been vastly criticised on the basis that it represents more a *consequence* than a *condition* for statehood,[454] and that it is not useful to distinguish between "states" and other international actors on the basis of the capacity to enter into international agreements since other entities also possess treaty-making powers.[455] Moreover, for the purpose of deciding which entity is a "state" under the *Vienna Convention on the Law of Treaties*, that last criteria is simply useless because it throws the reader into a recursive loop: the *Vienna Convention on the Law of Treaties* provides that a "state" can make treaties while the *Montevideo Convention* provides that a "state" is one of the things that can make treaties... Conceptions of statehood have in any event greatly evolved in the last century and no definitive and exhaustive criteria have yet been adopted by the whole of the international community for the purpose of deciding who or what should be regarded as a state.

It actually appears very likely that federated states could be included in the word "state" for the purpose of the *Vienna Convention on the Law of Treaties*. This should not be surprising, since many federated states do have recognized treaty-making powers without being qualified "sovereign states"[456]: Belgium's "Regions" and "Communities",[457]

---

[452] Ivan A. Shearer, ed., *Starke's International Law*, 11th ed. (London: Butterworths, 1994) at 722-28. T.D. Grant, "Defining Statehood: The Montevideo Convention and Its Discontents", *supra* note 433 at 436 also mentions the case of the French recognition of Poland and Czechoslovakia during World War I, both "entities that never before enjoyed any territorial control".

[453] Crawford demonstrates that Poland, Yugoslavia, Czechoslovakia, and Baltic states were still recognized as states by the Allied Powers after being annexed by Nazi Germany (James Crawford, *The Creation of States in International Law* (Oxford: Clarendon Press, 1979) at 78-79 [J. Crawford, *The Creation of States in International Law*].

[454] See for example: J. Crawford, *The Creation of States in International Law*, *ibid.* at 49; Ingrid Detter, *The International Legal Order* (Brookfield (VT): Dartmouth, 1994) at 43; Peter Malanczuk, ed., *Akehurst's Modern Introduction to International Law*, 7th ed. (New York, Routledge, 1997) at 79.

[455] See for example: D.P. O'Connell, *International Law*, *supra* note 435 at 284-85 and T.D. Grant, "Defining Statehood: The Montevideo Convention and Its Discontents", *supra* note 433 at 434-435.

[456] A report of the Venice Commission on this subject is very instructive. See Council of Europe, Venice Commission/Commission de Venise, European Commission For Democracy Through Law/ Commission européenne pour la démocratie par le droit, *Federated And Regional Entities And International Treaties: Report adopted by the Commission at its 41th meeting*, Venice, 10-11 December 1999, CDL-INF (2000) 3, online: Venice Commission <http://venice.coe.int/docs/2000/CDL-INF(2000)003-

E.asp?MenuL=E> [Council of Europe, *Federated And Regional Entities And International Treaties*].)

Also, there is a vast literature on the multi-layered diplomacy – diplomacy between international organisations, states, federated states or regions, etc. See for example: Ivo Duchacek, Daniel Latouche and Garth Stevenson, eds., *Perforated Sovereignties and International Relations: Trans-sovereign Contacts of Subnational Governments* (New York: Greenwood Press, 1988); Hans J. Michelmann and Panayotis Soldatos, *Federalism and International Relations: the Role of Subnational Units* (Oxford: Clarendon Press, 1990); Brian Hocking, *Localizing Foreign Policy: Non-Central Governments and Multilayered Diplomacy* (London (U.K.): Macmillan, 1993); Panayotis Soldatos, "Cascading Subnational Paradiplomacy in an Interdependent and Transnational World" in Douglas M. Brown and Earl Fry, eds., *States and Provinces in the International Economy* (Berkeley: Institute of Governmental Studies Press, 1993) 45; Liesbet Hooghe, ed., *Cohesion Policy and European Integration: Building Multi-Level Governance* (Oxford: Oxford University Press, 1996); Michael Keating and John Loughlin, eds., *The Political Economy of Regionalism* (London (U.K.): Frank Cass, 1997); Éric Philippart, "Le Comité des Régions confronté à la 'paradiplomatie' des régions de l'Union européenne", in Jacques Bourrinet, ed., *Le Comité des Régions de l'Union européenne* (Paris: Editions économica, 1997); Francisco Aldecoa and Michael Keating, eds., *Paradiplomacy in Action: The Foreign Relations of Subnational Governments* (London (U.K.): Frank Cass, 1999); Charlie Jeffery, "Sub-National Mobilization and European Integration: Does it Make Any Difference" (2000) 38 Journal of Common Market Studies 1; Bart Kerremans, "Determining a European Policy in a Multi-Level Setting: The Case of Specialized Co-ordination in Belgium" (2000) 10 Regional and Federal Studies 1; Stéphane Paquin, "La paradiplomatie identitaire en Catalogne et les relations Barcelone-Madrid" (2002) 33 Études internationales 57; Stéphane Paquin, *La paradiplomatie identitaire en Catalogne* (Québec: Presses de l'Université Laval, 2003); Stéphane Paquin, *Paradiplomatie et relations internationales. Théorie des stratégies internationales des régions face à la mondialisation* (Bruxelles: Peter Lang, 2004); Guy Lachapelle and Stéphane Paquin, eds., *Mastering Globalization: New Sub-States' Governance and Strategies* (London (U.K.): Frank Routledge, 2005).

[457] *Texte coordonné de la Constitution du 17 février 1994* (Moniteur belge, 17 février 1994, deuxième édition) et mis à jour au 17 avril 2005, art. 167:

§ 1er. Le Roi dirige les relations internationales, sans préjudice de la compétence des communautés et des régions de régler la coopération internationale, y compris la conclusion de traités, pour les matières qui relèvent de leurs compétences de par la Constitution ou en vertu de celle-ci.

...

§ 2. Le Roi conclut les traités, à l'exception de ceux qui portent sur les matières visées au § 3. Ces traités n'ont d'effet qu'après avoir reçu l'assentiment des Chambres.

§ 3. Les Gouvernements de communauté et de région visés à l'article 121 concluent, chacun pour ce qui le concerne, les traités portant sur les matières qui relèvent de la compétence de leur Parlement. Ces traités n'ont d'effet qu'après avoir reçu l'assentiment du Conseil.

§ 4. Une loi adoptée à la majorité prévue à l'article 4, dernier alinéa, arrête les modalités de conclusion des traités visés au § 3 et des traités ne portant pas exclusivement sur les matières qui relèvent de la compétence des communautés ou des régions par ou en vertu de la Constitution.

Argentina's provinces,[458] Austria's *Länders*,[459] Germany's *Länders*,[460] Swiss Cantons,[461] Bosnia and Herzegovina's two "Entities",[462] etc. And

---

§ 5. Le Roi peut dénoncer les traités conclus avant le 18 mai 1993 et portant sur les matières visées au § 3, d'un commun accord avec les Gouvernements de communauté et de région concernés.

Le Roi dénonce ces traités si les Gouvernements de communauté et de région concernés l'y invitent. Une loi adoptée à la majorité prévue à l'article 4, dernier alinéa, règle la procédure en cas de désaccord entre les Gouvernements de communauté et de région concernés.

[458] See *Constitución Nacional De La República Argentina*, Convención Nacional Constituyente, ciudad de Santa Fe, 22 de agosto de 1994, art. 124 (1):

Las provincias podrán crear regiones para el desarrollo económico y social y establecer órganos con facultades para el cumplimiento de sus fines y podrán también celebrar convenios internacionales en tanto no sean incompatibles con la política exterior de la Nación y no afecten las facultades delegadas al Gobierno federal o el crédito público de la Nación; con conocimiento del Congreso Nacional. La ciudad de Buenos Aires tendrá el régimen que se establezca a tal efecto.

A translation of the *National Constitution of the Argentine Republic* provided by the Political Database of the Americas, online: Edmund E. Walsh School of Foreign Service, Center for Latin American Studies, Georgetown University <http://www.georgetown.edu/pdba/Constitutions/Argentina/argen94_e.html> reads:

The provinces are empowered to set up regions for the economic and social development and to establish entities for the fulfillment of their purposes, and they are also empowered, with the knowledge of Congress, to enter into international agreements provided they are consistent with the national foreign policy and do not affect the powers delegated to the Federal Government or the public credit of the Nation. The City of Buenos Aires shall have the regime which is to be established to that effect.

[459] See *Österreichische Bundesverfassungsgesetze*, Bundes-Verfassungsgesetz (B-VG), Art. 16 § 1-3. Art. 16 §1 provides:

Die Länder können in Angelegenheiten, die in ihren selbständigen Wirkungsbereich fallen, Staatsverträge mit an Österreich angrenzenden Staaten oder deren Teilstaaten abschließen.

("In matters within their own sphere of competence the Laender can conclude treaties with states, or their constituent states, bordering on Austria." (Austrian Federal Chancellery, *Österreichische Bundesverfassungsgesetze (Auswahl) / Austrian Federal Constitutional Laws (selection) / Lois constitutionnelles de l'Autriche (une sélection)*, English transl. by Charles Kessler and Peter Krauth (Vienna: Herausgegeben vom Bundespressedienst, 2000) online: Legal Information System of the Republic of Austria (RIS) <http://www.ris.bka.gv.at/info/bvg_eng.pdf>)).

[460] *Grundgesetz für die Bundesrepublik Deutschland*, art. 32.3 provides "(3) Soweit die Länder für die Gesetzgebung zuständig sind, können sie mit Zustimmung der Bundesregierung mit auswärtigen Staaten Verträge abschließen." ("Insofar as the Länder have power to legislate, they may conclude treaties with foreign states with the consent of the Federal Government." (*Basic Law for the Federal Republic of Germany*, (Berlin: German Bundestag – Administration – Public Relations section, 2001), online: German Bundestag http://www.bundestag.de/htdocs_e/parliament/function/legal/germanbasiclaw.pdf))).

[461] *Constitution fédérale de la Confédération suisse du 18 avril 1999*, Art. 56 provides:

whatever you might want to call the federation-like polity that may arise out of the *Treaty of Lisbon*[463] that is currently being ratified, it is none-theless instructive to note that the text contemplates that while the European Union would have *exclusive* treaty-making powers in certain areas, the Union's constitutive units would keep their treaty-making powers in a vast array of jurisdictions.[464] After all, we have to remember

---

56. Relations des cantons avec l'étranger

1. Les cantons peuvent conclure des traités avec l'étranger dans les domaines rele-vant de leur compétence.

2 Ces traités ne doivent être contraires ni au droit et aux intérêts de la Confé-dération, ni au droit d'autres cantons. Avant de conclure un traité, les cantons doi-vent informer la Confédération.

3 Les cantons peuvent traiter directement avec les autorités étrangères de rang infé-rieur; dans les autres cas, les relations des cantons avec l'étranger ont lieu par l'intermédiaire de la Confédération.

[462] *Ustav Bosne i Hercegovine*, art. I § 3 provides that the two "Entities" are the Federa-tion of Bosnia and Herzegovina and the Republika Srpska. Art. III § 2 (a) and (d) provide:

a) Entiteti imaju pravo da uspostavljaju posebne paralelne odnose sa susjednim drzavama, u skladu sa suverenitetom i teritorijalnim integritetom Bosne i Hercego-vine. ...

d) Svaki entitet moze takodjer sklapati sporazume sa drzavama i medjunarodnim organizacijama uz saglasnost Parlamentarne skupstine. Parlamentarna skupstina moze zakonom predvidjeti da za odredjene vrste sporazuma takva saglasnost nije potrebna.

("a. The Entities shall have the right to establish special parallel relationships with neighboring states consistent with the sovereignty and territorial integrity of Bosnia and Herzegovina. ..." and "d. Each Entity may also enter into agreements with states and international organizations with the consent of the Parliamentary Assembly. The Parliamentary Assembly may provide by law that certain types of agreements do not require such consent." (*Constitution of Bosnia and Herzegovina*, English transl., online: Constitutional Court of Bosnia and Herzegovina < http://www.ustavnisud. ba/public/down/USTAV_BOSNE_I_HERCEGOVINE_engl.pdf >)).

[463] *Treaty of Lisbon*, OJ 2007/C306/1 [*Treaty of Lisbon*]. The *Treaty of Lisbon* amends the *Treaty on European Union*, consolidated version [2002] O.J. C 325/5 [*Treaty on European Union*] and the *Treaty establishing the European Community*, consolidated version [2002] O.J. C 325/33 [*Treaty establishing the European Community*] to bring significant changes to the institutional structures of the Union. Among them, there is the merger of the "three pillars" into one legal personality called the "European Un-ion".

[464] Under the *Treaty of Lisbon*, *ibid.*, the Union's treaty-making powers remain an attributive jurisdiction. The *Treaty of Lisbon*, *ibid.*, Art. 2 para. 170-174 modifies the *Treaty establishing the European Community*, *ibid.* by adding Art. 188 L to 188 O after Art. 188 K (see *Treaty on European Union and the Treaty on the Functioning of the European Union*, consolidated versions [2008] O.J. C 115/01, Art. 216-219 [*Treaty on European Union and the Treaty on the Functioning of the European Un-ion*, consolidated versions of 2008]) in which it specifies the scope and process of the Union's treaty-making powers. The *Treaty of Lisbon*, *ibid.*, Art. 2 para. 12 amends the *Treaty establishing the European Community*, *ibid.* by introducing an Art.2 B al.2

that a preliminary version of Art. 6 of the *Vienna Convention* – then Art. 5 (2) of the *Draft Articles on the Law of Treaties* – explicitly recognized a *jus tractatum* to federated states *on the condition that the federal constitution granted them such powers.*[465] The International Law Commission, commenting on the *Draft Articles on the Law of Treaties*, declared that it

> considered that it was desirable to underline the capacity possessed by every State to conclude treaties; and that, having regard to the examples which occur in practice of treaties concluded by member States of certain federal unions with foreign States in virtue of powers given to them by the constitution of the particular federal union, a general provision covering such cases should be included.
>
> ...
>
> Paragraph 2, therefore, is concerned only with treaties made by a unit of the federation with an outside State. More frequently, the treaty-making capacity is vested exclusively in the federal government, *but there is no rule of*

(*Treaty on European Union*, consolidated version of 2008, *ibid.*, Art. 3 para.) that reads:

> The Union shall also have *exclusive competence* for the conclusion of an international agreement when its conclusion is provided for in a legislative act of the Union or is necessary to enable the Union to exercise its internal competence, or insofar as its conclusion may affect common rules or alter their scope." (Emphasis added.)

While the new Art. 188 L (2) (*Treaty on European Union*, consolidated version of 2008, *ibid.*, Art. 216 para. 2) provides that "[international a]greements concluded by the Union are binding upon the institutions of the Union and on its Member States", the *Treaty of Lisbon*, *ibid.*, Art. 1, para. 35 (*Treaty on European Union*, consolidated version of 2008, *ibid.*, Art. 32), clearly contemplates that the constitutive units will retain their treaty-making powers:

> Member States shall consult one another within the European Council and the Council on any matter of foreign and security policy of general interest in order to determine a common approach. Before undertaking any action on the international scene or *entering into any commitment* which could affect the Union's interests, each Member State shall consult the others within the European Council or the Council. Member States shall ensure, through the convergence of their actions, that the Union is able to assert its interests and values on the international scene. Member States shall show mutual solidarity. (Emphasis added).

In the apparently defunct *Treaty Establishing a Constitution for Europe*, OJ 2004/C 310/1 [*Draft Constitution for Europe*], very similar arrangements allowing for treaty-making both at the European polity level and at the level of the polity's constitutive units were proposed. See *Draft Constitution for Europe*, Art. I-13 (2), Art. I-40 (5) and Art. III-323 to III-326.

[465] International Law Commission (ILC), *Draft Articles on the Law of Treaties with commentaries*, 18th Sess., Y.B.I.L.C. 1966, II, 177, 178, Art. 5 (2) ("States members of a federal union may possess a capacity to conclude treaties if such a capacity is admitted by the federal constitution and within the limits there laid down") [*Draft Articles on the Law of Treaties with commentaries*].

international law which precludes the component States from being invested with the power to conclude treaties with third States. Questions may arise in some cases as to whether the component State concludes the treaty as an organ of the federal State or in its own right. But on this point also the solution must be sought in the provisions of the federal constitution.[466]

Art. 5 (2) was dropped from the final version of the Convention after being voted down following the active lobbying of Canada and other countries.[467] However, the states that opposed the inclusion of Art. 5 (2) in the Convention did not do so on the basis that federated states could not make treaties, but rather opposed it mainly on the basis that making capacity solely dependent on the content of specific federal constitutions might be taken as an invitation to other states to pass judgment on the internal affairs of such federations.[468] At any rate, while Ivan Bernier and Gibran van Ert are of the view that the principles of the old Art. 5 (2) represents the orthodox position,[469] it appears that even this view may be too restrictive in light of current practices. As a matter of fact, it is dubious that *only* a "federal constitution" could grant treaty-making powers to constitutive sub-units, as the cases of the Faeroe Islands and Greenland in Denmark[470] and the projected "new" European Union illustrate.[471] At any rate, whether the criteria refer to the "federal consti-

---

[466] *Draft Articles on the Law of Treaties with commentaries, ibid.* at 192 (emphasis added).

[467] Edward McWhinney (Book Review of *Les États Fédéraux dans les Relations Internationales: actes du colloque de Bruxelles, Institut de sociologie, 26-27 février 1982 / Société belge de droit international (S.B.D.I.)* (1984) 80 A.J.I.L. 998) reports (at 999) that Art. 5 (2) "was deleted by a vote of the UN General Assembly in plenary session (66 votes to 28, with 13 abstentions)".

[468] J. S. Stanford, "United Nations Law of Treaties Conference: First Session" (1969) 19 U.T.L.J. 59, at 61.

[469] Ivan Bernier, *International Legal Aspects of Federalism* (London (U.K.): Longman, 1973) 82 and G. van Ert, "The Legal Character of Provincial Agreements with Foreign Governments", *supra* note 321.

[470] Council of Europe, *Federated And Regional Entities And International Treaties*, *supra* note 456 ("In almost all the states concerned, the entities' powers in relation to international affairs are based on the constitution. The only exception is *Denmark*, where the relevant powers of the Faeroe Islands and Greenland derive from laws on the self-governing status of those regions. In *Belgium*, the constitutional provisions are amplified by the special law on institutional reform of 8 August 1980 and by a number of "co-operation agreements" between the federal state and the regions or language communities.")

[471] Treaty-making powers are not granted to the European Union's constitutive states by the *Treaty of Lisbon, supra* note 463, quite the contrary. Treaty-making powers are taken to rest, by default, in the constitutive states of Europe and are thus recognized by their respective material constitutions. It is rather as a matter of exceptional devolution from the constitutive states to the European government that the latter would receive certain treaty-making powers through the *Treaty of Lisbon, ibid.* In other

tution" or other internal sources of law for the international recognition of the treaty-making powers of federated states, this again sends the federal government begging for the answer it was looking for: the international law rule ends up following what the domestic law will say. In other words, international law basically takes the view that it is up to domestic law to settle the issue as to whether or not sub-units will have the capacity to make treaties. Therefore, those who wanted to use international law to argue that the federal government necessarily had general treaty-making powers are again sent back to square one.

Before concluding on this point, a few words need to be added for those who worry that recognizing treaty-making powers to provinces might help those provinces in achieving international recognition in the event of a declaration of secession. It should have become clear to everyone as a result of the foregoing discussion that this is simply a *non sequitur*. Those who have expressed this fear have never been able to point to a single case in which the prior capacity to make treaties of a seceding federated unit has either been determinative or has made the slightest difference in the decision of other states to recognize or not that unit as a new "sovereign state". This is like hanging tightly to one's belt and suspenders out of fear of losing one's hat! Because of the difficulties in arriving at a fixed definition of what a "state" is in our rapidly changing international order, it appears however that the criteria for determining the existence of a state are no more than an incomplete list of "rules of thumb" for state recognition and that, in the end, what truly matters in the case of alleged secession is the political[472] and legally underdetermined act of recognition.[473]

---

words, it would not be the "federal constitution" that would grant constitutive states their treaty-making powers because those states already possess their own treaty-making powers by virtue of their own constitution, but the "federal constitution" would rather operate the limited devolution to the central government of certain powers to make treaties on its own.

[472] Sir Hersch Lauterpacht famously wrote in 1947 that "[a]ccording to what is probably still the predominant view in the literature of international law, recognition of states is not a matter governed by law but a question of policy" (Hersch Lauterpacht, *Recognition in International Law* (Cambridge (U.K.): Cambridge University Press, 1947) at 65).

[473] For a similar opinion, see Pierre-Marie Dupuy, *Droit international public* (Paris: Dalloz, 2004) at 98. American officials have been quite blunt about this. For example, Robert J. Delahunty and John C. Yoo, respectively former Special Counsel and former Deputy Assistant Attorney General, with the Office of Legal Counsel in the Department of Justice during Georges W. Bush's presidency, wrote (Robert J. Delahunty and John C. Yoo, "Statehood And The Third Geneva Convention" (2005) 46 Va. J. Int'l L. 131 at 153):

When one surveys the practice of the United States in recognizing, not recognizing, or derecognizing states, it is obvious that our Government does not apply the Montevideo Convention tests of statehood in a value-neutral manner. On the contrary,

After reviewing all the evidence, I come to the conclusion that none of the proposed legal arguments is sufficient to support the claim made that the federal government has plenary powers to make treaties. That being said, I will offer later[474] an alternative theory explaining how and why the federal government may, under certain conditions, conclude treaties in relation to provincial matters. This theory will prove more respectful of the general economy of the Constitution and the federalism principle.

2. The Solid Policy Arguments Against Plenary Federal Treaty-Making Powers

In addition to the weakness of the legal arguments in support to the federal claim, there are strong policy arguments *against* recognizing to the federal government a general power to make treaties that would cover both federal and provincial matters. This part of the book will highlight a selection of those arguments. In the following sections, I will first show that, to the extent that Canada gains from "speaking with one voice" in the international arena, this does not entail that the federal government should be the one speaking for all (II.A.2.i.). Once I have shown that there are no necessary connections between the needs for Canada to speak with a common voice and giving the federal government plenary treaty-making powers, I will further show why it would actually be detrimental to Canada to recognize such general treaty-making powers to the federal government. To do that, I will rely on a discussion of the needs to align power with expertise (II.A.2.ii.) and democratic accountability (II.A.2.iii.). Finally, I will explain why recognizing plenary treaty-making powers to the federal government would not be good for national unity (II.A.2.iv.).

i. Many Ways to "One Voice"

The general policy claim made by those who would like to see the federal government have plenary powers to make treaties can be summarized by the words of G.R. Morris: "international affairs today is too crucial, complex and all-pervasive to permit the possibility of the nation speaking formally with more than one voice in any international matters of significance".[475] While the importance, complexity and pervasiveness of international affairs today remains beyond doubt as a general notion,

---

our governmental practice reveals that the decision whether or not to recognize or derecognize a state is highly policy-laden.

[474] See section II.B.3.

[475] G.R. Morris, "The Treaty-Making Power: A Canadian Dilemma", *supra* note 22 at 497.

I do not believe, however, that this context necessarily calls for federal plenary treaty-making powers.

As a preliminary matter, it must be acknowledged that the federal government can, *in principle*, develop coherent positions on matters relevant to its own exclusive jurisdictions such as on matters relating to the military, navigation, fisheries, banking, copyrights, etc. However, as we will see later in the section dealing with the need to "align power with expertise" (II.A.2.ii.), there are institutional constraints that make that internal cohesion hard to attain. Thus, dissonance between specific positions defended by the different parts of the federal government is obviously to be expected. Although the federal government has internal mechanisms to achieve coherence, cases will inevitably exist where different departments will take inconsistent views until coherence is achieved by a central agency such as the Prime Minister's office. Because this is generally an undeniable difficulty for the "Canadian sovereignist"[476] position, I will examine it in more detail later. For the moment, I will simply deal more specifically in this section with Ottawa's apologists' worries about achieving coherence for international relations purposes on provincial matters.

I need to start by clearly pointing out that provincial and territorial presence in international relations does not, *per se*, preclude that singularity of a Canadian "voice". What would really have the effect of causing "cacophonic voices" would be the lack of adequate means to coordinate several provincial perspectives when an issue relates to their own exclusive competences, or the lack of an appropriate mechanism to develop common policies on issues that relate to matters of both federal and provincial jurisdictions. But it is not at all clear why the federal government, when it has no jurisdiction on an issue and when it has not been called upon to do the job, could effectively and legitimately decide which province's interests should trump which other province's interest when they may conflict. This is particularly true in contexts where the federal government is not necessarily in a situation to create the incentives necessary for harmonizing all the positions.

There are other means to achieve coherence than having decisions dictated by the federal government. If the problem is to find an institution capable of harmonizing provincial views, something akin to a modified Council of the Federation might very well do the trick. The Council of the Federation is an intergovernmental organisation made up of the Premiers of all Canadian provinces and territories.[477] The Council

---

[476] On "Canadian sovereignists", see *supra* at section I.D.7. and *infra* at section II.A.2.iv..

[477] I note immediately that while I will be discussing here and later certain actions undertaken by Canadian territories, I will not be discussing the issue of their constitu-

recognized that "[u]nder the Constitution, Canada's two orders of government are of equal status, neither subordinate to the other, sovereign within their own areas of jurisdiction; and accordingly, they should have adequate resources to meet their responsibilities".[478] Therefore, the Council aims, among other things, at "strengthening interprovincial-territorial co-operation",[479] "exercising leadership on national issues of importance to provinces and territories and in improving federal-provincial-territorial relations"[480] and "promoting relations between governments which are based on respect for the constitution and recognition of the diversity within the federation".[481] To the extent that the Council is only composed of the Premier of each province and territory, it would obviously gain from more democratic inputs. For example, if the Council were to become the institution through which provinces were to develop their common foreign policies in relation to their exclusive jurisdictions, it would certainly gain from including representatives of civil society somewhere in the process. In other words, the Council would gain legitimacy by moving from being simply a tool of "executive federalism" to a true institution of "federal democracy".[482] Be that as it may, the Council or a similar institution where provinces and territories are themselves represented could certainly achieve the goal of harmonizing views for the purpose of presenting a common vision to the world.

This would not be a first. In Belgium, for example, the three "regions"[483] are responsible for both developing the foreign policies of the country and representing the country in international institutions on matters that pertain to their jurisdictions. Thus, when an issue is a "regional" matter, representatives of the regional governments are the ones representing Belgium as a whole and not the central government. This could be done in Canada as well. In fact, this has been done in the past. Take for example, the "Council of Ministers of Education, Canada" (CMEC) that was created in 1967 to coordinate provincial and

---

tional powers and limitations in this essay. Those actions are simply presented as examples of what political sub-units do within the Canadian federation.

[478] Council of the Federation, *Founding Agreement, December 5, 2003* (Charlottetown: 5 September, 2003) online: Council of the Federation <http://www.councilofthe federation.ca/pdfs/850095003_e.pdf>, preamble [Council of the Federation, *Founding Agreement*].

[479] *Ibid.*, art. 3 (a).

[480] *Ibid.*, art. 3 (b).

[481] *Ibid.*, art. 3 (a), (c).

[482] For a critical overview of the current work of the Council of the Federation, see Jean Leclair, "Jane Austen and the Council of the Federation" (2006) 15 Const. Forum 51.

[483] "Regions" are the functional equivalents of provinces in Canada.

territorial actions in relation to education. According to CMEC's own website, "CMEC's mandate internationally is that of coordinating the collective responsibility of the provinces and territories for education where the activities concerned require experts, delegates or reports that speak for Canadian education authorities as a whole."[484] This international role of the CMEC has long been recognized by the federal government. In 1977, the federal Foreign Affairs Minister concluded an agreement with the CMEC to the effect that the latter would be able to recommend the composition of the Canadian missions and to decide who would lead the missions to any international event in relation to education.[485] Also, this protocol, to which all provinces agreed, provides that it is the provinces, through consensus, that determine the Canadian positions over educational matters.[486] The CMEC also maintains a permanent secretariat to sustain Canada's relations with education-related international organisations.[487]

Belgian regions have also developed mechanisms to produce such common policies. In order to deal with the possibility of not being able to achieve a common position on a subject, the three Belgian regions have found a powerful incentive to come up with an agreement: either they develop a common position or Belgium as a whole takes no position whatsoever on the issue.[488]

While certain subjects might be amenable to such all or nothing approach, others might be less so. And since there are more constitutive units in Canada than there are in Belgium, this mechanism would

---

[484] Council of Ministers of Education, Canada, *CMEC and education-related international activities*, online: Council of Ministers of Education <http://www.cmec.ca/international/indexe.stm>. [*CMEC and education-related international activities*].

[485] Stéphane Paquin, "Quelle place pour les provinces canadiennes dans les organisations et les négociations internationales du Canada à la lumière des pratiques au sein d'autres fédérations?" (2005) 48 Administration publique du Canada/Canadian Public Administration 477.

[486] *Ibid.*

[487] *Ibid.* The CMEC's website mentions that it has developed relations with a wide variety of education-related international organisations (*CMEC and education-related international activities*, *supra* note 484):

> CMEC's international activities have traditionally involved three major international organizations, the Organisation for Economic Co-operation and Development (OECD), the United Nations Educational, Scientific and Cultural Organization (UNESCO), and the Commonwealth. While other partnerships have been formed with the Southeast Asian Ministers of Education Organization (SEAMEO), the Council of Europe, the Asia-Pacific Economic Cooperation (APEC) Education Forum, the Organization of American States (OAS), and the Summit of the Americas process, both OECD and UNESCO, as well as the Commonwealth, continue to play a prominent role.

[488] I would like to thank Stéphane Paquin for informing me about this mechanism.

probably not be appropriate for most issues requiring a common position. However if we use a bit of our institutional imagination and knowledge of comparative law, we can easily design a further mechanism that would weaken the possibility of impasses (possibly, however, at the cost of limiting the incentives to harmonize positions). For example, in order to avoid deadlocks on certain issues, we could tamper the system by adding to it something similar to the principle of "constructive abstention" developed by the European Union. The principle was developed and adopted with the *Treaty of Amsterdam*[489] as a way out of a difficult conundrum in the development of rules relating to European defence and security policy: how to accommodate the idea that states should remain responsible for the decision of sending their own troops to combat while, at the same time, allowing Europe to develop common defence position even in the face of a lack of unanimity? The amendment to the Article J.10 of title V ("Provisions On A Common Foreign And Security Policy") of the *Treaty on European Union*[490] brought by Art. 1 (10) of the *Treaty of Amsterdam* was thus meant to solve that problem. It reads:

> Decisions under this Title shall be taken by the Council acting unanimously. Abstentions by members present in person or represented shall not prevent the adoption of such decisions.
>
> When abstaining in a vote, any member of the Council may qualify its abstention by making a formal declaration under the present subparagraph. In that case, it shall not be obliged to apply the decision, but shall accept that the decision commits the Union. In a spirit of mutual solidarity, the Member State concerned shall refrain from any action likely to conflict with or impede Union action based on that decision and the other Member States shall respect its position. If the members of the Council qualifying their abstention in this way represent more than one third of the votes weighted in accordance with Article 205(2) of the Treaty establishing the European Community, the decision shall not be adopted.[491]

We could build on this example to adopt a procedure aimed at constructing a common interprovincial position over certain specified matters of international import. According to this decision-making procedure, one or more provinces could decide to abstain from the common position and their abstention would not count as negative votes for the purpose of reaching unanimity. If a province "constructively

---

[489] *Treaty of Amsterdam amending the Treaty of the European Union, the Treaties establishing the European Communities and certain related acts*, 2 October 1997, [1997] OJ C340/1 (entered into force 1 May 1999) [*Treaty of Amsterdam*].

[490] *Treaty on European Union*, *supra* note 463.

[491] The amendment has been integrated in the consolidated version of the *Treaty on European Union*, 12 December 2002, [2002] O.J. C325/5, Art. 23 (1).

abstained" and made an official declaration pertaining to that abstention, that province would, moreover, not be bound by that decision. A treaty, for example, agreed upon by the other provinces would need to explicitly exclude the province in question from its application through a specific reserve. The minimum number of supporting provinces could be uniformly set or could vary according to the subject-matter of the decision to be taken. It might also be agreed, when setting up such a coordination mechanism, that provinces could still retain their powers to make their own arrangements with the targeted partners if they disagreed with the majority of the other provinces on certain subject-matters. One could think about issues related to language, for example. After all, it might be useful to achieve unity of voice on many issues but it might not be desirable, in light of Canada's diversity and minority rights, to always develop a single position on every issue; that is the reason why we chose a federal system after all! Following this line of reasoning, the agreement setting up this procedure could specify an exhaustive list of subject-matters over which the procedure would be applicable while leaving others to the discretion of provinces.

The purpose behind this brief sketch of institutional options is simply to demonstrate that the "one voice" trope does not necessarily lead to the conclusion that the federal government must necessarily have plenary powers to make treaties; there are many other ways to achieve that objective. While I do believe that the available options might constitute good starting points for negotiations that would lead to an agreement, I am not necessarily committed to any of those specific institutional arrangements. But at any rate, this type of decision-making procedure would certainly be much more attuned to the basic principle of Canadian federalism highlighted by the Council of the Federation ("Canada's two orders of government are of equal status, neither subordinate to the other, sovereign within their own areas of jurisdiction"[492]) than the federal sovereignist position too often advocated by Ottawa while at the same time respecting the possible imperative of univocality.

Given the existing alternatives, those who defend Ottawa's claim to plenary treaty-making powers must now demonstrate (i.) that the federal government is necessarily in a better institutional situation to achieve a "unity of voice", (ii.) that this Ottawa-controlled "unitary voice" will be able to rely on all the necessary expertise to accomplish its mission and that this institutional arrangement will be more respectful than others of the Canadian underlying constitutional values of (iii.) democracy and (iv.) federalism. I have raised questions about the first issue in this section and I will now present arguments demonstrating that the current

---

[492] Council of the Federation, *Founding Agreement, supra* note 478.

general position of the federal government also fails to meet the other three criteria ((ii.), (iii.) and (iv.)).

ii. The Need to Align Power with Expertise

Gerald Morris noted many years ago, when states were not organisations as complex as they are today, that "[e]ven a unitary state today has extreme difficulty in coordinating all aspects of its international relations."[493] While it is true, as Morris also pointed out, that "some measure of consistency is essential if a nation's influence is to be used with any effectiveness in the pursuit of its objectives",[494] consistency should not come at the expense of expertise. Indeed, it is often worse to be wrong and resolute than to be right and wavering.

Thus, one important weakness that affects the ability to negotiate appropriate international agreements for Canadians lies in the federal executive's assumed monopoly over such negotiations. In effect, to be effective, power has to be aligned with knowledge.[495] This raises an important challenge to the Canadian sovereignists since the federal government claims that it is under no obligation to consult provinces before concluding international agreements affecting provinces' legislative jurisdiction. The federal government has stated officially that it would not enter into treaties "dealing with matters within provincial jurisdiction ... without prior consultation with the Governments of the Provinces"[496] but refuses to recognize that it is bound by an obligation to consult.[497] If the federal government does not recognize an obligation to

---

[493] G.R. Morris, "The Treaty-Making Power: A Canadian Dilemma", *supra* note 22 at 503.

[494] *Ibid.*

[495] The following reflection was triggered by a discussion that I had with Andrew Petter and I would like to thank him for that.

[496] Canada, Legal Bureau of the Department of External Affairs, Letter February 1, 1985, *supra* note 60, from the Legal Bureau of the then Department of External Affairs responding to a Council of Europe questionnaire.

[497] A series of attempts at recognizing such obligation were made in Parliament. However, they have all failed. The latest occasion was with Bill C-260, *An Act respecting the negotiation, approval, tabling and publication of treaties*, 1st Sess., 38th Parl., 2004, cls. 3 and 4 (as passed first reading by the House of Commons 3 November 2004 and rejected on second reading by the House of Commons 28 September 2005) [*An Act respecting the negotiation, approval, tabling and publication of treaties*] stated explicitly that:

3. The Government of Canada may, without consulting the government of each province, negotiate and enter into a treaty in a sector within the exclusive legislative authority of Parliament that does not affect an area under the legislative authority of the legislatures of the provinces.

4. The Government of Canada shall not, without consulting the government of each province in accordance with the agreements entered into under section 5, negotiate or conclude a treaty

(*a*) in an area under the legislative authority of the legislatures of the provinces; or

(*b*) in a field affecting an area under the legislative authority of the legislatures of the provinces.

3. Le gouvernement du Canada peut, sans consulter les gouvernements provinciaux, négocier et conclure un traité dans un secteur relevant exclusivement de la compétence législative du Parlement qui ne touche pas un secteur de compétence législative provinciale.

4. Le gouvernement du Canada ne peut, sans consulter le gouvernement de chaque province conformément aux ententes conclues aux termes de l'article 5, négocier ou conclure un traité:

a) dans un secteur de compétence législative provinciale;

b) dans un domaine touchant un secteur de compétence législative provinciale.

The bill was defeated on the second reading over disagreements about the "consultation" requirement. In particular, the Liberal MPs, who were then forming a minority government, were adamantly opposed to the Bill because they believed that it would negate what they conceived as the exclusive federal treaty powers. For example, the Honorable Dan McTeague, Parliamentary Secretary to the Minister of Foreign Affairs said that "it is clear that the member's efforts build on work done in the past by other members of the Bloc Québécois, in order, for one, *to give the provinces powers that are clearly federal ones under the Constitution*. Not only is this set out in the Constitution but it was confirmed too by the Supreme Court of Canada in the 1930s." (*House of Commons Debates*, No. 101 (18 May 2005) at 1815, online: Edited Hansard <http://www2.parl.gc.ca/HousePublications/Publication.aspx?Language=E&Pub=Hansard&Mode=1&Parl=38&Ses=1&Doc=101#T1815> (Hon. Dan McTeague) (emphasis added) [*House of Commons Debates*, No. 101 (18 May 2005)]). But the crux of McTeague's opposition would come a few minutes later:

The bill before us creates nothing new in this regard, but forces a straitjacket on the Canadian government in having it consult its provincial partners.

The requirement to negotiate individual agreements with each province under the pressure of an artificial timeframe, which this bill would create, is not only useless, but the cost of it would be prohibitive and could produce unexpected results. It could, potentially, oblige us to replace an efficient system with something less flexible, creating uncertainty that does not currently exist.

The bill before us raises another major concern in constitutional terms. Its provisions would limit the government's power to conclude treaties in areas of federal jurisdiction without consultation with the provinces. Canadian constitutional law has provided for over 60 years that *the power to negotiate and conclude treaties lies exclusively with the federal government. This power is essential to Canada's speaking with a single voice internationally.*

Among the proposals made by the hon. member for Haute-Gaspésie—La Mitis—Matane—Matapédia in Bill C-260, one of them mentions the royal prerogative in right of provincial governments with respect to the negotiation and conclusion of treaties in an area under the legislative authority of the provinces.

I have to say, in no uncertain terms, this provincial prerogative does not exist at this time.

As I already mentioned, the prerogative to negotiate and sign any international treaties belongs only to the federal executive branch.

In that sense, Bill C-260 would violate the provision in the Constitution on the allocation of jurisdictions. *It bears repeating that the power of the provinces to negotiate and conclude treaties simply does not exist.*

An amendment of this scale to the constitutional order would require more than a debate in this chamber. It would involve significant and lasting changes to the Constitution. (Emphasis added.)

Mr. Wajid Kahn (Liberal) also held the view that "[u]nder our Constitution, the power to conclude treaties belongs exclusively to the executive branch of the federal government. This means that it is the federal executive that negotiates the treaties and agrees to commit Canada to international obligations." (*Ibid.* at 1840). Mr. Derek Lee (Liberal) repeated in almost the same words what the Honorable Dan McTeague had said a few days earlier ((*House of Commons Debates*, No. 122 (23 June 2005) at 1740, online: Edited Hansard <http://www2.parl.gc.ca/HousePublications/Publication.aspx? Language=E&Pub=Hansard&Mode=1&Parl=38&Ses=1&Doc=122#Int-1372283> (Derek Lee)), Don Boudrias (Liberal) also repeated the mantra that "Canadian constitutional law has provided for over 60 years that the power to negotiate and conclude treaties lies exclusively with the federal executive, to the governor in council. This power is essential to Canada's speaking with a single voice internationally, as it must." (*Ibid.* at 1805) and Ms. Yasmin Ratansi (Liberal) declared that "Canadian constitutional law clearly establishes that the negotiation of a treaty and signatory of a treaty are strictly in the purview of the federal executive." (*Ibid.* at 1810). While Ms. Alexa McDonough (New Democratic Party (NDP)) recognized the shortcomings of the current federal ratification mechanism that excludes Parliament, she claimed that (*ibid.* at 1750):

we have to be sure that we have preserved the ability of the federal government, the Parliament of Canada, to act in the national interest. If we create a process of consultation with provincial governments that is cumbersome and impractical and that in fact can make it almost impossible for the government to act in the national interest, then we have not created a solution. We have created yet another problem.

Pat Martin (NDP) expressed his reservations in even stronger terms (*ibid.* at 1820):

No one province should have too much control over a national treaty. This is where I find fault with the bill we are debating. There are good reasons that no one rogue province and no one rogue state should be able to unilaterally alter or compromise international treaties that exist between nation-states. There is only one nation-state that we are dealing with in the Parliament of Canada. It is the nation-state of Canada. That is all there is. I do not want to encourage or lend succour or support in any way to anyone who envisions some other nation-state within these hallowed chambers.

While the position of the Conservative Party of Canada (CPC) presented by Mr. Stockwell Day (*House of Commons Debates*, No. 101 (18 May 2005), at 1850-55) seemed, initially, to be supportive of the Bill, the CPC ended up leaving only the Bloc Québecois voting in favour of the Bill. The Bill was thus defeated 54 (yeas) to 216 (nays) [37 (absent or abstained)]. For previous efforts to have the obligation to consult, see among others: Bill C-313, *An Act respecting the negotiation, approval,*

consult provinces when it negotiates treaties on matters *affecting* provincial subject-matters, nor does it recognize that it has an obligation to get provinces' *consent* before forming such agreements *related to* provinces' legislative powers. This basically means that the federal government is of the view that it can conclude agreements on matters in which it has no expertise whatsoever. Apart from the valid constitutional arguments in favour of recognizing mandatory provincial involvement, it should by now be obvious that there are strong policy reasons for doing so.

In fact, Ottawa's current position is quite anachronistic in light of the federal government's own structure. In effect, now that foreign affairs are not simply about the "high politics" of war and peace, but rather involve a wide range of domestic issues, foreign affairs have been "domesticated" and are now conducted by a wide range of departments – that is, where the expertise on the subject-matter lies. For example, Environment Canada has been involved at different levels of international relations for quite sometime. On its website, Environment Canada describes as follows its international involvements:

> For its part, Environment Canada has long been a contributor to the Government of Canada's international environmental agenda by advancing and sharing science and know-how, as well as through negotiations and policy dialogue in international fora. To better address the environmental challenges of our global environment, an approach to enhance knowledge, innovation and partnerships, within Canada and internationally, has been initiated by Environment Canada.
>
> The International Relations Directorate (IRD) plays the central policy and coordination role for Environment Canada's international activities. It provides strategic advice on international relations, develops the strategic framework within which the Department's international activities are managed, participates in the negotiation and implementation of international agreements and MOUs [memorandum of understanding], and provides policy and operational support to the Minister, DM [Deputy Minister] and senior management on international activities. The directorate's responsibilities also include managing the Department's bilateral and regional relations (e.g. North American Agreement on Environmental Cooperation) as well as participation in international organizations such as the International Joint

---

tabling and publication of treaties, 1ˢᵗ Sess., 37ᵗʰ Parl., 2001, cls. 4 (first reading by the House of Commons 28 March 2001); Bill C-317, *An Act to provide for consultation with provincial governments when treaties are negotiated and concluded*, 1ˢᵗ Sess., 37ᵗʰ Parl., 2001, cls. 4 (first reading by the House of Commons 28 March 2001) and Bill C-214, *Act to provide for the participation of the House of Commons when treaties are concluded*, 2ⁿᵈ Sess., 36ᵗʰ Parl., 1999, cls. 4 (rejected on second reading by the House of Commons 13 June 1999).

Commission, the Organisation for Economic Cooperation and Development, and the United Nations Environment Program. [498]

Even foreign affairs as such are divided in several departments within the federal government: there is a Minister of Foreign Affairs, a Minister of International Trade, a Minister of National Defence, a Minister of International Cooperation.

Moreover, even the more purely technical knowledge about the conduct of "foreign affairs" is scattered across several departments. Take, for example, the strong expertise that the Department of Justice has developed on a variety of public international law issues. This is not hidden but displayed on plain view by the Department:

> The Department's international law work ensures integrated and proactive legal advisory, policy and litigation services to a range of governmental clients. The work covers issues central to Canada's interests, such as international human rights and humanitarian law; national security; anti-terrorism and transnational crime; international trade and investment law and intellectual property law; family law and other international private law matters; and international aviation, maritime and environmental law.
>
> International Cooperation
>
> The International Cooperation Group (ICG) promotes Canadian values of justice and good governance by implementing projects abroad.[499]

One might have thought that the Department of Foreign Affairs had inherited the capacity to coordinate all the federal departments in their international relations. However, this has not happened. Pierre Elliott Trudeau's attempt to transform the then External Affairs Department into a central agency akin to the Department of Finance, or the Treasury Board, failed in large part apparently because the Department had very little other power, other than persuasive reasons, to impose its position on other departments.[500]

Now, as Denis Stairs notes, "[s]ome of the Department [of Foreign Affairs]'s more reflective officials express concern that their role is now

---

[498] Canada, Environment Canada, *International Relations: Welcome*, online: Environment Canada <http://www.ec.gc.ca/international/index_e.htm>.

[499] Canada, Department of Justice, *The Department: Our Work*, online: Department of Justice <http://www.justice.gc.ca/en/dept/work.html>.

[500] Denis Stairs, "The Conduct of Canadian Foreign Policy and the Interests of Newfoundland and Labrador" in *Collected Research Papers of the Royal Commission on Renewing and Strengthening Our Place in Canada*, Vol. 2 (St. John's (NL): Royal Commission on Renewing and Strengthening Our Place in Canada, 2003) 147, online: Newfoundland & Labrador, Research Papers <http://www.gov.nf.ca/publicat/royalcomm/research/Stairs.pdf>, at 9. [Denis Stairs, "The Conduct of Canadian Foreign Policy and the Interests of Newfoundland and Labrador" with references to online version].

less about the making of foreign policy and more about providing support services to departments elsewhere in government."[501] That is because the federal government is also realizing that the Department of Foreign Affairs simply cannot replicate the substantive expertise of all the other departments. This is the reality of modern bureaucratic politics. And because globalization implies that the frontiers between the domestic and international politics are blurring, it would be senseless anyway to try to develop two parallel federal governments – one dealing with internal issues and the other dealing with the same issues externally.[502]

If the Department of Foreign Affairs cannot develop the expertise necessary to conduct federal relations with respect to subject-matters of federal jurisdiction, we can easily imagine the difficulties it faces in relation to provincial matters. And to the extent that provinces are not necessarily included in federal negotiations and that the federal government attempts to muzzle the provinces' international activity, Canada condemns herself at being, to a large extent, *reactive* and ill-informed on issues related to provincial jurisdiction. After all, initiatives are the products of expertise, means and incentives. And the federal government not only lacks the expertise to deal with provincial issues at an international level, but it also lacks the legitimate incentives to do so. This is what I will discuss in the next section.

---

[501] *Ibid.* at 6-7.

[502] The Canada School of Public Service Action-Research Roundtable on Managing Canada-US Relations has produced a very instructive compendium that offers a snapshot of the different channels of collaboration between certain federal institutions (Agriculture and Agri-Food Canada, Bank of Canada, Canada Border Services Agency, Canadian Food Inspection Agency, Canadian Space Agency, Citizenship and Immigration Canada, Competition Bureau, Environment Canada, Finance Canada, Fisheries and Oceans Canada, Foreign Affairs Canada, Health Canada, Industry Canada, International Joint Commission, International Trade Canada, Justice Canada, NAFTA Secretariat, National Defence, National Energy Board, Natural Resources Canada, Parks Canada, Privy Council Office, Public Safety and Emergency Preparedness Canada (Portfolio), Public Safety and Emergency Preparedness Canada (Emergency Management and National Security Branch), Royal Canadian Mounted Police, Standards Council of Canada, Statistics Canada, Transport Canada) and those of the United States. See Canada School of Public Service, CSPS Action-Research Roundtable on Managing Canada-US Relations, *Building Cross-Border Links: A Compendium of Canada-US Government Collaboration* by Dieudonné Mouafo, Nadia Ponce Morales, Jeff Heynen, eds. (Ottawa: CSPS Action-Research Roundtable on Managing Canada-US Relations, 2004) (Chair: Louis Ranger) [CSPS, *Building Cross-Border Links: A Compendium of Canada-US Government Collaboration*].

iii. The Need to Align Power with Democratic Accountability

To the extent that one considers democratic accountability an important value, allowing the federal government to make treaties in relation to provincial matters would be worrisome for at least two reasons.

The first one is that it would allow for an "accountability mismatch": voters would have a harder time identifying who is to praise (or who is to blame) for the policies associated with the adopted treaties. This could have the effect, for example, of limiting the efforts put towards the negotiation and adoption of a treaty that would be popular only in one or a few provinces when the population of the other provinces is indifferent to the issue, for the mere reason that the federal government would not gain much across the country from investing resources in such a project. This phenomenon could be further exacerbated if the treaty subject falls under the provincial jurisdiction and has no specific and stable constituency to which it would appeal.[503] On the other hand, this would allow the federal government to get the credit for making a popular, yet costly, treaty while shifting to the provinces the expenses of implementation and the blame for not doing so appropriately.

Second, this accountability mismatch has an important side-effect on the issue of state responsibility at international law. Since there are no formal agreements on the issue yet but only *ad hoc* arrangements when Canada's international responsibility is called into question because of provincial (in)action, this puts Canada in a delicate situation. While in the past, sanctions for not following international obligations were mostly diplomatic in nature, monetary damages are now more important as commercial and investment treaties have burgeoned. Until the federal government and the provinces come to an agreement on the general issue of how responsibility should be allocated, the federal government has very good reasons to avoid making treaties for which it cannot be sure that adequate implementation will follow. But apart from the financial concerns, the issue of principle here is that the proper *demos* should bear the costs of its international wrongdoings. When one province is breaching international law on a matter related to her jurisdiction, it is inappropriate to impose collective punishment on the population of all other provinces. If the federal government and the provinces are equal in status and they each embody distinct (although overlapping) political communities, responsibilities should fall squarely where it belongs.

---

[503] This would help to explain, for example, the Canadian government's hesitant participation in the work of the Hague Conference on Private International Law (see Renaud Dehousse, *Fédéralisme et relations internationales* (Bruxelles: Bruylant, 1991) at 190.

iv. The Subsidiarity Principle, Existential Communities and Functional Regimes

There is another reason why one should worry about democratic accountability, and this one is related to the democratic reasons that underlie the particular distribution of powers in the Canadian federation. To that effect, the Supreme Court wrote:

> The principle of federalism recognizes the diversity of the component parts of Confederation, and the autonomy of provincial governments to develop their societies within their respective spheres of jurisdiction. The federal structure of our country also facilitates democratic participation by distributing power to the government thought to be most suited to achieving the particular societal objective having regard to this diversity.[504]

Recognizing a general federal power to make treaties in relation to provincial matters in an era of globalization would simply ruin the federal principle. Subsidiarity, the hallmark of federalism, has been succinctly described by the Supreme Court as the "proposition that law-making and implementation are often best achieved at a level of government that is not only effective, but also closest to the citizens affected and thus most responsive to their needs, to local distinctiveness, and to population diversity."[505] Recognizing plenary making-powers to the federal government would turn subsidiarity into a thing of the past in Canada. While other parts of the world are now recognizing the increasing role of multilayered governance in order to better accommodate local needs and diversity with the mutually beneficial pooling of resources, Canada would to the contrary flatten its political landscape. Decisions relevant to one part of the political community would be taken by another part of that community. The legitimate voice of the provincial communities would be silenced to allow others to speak for

---

[504] *Reference Re Secession of Québec, supra* note 76 at para. 58. See also Rinfret J in *Nova Scotia (A.-G) v. Canada (A.-G.)*, [1951] S.C.R. 31[*Nova Scotia (A.-G) v. Canada (A.-G.)*] at 34, who wrote:

> The constitution of Canada does not belong either to Parliament, or to the Legislatures; it belongs to the country and it is there that the citizens of the country will find the protection of the rights to which they are entitled. It is part of that protection that Parliament can legislate only on the subject matters referred to it by section 91 and that each Province can legislate exclusively on the subject matters referred to it by section 92.

This quote is cited with approval by both the majority and the dissenting judges in the *Patriation Reference, supra* note 95.

[505] *114957 Canada Ltée (Spraytech, Société d'arrosage) v. Hudson (Town)*, [2001] 2 S.C.R. 241, 2001 SCC 40 at para. 3 (*per* L'Heureux-Dubé J, Gonthier, Bastarache and Arbour JJ. concurring). See the vigorous defence of the subsidiarity principle by the majority opinion in *Canadian Western Bank, supra* note 218 at para. 45.

them, to allow the federal government's "single voice". This would not be good for Canada's unity.

As we have seen earlier, there are more ways than one to achieve a "singular" Canadian voice in international relations. It seems, thus, that there is something more to the trope of the singular voice than purely functional reasons. The real reasons seem to have more to do with the fear that recognizing official roles to Québec in international relations would pull *Québécois* further away from the common federal project and would grant ammunitions to Québec's sovereignists in their bid for international recognition in the event that they would win a future referendum. This is an erroneous perception: it is mistaken at the legal level and it gets things totally in reverse at the political level. Let me explain.

As we have already seen, in the event of a "yes" vote in a future referendum on Québec's secession from Canada, the prior presence of Québec on the international scene would certainly not be determinant – or even be of any significant consequence – in other countries' decision to recognize or not recognize Québec as an independent country. Thus, the "legal" concern is misplaced. The international system already recognizes that international organisations and sub-national organisations can make treaties. Gone are the days when there was a single international status at international law. Thus, in the event of a "yes" vote, the relevant question would not be so much whether or not Québec would be recognized as an independent state, but rather what kind of rights and duties would be recognized and what changes would occur in the respective situations of Québec and Canada in the current web of transnational structures and expectations. After all, in today's globalized world, state independence is quite a relative idea. But so does belonging.

And this leads to the political question underlying the current lack of agreement between Canadian sovereignists and Québec federalists. In order to clarify the source of the problem and a possible way out, I need first to introduce a few conceptual tools.

We know that we now have, in the international arena, a multiplicity of legal statuses (covering states, federated states, "peoples", municipalities,[506] universities,[507] international organisations, non-governmental

---

[506] The *Fourth Municipal Leaders Summit on Climate Change* organized in Montréal in parallel to the 11th Session of the Conference of the Parties (COP11) and first Meeting of the Parties (MOP1) to the *United Nations Framework Convention on Climate Change*, 9 May 1992, 1771 U.N.T.S. 107, 31 I.L.M. 848 (entered into force 21 March 1994) [*UNFCCC*] (the United Nations Climate Change Conference – Montréal 2005) offered a recent example of the important international role that municipalities can play in international relations. Not only were the municipalities able to lobby their own governments, they also made commitments of their own including taking actions

organisations, multinational and transnational corporations, individuals, etc.) to which are attached different rights, duties and expectations that are often tailor-made to each type of status. In fact, the ontology of this new world order is made of a wide variety of entities ranging from what I would call *"existential communities"* to *"functional regimes"* that are standing in a variety of ways to one another. The multiplicity of types of actors and their different legal relations participate in what many are now calling the development of a form of loose "international federalism" of multi-layered governance.[508] Rights, duties and expectations of

---

to "3.1 ... achieve the emission reduction targets set forth in the International Youth Declaration of 30% by 2020 and 80% by 2050 based on 1990 levels, building upon the actions already taken by local governments that committed to a 20% reduction by 2010." Recognizing the multiplicity of international actors needed to be mobilized to achieve their objectives, they also committed to "3.6 Advancing partnerships and collaboration with national and sub national governments, non-governmental organizations, corporate and industrial sectors, as well as non-governmental organizations and community groups, in order to multiply reduction potential." They also requested, among other things, that "4.1 Local governments be recognized by the Conference of the Parties for the actions they have implemented and are continuing, tangibly to reduce greenhouse gas emissions. ...", "4.2 National and sub-national governments: recognize the fundamental role of local governments in mitigating and adapting to climate change; partner with them to enhance their technical, human and financial capacity and legislative authority; and fully engage them when making strategic decisions on climate change policies" and that "National and sub-national governments ensure that local governments have the opportunity to participate in emissions trading in accordance with evolving domestic and international trading systems." (See Fourth Municipal Leaders Summit on Climate Change, On the Occasion of the United Nations Climate Change Conference (COP 11 and COP/MOP 1), *World Mayors and Municipal Leaders Declaration on Climate Change* (Montréal: 7 December 2005), online: International Council for Local Environmental Initiatives (I.C.L.E.I.) – Local Government for Sustainability <http://www.iclei.org/index.php?id=2447>).

[507] Apart from the networks of scientific cooperation and student exchange programs, Universities are also becoming important international actors through their research and policy centers that work, for example, on codifying international law and through their international legal clinics that are actively involved in the international legal process. The Centre d'études sur le droit international de la mondialisation (C.É.D.I.M.) of the Université du Québec à Montréal, for example, hosted in 2006 an international conference "International Legal Clinics as New International Actors". The conference gathered key clinical players from around the world to discuss not only strategies and possible alliances but also the very role of university legal clinics in our current world order. The *Clinique internationale de défense des droits humains de l'U.Q.A.M.* (C.I.D.D.H.U.) was launched at about the same time. It is currently involved in cases related to human rights violations in Colombia, Guatemala, Haïti, Dominican Republic, Burkina-Faso, etc.

[508] See, for example, John O. McGinnis, "The Decline of the Western Nation State and the Rise of the Regime of International Federalism" (1996) 18 Cardozo L. Rev. 903; Kenneth W. Abbott, "Economic Issue and Political Participation: The Evolving Boundaries of International Federalism" (1996) 18 Cardozo L. Rev. 971; Peter J. Spiro, "Foreign Relations Federalism" (1999) 70 U. Colo. L. Rev. 1223; Daniel J. Elazar, "The State System + Globalization (Economic Plus Human Rights) = Federal-

the diverse entities that now populate our world order will depend in part on their perceived situation on the spectrum between the *existential* and the *functional*.

"Existential communities" are communities through which individual' selfhood is constituted by a deep sense of "love",[509] of loyalty and of identity, etc. to the other members of the group. In other words, an existential community is what makes it possible for the self to transcend the individual. Those communities, from the internal point of view of committed members, are ends and not means. A paradigmatic case here would be the Catholic view of the Church as the "corpus mysticum" of Christ.[510] At the other end of the spectrum, "functional regimes" are institutional mechanisms that are meant to solve functional problems like coordination of behaviour. Those collective institutions are means to achieve certain ends. A paradigmatic case here would be the International Organization for Standardization (ISO). If any sense of identity results in the participation in the functional regime, this is simply an incidental effect (except if the regime has been put in place specifically for the purpose of inducing a sense of identity to its participants). Obviously, whether an institution is primarily an existential one or a functional one can be the object of heated controversy for people participating in that institution.

These ideas help to explain the constant misunderstanding between Québec and what is often referred to as the "rest of Canada" (ROC) by *Québécois*. Although the "nation-state" is often taken to be an existential institution, multinational states are not necessarily seen as such by all their members. This helps to understand both the comment of the then sovereignist Premier of Québec Lucien Bouchard in 1996 to the effect that "Canada is divisible because it is not a real country"[511] and

---

ism (State Federations Plus Regional Confederations)" (1999) 40 S. Tex. L. Rev. 555. This idea of nested political organisations is not new nor is it associated with a single ideological current. In effect, versions of those views can be found in the works of Johannes Althusius, *Politica Methodice Digesta* (1603), trans. by Frederick S. Carney (Indianapolis: Liberty Press, 1995) or Pierre-Joseph Proudhon, *Le principe fédératif (1863)* (Paris: M. Rivière, 1959). For two thought-provoking reflections on polyarchy, see Roderick Macdonald, "Kaleidoscopic Federalism" in Jean-François Gaudreault-DesBiens and Fabien Gélinas, eds, *Le fédéralisme dans tous ses états / The States and Moods of Federalism* (Cowansville (Qc): Yvon Blais, 2005) 261 and Roberto Mangabeira Unger, *What Should Legal Analysis Become* (London (U.K.): Verso, 1996) at 148-163.

[509] I do not intend to refer here to romantic love but rather something more transcending than *philia* but not necessarily universal as *agape*.

[510] See E. Kantorowicz, *The Kings Two Bodies, supra* note 83.

[511] Philip Authier, "Bouchard says no to partition" The [Montreal] Gazette (28 January 1996) A1.

the ensuing furious reactions by Canadian nationalists. One can read Bouchard's statement as meaning that Canada is not an existential community but a mere functional regime. Thus, Canada could be fragmented at will by the existential communities for which that regime was set up. For Canadian nationalists, that was not only wrong descriptively but it was an insult to their sense of identity because it negated their political existence. The reverse happens when English-speakers do not understand why francophones in Québec want to take special measures to protect the French language as opposed to simply letting the "linguistic market" do its job. Language for many francophones in Québec is not a mere instrument of communication; it is constitutive of the transcendent self.

Many political controversies unconsciously flow from disagreement over whether a specific institution is primarily existential or whether it is primarily functional. The current constitutional framework is imagined by "Canadian sovereignists" as instituting one Canadian existential community (Canada) and ten mostly functional regimes (provinces), while "Québec sovereignists" imagine Québec as their existential community being stuck in a larger functional regime. Each desire a strong nation-state but they can't agree on which institution embodies it. And to make matters a bit more complicated, it appears that, to a large degree, even Québec federalists tend to see themselves primarily as *Québécois*.[512]

---

[512] For example, a Léger Marketing poll conducted for The Globe and Mail and Le Devoir among 1,008 respondents throughout Québec between April 20 and April 24, 2005 found that 18% of respondents saw themselves as Québécois only and 32% as more Québécois than Canadian, for a total of 50% of respondents who saw themselves more as Québécois than Canadian. Then, 35% of the respondents said that they are as much Québécois as they are Canadian. Only 7% of the respondents said that they were more Canadian than Québecois and 6% identified themselves as Canadian only. (The maximum margin of error is ± 3.1%, 19 times out of 20. The poll results are available at Léger Marketing, The Globe and Mail and Le Devoir, Press Release, "Québec Poll" (27 April 2005), online: Léger Marketing: <http://legermarketing. com/documents/spclm/050427ENG.pdf>). Another poll conducted by Léger Marketing (for The Gazette and Le Journal de Montréal) among 2008 respondents throughout Québec found that 58% of the respondents identified themselves as "autonomiste" while other terms gathered much less support ("nationaliste" (55%), "souverainiste" (45%) and "fédéraliste" (33%)). The poll also found that 92% of the respondents were "proud to be Québécois" and 75% were "proud to be Canadians". These numbers were surprisingly obtained while 54% of the respondents also said that they would have voted "for sovereignty if a referendum on sovereignty with an offer of economic and political partnership with the rest of Canada had been held" in the previous week. (The maximum margin of error is ± 2.2%, 19 times out of 20. The poll results are available at Léger Marketing, The [Montreal] Gazette and Le Journal de Montréal, Press Release, "Quebec Survey" (14 May 2005), online: Léger Marketing <http://legermarketing.com/documents/SPCLM/050516ENG.pdf>).

There are two elements that result in increasing the tension between the *Québécois* and other Canadians that are relevant here. The first element is related to the way we conceive states as existential communities and the second is associated with the political psychology that flows from those conceptions.

In effect, one source of the Canadian problem is that many politicians in Canada and Québec are in fact "sovereignists". And here, I mean both Québec independentists and many Canadians who mistakenly call themselves "federalists". In fact, whether or not they call themselves "sovereignists", they both use an arcane notion of sovereignty to frame their political claims. In effect, the notion of sovereignty used by both Canadian sovereignists (who claim that Canada must necessarily "speak with one voice", the federal government's voice) and Québec sovereignists (who claim that Québec has reached her maturity and must walk entirely on her own) is based in large parts on the "personification" metaphor. The sovereign state is conceived as a "person" that has her "head", "arms", "organs" and "members" that make a "body politic" with its own "will", "interests", "dignity", etc. The state also acts as a person: it "protects" its "members" from "rogue states" and other "enemies", it "demands" loyalty, its "organs" "provide" its "members" with "support", it "educates" us, it "puts in place" market conditions, etc. That "person" can be a "mother" or a "father",[513] but an "uncivilised" or "underdeveloped" one is like a child that needs help, perhaps a "tutor", a "protector" or a "mandator" to gain its autonomy and to join the "international family". Canada's independence was portrayed that way: *she* became mature enough to become independent from the "mother country". In fact, the federal government's position in the *Labour Conventions* case was precisely couched in terms of the "succession" from the "mother country". But in all those cases, the political community is conceived as *one unitary* person: *she* "must speak with one voice".

That frame leaves little space for conceiving of the possibility of membership in multiple existential communities. In fact, this conceptual metaphor does not leave space for conceiving of a true federalism; federalism as the institutional expression of the idea that individuals can belong to more than one existential community simultaneously. Federalism, framed through that personhood metaphor, looks like a *monster*: it is a hydra, or Siamese twins,[514] with multiple heads. Conceived that way,

---

[513] Not only is the state sometimes said to be "*pater*nalistic", but to it is even sometimes called the "fatherland".

[514] Not surprisingly, that image of the Siamese twins has been used in Québec literature to describe the Canada/Québec situation. See for example Jacques Godbout's metaphorical novel *Les têtes à Papineau* (Paris: Le Seuil, 1981) where Siamese twins shar-

federalism is necessarily pathological, it is an unstable system that is called to reach its point of equilibrium either through supremacy of the center or through independence of its components. From that conceptual framework, dual loyalties are not conceivable. [515]

We need to understand the consequences of this "sovereignist" framework on political psychology. This conception of sovereignty forces people to choose camps either for Canada or for Québec. That means not only that people have to choose between two existential communities, but that the stakes of losing are incredibly high. Losing means losing one's identity, one's chance of surviving one's death. Thus, this conception turns the situation into a zero-sum game. Any compromise is thus seen as treason. And this leads Canadian sovereignists to perceive themselves as being involved in a "war" against Québec sovereignists. [516] Therefore, cooperation and equal coexistence of

---

ing one single body debate whether or not they should undergo a surgery to be separated from each other. However, this idea of a "body politic" that would have more than one "head" would be "monstrous" is far from a new one. Otto Gierke described how, during the Middle Age, the ecclesiastical party argued against the imperial party for a single "head" to the "mystical body" that formed mankind in those very terms (see Gierke, *Political Theories of the Middle Age, supra* note 5 at 22). It is not without irony that, today, it is the "statistically Catholic" province that is countering the "one body, one head" argument coming from provinces where Protestants are the majority.

[515] For other criticisms of the state as person metaphor, see Edward L. Rubin, *Beyond Camelot: Rethinking Politics and Law for the Modern State* (Princeton: Princeton Universtity Press, 2005). However, while I think that Rubin's criticisms are enlightening, I am not convinced that his alternative metaphors taken from the fields of management and engineering will do the job because they overemphasise the functional nature of the institutional forms that existential communities may take. Doing so only highlights the fact that such institutional arrangements attempt to meet the functional needs of individuals but completely hides the fact that state institutions are meant to be the embodiment of collective selves. If state institutions are nothing but service providers, then there is little to differentiate them from any other service providers. The possibility of individual sacrifice makes little sense in that context and is rather replaced by the question as to whether one gets at least as much as one is giving. In that context, the strongest have little interests in putting in place institutions that will weaken their positions. However, if the state is conceived as the embodiment of a collective identity that transcends the life of individuals, the possibility of solidarity based on something more than reciprocity opens up. From that perspective, the individual is a part of a project that is bigger than her. Giving to others makes sense as an act of accomplishing one's role in the narrative of the collective life. These thoughts make possible the idea of the survival of one's identity despite one's individual death. In other words, the technical metaphors used to frame state institutions might properly highlight their functional uses but they do so at the cost of hiding the assumptions about collective transcendence that made them acceptable in the first place.

[516] This was clearly the vision behind the now infamous "sponsorship program" developed after the 1995 referendum by the federal Liberals. That special sponsorship program was put in place by Prime Minister Jean Chrétien as a response to the rise of Québec sovereignism. The idea behind the program was that the Canadian govern-

the federal government and the provinces are not truly intelligible from that frame of mind. This leads to strategies that only increase tensions. In particular, Canadian sovereignists, fearing the loss of their country and their identity, understand their position as one of having to "fight" provinces' demands to have their jurisdiction respected.

Paradoxically, to the extent that the Canadian sovereignist strategy is built on the idea that they have to "fight against" any legitimization of provinces' autonomy, they also offend the very people that they are trying to bring into their camp. In other words, their conceptual framework makes it harder for them to remember that membership in an existential community is a matter of emotional attachment, of "love"[517] and that such disposition cannot be imposed in a confrontational way. "Love me or else!" is not terribly effective. The only possibility for a common future will reside in finding ways to accommodate those conflicting senses of belonging.

The challenge of reconciling "diversity with unity"[518] is not simply an empty slogan. What is at stake with the idea of self-government is primarily the idea that rules ought to come from the self (thus, the existential community). At the same time, the very idea of government is associated with the need for efficient collective decision-making and effective implementation of collective policies (thus, the state is also a functional regime). Federalism is an attempt to achieve the successful marriage of the existential longings of different communities with their respective functional needs.

Giving more powers to the federal government while rejecting calls for needed provincial powers has the exact opposite effects than what is hoped for by Canadian sovereignists: the centripetal move causes a centrifugal reaction in Québec. Keeping Québec in the federation will

---

ment needed to be more visible in Québec so as to increase the sense of belonging to Canada among Québeckers. However, the program was plagued with financial improprieties, and corruptions charges flew around. Among other things, it was recognized that public funds were diverted to the federal Liberal party. Jean Chrétien's successor, Paul Martin, set up a commission of inquiry to look into the matter. As a result, many participants in the program faced criminal charges and were convicted. However, what matters here is that even as many witnesses recognized improprieties, they attempted to justify them by claiming that they "were at war", and in those situations the ends justify the means. For example, Charles Guité, the civil servant in charge of managing the program from 1996 to 1999, said during his testimony to the commission "[w]e were basically at war trying to save the country... When you're at war, you drop the book and the rules and you don't give your plan to the opposition." (Daniel Leblanc, "Guité: 'When you're at war you drop... the rules'" Globe and Mail (Saturday, April 03, 2004) A1).

[517] See *supra* note 509 for the meaning with which I use the term here.

[518] *Reference Re Secession of Québec, supra* note 76 at para 43.

mean finding ways to reconcile and, hopefully, harmonize the conflict-ing senses of what are the proper existential communities in Canada. To do so, I will have to revisit the metaphors we use to make sense of our "being-together".

Even if we were to attempt to reframe the metaphor of the multiple "heads" of the "body politic" by talking instead of the different "brain hemispheres", that will not do. The goal will not be achieved by continuing to compare Canada to a "person". Reconceptualising the Canadian state as a "body politic" with one brain made of one right hemisphere and ten left hemispheres might seem like a good start but it would still be quite misleading. The problem is not only with the head but also with the heart. Since the sense of collective self is not being situated at the same place for everyone, the perceived legitimacy of different state actions will not only depend on the general ideological positions of individuals (right or left) but will also depend on the institu-tions that will carry them out. For example, progressives have tradition-ally been moved to build a strong national government for the purpose of enhancing its capacity to foster welfare. However, the problem has been that progressives in Québec and progressives in the rest of Canada do not agree on which one is the "national government".[519]

That is why "asymmetrical federalism" has been proposed as a solu-tion to this differential sense of political belonging. It is not that other provinces do not represent existential communities. They certainly do. However, in a contest of identity between Canada and those provinces, it is plausible that the federal state might come on top more often for a majority of the citizens of those other provinces than it would be the case in Québec. In any case, if that situation were to change – and there are presently signs of that coming from Alberta –, there will be demands coming from other corners than Québec asking for a limitation of fed-eral interventions in provincial jurisdictions and an increased demand for provincial leadership. For the moment, however, the Québec de-mands are the only ones coming from a province that are primarily based on identity claims and not functional needs.[520]

This helps to understand why Québec might have, today, a more driven attitude towards international relations than other provinces. Recognizing Québec's claims should not be seen as a threat to the Canadian federation but rather as a sign that the federation is capable of accommodating multiple senses of belonging within its institutional setting. In other words, it should be seen as evidence that the federation is capable of being flexible enough to suit multiple interwoven existen-

---

[519] I would like to thank Pierre Ducasse for suggesting this formulation to me.

[520] I note that many Aboriginal demands flow from the same reasoning.

tial communities. It should be seen as a sign of success rather than failure.

*

* *

To summarize the first part of this section, I would say that it is clear that the federal government cannot count on any constitutional sources to justify its claim to a plenary treaty-making power, nor would it be a sound policy position to take in any event. Building upon what has already been said in this past section, the next section will be devoted to a discussion of the case for the recognition of provincial treaty-making powers.

B. Making the Case for Provincial Treaty-Making Powers

In 1968, Gabon's National Minister of Education officially invited his Québec counterpart to participate in the annual conference of education ministers of francophone countries.[521] The invitation was sent directly to Québec instead of going through Ottawa. The then Québec education Minister accepted, took part in the conference and was treated with all the honours usually bestowed upon representatives of sovereign states. Although education is clearly a provincial matter,[522] Ottawa was quite upset: Lester B. Pearson wrote a letter protesting to Gabon's government that it did not act according to international law, and Canada subsequently broke off her diplomatic relations with Gabon. The situation grew even tenser between Ottawa and Québec after the follow-up education conference held in Paris in the same year, to which Québec was again invited.[523] These were combined with several other incidents that increased the tensions between Ottawa and Québec in that period.[524]

---

[521] A summary of these events can be found in Prof. Jean-Herman Guay's historical project *Bilan du siècle: une base intégrée d'information sur le Québec* (Anonymous, "1968 Participation du Québec à la conférence de Libreville" in Jean-Herman Guay *et al.*, *Bilan du siècle: une base intégrée d'information sur le Québec*, online: Université de Sherbrooke, Faculté des lettres et sciences humaines, Bilan du siècle <http://bilan.usherbrooke.ca/bilan/pages/evenements/1934.html>).

[522] S. 93 of the *Constitution Act, 1867*, *supra* note 39: "In and for each Province the Legislature may exclusively make Laws in relation to Education ...".

[523] While Ottawa, again, expressed its discontent with the situation, the federal government did not break its diplomatic relations with Paris. See Anonymous, "22 avril 1968 – Participation du Québec à une conférence sur l'éducation à Paris" in Jean-Herman Guay *et al.*, *Bilan du siècle: une base intégrée d'information sur le Québec*, online: Université de Sherbrooke, Faculté des lettres et sciences humaines, Bilan du siècle < http://bilan.usherbrooke.ca/bilan/pages/evenements/1902.html>.

[524] For example, Québec also participated in the creation, in 1969, of the "Conférence des ministres de la Jeunesse et des sports des pays de langue française" (Confejes) (Anonymous, "1969 – Création de la Conférence des ministres de la Jeunesse et des sports

181

Edward McWhinney, both a constitutionalist and an internationalist trained in the views of the "New Haven school of international law", wrote in 1969 about this controversy that:

> Looking back, it may be suggested that unedifying public quarrels ... have been rather damaging to all of the parties involved, for they reveal a preoccupation with old-fashioned, abstract and theoretical, questions of where sovereignty lies and whether it is divisible in any sense – in short, an atavistic preoccupation with the "symbols" of government at the expense of the substance ...[525]

Such conflicts are reminiscent of the controversies over diplomatic representation and ceremonials in the decades that followed the Westphalian treaties and that prompted the invention of the notion of *"persona jure gentium"* or, as we often translate it (anachronistically[526]): "international legal personality".[527] Contrary to what is too often as-

---

des pays de langue française" in Jean-Herman Guay *et al.*, *Bilan du siècle: une base intégrée d'information sur le Québec*, online: Université de Sherbrooke, Faculté des lettres et sciences humaines, Bilan du siècle <http://bilan.usherbrooke.ca/bilan/pages/evenements/2073.html>) and sent a separate delegation from that of Ottawa to the 1969 international "francophonie" conference held in Niamey (Niger) (Anonymous, "17 février 1969 – Ouverture de la conférence internationale de la francophonie" in Jean-Herman Guay *et al.*, *Bilan du siècle: une base intégrée d'information sur le Québec*, online: Université de Sherbrooke, Faculté des lettres et sciences humaines, Bilan du siècle <http://bilan.usherbrooke.ca/bilan/pages/evenements/2025.html>).

[525] Gibran van Ert refers to this quote in G. van Ert, *Using International Law in Canadian Courts*, *supra* note 41 at 87-88. The initial reference is E. McWhinney, "Canadian Federalism and the Foreign Affairs and Treaty Power: The Impact of Québec's Quiet Revolution", *supra* note 41 at 13-14.

[526] The Latin word *"gentium"* does not translate literally into "international". In fact, the very concept of "international" was not known at the time. In a theoretically sophisticated and intellectually rewarding genealogy of sovereignty, Jens Bartelson writes about the expression "international system":

> To be sure, if we extend the range of application of the term international to cover everything that takes place between states, we are entitled to speak of something international in the Classical Age, even if the term itself was never used by classical authors. By the same token, we are entitled to speak of a system, since both Grotius and Pufendorf use the term to convey the sense of a fundamental moral or legal unity underlying the accentuated division into particular states. But if we by international system mean a totality which is something more than the sum of its constituent parts, yet something presumably distinct from a universal *Respublica Christiana*, we have to wait another 200 years for its emergence within political knowledge.

(Jens Bartelson, *A Genealogy of Sovereignty* (Cambridge: Cambridge University Press, 1995) at 137 (footnotes omitted)). The author presents a genealogy of the idea of "international" at 209-236 (*ibid.*).

[527] The remaining of the current paragraph owes a great deal to the information presented in Janneke Nijman's erudite paper "Leibniz's Theory of Relative Sovereignty and International Legal Personality: Justice and Stability or the Last Great Defence of the

sumed, the Westphalian treaties did not so much establish the "modern sovereign state" as they established a division of powers between the Emperor and the Princes in an effort to salvage both the Holy Roman Empire and recognize the new authority of other political[528] players.

Holy Roman Empire" IILJ Working Paper 2004/2 (History and Theory of International Law Series) online: New York School of Law, Institute for International Law and Justice (I.I.L.J.) <http://www.iilj.org/papers/2004/2004.2%20Nijman.pdf> [J. Nijman, "Leibniz's Theory of Relative Sovereignty and International Legal Personality"].

[528] This is clear from Art. 62-63 of the *Peace Treaty between the Holy Roman Emperor and the King of France and their respective Allies*, 24 October 1648 (*Instrumentum Pacis Monasteriensis*), Die Westfälischen Friedensverträge vom 24. Oktober 1648. Texte und Übersetzungen (Acta Pacis Westphalicae. Supplementa electronica, 1), online: <http://www.pax-westphalica.de/>; Yale Law School, Avalon Project <http://www.yale.edu/lawweb/avalon/westphal.htm> [*IPM*] and Art. VIII, 1 and VIII, 2 of the *Peace Treaty between the Holy Roman Emperor and the King of Sweden*, 24 October 1648 (*Instrumentum Pacis Osnabrugensis*), Die Westfälischen Friedensverträge vom 24. Oktober 1648. Texte und Übersetzungen (Acta Pacis Westphalicae. Supplementa electronica, 1), online: <http://www.pax-westphalica.de/> [*IPO*]:

[Art. VIII,1 IPO = § 62 IPM] Ut autem provisum sit, ne posthac in statu politico controversiae suboriantur, omnes et singuli electores, principes et status Imperii Romani in antiquis suis iuribus, praerogativis, libertate, privilegiis, libero iuris territorialis tam in ecclesiasticis quam politicis exercitio, ditionibus, regalibus horumque omnium possessione vigore huius transactionis ita stabiliti firmatique sunto, ut a nullo unquam sub quocunque praetextu de facto turbari possint vel debeant.

[Art. VIII,2 IPO = § 63 IPM] Gaudeant sine contradictione iure suffragii in omnibus deliberationibus super negotiis Imperii, praesertim ubi leges ferendae vel interpretandae, bellum decernendum, tributa indicenda, delectus aut hospitationes militum instituendae, nova munimenta intra statuum ditiones extruenda nomine publico veterave firmanda praesidiis nec non ubi pax aut foedera facienda aliave eiusmodi negotia peragenda fuerint. Nihil horum aut quicquam simile posthac unquam fiat vel admittatur nisi de comitiali liberoque omnium Imperii statuum suffragio et consensu.

Cumprimis vero ius faciendi inter se et cum exteris foedera pro sua cuiusque conservatione ac securitate singulis statibus perpetuo liberum esto, ita tamen, ne eiusmodi foedera sint contra Imperatorem et Imperium pacemque eius publicam vel hanc inprimis transactionem fiantque salvo per omnia iuramento, quo quisque Imperatori et Imperio obstrictus est.

[Art. VIII,1 IPO = § 62 IPM] VIII. And in order to prevent for the future all Differences in the Political State, all and every the Electors, Princes, and States of the Roman Empire shall be so establish'd and confirm'd in their antient Rights, Prerogatives, Liberties, Privileges, free Exercise of their Territorial Right, as well in Spirituals and Temporals, Seigneuries, Regalian Rights, and in the possession of all these things, by virtue of the present Transaction, that they may not be molested at any time in any manner, under any pretext whatsoever.

Art. VIII,2 IPO = § 63 IPM] 1. That they enjoy without contradiction the Right of Suffrage in all Deliberations touching the Affairs of the Empire, especially in the matter of interpreting Laws, resolving upon a War, imposing Taxes, ordering Levies and quartering of Soldiers, building for the publick Use new Fortresses in the Lands

Thus, that era was characterised by the opening up of the political space for a multitude of authoritative institutions that were to different degrees autonomous from the Emperor and the Pope. In light of the need to engage in diplomatic relations after the Thirty Years War with different types of authorities, there were controversies as to who could send different types of diplomats and what honours could be bestowed on them. For example, there was a controversy as to whether the Duke of Brunswick-Lüneburg in Hanover – who was a prominent prince of the Empire (*Reichsfürsten*) but not an Elector (*Kurfürst*) – could send ambassadors to the Nijmegen peace negotiations (1677-1679). The Duke claimed to be the equal of the Electors, but France wanted to maintain a distinction between the two statuses.[529] Because the political landscape was evolving rapidly, diplomatic usages were suffused with confusion. It is in that context that Leibniz, who was a counsel to the Duke of Brunswick-Lüneburg, came up with the concept of "international legal personality" as a solution to the changing ontology of world politics.[530] Thus, the concept of "international legal personality" was *not* developed to deal with "absolute sovereigns" but rather precisely for the opposite reason: it was developed to deal with entities enjoying different degrees of autonomy. In other words, the introduction of the concept of "international legal personality" was a pragmatic solution to the problem that arose from the need of different political players to engage with other political players of different nature. And that solution involved the recognition of interlocking governments with no absolute powers but rather powers distributed according to specific fields of competence.

A similar strategy was adopted in 1971 between the federal government and the Québec government: many of the tensions between Ottawa and Québec decreased when both levels of government disentangled

---

of the States, and reinforcing old Garisons, making of Peace and Alliances, and treating of other such-like Affairs; so that none of those or the like things shall be done or receiv'd afterwards, without the Advice and Consent of a free Assembly of all the States of the Empire: That, above all, each of the Estates of the Empire shall freely and for ever enjoy the Right of making Alliances among themselves, or with Foreigners, for the Preservation and Security of every one of them: provided nevertheless that these Alliances be neither against the Emperor nor the Empire, nor the publick Peace, nor against this Transaction especially; and that they be made without prejudice in every respect to the Oath whereby every one of them is bound to the Emperor and the Empire. (Anonymous translation (1713)).

[529] J. Nijman, "Leibniz's Theory of Relative Sovereignty and International Legal Personality", *supra* 527 at 10-12.

[530] Janneke Nijman demonstrates convincingly that (*ibid.* at 4) "Leibniz' introduction of the concept [of "international legal personality"] resulted from an original attempt to preserve the universal (medieval) structures propagated by the Pope and Emperor while accommodating the emergence and the inclusion of new participants in the diplomatic community and on the European stage."

themselves from the conceptual web of "sovereignty" and agreed on the modalities of Québec's admission to the international "Agence de coopération culturelle et technique de la francophonie" (now the "Agence intergouvernementale de la Francophonie"). The agreement[531] provided that Québec would have the status of a participating government with her own distinct representation from the Canadian delegation, thus allowing Québec to have an identified presence and her own voice on matters related to her own legislative competences.[532]

In fact, the conceptual framework built around the notion of "sovereignty" hinders more than it helps in the search for pragmatic solutions to pragmatic problems. As McWhinney recently wrote,

> la notion de souveraineté, cette formulation politique qui remonte au XVIIᵉ siècle et qui a été érigée en impératif catégorique constitutionnel et international dès la fin du XIXe siècle. Inutile de dire que la notion classique de souveraineté s'avère de plus en plus inadaptée – tant en droit international qu'en droit constitutionnel – dans une Amérique du Nord où la communication est instantanée, où la transmission des données traverse les frontières et où les décisions, qu'il s'agisse de questions cruciales de politique économique et financière ou de politique de défense et de sécurité, se prennent à un niveau transnational.[533]

Thus, if we do not entirely rid ourselves of the idea of "sovereignty", at least, we should not let it hinder us in our search for the proper institutional settings that will satisfy our current needs as overlapping existential communities.

While the case can be certainly made for completely leaving behind the old concept of sovereignty, this argument will have to be left for some other occasion. What matters for the moment is to recognize the following things: (1) "International status" does not necessarily rhyme

---

[531] Québec, Secrétariat aux affaires intergouvernementales, Bureau des ententes, Ententes intergouvernementales canadiennes déposées au bureau des ententes, *Entente Canada-Québec concernant la participation du Québec aux programmes de l'agence de coopération culturelle et technique (ACCT)*, 1971-024; reproduced as *Modalités selon lesquelles le gouvernement du Québec est admis comme gouvernement participant aux institutions, aux activités et aux programmes de l'Agence de coopération, culturelle et technique, convenues le 1ᵉʳ octobre 1971, entre le gouvernement du Canada et le gouvernement du Québec* in Jaques-Yvan Morin, Francis Rigaldies and Daniel Turp, eds., *Droit international public: Notes et documents*, t. 2, 3ʳᵈ ed. (Montréal: Thémis, 1997) at 462, Doc. No. 114A.

[532] New Brunswick was also recognized a similar status in 1977. See Organisation internationale de la Francophonie, "Canada Nouveau-Brunswick", online: Organisation internationale de la Francophonie <http://www.francophonie.org/oif/pays/detail-pays.cfm?id=118>.

[533] Edward McWhinney, "Point de départ d'un dialogue fructueux" *Le Devoir* (12-13 July 2003) B5.

with "sovereignty".[534] Thus, it should not be controversial to say that provinces have attained a certain international personality.[535] This does not mean that they are *independent* or *"sovereign"*. It simply means that foreign states and other international actors interested in dealing with the provinces have recognized that provinces have a degree of internal and external autonomy in their decision-making processes that makes it both possible and desirable to directly engage with them as distinct international entities.[536] (2) The flipside of this is that the ways in which provinces portray themselves as potential international actors plays an important role in how other international actors will consider possible interactions with them.

It is in light of the practical need to engage with other governments and international actors, in order to successfully accomplish their domestic missions, that provinces have started engaging in international relations and have started portraying themselves as international actors. In the next two sections, I will give a brief overview of the current international activities of provinces as presented by the provinces themselves (II.B.1.) and the nature of the international agreements that they may conclude (II.B.2.).

1. The Self-Portraits of Provincial Involvement in International Relations

Provinces and territories have developed their own international policies and institutions to implement them. Thus, what I presented earlier as a brief overview of Québec's international activities[537] is not exceptional in the Canadian federation. This section will now simply paint a quick portrait of how provinces and territories[538] describe their own international practices. This should help in understanding that the domestication of international relations is not a mere abstraction but has a rather concrete impact on the ways provincial and territorial governments go about fulfilling their missions. It will also highlight the ways in which those institutions send an image of themselves to potential partners.[539]

---

[534] See section II.A.1.iv.

[535] A.L.C. de Mestral, "Le Québec et les relations internationales", *supra* note 41 at 219-223 and J.-Y. Morin, "La personnalité internationale du Québec" *supra* note 41 at 303.

[536] J.-Y. Morin, "La personnalité internationale du Québec", *ibid.* at 274.

[537] See *supra* note 42ff and accompanying text.

[538] See warning concerning "territories" at note 477.

[539] Obviously, these self-images are not still lifes; they are continually evolving. However, for the purposes of this essay, it appeared sufficient to highlight the vivacity of the diverse self-expressions of provinces and territories as evidenced by specific arte-

British Columbia's Intergovernmental Relations Secretariat has an "International Relations Section". That section "has overall responsibility for British Columbia's relations with international governments."[540] The government of British Columbia claims that "[t]he activities of this section are an acknowledgement by the provincial government of the strategic importance of sound international relations to the economy and the citizens of British Columbia."[541] Among the objectives of that branch, one finds:

To work across government in leading and co-ordinating the development of a strategic approach to British Columbia's international relations

To liaise with foreign governments, neighbouring U.S. States and other Canadian jurisdictions on issues pertaining to British Columbia's international relations

To support Ministries and Crown Corporations on specific international issues, particularly those spanning a number of government agencies

To support the Premier for international visits

To act as the principal liaison between the Province of British Columbia and the federal Department of Foreign Affairs and International Trade (DFAIT)

To assert a provincial role in international agreements and negotiations that have a direct impact upon British Columbia

To maintain co-operation and economic arrangements with various subnational entities around the world, such as Eastern Cape Province in South Africa

To maintain a dialogue with the United States (the western states in particular) on subjects of transportation, trade, environment, and other fields in order to foster international co-operative efforts

To promote the regional interests of BC by maintaining a provincial presence as a member of the Pacific North West Economic Region (PNWER), the Council of State Governments (West), the Western Governors' Association, and other regional organisations which offer a framework for ongoing regional co-operation and interaction[542]

---

facts relating to their external self-image, which they produced at a specific point in time in the early 21st century. The specific activities in which each province and territory are engaged in are not as important as the variety of such activities taken as a whole and the active self-representations manifested by all of those institutions. (The information for this section was first gathered in December 2005 and was updated in early April 2007.)

[540] British Columbia, Intergovernmental Relations Secretariat, "International Section", online: Government of British Columbia <http://www.gov.bc.ca/igrs/prgs/#inter>.

[541] *Ibid.*

[542] *Ibid.*

As it is clear from this language, British Columbia considers those efforts as "pertaining to British Columbia's international relations".[543] The same perspective is adopted by just about every province.[544]

Alberta has a Minister of International and Intergovernmental Relations whose mission is to "[a]dvanc[e] Alberta's interests internationally by building strategic relationships with governments outside of Canada."[545] The government of Alberta does maintain direct contact with foreign governments[546] and has an office in Washington co-located in the Canadian embassy.[547] Alberta has also developed "twinning" relations with fourteen regions or federated states abroad.[548]

Saskatchewan's Ministry of Government Relations has an "International Relations Branch" responsible "for the coordination, development and implementation of policies and programs for Saskatchewan's relations with foreign governments and international organizations."[549] In particular, that branch has the responsibility to:

> Lead in the development, negotiation and implementation of multi-sectoral international agreements; Develop, coordinate and implement the government's strategic framework for international relations, in collaboration with Departments/Agencies; Staff the Premier and Minister on missions abroad involving intergovernmental and multi-sectoral interests; Co-manage, with the Protocol Office, the province's International Visitors' Program; Manage the province's international development assistance initiatives; and, Provide

---

[543] *Ibid.*

[544] As we will see below, only Prince Edward Island is more vague on the issue. The government talks about both national and regional relations. Those regional relations include collaborations with the New England Governors. See Prince Edward Island, Executive Council Office, "Intergovernmental Affairs", online: Government of Prince Edward Island <http://www.gov.pe.ca/eco/ia-info/index.php3> [Prince Edward Island, "Intergovernmental Affairs"].

[545] Alberta, Ministry of International and Intergovernmental Relations, "Our Mission – International Relations", online: Government of Alberta <http://www.iir.gov.ab.ca/international_relations/our_mission.asp>.

[546] See Alberta, *Framework for Alberta's International Strategies* (Edmonton: Alberta International and Intergovernmental Relations, 2000) reproduced online: Government of Alberta <http://www.iir.gov.ab.ca/international_relations/pdfs/3.1.1-%20AB_International_Strategies.pdf>.

[547] Alberta, Ministry of International and Intergovernmental Relations, "Alberta Washington Office", online: Government of Alberta <http://www.iir.gov.ab.ca/international_relations/alberta_washington_office.asp>.

[548] Alberta, Ministry of International and Intergovernmental Relations, "Twinning Relations", online: Government of Alberta <http://www.iir.gov.ab.ca/international_relations/twinning_relations.asp>.

[549] Saskatchewan, Government Relations, "Intergovernmental Affairs", online: Government of Saskatchewan <http://www.gr.gov.sk.ca/intergovernmental.htm>.

strategic and operational advice and support to other Departments/Agencies in pursuit of their international interests.[550]

Manitoba's international relations strategy is developed in a governmental document entitled "Reaching Beyond Our Borders: The Framework For Manitoba's International Activities".[551] Manitoba identified as a key goal of her strategy the creation of

> ... opportunities for the involvement of the Province's partners in creating a fully integrated and coordinated approach to international activities. The Province will work with advisory bodies, Crown Corporations, Manitoba's business community, educational institutions, non-government organizations, the Government of Canada, and Manitoba's municipalities to position Manitoba on the international stage.[552]

Up until September 2006, Manitoba had a Department of Intergovernmental Affairs and Trade whose Minister was also responsible for International Relations Co-ordination. That Department, among other things, "participate[s] in strategic partnerships with private sector and non-government organizations and intergovernmental alliances."[553] In November 2003, the government of Manitoba created a "Federal-Provincial and International Relations and Trade Division" in the Department of Intergovernmental Affairs and Trade "to coordinate resources and expertise in international relations and business development" and to coordinate the implementation of her "Reaching Beyond Our Borders" strategy.[554] Among the core functions of this Division were to

> ... coordinat[e], monito[r] and repor[t] on the international activities undertaken by provincial departments. This branch works with other departments to provide strategic policy advice, analysis and support to manage relationships with the United States and other international jurisdictions and fosters strong, positive, and cooperative relationships with key international partners. The branch supports the Province's involvement with the Western Governors' Association, the Legislators' Forum, the Midwestern Legislative Conference of the Council of State Governments, and bilateral relationships

---

[550] *Ibid.*

[551] Manitoba, Reaching Beyond Our Borders: The Framework For Manitoba's International Activities, online: Government of Manitoba <http://www.gov.mb.ca/international/index.html> [Manitoba, Reaching Beyond Our Borders: The Framework For Manitoba's International Activities].

[552] *Ibid.*

[553] Manitoba, Intergovernmental Affairs and Trade, "Role and Mandate", online: Government of Manitoba <http://www.gov.mb.ca/ia/aboutus/mandate.html>.

[554] Manitoba, *Reaching Beyond Our Borders: The Framework For Manitoba's International Activities*, "Objective One: Ensure a Strategic & Corporate Approach", online: Government of Manitoba <http://www.gov.mb.ca/international/objective1.html>.

with individual states. This branch also houses the International Projects Initiative that coordinates the Province's involvement in international development projects and helps our local firms to bid successfully on them.[555]

With the Cabinet shuffle of September 2006, Mr. Scott Smith, who had been Minister of Intergovernmental Affairs and Trade, was appointed to the newly created Department of Competitiveness, Training and Trade.[556] This Department is now in charge of carrying the "Reaching Beyond Our Borders" strategy.

One of the divisions in Ontario's Ministry of Intergovernmental Affairs is the Office of International Relations and Protocol (OIRP). The OIRP is responsible for leading

> ... the conduct of Ontario's relations with foreign jurisdictions, and co-ordinates official government events and ceremonies. It provides advice and service to the Premier, the Minister, other ministers and the Lieutenant Governor. OIRP works to advance Ontario's international objectives, which are principally economic, by building and supporting Ontario's relations with foreign jurisdictions, Foreign Affairs Canada and Canadian foreign missions, the diplomatic and consular corps, and non-government organizations with international activities.[557]

The Ministry of Economic Development and Trade has established "International Marketing Centres" (IMCs) that are co-located in various Canadian diplomatic and consular missions. There are IMCs in London, Los Angeles, Munich, New Delhi, New York, Shanghai and Tokyo.[558] Ontario also offers the services of "In-market Trade Development Consultants" to help Ontario exporters develop markets in Brazil, Chile and Mexico.[559] It should however be noted that Ontario's websites are very quiet about her international involvements. For example, one has to go to the Ministry of Natural Resources' website and click on "Protecting Great Lakes Basin Waters"[560] to learn that Ontario is a participating

---

[555] *Ibid.*

[556] Government of Manitoba, News Release, "Infrastructure And Economic Competitiveness Focus Of New Cabinet: Doer" (21 September 2006) online: Government of Manitoba < http://www.gov.mb.ca/chc/press/top/2006/09/2006-09-21-05.html>.

[557] Ontario, Ministry of Intergovernmental Affairs, "About the Ministry", online: Government of Ontario <http://www.mia.gov.on.ca/english/about/aboutmia_en.html>.

[558] Ontario, Ministry of Economic Development and Trade, "International Marketing Centres", online: Government of Ontario < http://www.ontarioexports.com/oei/ redirect.jsp?page=English/Target_Your_Market/IMC.html>.

[559] Ontario, Ministry of Economic Development and Trade, "In-Market Support", online: Government of Ontario <http://www.ontarioexports.com/oei/redirect.jsp?page= English/Target_Your_Market/Ontario_Abroad.html>.

[560] Ontario, Ministry of Natural Resources, "About the Ministry of Natural Resources", online: Government of Ontario <http://www.mnr.gov.on.ca/MNR/>.

member to the very important intergovernmental water management regime put in place on the basis of the *Great Lakes Charter (1985)*,[561] the *Great Lakes Charter Annex (2001)*[562] and the *Great Lakes—St. Lawrence River Basin Sustainable Water Resources Agreement (2005)*.[563] The latter agreement provides for the creation of the Great Lakes—St. Lawrence River Basin Water Resources Regional Body, an innovative intergovernmental body responsible for overseeing the implementation of the agreement.[564] Premier McGuinty has been appointed chair of that body for 2007.[565] When one digs a bit more, one finds that Ontario and Québec are also "associate members" of the Great Lakes Commission composed of eight American states, Québec and Ontario.[566] The relative silence that Ontario displays about her international activities might be in part explained by the important reduction of her involvement in the world with the dismantlement, in the 1990s, of Ontario's network of bureaus abroad. But it might also be seen as an indicator of her degree of satisfaction with the work done by the federal government in defending her interests. Obviously, times have changed for Ontario since the *Labour Conventions* case.

While all provinces and territories are actively and explicitly engaged in the realm of international relations, it is mainly Québec's actions that have been the focus of most of the political and scholarly attention in the last forty years. This is in part because Québec has been the most outspoken province about her international relations since the 1960s. However, Québec's activities abroad started much earlier than that, as the *Ministère des Relations internationales* reminds us:

---

[561] *The Great Lakes Charter*, Illinois, Indiana, Michigan, Minnesota, New York, Ohio, Ontario, Québec, Pennsylvania and Wisconsin, 11 February 1985, Council of Great Lakes Governors, online: <http://www.cglg.org/projects/water/docs/GreatLakes Charter.pdf>.

[562] *The Great Lakes Charter Annex: A Supplementary Agreement to The Great Lakes Charter*, Illinois, Indiana, Michigan, Minnesota, New York, Ohio, Ontario, Québec, Pennsylvania and Wisconsin, 18 June 2001, Council of Great Lakes Governors, online: < http://www.cglg.org/projects/water/docs/GreatLakesCharterAnnex.pdf>.

[563] *Great Lakes—St. Lawrence River Basin Sustainable Water Resources Agreement*, Illinois, Indiana, Michigan, Minnesota, New York, Ohio, Ontario, Québec, Pennsylvania and Wisconsin, 13 December 2005, online: Council of Great Lakes Governors < http://www.cglg.org/projects/water/docs/12-13-05/Great_Lakes-St_Lawrence_ River_Basin_Sustainable_Water_Resources_Agreement.pdf>.

[564] *Ibid.*, ss. 400-401.

[565] Ontario, Ministry of Natural Resources, "Great Lakes-St. Lawrence River Basin Sustainable Water Resources Agreement", online: Government of Ontario <http://www.mnr.gov.on.ca/mnr/water/greatlakes/index.html#PGL>.

[566] Great Lake Commission des Grands Lacs, "Associate Members", online: < Great Lake Commission des Grands Lacs http://www.glc.org/about/associate.html>.

In 1871, Québec began sending immigration officers to the United Kingdom, continental Europe and the United States. From 1880 to 1883, Québec's representative in London also provided assistance to Québec exporters. In 1882, the government appointed Hector Fabre as its agent-general in Paris to act as "the accredited representative of the government of Quebec for all negotiations falling within the jurisdiction of the province." The appointment came with a broad mandate, relatively clear instructions and a high level of responsibility, since Hector Fabre reported directly to the Premier of Québec. Québec appointed an agent-general to London in 1911 and then to Brussels three years later. In 1940, the *Act respecting the Agents-General for the Province* provided for appointments "to all countries and all places in the Dominion and abroad." Its goal was to promote Québec's development through exports, immigration, tourism, investment from abroad, and relations with financial markets. Under this Act, the government appointed an agent-general to New York City in 1943. Since June 1940, the appointee had held the post of Secretary at Québec's Trade and Tourism Bureau in New York.[567]

Morevover, as we saw in the introduction, Québec has not been sitting on her hands since the 1960s either. Willing to reaffirm its traditional positions and to clarify its new objectives and strategies, the Québec government released in 2006 an important policy document entitled "Working in Concert", in which it reminds the readers that

> Québec ... considers itself enabled to exercise the external attributes of the functions it exercises internally. Over the years, it has put into place the appropriate legal and institutional instruments to those ends. It has mandated the *Ministère des Relations internationales* to lead the Government's international initiatives, coordinate the actions of departments and agencies in this regard, manage a network of representatives abroad, as well as negotiate and enforce international agreements.

> Today, Québec has nearly thirty delegations, offices, and local representatives in eighteen countries. More than 300 bilateral agreements are now in effect with the national governments and federated states of nearly 80 countries. The Government of Québec is a participating member of La Francophonie and carefully monitors the work of international organizations in matters regarding its jurisdiction and interests.[568]

Among other things, Québec's "Working in Concert" recognizes the impact that an increasing number of international instruments have on

---

[567] Québec, *Ministère des Relations internationales*, "Legal and Historical Foundations" (August 2006) 2 Québec's International Initiatives 1 at 3; online: Gouvernement du Québec <http://www.mri.gouv.qc.ca/en/pdf/action_internationale2.pdf>.

[568] Québec, Ministère des Relations internationales, Québec's International Policy: Working in Concert (Québec: Ministère des Relations internationales, 2006) at 5; online: Gouvernement du Québec <http://www.mri.gouv.qc.ca/en/pdf/Politique.pdf>.

the government of Québec's capacity to make collective choices, and the concomitant need to participate in the decision-making processes that lead to the creation of such instruments.[569] It also acknowledges, among other things, that Québec's economy depends a great deal on foreign trade,[570] that new security concerns necessitate increased collaboration among different jurisdictions,[571] that the promotion of Québec's culture and identity requires the capacity to "reach out to the world",[572] and that Québec can contribute to the "cause of international solidarity".[573] In light of this, the government of Québec wants to increase its participation in different international organisations[574] and in the negotiations of international, regional and bilateral agreements that affect its interests.[575] It also wishes to build stronger ties with other federated states and regions[576] and to "create a greater synergy" with the organised groups of the civil society in Québec that are active internationally.[577]

"The Province of New Brunswick", unsurprisingly, "is increasingly involved in international activities."[578] Her Department of Intergovernmental Relations is divided into many branches. The International Relations unit, for example, "facilitates inter-departmental coordination of the Province's international activities with the aim of focusing efforts towards the Province's strategic interests and achieving a higher level of presence and success in the global community."[579] One of the ways in which that unit advances those goals is by providing "guidelines and support to departments and agencies of the Province in negotiations and implementation of bilateral and multilateral arrangements with international partners."[580] New Brunswick is also quite involved in the "Organisation internationale de la francophonie". There is a division of the Department of Intergovernmental Relations, called the "Francophonie and Official Languages Branch" (FOLB), which is specifically respon-

---

[569] *Ibid.* at 27.

[570] For example, the policy paper highlights the fact that 52.8% of Québec's GDP is due to exports (*ibid.* at 43). See, in general, *ibid.* at 41-63.

[571] *Ibid.* at 65-77.

[572] *Ibid.* at 6, 79-89.

[573] *Ibid.* at 91, 93-101.

[574] *Ibid.* at 28-30.

[575] *Ibid.* at 30-35.

[576] *Ibid.* at 36.

[577] *Ibid.* at 37.

[578] New Brunswick, Department of Intergovernmental Affairs, "International Relations": Government of New Brunswick <http://www.gnb.ca/0056/International/index-e.asp>.

[579] *Ibid.*

[580] *Ibid.*

sible for the coordination and promotion of the activities of the New Brunswick government within the provincial, Canadian, and international Francophonie.[581]

In December 2005, Nova Scotia's Department of Intergovernmental Affairs presented itself as being "responsible for coordinating the Province's relations with the Federal government, other Provinces and Territories and *foreign governments at the national and subnational levels.*"[582] One of the self-proclaimed goals of that Department is to "Expand Nova Scotia's international linkages to support and promote Nova Scotia's interests abroad."[583]

Newfoundland and Labrador's "Intergovernmental Affairs Secretariat" is "responsible for the coordination of all policies, programs and activities of the Government of Newfoundland and Labrador in relation to *other sovereign governments.*"[584] Among other things, it "takes lead responsibility for the development of provincial policy in matters which do not fall under the responsibility of other departments (including defence, regional development, and foreign affairs)".[585]

---

[581] New Brunswick, Department of Intergovernmental Affairs, "Francophonie/Offical Languages": Government of New Brunswick <http://www.gnb.ca/0056/Francophonie/index-e.asp>.

[582] Nova Scotia, Department of Intergovernmental Affairs, "Welcome to the Department of Intergovernmental Affairs", online: Government of Nova Scotia <http://www.gov.ns.ca/iga/> (emphasis added); archived online at Internet Archive, *Wayback Machine*, online: Internet Archive <http://web.archive.org/web/20051228064032/http://www.gov.ns.ca/iga/>. As of 18 April 2007, the Department of Intergovernmental Affairs website (Nova Scotia, Department of Intergovernmental Affairs, "Welcome to the Department of Intergovernmental Affairs", online: Government of Nova Scotia <http://www.gov.ns.ca/iga/>) read: "IGA coordinates the Province's relations with federal, provincial and territorial governments as well as with *other* governments" (emphasis added), thus dropping the specification about the nature of those "other" governments (i.e. "foreign governments at the national and subnational levels").

[583] Nova Scotia, Department of Intergovernmental Affairs, "About Us", online: Government of Nova Scotia <http://www.gov.ns.ca/iga/aboutus.htm>.

[584] Newfoundland & Labrador, Intergovernmental Affairs Secretariat, "Overview", online: Government of Newfoundland & Labrador <http://www.exec.gov.nl.ca/exec/iga/iga-ovr.htm> (emphasis added).

[585] *Ibid.* Since s. 91 (7) of the *Constitution Act, 1867* gives Parliament powers over "Militia, Military and Naval Service, and Defence", reference to the latter might seem surprising in a list of tasks of a provincial authority. However, this is a good example where provinces might have an interest in dialoguing and negotiating with the federal government. The provincial departments' activity on defence matters is described in the following way by Newfoundland and Labrador: "in consultation with other provincial departments and agencies, Intergovernmental Affairs coordinates discussion with military officials and local representatives related to planning issues and provincial interests. In recent years, defense activity has focused upon flight training by allied forces in Goose Bay" (*ibid.*)

And in Prince Edward Island, where the population is of about 138 000 habitants,[586] the Premier is also the "Minister Responsible for Intergovernmental Affairs",[587] whose responsibility is to "ensure that the province's interests are represented in national and regional policy discussions."[588] Among the tasks given to the staff of this department, we find the following:

- coordinating and/or preparing briefing materials required for meetings such as First Ministers Meetings, Annual Premiers Conferences, Council of Atlantic Premiers, New England Governors and Eastern Canadian Premiers;
- advancing and promoting the Province's interests in regional discussions, initiatives and agreements;
- developing and implementing the Action Plan for Atlantic Regional Cooperation and New England Governors-Eastern Canadian Premiers resolutions ...

So even the smallest province in Canada is actively involved with outside partners.

It is worth noting that "territories" – while their constitutional statuses do not raise the same issues as that of the provinces – are also engaged in one form or another of international relations. For example, Yukon's Executive Council Office "works to build strong "government-to-government" relationships between the Yukon and Yukon First Nation governments, and to foster effective relations with the governments of Canada, the provinces and territories, and with other circumpolar jurisdictions such as the State of Alaska."[589] In 2006, the government of the Northwest Territory relied on its "Intergovernmental Relations and Strategic Planning" division, to "develo[p], promot[e] and maintai[n]" "relations with federal, provincial, territorial, Aboriginal and international governments".[590] Changes were recently brought to the

---

[586] As of July 1, 2005, Prince Edward Island's preliminary data indicated that the population was 138, 113. See Prince Edward Island, Provincial Treasury (Economics, Statistics and Federal Fiscal Division), *32nd Statistical Review 2005* (Prince Edward Island: Document Publishing Center, 2006) at 6; reproduced at Government of Prince Edward Island, online: Annual Statistical Review <http://www.gov.pe.ca/photos/original/32annualreview.pdf>.

[587] Prince Edward Island, Executive Council Office, "Members of the Executive Council", online: Government of Prince Edward Island <http://www.gov.pe.ca/eco/>.

[588] Prince Edward Island, Executive Council Office, Intergovernmental Affairs, online: Government of Prince Edward Island <http://www.gov.pe.ca/eco/ia-info/index.php3>.

[589] Yukon, Executive Council Office, "Executive Council Office", online: Government of Yukon <http://www.gov.yk.ca/depts/eco/index.html>.

[590] Northwest Territories, Department of the Executive, "Department of the Executive", online: Government of the Northwest Territories <http://www.executive.gov.nt.ca/>; archived online at Internet Archive, *Wayback Machine*, online: Internet Archive <http://web.archive.org/web/20051231153516/http://www.executive.gov.nt.ca/>.

structure of the Northwest Territories' government, which created a new Department of Aboriginal Affairs and Intergovernmental Relations. Among other things, it "is responsible for managing the government's relationships with federal, provincial and territorial governments and with circumpolar countries in all matters of intergovernmental significance."[591] Finally, in Nunavut, the "Intergovernmental Affairs Division of the Executive is responsible for the management and development of government strategies, policies and initiatives relating to federal, provincial, territorial, circumpolar and aboriginal affairs."[592]

From this overview one can draw a straightforward conclusion: gone are the days (if they ever existed) when provinces and territories could simply act locally to accomplish their domestic mandates, without caring about what might be going on outside of their borders. Now, provinces and territories actively portray themselves as international actors and they find willing counterparts ready to recognize them as potential partners and interested in engaging in mutually beneficial actions.[593] In short, provinces need to deal with international partners, they officially recognize that need, and they find willing partners to satisfy this need.

2. The Legality of Provincial International Involvements and Treaty-Making

i. At Canadian Constitutional Law

As we have seen earlier, the text of the Canadian constitution is silent about either federal or provincial treaty-making powers. However, as we have also seen, treaty-making is a prerogative of the Crown.[594] Therefore, for provinces to possess treaty-making powers, they must possess them through the Crown's prerogatives.

R. J. Delisle opposed the idea that provinces could have inherited the prerogative to make treaties. He wrote:

> The position of provincial Lieutenant-Governors precludes the possibility of the prerogative power being delegated to them. They are appointed not by

---

[591] Northwest Territories, Department of Aboriginal Affairs and Intergovernmental Relations, "Intergovernmental Relations", online: Government of the Northwest Territories <http://www.daair.gov.nt.ca/who-we-are/intergovernmental-relations.html>.

[592] Nunavut, Executive and Intergovernmental Affairs, "Intergovernmental Affairs", online: Government of Nunavut <http://www.gov.nu.ca/Nunavut/English/ departments/ EIA/ia.shtml>.

[593] For a detailed overview of the collaboration channels developed by provinces and territories with American institutions, see CSPS, *Building Cross-Border Links: A Compendium of Canada-US Government Collaboration*, *supra* note 502 at 155-217.

[594] See I.D.1..

the Sovereign but by the Governor-General-in-Council by instrument under the Great seal of Canada.[595] They are removable by the Governor-General and their salaries are fixed and provided by the parliament of Canada. There is no direct contact with the Sovereign and, therefore, the Royal Prerogative of treaty-making cannot directly descend upon them by any delegation through Letter Patent or usage.[596]

In short, Delisle claimed that the Lieutenant-Governors are the instruments of the Governor-General.

But all this is to forget the Privy Council's opinions in the *Liquidators of the Maritime Bank of Canada,*[597] in *Re The Initiative and Referendum Act*[598] and in *Hodge v. R.*[599] Most importantly, this line of arguments was explicitly rejected by the Supreme Court of Canada about twenty years before Delisle made his claims. It is worth quoting at length here the very important statement made by the Supreme Court of Canada in 1948:

> As a consequence of these judicial pronouncements, the nature of the federal and provincial legislative and executive powers is clearly settled, and a Lieutenant-Governor, who "carries on the Government of the Province", manifestly does not act in respect of the Government of Canada. All the functions he performs are directed to the affairs of the Province and are in

---

[595] I note that a similar point was made by B. Laskin, "The Provinces and International Agreements", *supra* note 40 at 108 to suggest that only the federal government may have powers over foreign affairs.

[596] R. J. Delisle, "Treaty-Making Power in Canada", *supra* note 319 at 132 (footnotes omitted).

[597] *Liquidators of the Maritime Bank, supra* note 23:

> There is no constitutional anomaly in an executive officer of the Crown receiving his appointment at the hands of a governing body who have no powers and no functions except as representatives of the Crown. The act of the Governor General and his Council in making the appointment is, within the meaning of the statute, the act of the Crown; and a Lieutenant-Governor, when appointed, is as much the representative of Her Majesty for all purposes of provincial government as the Governor General himself is for all purposes of Dominion government.

[598] *In re The Initiative and Referendum Act, supra* note 233 at 942:

> [t]he scheme of the Act passed in 1867 was thus, not to weld the Provinces into one, nor to subordinate Provincial Governments to a central authority, but to establish a central government in which these Provinces should be represented, entrusted with exclusive authority only in affairs in which they had a common interest. Subject to this each Province was to retain its independence and autonomy and to be directly under the Crown as its head. Within these limits of area and subjects, its local Legislature, so long as the Imperial Parliament did not repeal its own Act conferring this status, was to be supreme, and had such powers as the Imperial Parliament possessed in the plenitude of its own freedom before it handed them over to the Dominion and the Provinces, in accordance with the scheme of distribution which it enacted in 1867.

[599] *Hodge v. R., supra* note 14 and opinion quoted thereof.

no way connected with the Government of Canada, and it is the functions that he performs that must be examined in order to determine the nature of his office. ...

It has been argued that the Honourable Mr. Carroll came within the provision of the Act, because he was appointed by the Governor General in Council, and because his salary was paid out of the Consolidated Fund of Canada. The Governor General in Council is of course the instrumentality through which, in view of the *B.N.A. Act*, a Lieutenant-Governor is appointed to represent directly His Majesty. And the Dominion Government is also, under a provision of the same Act, obligated to pay the salary of the Lieutenant-Governor. But I fail to see how this can affect the nature of the functions performed. That the Lieutenant-Governor is appointed and paid by the Dominion, does not alter the essentially provincial character of his office, which is to carry on the Government of the Province.

The additional provisions of the Constitution, namely, that the Lieutenant-Governor receives instructions from the Governor General, that bills may be reserved for the signification of the Governor General's pleasure, that an Act that has been sanctioned, may be disallowed by the Governor General in Council, and finally that the Lieutenant-Governor may be removed from office by the same authority, have I think, no important signification.[600]

Those cases not only made it clear that provinces enjoyed Crown prerogatives, but confirmed that those prerogative powers are not "delegated" to them but are instead "first-hand" prerogatives.

Moreover, as we have seen, in Canada, the prerogatives follow the division of legislative jurisdictions. Whereas some might have doubted after the *Liquidators of the Maritime Bank of Canada*[601] whether that case had established a general principle or simply a rule applicable to the case at hand, the wide range of subsequent decisions restating the principle in the widest possible terms should have put those doubts to rest.[602]

Some authors, however, have attempted to argue that the foreign affairs prerogatives are different from others. For example, Gerald Morris has claimed that

... the treaty-making power is an integral part of the broader foreign affairs power and in actual practice it cannot be artificially separated from it. Nor can general responsibility for foreign affairs be divided up into watertight federal and provincial compartments on any sensible basis.[603]

---

[600] *Canada v. Carroll, supra* note 299 at 130-31.

[601] *Supra* note 23.

[602] See *supra* notes 299ff and accompanying text.

[603] G.R. Morris, "The Treaty-Making Power: A Canadian Dilemma", *supra* note 22 at 490.

While I do agree with Morris that treaty-making powers – being such an important tool in the foreign affairs toolkit – are hardly detachable from the capacity to engage in international relations, international experience as well as our own Canadian experience has shown that foreign affairs, to the extent that they are the external extension of internal governing tools, are indeed as divisible as internal matters.[604]

It is important to note here that the divisibility of the prerogatives in no way threatens the federal government's powers over defence since s. 91(7) of the *Constitution Act, 1867* provides Parliament with the exclusive powers over "Militia, Military and Naval Service, and Defence." But the "High Politics" of war and peace are no longer occupying the place that they used to in the everyday life of international relations; economic integration and transnational regulation of "domestic" issues have taken the prime place. That is indeed why, as we have seen, provinces have for decades engaged in a variety of diplomatic relations to fulfill their own domestic missions. Diplomacy, like treaty powers, is not, *in se*, within federal plenary and exclusive jurisdiction.

In light of this, there are simply no constitutional reasons for denying provinces prerogative powers to make treaties.

ii. At International Law

As we saw earlier, the *Vienna Convention on the Law of Treaties*[605] provides at Art. 6 that every "state" possesses the capacity to conclude treaties, and federated states satisfy that requirement.[606] To the extent that foreign states rely on Canadian constitutional law to determine if provinces have the power to conclude treaties, it should be more clearly acknowledged that provinces do have the capacity to conclude treaties with those foreign states.

However, while most states officially rely on the constitutional rules applicable to federated states to determine their international capacity to conclude international agreements, it is important to note that those foreign states will, to a large degree, consider the federated states' practical capacities to commit themselves. States do not conclude agreements for their mere pleasure; they do so because they believe that those agreements will advance their interests. The flipside of this is that even if federated states did not count as "states" for the purposes of the *Vienna Convention on the Law of Treaties*, certain states might still be

---

[604] See, section II.A.2.ii. See also G. van Ert, "The Legal Character of Provincial Agreements with Foreign Governments", *supra* note 321 at 1112 and G. van Ert, *Using International Law in Canadian Courts, supra* note 41 at 82-83.

[605] *Vienna Convention on the Law of Treaties, supra* note 447.

[606] See section II.A.1.iv.

willing to conclude agreements with them if they consider that such agreements will further their interests. International law would not oppose it. We have to remember that Art. 3 a) of the *Vienna Convention on the Law of Treaties* clearly specifies that it does not affect the legal validity of any other international agreements concluded between a state and any other subject of international law. Thus, the *Vienna Convention on the Law of Treaties* is not meant to be exhaustive. This means that there could be treaties between international entities that are not "states" within the ambit of the *Vienna Convention on the Law of Treaties*. As we have seen earlier in section II.A.1.iv., there is little doubt that federated states could be considered international subjects. This is more concretely the case if a foreign state is willing to consider a federated state as an international subject for the purpose of concluding mutually beneficial agreements.

The fact that there might be treaties between states and other international entities should only be surprising to those who still imagine treaties as being the highly formal agreements between monarchs otherwise living in a quasi-state of nature mainly controlled by customs and force. Times have changed and the ontology of that international arena has changed as well. Monarchs are no longer the only actors inhabiting that space and the needs of all the actors occupying that space require much more than a rudimentary social contract of non-aggression. The *Vienna Convention on the Law of Treaties* recognized that. Additionally, it is important to remember that, for the purposes of the *Vienna Convention on the Law of Treaties*, a "treaty" "means an international agreement concluded between States in written form and governed by international law, whether embodied in a single instrument or in two or more related instruments and *whatever its particular designation*".[607] "Head of State" treaties are thus no longer the main treaties used in the international arena. The abandonment of "Head of State" treaties in favour of intergovernmental treaties reflects a change in the way we conceive the state and its roles. While in the past, a treaty represented the solemn accord between two or more sovereigns to settle *inter*-state issues, nowadays, international agreements deal with internal issues as much as they deal with external issues, if not more. In fact, the primary function of the vast majority of international agreements is no longer to set up and maintain *the conditions for internal governance* by protecting polities from external interventions; the bulk of international agreements are now meant to be, *by themselves, instruments of governance*. That shift explains in part why international law as a whole has evolved from

---

[607] *Vienna Convention on the Law of Treaties, supra* note 447, Art. 2§1(a) (emphasis added.)

a system mostly based on custom to a system embodied in treaties.[608] This is not to say however, as some "hyperglobalisationists" would have it, that agreements of the traditional sort are disappearing. They are not. But it is to say that they no longer constitute the object of the majority of international negotiations. And since international agreements are no longer used primarily to seal the peace but rather to make all sorts of functional arrangements, this also helps to explain the general trend in international law to move away from treaty formalism, towards the use of a multitude of more flexible instruments to facilitate and institutionalize functional agreements between a variety of governing institutions. In that context, treaty formalism is considered more of a hindrance to the ability of governments to take concerted actions effectively to accomplish their missions.

It is against the backdrop of the changes in international law that I have just presented that I would like to lay out additional arguments in favour of recognizing that agreements between a province and a foreign state can be "treaties".

a. Cooperation, Incentive Structures and Bindingness
   at International Law

International relations are now a necessary aspect of any state's governance. Because our modern means of communication and transportation have increased our mobility, and because our economies are subject to evermore integrative forces, traditional domestic issues increasingly contain transnational aspects. That is the main reason why Canadian provinces have made intergovernmental agreements – both inside and outside Canada – on issues such as "economic cooperation, cultural relations, family maintenance orders, succession duties, the environment",[609] and other such areas of regulation affected by transnational factors. For example, agreements ensuring mutual assistance in the administration of securities laws – a matter of provincial jurisdiction[610] – have proven necessary since, as the Supreme Court of Canada recently noted, "[t]here can be no disputing the indispensable nature of inter-

---

[608] Over 158,000 treaties or international agreements entered into by Members of the United Nations since the entry into force of the UN Charter (Dec. 14th, 1946) have been registered with the Secretariat. See United Nations, United Nation Treaty Series, "Overview", online: United Nations <http://untreaty.un.org/English/overview.asp>.

[609] G. van Ert, *Using International Law in Canadian Courts*, *supra* note 41 at 72 (footnotes omitted.)

[610] *Smith v. R.*, [1960] S.C.R. 776; *Multiple Access Ltd. v. McCutcheon*, [1982] 2 S.C.R. 161; *Global Securities Corp. v. British Columbia (Securities Commission)*, [2000] 1 S.C.R. 494 [*Global Securities Corp. v. British Columbia (Securities Commission)*]; *Lymburn v. Mayland*, [1932] 2 D.L.R. 6; *Gregory & Co. v. Quebec Securities Commission*, [1961] S.C.R. 584; *R. v. W. McKenzie Securities Ltd.*, (1966) 56 D.L.R. (2d) 56.

jurisdictional co-operation among securities regulators today."[611] The Court added:

> ... administrative arrangements between provinces and foreign authorities are quite common. Without commenting on the constitutionality of any of these arrangements, I would note simply that where, as here, there is a clearly dominant intraprovincial purpose, the mere fact that the province is co-operating with a foreign authority in the pursuit of that purpose will not change the law's pith and substance ... [612]

While validating the impugned statute, the Court held that "[o]btaining reciprocal cooperation and uncovering violations abroad are both aspects of the Commission's mandate, which fits easily within s. 92(13)."[613]

But for there to be *cooperation*, the instruments produced by the contracting parties will often need to contain more than mere predictions of what the parties will do in specified circumstances. In other words, such agreements will often have to be understood as true commitments in order to be effective. And that is because of the different forms of "collective action problems" that such agreements are trying to solve. Among those problems, there are those that arise from the difficulty of coordinating actions simultaneously, and others that arise from the difficulty of ensuring iterated cooperation over an extended period of time. Those different problems will call for different solutions.

In that sense, it is true that informative statements about what other players will do in specific future circumstances help to *coordinate* reciprocal actions by creating a focal point around which players can adjust their behaviour. In a classic coordination problem, it matters more to the players that everyone chooses an identical strategy, than what that specific strategy is. A good example of a coordination problem concerns the choice of the side of the road on which cars should be driving. If we assume that there are no intrinsic reasons for choosing one side over another, that is, that there are no reasons for preferring driving on one side or another apart from the behaviour of the other drivers, the problem becomes one of coordinating everyone's individual choice to avoid frontal crashes and to ensure the efficient use of the road.[614] In such

---

[611] *Global Securities Corp. v. British Columbia (Securities Commission)*, *ibid.* at para. 27. The Court also cited Elizabeth R. Edinger, "The Constitutional Validity of Provincial Mutual Assistance Legislation: *Global Securities v. British Columbia (Securities Commission)*" (1999) 33 U.B.C. L. Rev. 169 at 176.

[612] *Global Securities Corp. v. British Columbia (Securities Commission)*, *ibid.* at para. 38.

[613] *Ibid.* at para. 44.

[614] Obviously, this factual assumption may prove to be false. There might be physiological reasons to favour one side of the road to the other. For example, empirical experiments might one day demonstrate that the brain of most drivers is hardwired to react

circumstances, receiving information about the focal point should be sufficient for rational players to fall into line, since coordinating will bring about the biggest payoff for each one of them. In effect, in such situation, if one player does not act according to the coordinated solution, every player loses, including the defector. Thus, there are cases where it is true that parties might not want to be bound by any obligation but merely want to exchange information about the future behaviour of the players involved so as to adjust their own. But this particular case is far from covering all the possible contexts where cooperation is sought. Coordination is far from exhausting the range of problems that cooperation can address.

If we look at the mutual assistance agreement concerning securities regulation discussed above, one sees immediately that it does not fit into the simple coordination model. In effect, if we consider the United States Securities and Exchange Commission (S.E.C.)'s request in isolation from the future behaviour of its own or other players' behaviour, it could appear cheaper for British Columbia to simply ignore the request made by the S.E.C., than to go through the procedures necessary to provide the United States agency with the requested information. Contrary to the coordination problem illustrated above, here, British Columbia would increase – or at least not decrease – her payoff by not following the statement it gave about her future behaviour. Thus, to understand why British Columbia did go ahead with the request – and even fought Global Securities Corp. challenges up to the Supreme Court –, we need to have recourse to a wider range of models.

"Game theory"[615] has developed a series of models to analyse cooperation problems and examine ways to solve those problems. One such model is the famous "prisoner's dilemma"[616], in which there are four possible outcomes to a two player game: (1) if A cooperates, but B

---

more swiftly to fast-moving objects coming from the left side than from the right (or vice versa). Also, it must be noted that once the habit of driving on one side of the road has acquired a certain degree of automatism among drivers, quitting that habit constitutes a significant cost that will go against switching sides.

[615] This interdisciplinary field, developed at the confines of mathematics, economics and politics, grew out of the path-breaking 1944 book by John von Neumann and Oskar Morgenstern entitled *Theory of Games and Economic Behavior*. Princeton University Press recently released a new edition of that classic: John von Neumann and Oskar Morgenstern, *Theory of Games and Economic Behavior*, 60th anniversary ed., introduction by Harold Kuhn and afterword by Ariel Rubinstein (Princeton: Princeton University Press, 2004).

[616] We apparently owe the name of this non-zero sum game to the Princeton mathematics professor Albert William Tucker. However, the matrix itself was first introduced by Merrill Flood and Melvin Drescher of the RAND Corporation. See William Poundstone, *Prisoner's Dilemma* (New York: Doubleday, 1992) at 8, 116-119.

defects, B gets the highest possible payoff and A the lowest; (2) if B cooperates and A defects, we get the reverse result; (3) if A and B cooperate, they each get a bigger payoff than what cooperation paid in the previous two outcomes, but one that is lower than defection in the previous two outcomes; finally (4) if A and B defect, they each get a higher payoff than if they had been the only one to cooperate (as in the first two outcomes), but they each get a lower payoff than if they had both cooperated. This could be illustrated in the following matrix where each payoff is represented by a numeral:

	B cooperates	B defects
A cooperates	A (3), B (3)	A (0), B (5)
A defects	A (5), B (0)	A (1), B (1)

If this game is played only once (or if players know in advance how many rounds there will be) and there is no third party to enforce any promise that they may have made to each other before playing, both players will rationally opt for defection despite any cheap talk that they would have engaged in prior to the play. That is because they will want to maximise their minimal payoff. But the problem here is that the equilibrium lies at a point that is suboptimal for all participants.[617] In fact, A and B would be both better off if they could cooperate. So what players would like is to achieve full cooperation to obtain the highest possible payoff.

This model seems closer to the problem that British Columbia had to solve in relations to securities regulation. If the British Columbia Securities Commission and the S.E.C. cooperate, they will both achieve their respective objectives in a way that will offset the costs of making the agreement and of providing the securities information sought by the other player. But if only one cooperates, the cooperating party will have to pay for both the costs of making the agreement and of providing the information, without receiving anything in return, while the defecting party will have gained the same benefit as if both parties had actually cooperated but without paying for the costs of providing the information to the other player. Knowing this, both parties would rationally defect. If both parties defect, they only incur the costs of making the agreement and no one gains any benefit. But how could British Columbia ensure

---

[617] It is in fact at a suboptimal Pareto level. "Pareto optimization" happens when a reallocation of goods makes at least one individual better off without making any other individual worse off. A situation is "Pareto optimal" when no Pareto optimization is possible.

that the S.E.C. would cooperate so that they could both achieve their optimal payoffs?

The first part of the answer is to be found in the fact that international players are rarely engaged in one-shot games but are rather engaged in repeated games. While this makes no difference for the coordination problem discussed initially – that is, the fact that one drives one's car more than once does not change one's strategy –, it makes a big difference in this context. In *iterated* "prisoner's dilemma" types of situation when the number of games is not known in advance, it might actually become rational for all players to cooperate right from the start if they are playing with the right players. The reason is that the possibility of punishment in the following round will threaten to diminish the total payoffs of the defector. Thus, the two players receive high payoffs over the long term as long as they are both capable of resisting the short-term temptation to defect. For this to be the case, it is important that players do not know in advance the number of iterations of the game. In effect, if players know ahead of time the number of iterations of the game, they will no longer have reasons to cooperate in the last round since there will be no possibility of future retaliation; and since everyone should rationally defect in the last round, there will be no reasons not to defect in the second to last, and the same reasoning applies back up to the first round. The same reasoning applies moreover if one player can unilaterally put an end to the iterated game. In other words, in such situations as when a player does not intend or is not seen as intending to participate in the iterated game, cooperation will not be possible because future defection will be assumed. That is why, for cooperation to be possible, it is necessary for players to be convinced that others are taking part in the iterated game. In fact, the very issue of keeping the game going or not can itself be conceptualised as being part of a larger collective action problem. So how can players ensure that they can be taken seriously when they inform the other party that they truly intend to participate in an iterated game?

In the absence of a third-party enforcer in international relations, different mechanisms have been developed over time to ensure that promises could be made credible. The classic example is that of the monarchs who exchange sons to guarantee a Peace Treaty.[618] They make their

---

[618] This example is taken from Alan O. Sykes, "The Economics of Public International Law" (July 2004) U Chicago Law & Economics, Olin Working Paper No. 216, at 19-20, online: Social Science Research Network <http://ssrn.com/abstract=564383>. Thomas Schelling had mentioned hostage exchanges as a commitment device in a footnote to his article "An Essay on Bargaining" (1953) 46 American Economic Review 281 at 300 but we had to wait for Oliver E. Williamson to give us a more detailed examination of the use of "hostages" as a credible commitment device (see

promise credible by making defection more costly to their own eyes than any possible benefit they may reap from defecting. Today's equivalent strategy is bond posting. If governments do not necessarily post bonds in the form of hard cash when they want to cooperate with others, they do something functionally equivalent: they enlarge "the shadow of the future"[619] by explicitly recognizing their engagement and thereby putting their reputation as trustworthy partners on the line.[620] In other words, they can turn their cheap talk into something credible by "bond posting" their reputation through formal acknowledgment of their engagement. If a government defects, not only does it risk retaliation in the form of "tit for tat",[621] but the other government gains the capacity to damage one important asset of the defector: its reputation as a good partner. On the flipside, the readiness to grant to the other party such a power over one's important asset signals one's "low discount rate".[622] It is important for "good players" to signal their low discount rate in order to attract similar potential partners.

But for all this to happen, there must be an *agreement* and that agreement must be publicly known, otherwise the players' reputation has not been made vulnerable. In effect, one's reputation could not be tarnished by the fact of not abiding by something by which she or he was not publicly known to be bound to abide by.[623] In other words, the

---

Oliver E. Williamson, "Credible Commitments: Using Hostages to Support Exchange" (1983) 73 American Economic Review 519).

[619] The expression is taken from Robert Axelrod, *The Evolution of Cooperation* (New York: Basic Books, 1984) at 124. Axelrod uses that expression many times in his book.

[620] Because "reputation" is information about one's character as a game partner, it is highly valuable. The more a player has a good reputation for cooperation, the easier it might be to find willing partners to play with him. Thus, putting one's reputation on the line is a strong self-imposed deterrent against defection. That is why the willingness of the player to put such a valuable thing at the mercy of the other player also signals to them that he is committed to cooperate.

[621] "Tit for tat" is a classic strategy in iterated prisoner's dilemma games whereby one plays the same move as the other player played in the previous round: if the other player cooperated in the last round, one cooperates, if the other player defected, one defects in this round.

[622] The concept of "discount rate" corresponds to the value attributed by an agent to future utility as opposed to present utility. An agent with a "low discount rate" is an agent that does not discount much the value of future utility as opposed to present one. The opposite, an agent with a high discount rate is an agent for which the present utility is worth much more than a future one. The highest the discount rate of an agent, the highest is the possibility for that agent to defect for a short-term benefit.

[623] The analysis as to whether or not a player intended to be bound is contextual. Each instrument must be examined on a case by case basis independently from "its particular designation" (*Vienna Convention on the Law of Treaties, supra* note 447, Art.1

agreement must be thought to create *valid obligations*. Thus, these formal and public engagements increase the costs of defecting to a point that might make it more expensive to defect than to cooperate (in that sense, it restricts the possible actions of a short-term utility-maximiser) and signal to other possible partners that the players have a low discount rate, manifest in that they accept to post bond with their partners through the acceptation of obligations.

But logically, for an *obligation* to arise, something more than the mere acts of will of the partners is necessary: there needs to be a secondary rule recognizing that these types of promises give rise to obligations. Otherwise, the mutual promises remain simple predictions about the players' future acts. H.L.A. Hart summarized that point nicely when he wrote:

> ... in order that words, spoken or written, should in certain circumstances function as a promise, agreement, or treaty, and so give rise to obligations and confer rights which others may claim, *rules* must already exist providing that a state is bound to do whatever it undertakes by appropriate words to do. Such rules presupposed in the very notion of a self-imposed obligation obviously cannot derive *their* obligatory status from a self-imposed obligation to obey them.[624]

Because we are talking about agreements between distinct international subjects that may not otherwise be subjected to the same "domestic law", the secondary rules that create those obligations are thus of an international character.

Thus, binding oneself does not necessarily mean diminishing one's capacity. In fact, it can be quite the opposite. While on the face of it, constraints are limits imposed on one's action, certain constraints can in fact prove capacity-enhancing.[625] As we have just seen, international agreements may bring the benefits of cooperation, which would not be otherwise available. But a party will not necessarily be ready to convey to another a benefit unless that first party can be reasonably assured that the other party will hold its end of the bargain. Thus, the ability to

---

(1)) Thus, whatever the agreement is called, the decisive factor should be the intention of the parties in determining whether it has a binding effect.

[624] H.L.A. Hart, *The Concept of Law, supra* note 384 at 225.

[625] There are many ways in which constraints can prove to be capacity-enhancing. Different forms of constraints can work to overcome passions, self-interest, hyperbolic discounting of future gains, or strategic time-inconsistency, and can be used to neutralize preference changes over time. See the two classics by Jon Elster on the topic: Jon Elster, *Ulysses and the Sirens: Studies in Rationality and Irrationality*, rev. ed. (Cambridge (U.K.): Cambridge University Press, 1984) and Jon Elster, *Ulysses Unbound: Studies in Rationality, Precommitment, and Constraints* (Cambridge (U.K.): Cambridge University Press, 2000).

commit oneself and to offer some guarantees of such commitment are often necessary to be taken seriously by would-be partners. Thus, the capacity to *effectively* commit oneself enhances one's capacity to obtain the benefits of cooperation.[626] Provinces do need these benefits in our current world order.

The function of binding agreements in international cooperation is the reason why many agreements have to be more than mere information about what one will do in future circumstances. As Paul Gérin-Lajoie rhetorically asked in his famous speech pronounced in 1965 before the Consular Corps in Montréal: "Une entente n'est-elle pas conclue dans le but essentiel d'être appliquée ...?"[627] That is also why it is so artificial to simply talk about "non-binding" agreements concluded by provinces. Many of those agreements can only work because they have sufficiently raised expectations of cooperation through the making of public commitments. Obviously, not all such international instruments are meant to be binding, but the binding or non-binding character of an instrument ought to be decided with the help of ordinary rules of treaty interpretation and not preconceptions about the capacity of provinces to make treaties.

b.   The Necessary Bindingness of Constitutive Rules

There is a deeper argument in favour of recognizing that provinces sometimes enter into truly binding agreements. The previous argument emphasised the fact that the incentive structures for governments to enter into many cooperative enterprises require that provincial governments be able to enter into true agreements instead of merely making predictive statements about their own future behaviour. One could simply deduce that provinces possess the required capacity to enter into such agreements from the fact that they have entered into many cooperative enterprises. And because many of these agreements are only possible to the extent that parties undertake obligations, there must be international secondary rules that underlie those agreements to turn them into obligations. Now, the argument that I will highlight is related to the fact that many forms of cooperative enterprises in which provinces are engaged in require an agreement as a necessary condition of their existence. In other words, I am not talking about cases where parties would not be willing to cooperate without an agreement, but rather about cases where certain forms of cooperation would not even be possible, even *in principle*, without an agreement.

---

[626] Obviously, putting one's reputation on the line and other forms of "bonds" will not always suffice to ensure respect for agreements and no general mechanism has yet been developed in the international arena to prevent all possible cases of "efficient breach".

[627] Paul Gérin-Lajoie, *Address to the Consular Corps, supra* note 6.

The cases where such situations arise are those in which the agreement does not merely state the mutual obligations of the parties but rather *constitute* the instrument by which cooperation will be made possible. Institutionalised mutual trust through intergovernmental "committees", "councils", "commissions", "agencies" is often necessary to coordinate governmental actions to deal with cross-jurisdictional issues in our increasingly integrated world. Pure statements of intentions are not sufficient to set up those institutions. This we have known at least since H.L.A. Hart's famous criticisms of John Austin's command theory of law.[628] In these situations, a form of intergovernmental agreement is necessary to constitute those joint institutions because mere acts of will are not sufficient. For an institution to be "created", there must be secondary rules setting it up and specifying its powers. Those rules are "constitutive" in the sense that they specify the criteria for the existence of the institution *qua* institution. Because agreements setting up those institutions are constitutive, they are necessarily binding as the rules of chess are binding on chess players; not following the rules does not necessarily mean that sanctions will be imposed, it simply means that one is not participating in the common endeavour. In that context, failing to respect the constitutive rules will mean failing to participate in the common collaborative project that gave rise to the institution. Thus, bilateral or multilateral agreements between federated states setting up institutions are necessary "binding" if those institutions are to exist.

   c.   International Law and Legal Pluralism

I would suggest that many of the provincial agreements that take the forms discussed in the last two sections could meet the requirements of the *Vienna Convention on the Law of Treaties*[629]. However, even if they did not, they could still qualify under other international norms. Whether an agreement otherwise binding in the senses explored in the previous sections, but not satisfying the *Vienna Convention on the Law of Treaties*[630] could be seen as *legally* binding at international law might appear at first a complex matter because it seems to require us to identify precisely what international law is. In effect, agreements cannot be "legally" binding in the abstract; they can only be so in reference to a legal order. Thus, before examining the question as to whether or not an agreement might be binding within a specific legal order, one has to settle the question of the relevant legal order involved.

International law – or law*s* – cannot rely on centralised hegemonic institutions to maintain a monistic view of law, and it is therefore more

---

[628] H.L.A. Hart, *The Concept of Law, supra* note 384.

[629] *Vienna Convention on the Law of Treaties, supra* note 447.

[630] *Ibid.*

openly pluralistic than many modern domestic state legal systems. H.L.A. Hart wrote, about forty years ago "that there is no basic rule providing general criteria of validity for the rules of international law, and that the rules which are in fact operative constitute not a system but a set of rules, among which are the rules providing for the binding force of treaties".[631] I would suggest that this statement remains largely true today; there is not a unique rule of recognition that unifies exhaustively the rules of international law into a single system. The multiplication of specialized international regimes (e.g. trade regimes, human rights regimes, water management regimes, etc.) is a testimony to that fact. There might be rules of recognition that give unity to specialized international legal regimes and there might be free-floating primary and secondary rules that surround and sometimes penetrate those overlapping regimes; but there is no single rule of recognition that currently unifies the whole body of rules and institutions into a single system. In the absence of a totally unified international legal system that would encompass all international legal regimes, there is no point in denying the legal nature of provincial agreements and other international subjects anymore than there is in denying the legal nature of any other international norm.

The absence of an effective third-party enforcer to sanction violations of the agreements concluded by federated states should not distract us either. The same could be said for most fields of international law. We have to remember that international law is not exactly like domestic law: there is no true central legislative power and no general compulsory jurisdiction at international law.

In the end, what matters is whether or not there is a secondary rule that can transform the statements made by negotiating parties into obligations. Obviously, to the extent that entities that are parties to the agreement consider the agreement legally binding, there is no point in looking further. The question may remain as to whether one party could challenge the binding nature of an agreement, the terms of which it is no longer interested in fulfilling. It appears in any event that, when one looks at the state practices alluded to earlier and the observed willingness of states to be bound by agreements with federated states, there is enough evidence to find a custom recognizing that treaties are possible between a state and a federated state.

---

[631] H.L.A. Hart, *The Concept of Law, supra* note 384 at 238.

3. *A Plausible Legal Foundation for Federal Treaty Powers in Relation to Provincial Matters: Provincial Delegation*

After having demonstrated that the federal government does not possess exclusive and plenary treaty-making power in relation to provincial matters, and after having shown that provinces are capable of concluding treaties according to both Canadian constitutional law and international law, it is now time to suggest a possible source for the federal treaty-making power that is sometimes exercised by the federal government in relation to provincial matters.

As we know, cooperative federalism allows for flexibility through all sorts of delegation mechanisms. In light of the changing nature of the state – moving from a "public order" state to a regulation and welfare state, many provinces were often glad to be able to benefit from economies of scale that came with centralisation. Nova Scotia, for example, even attempted to adopt legislation allowing for a delegation of legislative powers to the Parliament on any "matter relating to employment in any industry, work or undertaking in respect of which such matter is, by Section 92 of The British North America Act, 1867, exclusively within the legislative jurisdiction" of the province. Such attempt at "horizontal delegation" was declared unconstitutional by the Supreme Court.[632] The following year, however, the Supreme Court allowed "diagonal delegation" (i.e. delegation of regulatory power to agencies managed by the other level of government).[633] If such delegation is possible, then nothing stops provinces from delegating either expressly and under certain conditions a part, or the totality, of the *exercise*[634] of their treaty powers to representatives of the federal government – as Québec has done by adopting s. 22.1 of *An Act respecting the Ministère des Relations internationales*[635] – or implicitly through acquiescence.[636]

---

[632] *Nova Scotia (A.-G) v. Canada (A.-G.)*, *supra* note 504.

[633] *Prince Edward Island (Potato Marketing Board) v. H.B. Willis Inc.*, [1952] 2 S.C.R. 392.

[634] The provinces could delegate the *exercise* of their treaty-making prerogative but could not transfer the prerogative itself to the federal government without a proper constitutional amendment. See section III.D.

[635] *An Act respecting the Ministère des Relations internationales*, *supra* note 35. In particular, s. 22.1 provides that

This legal proposition intensifies only slightly the role of the provinces in the federal government's action abroad, and formalises the federal government's official commitment, i.e. not to enter into treaties "dealing with matters within provincial jurisdiction ... without prior consultation with the Governments of the Provinces".[637] The obligation to consult provinces when negotiating an international agreement that will merely *affect* their jurisdiction might flow as much from courtesy as from constitutional law. However, Rinfret J.'s position in the *Labour Conventions* case – *SCC* makes it clear that provincial consent over treaties *in relation to* their legislative competence could be derived from provinces' prerogatives and is therefore necessary.[638]

The [Québec] Minister [of International Relations] may agree to the signing of such an accord by Canada.	Le ministre [des Relations internationales du Québec] peut donner son agrément à ce que le Canada signe un tel accord.
The Government must, in order to be bound by an international accord pertaining to any matter within the constitutional jurisdiction of Québec and to give its assent to Canada's expressing its consent to be bound by such an accord, make an order to that effect. The same applies in respect of the termination of such an accord.	Le gouvernement doit, pour être lié par un accord international ressortissant à la compétence constitutionnelle du Québec et pour donner son assentiment à ce que le Canada exprime son consentement à être lié par un tel accord, prendre un décret à cet effet. Il en est de même à l'égard de la fin d'un tel accord.

[636] For provincial purposes, this turns on its head Bora Laskin's views according to which "[i]n the present state of Canadian constitutional law and applicable international law, a province can engage in dealings with a foreign government only through the authority of the national government, and it would in that respect be really a delegate of the national government. The latter is entitled to determine how and by whom it will be represented abroad." (B. Laskin, "The Provinces and International Agreements", *supra* note 40 at 111. Obviously, the federal government would not need such a provincial delegation of powers when its actions are related to its own jurisdiction.

[637] Canada, Legal Bureau of the Department of External Affairs, Letter February 1, 1985, *supra* note 60 from the Legal Bureau of the then Department of External Affairs responding to a Council of Europe questionnaire.

[638] This seems to be more solid ground on which to base that obligation than the one suggested by Allan Gotlieb and Eli Lederman, "Ignoring the provinces is not Canada's way" National Post (3 January 2003) A14 who claimed that:

> ... by ratifying the Kyoto Protocol without first consulting with and obtaining the support from the provinces, the federal government has departed from a long-standing practice, so consistent in nature and fundamental to the Canadian Constitution that it may be considered a constitutional convention, or arguably, an unwritten constitutional rule.

At any rate, I will not pass judgment here on the capacity of the Parliament to implement the *Kyoto Protocol to the United Nations Framework Convention on Climate Change*, 11 December 1997, UN Doc. FCCC/CP/1997/L.7/Add.1, 37 I.L.M. 22, online: United Nations Framework Convention on Climate Change <unfccc.int/essential_ background/Kyoto_protocol/items/1678.php> (entered into force 16 February 2005).

While these legal propositions will obviously make "Canadian sovereignists" unhappy, they are the ones with the surest legal foundations and the ones that lead to more democratic outcomes. It is true that Canada might be forced to abstain from concluding certain treaties because of a lack of provincial support in certain areas, but the use of a "federal clause" or a "reservation" are ways to minimise the effect of such abstention by certain provinces. These tools show that, contrary to what Dean Rand (as he then was) feared, a divided treaty power does not necessarily amount to giving provinces a veto power that risks "sterilising national action".[639] One might complain that those consultations and internal negotiations could cause additional delays, but this is not necessarily something to be lamented since such a process may promote better informed consent and stronger commitments.[640]

Institutionally speaking, I would suggest, however, that in order to develop more effective coordination mechanisms between provinces and the federal government, a common agreement should be negotiated.[641]

On a supposed uniform practice of seeking consent from provinces before ratifying international agreements related to their jurisdiction, see also Allan Gotlieb, "Only one voice speaks for Canada" The Globe and Mail (5 October 2005) A23 where Gotlieb, writing in an otherwise distinctive Canadian sovereignist tone, nonetheless claims that Ottawa ratifies agreements in areas of provincial concern "only after receiving the concurrence of the provinces". Max Yelden, "Quebec Already Speaks for Canada" The Globe and Mail (17 October 2005), online: The Globe and Mail (web-exclusive comment) <http://www.theglobeandmail.com/servlet/story/RTGAM. 20051017.wcomment1017/BNStory/National/> also writes that "[a]s to Madame Gagnon-Tremblay's fourth point, that Quebec's consent be obtained before treaties are signed, Mr. Gotlieb makes clear that treaties in areas of domestic provincial jurisdiction are not ratified without provincial consent and prior consultation. This has been the case for a very long time." Benoît Pelletier, Québec's current Liberal Minister of Intergovernmental Affairs disagreed with Gotlieb and others on whether or not, *in fact*, "Canada has ... always effectively sought provincial and territorial concurrence before signing and ratifying international treaties dealing in matters of provincial jurisdiction." (Benoît Pelletier, "To refuse provincial input in international negotiations is to condemn our federation to a state of perpetual stagnation" The Globe and Mail (12 October 2005), online: The Globe and Mail (update) <http://www. theglobeandmail.com/servlet/story/RTGAM.20051011.wwebex1012/BNStory>.) However, it is clear from Pelletier's complaint that he does not disagree with the *principle*.

[639] I.C. Rand, "Some Aspects of Canadian Constitutionnalism", *supra* note 41 at 143. Rand also feared that such division would result in an "inverting of the underlying scheme of Dominion and provincial relations." (*Ibid.*) However, if both levels are constitutionally equals, there is simply no logical space for such inversion.

[640] A.L.C. de Mestral, "L'évolution des rapports entre le droit canadien et le droit international un demi-siècle après l'affaire des conventions internationales de travail", *supra* note 112 at 310-311.

[641] I have mentioned possible elements that might contain such an agreement in sections II.A.2.i. and II.A.2.ii. Of course, as long as the agreement would not be entrenched, it would only have political weight (see *Reference Re Canada Assistance Plan (B.C.)*,

The willingness of provinces to negotiate a compensation mechanism in case they are held responsible for Canada's violation of an international obligation should be a serious incentive for the federal government to participate in such negotiations. Apart from compensation schemes that could be developed, one could also think of creating external incentives towards compliance, by using what has been called "double-decker treaties" (e.g. treaties that are ratified by both levels of government).[642] Finally, it has been argued that "[t]he more important the treaty to a foreign government, and the more substantial the pecuniary interests involved, the more resolute would be the demand that Ottawa be the guarantor of the undertaking."[643] The institutional schemes suggested here adequately respond to that argument. In the end, what foreign governments will want is adequate assurance that treaty obligations will be respected and, as first-year law students learn very quickly, they will be happy to find out that there is more than one entity that can be called to answer in case of a breach!

*

* *

What we have seen in this chapter should be enough to refute the arguments of the "Canadian sovereignists" who want all foreign affairs powers in the hands of the federal government. Their position is wrong

---

[1991] 2 S.C.R. 525) but it could be transformed into a constitutional convention. After being tested over a certain period of time and improved in light of experience, that agreement could also be entrenched when the political conditions would be favourable.

[642] On "double decker" treaties, see C. Schreuer, "The Waning of the Sovereign State: Toward a New Paradigm of International Law?", *supra* note 104 at 457:

> The European Community has developed a different technique to deal with treaties straddling State and Community competences. These treaties are concluded in the form of 'mixed agreements' to which the Members as well as the Community are formal parties. This 'double decker' method may be an interesting model for future solutions. (Footnotes omitted.)

The author also refers to other examples, such as the "ratifications of multilateral treaties by Byelorussia (now Belarus) and the Ukraine while they were still Soviet Republics, in addition to the Soviet Union". For further readings on "mixed agreements", Christoph Schreuer suggests: Henry G. Schermers, "International Organizations as Members of Other International Organizations" in Rudolf Bernhardt *et al.*, eds., *Völkerrecht als Rechtsordnung, internationale Gerichtsbarkeit, Menschenrechte: Festschrift für Hermann Mosler* (Berlin: Springer Verlag, 1983) 823 at 826-831 and David O'Keefe and Henri G. Schermers, eds., *Mixed Agreements* (Boston: Kluwer Law and Taxation Publishers, 1983). On the issue of mixed agreements, see also Joni Heliskoski, *Mixed Agreements As A Technique For Organizing The International Relations Of The European Community And Its Member States* (New York: Kluwer Law International, 2001).

[643] G.R. Morris, "The Treaty-Making Power: A Canadian Dilemma", *supra* note 22 at 501.

in terms of public policy and it is legally without foundations, unless, of course, the *Labour Conventions* case is reversed. The following chapter will present the legal arguments offered in favour of reversing that decision and will show that they are all ill-founded. In particular, I will show how reversing the *Labour Conventions* case would drastically alter Canadian constitutionalism.

CHAPTER III

Treaty Implementation
in the Canadian Federation

Despite renewed approval of the *Labour Conventions* case[644] by the courts,[645] constant support for it by all successive Québec governments (sovereignists and federalists alike), and general endorsement of it by Francophone constitutionalists, the decision has often been seen as a mistake in English Canada. In fact, many English-speaking writers would ultimately like to see the decision reversed. The argument most often made by those who support a reversal is that the federal government must have plenary and exclusive powers over both treaty-making and treaty implementation; otherwise Canada's negotiation position is weakened and her ability to enter treaties is severely diminished. However, I have never seen this claim substantiated with any concrete example. Those who argue that the current system weakens Canada's ability to negotiate effectively have yet to come up with the empirical evidence to support such claim. At least *prima facie*, the claim seems baseless from the sheer number of international agreements to which Canada has agreed. In fact, I am tempted to suggest that, on this issue, things have not changed much since Justice La Forest said in the 1970s that the

---

[644] *Labour Conventions* case, *supra* note 19.

[645] As we have seen earlier, there is L'Heureux-Dubé and McLachlin JJ.'s recent (albeit confusing) support for the decision's rule on the division of legislative powers in *Thomson v. Thomson, supra* note 265 at 611. For further approvals of the decision, see for example: *Patriation Reference, supra* note 95 (Martland and Ritchie JJ., dissenting opinion but not on this point); *Foreign Legations case, supra* note 396 (three separate opinions of Taschereau J. (in the majority), Kerwin and Hudson JJ. (dissenting) of a panel of five); *Saxena v. Thailand (Kingdom)*, [1997] B.C.J. No. 1511, at para. 15 (unanimous decision of the B.C. C.A.); *Alberta Union of Provincial Employees v. Alberta* [1980] 120 D.L.R. (3d) 590 (Alta. Q.B.) (affirmed 130 D.L.R. (3d) 191, leave to appeal to the Supreme Court of Canada (Martland, Ritchie and Dickson JJ.) refused December 7, 1981); *British Columbia Packers Ltd. v. Canada (Labour Relations Board)*, [1974] 2 F.C. 913 at paras. 48-49. The Supreme Court had expressed doubts about the *Labour Conventions* case, *supra* note 19 in earlier decisions (see *MacDonald v. Vapor Canada Ltd.*, [1977] 2 S.C.R. 134 [*MacDonald v. Vapor Canada Ltd.*] and *Schneider v. The Queen*, [1982] 2 S.C.R. 112). However, as we will see later, despite the marked willingness to overrule older precedents that characterized that period, the Court has decided that it is wiser to leave the rules expounded by the 1937 Privy Council decision in place.

important role that Canada plays in international relations should be sufficient to put to rest the claim that the *Labour Conventions* case crippled Canada's ability to negotiate effectively.[646]

In this chapter, I will show why reversing the *Labour Conventions* case would be a terrible thing for the general economy of the Canadian constitution and for federalism in particular. To do so, I will examine each of the different sources invoked by those who want to reverse the decision and show why it does not make sense to follow them. Thus, in section III.A., I will begin by explaining why s. 132 of the *Constitution Act, 1867* should not be revived. The following section (III.B.) will be devoted to showing why we should not use the "national concerns" doctrine of s. 91 to create a plenary federal power to implement treaties. Section III.C. will respond to arguments based on the federal Parliament's exclusive extra-territorial legislative powers. Finally, in section III.D., I will comment on the difficulties of using the amending formula of the Constitution to reverse the effects of the *Labour Conventions* case and what such difficulties should tell us about the illegitimacy of a potential judicial reversal of that precedent. As Gerard La Forest has pointed out, the balance struck in the latter case took into account many factors and is secured by historical, cultural, political and geographical considerations and it should not be lightly tampered with.[647]

A. Section 132 Cannot Be Judicially Revived

Let me begin by addressing arguments about judicially reviving s. 132 that are presented at frequent intervals.[648] Usually, those supporting such change are convinced that this would be a good idea as a matter of policy and not much time is spent developing legal arguments that would support their position. However, to reverse a Privy Council precedent that has been in place for three quarter of a century and upon which reliance has been put (including by the federal government and its

---

[646] G.V. La Forest, "Labour Conventions Case Revisited", *supra* note 112 at 148. See also A.L.C. de Mestral, "L'évolution des rapports entre le droit canadien et le droit international un demi-siècle après l'affaire des conventions internationales de travail", *supra* note 112 at 310-311.

[647] G.V. La Forest, "Labour Conventions Case Revisited", *ibid.* at 147-150. See also: A.L.C. de Mestral, "L'évolution des rapports entre le droit canadien et le droit international un demi-siècle après l'affaire des conventions internationales de travail", *ibid.* at 321.

[648] See for example, V.C. MacDonald, "The Canadian Constitution Seventy Years Later", *supra* note 112 at 416; Torsten H. Strom and Peter Finkle, "Treaty Implementation: The Canadian Game Needs Australian Rules" (1993) 25 Ottawa L. Rev. 39 at note 74 and accompanying text.

international partners[649]), one must have very strong arguments. These do not exist. Instead, I think that there are strong arguments *against* reversing the Privy Council.

To better understand the original purpose of s. 132,[650] it is useful to examine how the Framers arrived at its current wording. Initially, Resolution 30, adopted at the Conference of Delegates from the Provinces of Canada, Nova Scotia, New Brunswick, Newfoundland and Prince Edward Island held in Québec in October 1864, read:

> The General Government and Parliament shall have all powers necessary or proper for performing the obligations of the *Federated Provinces*, as part of the British Empire, to Foreign Countries, arising under Treaties between Great Britain and such Countries.[651]

Nothing was said about Parliament's power to enact laws to implement Imperial treaty obligations relating to the federal field of powers. The Delegates must have assumed that such a provision was not necessary since Parliament would already have the powers to implement such obligations within its regular legislative jurisdiction. Thus, the Delegates assumed that, without a specific indication to the contrary, treaty implementation would normally be the responsibility of the legislature that has jurisdiction over the subject-matter of the treaty in question.

Then, at the London Conference of Delegates from the Provinces of Canada, Nova Scotia and New Brunswick held at the Westminster Palace Hotel in December 1866, the Delegates adopted a modified version of the initial resolution that replaced the expression "Federated Provinces" by "Confederation".[652] While this new expression was more concise, it was also more ambiguous. Was the expression "Confederation" meant to include both the "General Government" as well as the

---

[649] See Canada, Legal Bureau of the Department of External Affairs, Letter February 1, 1985, *supra* note 60.

[650] The "purpose" of a constitutional provision is not determined by the subjective beliefs of politicians who pushed for the adoption of that provision (see H. Cyr, "L'interprétation constitutionnelle, un exemple de postpluralisme", *supra* note 169). However, because we presuppose that constitutional provisions are adopted for a reason, we assume that they reflect a certain purpose. The initial purpose of a provision is thus a theoretical construction based on the circumstances of its adoption and created with the help of a series of interpretative heuristics (e.g. statements of intention, mischief rule, expected effects of the provision, etc,). As most theories, the best ones will be the ones that are coherent, simple, exhaustive in their explanation, etc.

[651] *The Québec Resolutions, October 1864* (The 72 Resolutions), reproduced in William P.M. Kennedy, *Statutes, Treaties and Documents of the Canadian Constitution, 1713-1929*, 2nd ed. (Toronto: Oxford University Press, 1930) at 544 (emphasis added) [W.P.M Kennedy, *Statutes, Treaties and Documents of the Canadian Constitution, 1713-1929*].

[652] *Ibid.* at 614.

provinces? If so, why change the wording if they assumed that the General Government would normally have the power to implement Imperial treaty obligations with respect to subject-matters falling within its own jurisdiction? It was certainly not because the Delegates did not want the Imperial Parliament to intervene in Canadian domestic affairs to perform Great Britain's obligations. In effect, it simply stated that Parliament would have such powers but did not propose to amend s. 1 of the *Colonial Laws Validity Act, 1865*[653] adopted less than two years earlier and that provided that "An Act of Parliament or any Provision thereof shall in construing this Act be said to extend to any Colony when it is made applicable to such Colony by the express Words or necessary Intendment of any Act of Parliament". A plausible interpretation for this change of wording is that it intended to mark a complete unitary integration of authority in the "General Government" in relation to any international obligations arising from membership to the Empire.

But the final version of the project got rid of the ambiguity and provided that

> The *Parliament and Government of Canada* shall have all Powers necessary or proper for performing the Obligations of *Canada or of any Province* thereof, as Part of the British Empire, towards Foreign Countries, arising under Treaties between the Empire and such Foreign Countries.[654]

The first thing to notice is that the drafters left behind the expression "General Government" and replaced it with "Government of Canada". Also, it clearly separated the "Obligations of Canada" from those of "any Province" arising under Treaties between the Empire and foreign countries. But why then include the expression "Obligations of Canada" if we already know that Parliament could legislate to implement such obligations? A possible explanation lies in the substitution of the expression "General Government" by "Government of Canada". The former expression portrayed the federal government as a "General Government" that would sit above the "Federated Provinces" in a hierarchically integrated unity. This is no longer the case with the expression "Government of Canada". The expression "Government of Canada" is open to more than one conception of the role of the federal government in the constitutional architecture. We can read s. 132 as giving us a clue as to the nature of that government in that structure: by stating that both "Canada" and "any Province" may have obligations of their own as parts of the British Empire, s. 132 indicates that the federal government has a distinct existence from that of the provinces and that it may have obligation of its own. In other words, s. 132 highlights the fact

---

[653] *Colonial Laws Validity Act, 1865* (U.K.), 28 & 29 Vict., c. 63.

[654] *Constitution Act, 1867*, *supra* note 39, s. 132 (emphasis added).

that Canada is neither a *confederation* in which the provinces have delegated powers to a central institution while keeping for themselves the entire attributes of "self-governing colonies", nor is it a *unitary* state in which provinces are delegates or subordinates[655] of the "General Government". Section 132 confirms that Canada is a federation. And again, the fact that s. 132 was deemed necessary to grant legislative power to Parliament to perform Imperial obligations related to provincial subject-matters simply confirms that it was expected that, without such express provision, Parliament would not otherwise have such power.

But whether they were dealing with Canada's obligations or the provinces', the drafters were concerned with those obligations that were flowing from their participation in the *British Empire* and not any other. Thus, the initial purpose of s. 132 was to ensure the performance of international obligations undertaken by the *Imperial government* in respect to the Dominion and the provinces. As I said earlier, at the time the *Constitution Act, 1867* was adopted, it was not anticipated that Canada and the provinces would one day be directly involved in international relations.[656] They were subordinated to the greater interests of the Empire. Thus, only the Imperial government was thought able to incur international obligations. And only the Imperial government was thought to be able to incur responsibility for failing to respect the obligations undertaken. This means that s. 132 had little to do with either the provinces or the "Dominion" self-governance but rather to do with the international situation of the Imperial government. Thus, s. 132 was adopted for the purpose of ensuring that the *Imperial government* would not be held in violation of her international obligations. As we have seen earlier in the *Aeronautics Reference*, the Dominion was meant not only to have the right to perform Imperial obligations for her and the provinces, "*but also the obligation*, to provide by statute and by regulation that the terms of the Convention shall be duly carried out."[657]

Therefore, the initial purpose of that section was to grant the necessary powers to protect the Imperial government from violations of its international obligations by its subordinates. Now that the Empire has vanished, that initial purpose has expired since the entity that was meant to be protected no longer exists. To be clear, this is not a case like the

---

[655] I distinguish here "subordinate" entities from "delegated" entities. The first type is taken to have at least some authority independently from a grant of power by its political superior while the second type of entity refers to an entity that receives all of its authority from that political superior.

[656] See *supra* note 61 and accompanying text.

[657] *Aeronautics Reference, supra* note 125 at 77 (emphasis added).

issue of changing how "banking" works,[658] rather this is a case more like the one we would face if banking were to simply disappear. It is not simply that the mode of being of the initial object has changed; it is rather that the object itself no longer exists.

Those who want a new version of s. 132 to be revived suggest that purposive interpretation is not enough. As Lord Sankey famously stated, the Constitution is a "living tree capable of growth and expansion within its natural limits".[659] As I have written elsewhere, I agree with "progressive interpretation" of the Constitution.[660] However, the use of progressive interpretation is more limited in the context of federalism than in the context of *Charter* rights because the extension of one jurisdiction risks affecting the political balance achieved by the framers. And in that context, "progressive interpretation" might create a fear of the "bait and switch" phenomenon, thus hindering future revisions of the scope of provincial and federal jurisdictions.[661]

---

[658] *Alberta (A.G.) v. Canada (A.G.)*, [1947] A.C. 503 [*In re* Alberta Bill of Rights Act] at 516-17:

> The question ... is whether operations of this sort fall within the connotation of "banking" as that word is used in s. 91 of the British North America Act. Their Lordships entertain no doubt that such operations are covered by the term "banking" in s. 91. *The question is not what was the extent and kind of business actually carried on by banks in Canada in 1867, but what is the meaning of the term itself in the Act.* To take a what may seem a frivolous analogy, if "skating" was one of the matters to which exclusive legislative authority of the Parliament of Canada extended, it would be nothing to the point to prove that only one style of skating was practised in Canada in 1867 and argue that the exclusive power to legislate in respect of subsequently developed styles of skating was not expressly conferred on the central legislature. (Emphasis added).

[659] *Edwards*, *supra* note 82 at 136.

[660] See for example, Hugo Cyr, "Why The Rules Governing The Division Of Legislative Powers Over Marriage And Divorce Favour The Recognition Of Same-Sex Marriages", brief presented to the House of Commons Standing Committee on Justice and Human Rights (Ottawa: 8 April 2003) and Hugo Cyr, "La conjugalité dans tous ses états: la validité constitutionnelle de 'l'union civile' sous l'angle du partage des compétences législatives" in Pierre-Claude Lafond et Brigitte Lefebre, eds., *L'union civile nouveaux modèles de conjugalité et de parentalité au 21ᵉ siècle* (Cowansville: Yvon Blais, 2003) 193 [H. Cyr, "La conjugalité dans tous ses états: la validité constitutionnelle de 'l'union civile' sous l'angle du partage des compétences législatives"].

[661] The "bait and switch" phenomenon happens in two stages. First, law-makers are induced to act in a certain way because expectations are created that if they do so certain consequences will (or will not) follow. Once the law-makers act according to the inducement, either those who created the expectations or other participants who remained silent during the inducement phase act wilfully in such a way that the consequences expected by the law-makers will not be realized. The law-makers are thus fooled into adopting something they do not necessarily want. See for example, William N. Eskridge, Jr. *Dynamic Statutory Interpretation* (Cambridge (Mass.): Harvard

Recently, Deschamps J. wrote for a unanimous Supreme Court in *Reference re* Employment Insurance Act *(Can.), ss. 22 and 23* that "[a] progressive interpretation cannot ... be used to justify Parliament in encroaching on a field of provincial jurisdiction."[662] How could the extension of one jurisdiction not encroach on the other if the division of powers is exhaustive?

The solution is to increase the size of the pie instead of redistributing its shares. In other words, this is made possible when the extension of power of one jurisdiction does not diminish the sphere of powers of the other and it does not create new areas for exercising an overriding power over the other jurisdiction. A good example of this type of situation is the progressive interpretation of s. 91 (26) granting Parliament power over "marriage and divorce" to include same-sex marriages.[663] That was a case in which the extension of the federal power was in line with the initial objective of maintaining the stability of the matrimonial status of persons moving from one part of the country to another. The progressive interpretation did not restrict in any way the provinces' powers to adopt laws on other forms of civil statuses[664] and it did not create new areas for

---

University Press, 1994) at 284-85 where he illustrates how the American Congress can been frustrated by courts shifting interpretive rules. And once burnt, twice shy.

Arguably, the fear of the "bait and switch" phenomenon was partly responsible for the failure of the Meech Lake Accord. In effect, many opponents to the Accord feared that no matter how much the "distinct society" clause may have been described as mainly "hortatory or symbolic" (Peter W. Hogg, *Meech Lake Constitutional Accord Annotated* (Toronto: Carswell, 1988) at 13) at the time of its adoption by many of its supporters outside Québec, the clause might still allow the judiciary to extend Québec's legislative jurisdiction in unwanted directions.

A majority of the Supreme Court recognized the "bait and switch" problem in the slightly different context of private orderings between insurance companies in their interprovincial dealings when it wrote:

> The courts should strive to give full effect to voluntary, interprovincial arrangements that seek to overcome some of the practical difficulties inherent in our federal structure. *The danger, however, is that if the courts overstate the effect of these voluntary arrangements, and thereby impose on the parties obligations that were never in their contemplation, cooperation may no longer be forthcoming.* (Emphasis added).

(Unifund Assurance Co. v. Insurance Corp. of British Columbia, [2003] 2 S.C.R. 63, 2003 SCC 40 at para. 103 (Justice Binnie for McLachlin C.J. and Iacobucci and LeBel JJ.) [*Unifund Assurance Co. v. Insurance Corp. of British Columbia*]

[662] *Reference re* Employment Insurance Act, *supra* note 97 at para. 10. Deschamps J. repeats that principle in the conclusion to her judgment (para. 76): "The evolution of the scope of a constitutional head of power cannot result in encroachment on a power assigned to another level of government."

[663] *Reference re Same-Sex Marriage*, [2004] 3 S.C.R. 698.

[664] See H. Cyr, "La conjugalité dans tous ses états: la validité constitutionnelle de 'l'union civile' sous l'angle du partage des compétences législatives", *supra* note 660.

overriding federal legislation. But here, the extension of federal power that would result from bringing back a modified form of s. 132 would not only "encroach on a field of provincial jurisdiction", it would simply allow for the invasion of the *entire jurisdiction*. I think that we could end the analysis right here. However, for the sake of dealing with the issue once and for all, I will examine it further.

Justice Deschamps also wrote in *Reference re* Employment Insurance Act that "[i]f an issue [of federalism] comes before a court, the court must refer to the framers' description of the power in order to identify its essential components, and must be guided by the way in which courts have interpreted the power in the past."[665] The Supreme Court wants to ensure that legislative powers will evolve only incrementally and that changes can still be related to an initial purpose or that it will at least be in line with a general body of case law. Here, reviving s. 132 can rely on none of these rationales. In fact, as we have seen earlier, far from being an incremental change of minor importance, a revival of a new version of s. 132 would mean the destruction of Canada's federal structure. We would not be doing away with only one essential component of one head of power but with the very idea of "heads of powers" for the federal Parliament.

It is true, however, that while courts tend to refuse the "shifting purposes" doctrine for statutes,[666] the Supreme Court has been willing, in the past, to accept that the initial purpose of a section might not be

---

[665] *Reference re* Employment Insurance Act, *supra* note 97 at para. 10.

[666] *R. v. Big M Drug Mart Ltd.*, [1985] 1 S.C.R. 295 at 335 (for the Court, Dickson J., as he then was): "Furthermore, the theory of a shifting purpose stands in stark contrast to fundamental notions developed in our law concerning the nature of "Parliamentary intention". Purpose is a function of the intent of those who drafted and enacted the legislation at the time, and not of any shifting variable." See also *R. v. Edwards Books and Art Ltd.*, [1986] 2 S.C.R. 713 at para. 86 (Dickson C.J., Chouinard, Le Dain JJ.); *Irwin Toy Ltd. v. Québec (A.G.)*, [1989] 1 S.C.R. 927 at para. 48 (Dickson C.J., Lamer and Wilson JJ.); *R. v. Zundel, supra* note 421 at para. 45ff. (McLachlin J. as she then was, *per* La Forest, L'Heureux-Dubé, Sopinka JJ); *M. v. H.*, [1999] 2 S.C.R. 3 at para. 197 (Gonthier J., dissenting); *Delisle v. Canada (Deputy A.G.)*, [1999] 2 S.C.R. 989 at para. 77 (Cory and Iacobucci JJ., dissenting). However the Supreme Court has qualified that doctrine by accepting that there might be multiple initial purposes to a statute (*R. v. Malmo-Levine*, [2003] 3 S.C.R. 571 at para. 65 (Gonthier and Binnie JJ., *per* McLachlin C.J., Iacobucci, Major, Bastarache JJ. concurring, Deschamps J. dissenting in part but concurring on this point (see para. 284) [*R. v. Malmo-Levine*]) and by describing the initial purpose in more general terms than might have been used to describe the purpose initially in order to allow for the possibility of "shift in emphasis" (*R. v. Butler*, [1992] 1 S.C.R. 452 at paras. 84-86 (Sopinka J. *per* Lamer C.J. and La Forest, Cory, McLachlin, Stevenson and Iacobucci JJ.); *R. v. Zundel, supra* note 421 at paras. 190-195 (dissent by Cory and Iacobucci JJ, Gonthier J.); *R. v. Malmo-Levine, ibid.* ("The purpose and character of the legislation remained the same, but new means were added to advance the original objectives of health and public safety.")).

determinative for its validity. The Supreme Court, in certain circumstances, might sometimes be willing to re-think partially its interpretation of the division of powers. It is true, for example, that Chief Justice Laskin wrote in 1978 in *R. v. Zelensky*[667]:

> New appreciations thrown up by new social conditions, or re-assessments of old appreciations which new or altered social conditions induce make it appropriate for this Court to re-examine courses of decision on the scope of legislative power when fresh issues are presented to it, always remembering, of course, that it is entrusted with a very delicate role in maintaining the integrity of the constitutional limits imposed by the *British North America Act.*

But this statement by Chief Justice Laskin, put in its historical context, also casts light on the issue before us. 1978 was a particularly difficult year for the doctrine of precedents in the Supreme Court. The Chief Justice had voted for expressly overruling at least four Privy Council or Supreme Court precedents[668] in that year and bluntly stated in a fifth case that "this Court is not bound by judgments of the Privy Council any more that it is bound by its own judgments".[669] That last case is of particular interest to us: *Capital Cities Communications v. C.R.T.C.*[670] At issue in that case was, *inter alia*, Parliament's power to regulate television signals coming from outside Canada and to regulate the further retransmission of such signals within Canada. Chief Justice Laskin, writing for the majority, referred to the *Radio Reference*.[671] He recalled that both the *Aeronautics Reference*[672] and the *Radio Reference* "invited a consideration of federal treaty-implementing powers".[673] Although he thought that the Privy Council in the *Radio Reference* had said that Parliament could implement treaties by virtue of its "Peace, Order and

---

[667] *R. v. Zelensky*, [1978] 2 S.C.R. 940 at 951 [*R. v. Zelensky*]. See also *Clark v. Canadian National Railway Co.*, [1988] 2 S.C.R. 680 at paras. 42-43 [*Clark v. Canadian National Railway Co.*]

[668] *Reference re: Agricultural Products Marketing Act, 1970 (Canada)*, [1978] 2 S.C.R. 1198 (Laskin C.J. overruling *Lower Mainland Dairy Products Sales Adjustment Committee v. Crystal Dairy*, [1933] A.C. 168); *Hill v. R.*, [1977] 1 S.C.R. 827 (Laskin C.J., in dissent, voting to overrule *Goldhar v. R.*, [1960] S.C.R. 60); *McNamara Construction (Western) Ltd.*, *supra* note 280 (Laskin C.J. overruling *Farwell v. R.*, (1893) 22 S.C.R. 553); *Paquette v. R.*, [1977] 2 S.C.R. 189 (Martland J. for the Court overruling in part *Dunbar v. R.*, (1936) 67 C.C.C. 20, [1936] 4 D.L.R. 737).

[669] *Capital Cities Communications v. C.R.T.C.*, *supra* note 221 at 161.

[670] *Ibid.*

[671] *Radio Reference*, *supra* note 130.

[672] *Aeronautics Reference*, *supra* note 125.

[673] *Capital Cities Communications v. C.R.T.C.*, *supra* note 221 at 154.

Good Government" powers,[674] he nonetheless stated that he needed "not pursue that aspect for the purposes of the present case."[675] Laskin C.J. simply stated that "[a]lthough this Court is not bound by judgments of the Privy Council any more that it is bound by its own judgments, I hold that the *Radio* case was correctly decided under the terms of ss. 91 and 92(10)(a)".[676] That was an interesting opinion in light of his serious doubts expressed about the *Labour Conventions* case[677] in his *obiter* in *MacDonald v. Vapor Canada Ltd.*![678] I will come back to this point a little later. But first, let's see how far the *R. v. Zelensky* argument could lead us.

When we examine the use to which *R. v. Zelensky* has been put, we discover that it has only been used once by the Supreme Court to interpret any other legislative heads of power than 91 (27) ("criminal law").[679] In *Clark v. Canadian National Railway Co.*,[680] the Supreme Court had to decide whether the limitation period against personal injuries in the federal *Railway Act*[681] was *ultra vires*. The Court notes (before discussing the changing circumstances that may justify revisiting a previous case that had found a similar section to be valid) that:

> In this Court, the characterization of the manner in which the Court dealt with the issue some seventy years ago is, of course, not determinative. It

---

[674] *Ibid.* at 154-55 ("[The Privy Council did hold in the *Radio* case that federal legislation implementing the International Radiotelegraph Convention of 1927, to which Canada was a party as an independent signatory, was competent to Parliament as being for the peace, order and good government of Canada, since it dealt with a matter that was not explicitly mentioned in s. 91 or s. 92 of the *British North America Act.*]")

[675] *Ibid.* at 154.

[676] *Ibid.* at 161.

[677] *Labour Conventions* case, *supra* note 19.

[678] *MacDonald v. Vapor Canada Ltd.*, *supra* note 645 at 169 ("Although the foregoing references would support a reconsideration of the *Labour Conventions* case, I find it unnecessary to do that here because, assuming that it was open to Parliament to pass legislation in implementation of an international obligation by Canada under a treaty or Convention (being legislation which it would be otherwise beyond its competence), I am of the opinion that it cannot be said that s. 7 was enacted on that basis.")

[679] See for example, *R. v. S. (S.) [S.S.]*, [1990] 2 S.C.R. 254; *RJR-MacDonald Inc. v. Canada (A.G.)*, [1995] 3 S.C.R. 199 at para. 28 (La Forest J., L'Heureux-Dubé and Gonthier JJ, dissenting) ("In developing a definition of the criminal law, this Court has been careful not to freeze the definition in time or confine it to a fixed domain of activity"); *R. v. Hinchey*, [1996] 3 S.C.R. 1128 at para. 30 ("I agree with this description. Parliament, therefore, retains the power to designate the specific acts which it considers harmful to the State. The criminal law is not "frozen as of some particular time": *R. v. Zelensky*, [1978] 2 S.C.R. 940 at p. 951.").

[680] *Clark v. Canadian National Railway Co.*, *supra* note 667.

[681] *Railway Act*, R.S.C. 1970, c. R.-2.

remains, however, that the Court would be less willing to interfere with a decision arrived at after full argument and deliberation ...[682]

This poses a serious problem to those who would want to bring back s. 132 from the dead; the "new social conditions" – Canada's international independence from the United Kingdom and Canada's autonomous treaty-making activities – were already there in the early 1930s and were appreciated and taken into serious consideration by the Privy Council when they decided the *Radio Reference*[683] in 1932 and the *Labour Conventions* case in 1937.[684] Moreover, the Court reversed its old precedent in *Clark v. Canadian National Railway Co.*, because it did not fit anymore with the general body of constitutional law that had grown around the issue of application of general provincial laws to s. 92 (10) undertakings. That was the type of situation that Deschamps J. was referring to earlier without mentioning this case. Again, I repeat, nothing of that sort has happened here. Quite the contrary; s. 132's obsolescence is well integrated in the Canadian constitutional fabric.

That being said, let's return to the restraint shown by Laskin C.J. in *Capital Cities Communications v. C.R.T.C.*[685] and *MacDonald v. Vapor Canada Ltd.*[686] considering its well-know opposition to the decision of the Privy Council in the *Labour Conventions* case. This restraint might be quite surprising coming from a judge who did not hesitate to overrule precedents. But to better understand Laskin C.J.'s reluctance to reverse the *Labour Conventions* case and the *Radio Reference*, [687] at least with regard to s. 132, one has to recall what he said in *R. v. Zelensky* about the Supreme Court's duty to always remember that "it is entrusted with a very delicate role in maintaining the integrity of the constitutional limits imposed by the *British North America Act*". And when one reads his previous writings, things get even clearer: Bora Laskin had written that s. 132 is "obsolete unless its words are tortured to meet the present international position, and this is too much to expect of the Courts".[688]

In effect, there are strong textual arguments against *frankensteinisation* of s. 132. Even if we wanted to give the most evolving purposive interpretation to that section, we would need to have that interpretation

---

[682] *Clark v. Canadian National Railway Co.*, *supra* note 667 at para. 39.

[683] *Radio Reference*, *supra* note 130.

[684] *Labour Conventions* case, *supra* note 19.

[685] *Capital Cities Communications v. C.R.T.C.*, *supra* note 221.

[686] *MacDonald v. Vapor Canada Ltd.*, *supra* note 645.

[687] *Radio Reference*, *supra* note 130.

[688] Bora Laskin, *Laskin's Canadian Constitutional Law: Cases, Text and Notes on Distribution of Legislative Power*, rev. 4th ed. by Albert S. Abel and John I. Laskin (Toronto: Carswell, 1975) at 218.

square off with the explicit text of the provision. To revive s. 132 in order to apply it to modern days would require us to *read down* the expressions "as Part of the British Empire". Chopping five words from a provision of the *Constitution Act, 1867* without a formal constitutional amendment is already quite demanding. Once there, we are not far away from the seven words that compose "Property and Civil Rights in the Province" of s. 92 (13)... And it is not all; we would also need to take out a sixth word: the second "Empire" would also have to go. But we could not just take that last word out; we would have to replace it by something else lest the sentence becomes meaningless. What should it be replaced by? "Canada or any Province" or only "Canada"? Reading in one or the other would also force us not only to decide whether the federal executive has the capacity to conclude treaties in relation to matters within provinces' legislative jurisdiction, but also whether provinces have the constitutional capacity to conclude international agreements. Not that I want to be too much of a textualist, but it seems that such changes require more than a little creative reading.

Therefore, any attempt to revive s. 132 judicially ought to be defeated. The only way to achieve that goal would be through a formal constitutional amendment. This is clearly unrealistic at the moment. Not only because there would not be that much enthusiasm on the part of provinces for such a change, but also because it would not simply require a technical change in the constitution; it would mean changing the deep structure of the Constitution and, to a large extent, do away with federalism as an entrenched constitutional principle.[689]

B. Section 91 and the Federal Power Over "Peace, Order and Good Government"

It is well-established that by virtue of the words "Peace, Order and Good Government" found in the introductory paragraph of s. 91 of the *Constitution Act, 1867*,[690] the federal Parliament has the necessary powers to adopt legislation in relation to provincial matters in cases of

---

[689] *Reference Re Secession of Québec, supra* note 76.

[690] The introductory paragraph of s. 91 of the *Constitution Act, 1867* reads:

> It shall be lawful for the Queen, by and with the Advice and Consent of the Senate and House of Commons, to make Laws for the Peace, Order, and good Government of Canada, in relation to all Matters not coming within the Classes of Subjects by this Act assigned exclusively to the Legislatures of the Provinces; and for greater Certainty, but not so as to restrict the Generality of the foregoing Terms of this Section, it is hereby declared that (notwithstanding anything in this Act) the exclusive Legislative Authority of the Parliament of Canada extends to all Matters coming within the Classes of Subjects next hereinafter enumerated; that is to say,
>
> ...

emergency – including economic emergency.[691] That being the case, suffice it to say here that, except in the most curious circumstances,[692] Parliament could not invoke its emergency powers to justify implementing treaty obligations that would otherwise fall within the jurisdiction of provinces. In effect, if there is ever again a situation in which legislative measures to be taken by Parliament are made "temporarily necessary to meet a situation of ... crisis imperilling the well-being of Canada as a whole and requiring Parliament's stern intervention in the interests of the country as a whole",[693] that exceptional crisis of a national magnitude would not, in all likelihood, be caused by the specific need to implement any particular treaty. Rather, it will be caused by a truly concrete emergency situation that will require a stern federal legislative action of a temporary nature. Nobody could seriously suggest that treaty implementation, in itself, could constitute an emergency in the constitutional sense, nor even in the colloquial one.

Thus, what is more relevant for our purposes here is to examine the other branch of the "Peace, Order and good Government" powers that has been called the "national concerns" doctrine.[694]

Historically, two opposite interpretations were given to that doctrine. According to the first one – very favourable to a high degree of centralisation –, Parliament could adopt uniform laws for the entire country on any matter of "national concern". I will call this interpretation the "Canadian Sovereignist Position". According to the second interpretation – more restrictive than the first one and more in line with the federal principle –, the federal Parliament only has jurisdiction over matters of "national concern" to the extent that those matters have not in any way been granted to provincial legislatures. In other words, the existence of a "national concern" might be necessary but it is not a sufficient condition for the existence of a federal power in relation to that matter; there is also the need to establish the residual character of the specific power claimed. I will call this interpretation the "Canadian Federalist Position".

The following excerpts from the famous *Russell v. R.* and the *Local Prohibition* case will illustrate those two interpretations very well:

---

[691] *Reference re Anti-Inflation Act*, [1976] 2 S.C.R. 373 [*Reference re Anti-Inflation Act*].

[692] The only possible circumstances that I could imagine for that being the case would be if (a) another state credibly threatened Canada with invasion if it did not implement a specific treaty and provinces were refusing to do so, or (b) if provinces were unwilling to implement essential conditions of a peace treaty between Canada and a belligerent country and the provinces' unwillingness to abide by the treaty threatened to continue the armed conflict. These appear to be improbable scenarios.

[693] *Reference re Anti-Inflation Act*, *supra* note 691 at 425.

[694] See *supra* notes 169, 242-260 and accompanying text.

Russell v. R. as a "Canadian Sovereignist Position":

The declared object of Parliament in passing the Act [the *Canada Temper-ance Act*] is that there should be uniform legislation in all the provinces re-specting the traffic in intoxicating liquors, with a view to promote temper-ance in the Dominion. Parliament does not treat the promotion of temperance as desirable in one province more than in another but as desir-able everywhere throughout the Dominion.[695]

Local Prohibition case as a "Canadian Federalist Position":

... [T]he exercise of legislative power by the Parliament of Canada, in regard to all matters not enumerated in s. 91, ought to be strictly confined to such matters as are unquestionably of Canadian interest and importance, and ought not to trench upon provincial legislation with respect to any of the classes of subjects enumerated in s. 92. *To attach any other construction to the general power which, in supplement of its enumerated powers, is conferred upon the Parliament of Canada by s. 91, would, in their Lordship's opinion, not only be contrary to the intendment of the Act, but would practically destroy the autonomy of the provinces. If it were once conceded that the Parliament of Canada has authority to make laws applicable to the whole Dominion, in relation to matters which in each province are substantially of local or private interest, upon the assumption that these matters also concern the peace, order, and good government of the Dominion, there is hardly a subject enumerated in s. 92 upon which it might not legislate, to the exclusion of the provincial legislatures.*[696]

I must add immediately that the tension that existed between the two interpretations has been authoritatively resolved in favour of the *Cana-dian Federalist Position* in the *Reference re Anti-Inflation Act*.[697] In effect, Justice Beetz, for the majority on this point,[698] clearly decided in favour of the second interpretation, the federalist position. It is worth reproducing here a relevant excerpt:

I fail to see how the authorities which so decide lend support to the first submission [that the containment and the reduction of inflation fall within

---

[695] *Russell v. R.*, *supra* note 168 at 841. Again in relation to the *Canada Temperance Act*, that position was taken in *Reference re Canada Temperance Act*, *supra* note 169 at 205 where Viscount Simon wrote:

> In their Lordships' opinion, the true test [of the Peace, Order and good Government power] is the real subject matter of the legislation: if it is such that it goes beyond local or provincial concerns or interests and must from its inherent nature be the concern of the Dominion as a whole ... . Then it will fall within the competence of the Dominion Parliament as a matter affecting the peace, order and good govern-ment of Canada, though it may in another aspect touch on matters specially re-served to the provincial legislatures.

[696] *Local Prohibition* case, *supra* note 169 at 360 (*per* Lord Watson (emphasis added)).

[697] *Reference re Anti-Inflation Act*, *supra* note 691.

[698] With the concurrence of Martland, Ritchie, Pigeon and de Grandpré JJ.

the competence of Parliament as matters affecting the peace, order and good government of Canada]. They had the effect of adding by judicial process new matters or new classes of matters to the federal list of powers. However, this was done only in cases where a new matter was not an aggregate but had a degree of unity that made it indivisible, an identity which made it distinct from provincial matters and a sufficient consistence to retain the bounds of form. The scale upon which these new matters enabled Parliament to touch on provincial matters had also to be taken into consideration before they were recognized as federal matters: if an enumerated federal power designated in broad terms such as the trade and commerce power had to be construed so as not to embrace and smother provincial powers (Parson's case) and destroy the equilibrium of the Constitution, the Courts must be all the more careful not to add hitherto unnamed powers of a diffuse nature to the list of federal powers.

The "containment and reduction of inflation" does not pass muster as a new subject matter. It is an aggregate of several subjects some of which form a substantial part of provincial jurisdiction. It is totally lacking in specificity. It is so pervasive that it knows no bounds. Its recognition as a federal head of power would render most provincial powers nugatory.[699]

Thus, the question to be asked here is whether the implementation of treaties related to provincial matters is a "new subject matter" of "national concern" in the sense of the Supreme Court's ruling. If the containment and reduction of inflation "is an aggregate of several subjects some of which form a substantial part of provincial jurisdiction",[700] the implementation of treaties related to provincial subject-matters is certainly also an aggregate of subjects of exclusive provincial jurisdiction which could hardly be seen as a new subject-matter.

Such was the view of the Privy Council in the *Labour Conventions* case.[701] As we have already seen, the Privy Council interpreted its opinion in the *Radio Reference*[702] and said that there were no separate and specific legislative competences over implementation of treaties. The legislature that had jurisdiction over the subject-matter of a treaty also had the jurisdiction to implement the treaty.[703] Many English-speaking commentators have questioned the soundness of that apparent

---

[699] *Reference re Anti-Inflation Act, supra* note 691 at 458.

[700] *Ibid.*

[701] *Labour Conventions* case, *supra* note 19.

[702] *Radio Reference, supra* note 130.

[703] *Labour Conventions* case, *supra* note 19 at 353:

> For the purposes of ss. 91 and 92, i.e., the distribution of legislative powers between the Dominion and the Provinces, there is no such thing as treaty legislation as such. The distribution is based on classes of subjects; and as a treaty deals with a particular class of subjects so will the legislative power of performing it be ascertained.

reversal.[704] Those commentators have argued that s. 92 does not grant treaty implementation powers to provinces[705] and that "it seems absurd to say that a matter which has become the subject of international agreement can yet be considered a matter of a private and local nature".[706] They seem convinced that the proper reading of Viscount Dunedin's view in the *Radio Reference*[707] is that there being no specific provisions dealing with the implementation of treaties binding on Canada (and the provinces), there is a gap that should be filled by the "Peace, Order an Good Government" powers of the Parliament. Opposed to those views, Gibran van Ert has recently argued in a very thoughtful article that: "[i]t is mistaken to assume that the content of treaty obligations cannot be local or private. States today conclude treaties that have as much to do with their own internal affairs as they do with international affairs."[708] Let's dig a little deeper.

---

[704] See, for representative examples, V.C. MacDonald, "The Canadian Constitution Seventy Years Later", *supra* note 112; F.R. Scott, "The Consequences of the Privy Council Decisions", *supra* note 112 and P. Hogg, *Constitutional Law of Canada*, 2002, *supra* note 217 at § 17.2.

[705] F.R. Scott, "The Consequences of the Privy Council Decisions", *ibid.* at 486, commenting on the *Labour Conventions* case, *supra* note 19, ironises that "Section 92 of the British North America Act, enumerating the provincial powers, has thus a new subsection added to it, namely 'The implementing by legislation of treaties between Canada and foreign countries relating to property and civil rights in the provinces.'" Nonetheless, Scott was forced to recognize that the state of the law was that "the implementation of treaties and conventions is split between Dominion and provinces in accordance with the judicial view of its subject matter under the headings of sections 91 and 92" (Frank R. Scott, "Constitutional Adaptations to Changing Functions of Government" (1945) 11 Canadian Journal of Economics and Political Science / Revue canadienne d'économique et de science politique 329 at 332). The centralist element of Scott's Canadian Sovereignist constitutional thought was quite in evidence in the latter article. In effect, he argued in that article, among other things, that "[w]hile an established convention leaves little doubt that we can amend our constitution whenever a mere majority of our Senate and House of Commons demand it (even when, as the opposition of Québec to the amendment of 1943 showed, a provincial legislature opposes the change) nevertheless the practice of travelling abroad for such national legislation seems too incongruous to survive for long even among a people so constitutionally afraid of changing their constitution as are the Canadians." (*Ibid.* at 331). If the Federal Parliament had been able to amend the Constitution as it saw fit without giving any weight to the will of provinces, Canada would no longer have been a federation but would have been transformed into a unitary state in which provinces would be mere delegates of the centre. It is thus not surprising that someone ready to turn Canada into such a unitary state did not have quandaries about centralising treaty implementation powers.

[706] V.C. MacDonald, "The Canadian Constitution Seventy Years Later", *supra* note 112 at 417.

[707] *Radio Reference, supra* note 130.

[708] G. van Ert, "The Legal Character of Provincial Agreements with Foreign Governments", *supra* note 321 at 1108.

It is useful to recall here that when the "national concern" doctrine is applied, it entails the recognition of a *permanent* and *exclusive* jurisdiction to the federal Parliament. That was the opinion of the Privy Council[709] and the majority's view in the *Reference re Anti-Inflation Act.*[710] In effect, as Justice Beetz wrote:

> Furthermore, all those powers would belong to Parliament permanently; only a constitutional amendment could reduce them. Finally, the power to regulate and control inflation as such would belong to Parliament to the exclusion of the Legislatures if, as is contended, that power were to vest in Parliament in the same manner as the power to control and regulate aeronautics or radio communication or the power to develop and conserve the national capital (*Aeronautics, Radio, Johannesson and Munro* cases); the provinces could probably continue to regulate profit margins, prices, dividends and compensation if Parliament saw fit to leave them any room; but they could not regulate them in relation to inflation which would have become an area of exclusive federal jurisdiction.[711]

Considering that in the present state of development of international law, treaties have much to do with domestic affairs, the Privy Council's warning in the *Labour Conventions* case that giving Parliament powers to implement treaties relative to provincial matters "would appear to undermine the constitutional safeguards of provincial autonomy"[712] rings even louder today.

If we want to take the measure of what would have been the consequences of accepting the doctrine defended by the Dominion in the *Labour Conventions* case in today's world, we can take two simple examples. We can easily see how absurd the results of that doctrine would have been by considering the impact a federal power to implement the *International Covenant on Economic, Social and Cultural Rights [I.C.E.S.C.R.]*[713] and the *International Covenant on Civil and Political Rights [I.C.C.P.R.]*[714] would have had on provincial legisla-

---

[709] See *Local Prohibition* case, *supra* note 696 and accompanying text.

[710] *Reference re Anti-Inflation Act, supra* note 691.

[711] *Ibid.* at 444. In *R. v. Crown Zellerbach Canada Ltd.*, [1988] 1 S.C.R. 401 at 433 [*R. v. Crown Zellerbach Canada*], Le Dain J. for the majority wrote:

> ... what was emphasized by Beetz J. in the *Anti-Inflation Act reference* – that where a matter falls within the national concern doctrine of the peace, order and good government power, as distinct from the emergency doctrine, Parliament has an exclusive jurisdiction of a plenary nature to legislate in relation to that matter, including its intra-provincial aspects.

[712] *Labour Conventions* case, *supra* note 19 at 352.

[713] *International Covenant on Economic, Social and Cultural Rights*, 16 December 1966, Can. T.S. 1976 No. 46, 993 U.N.T.S. 3 (entered into force 3 January 1976) [*I.C.E.S.C.R.*].

[714] *I.C.C.P.R., supra* note 428.

tures. Because Art. 2 (1) of the *I.C.E.S.C.R.* provides that "Each State Party to the Covenant undertakes to take steps … with a view to achieving progressively the full realization of the rights recognized in the present Covenant by all appropriate means, including particularly the adoption of legislative measures", it would mean that provinces could no longer adopt statutes "with a *view to achieving progressively the full realization of [those] rights*". In effect, according to the residual powers doctrine, those powers are *exclusive*. Therefore, provinces could no longer adopt laws striving to recognize the "right to work, which includes the right of everyone to the opportunity to gain his living by work which he freely chooses or accepts",[715] and in that context, they could not establish programs that "include technical and vocational guidance and training programmes, policies and techniques to achieve steady economic, social and cultural development and full and productive employment under conditions safeguarding fundamental political and economic freedoms to the individual."[716] In fact, provinces could no longer adopt statutes on a large array of work-related issues: fair wages, health and safety measures in the workplace, limitation of working hours, public holidays,[717] trade unions,[718] etc. Gone would be the provincial measures on social security.[719] Gone would be the provincial maternity leaves programs, the child protection programs.[720] To put it even more bluntly, gone would be all provincial measures intended to ensure that everyone has "an adequate standard of living for himself and his family, including adequate food, clothing and housing, and to the continuous improvement of living conditions."[721] I am not even talking about the total provincial exclusion from the health sector,[722] from education[723] and from "the conservation, the development and the diffusion of science and culture."[724] And when Canada ratified the *International Covenant on Civil and Political Rights* – if we were to follow the federal view defended in the *Labour Conventions* case –, provinces would have also lost the power to adopt laws protecting life,[725]

---

[715] *I.C.E.S.C.R.*, *supra* note 713, Art. 6 (1).

[716] *Ibid.*, Art. 6 (2).

[717] *Ibid.*, Art. 7.

[718] *Ibid.*, Art. 8.

[719] *Ibid.*, Art. 9.

[720] *Ibid.*, Art. 10.

[721] *Ibid.*, Art. 11 (1).

[722] *Ibid.*, Art. 12.

[723] *Ibid.*, Art. 13-14.

[724] *Ibid.*, Art. 15 (2).

[725] *I.C.C.P.R.*, *supra* note 428, Art. 6.

protecting freedom of thought, conscience and religion,[726] of expression,[727] of peaceful assembly,[728] of association (including to form and join trade unions).[729] They would have lost power to adopt measures protecting against medical or scientific experimentation without free consent[730] and protecting against forced labour and personal servitudes.[731] Provincial powers in relation to "property and civil rights" would also be drastically reduced since they could no longer provide rules to protect families,[732] nor could they put in place property regimes that would ensure one's freedom to choose one's residence.[733] Provinces could no longer protect individuals against "arbitrary or unlawful interference with [their] privacy, family, home or correspondence" nor against "unlawful attacks on [their] honour and reputation".[734] Provinces would have lost control over all judicial, legislative and administrative means to ensure that remedies are available in case any of those rights were infringed.[735] Even more fundamentally, provinces could no longer grant legal personality[736] to physical persons! This absurdity seems to know no limits. If Parliament had plenary powers to implement this Covenant, provinces would no longer be able to establish their own electoral laws and they would no longer be able to regulate through law the hiring of their own employees![737]

This is a very small sample of the possible consequences that would have flowed from acceptance of Ottawa's position here. And as we know, international law has been dramatically transformed in the last seventy-five years by a shift from a legal system primarily based on customs to one increasingly based on treaties. To give us an idea of the order of magnitude of the phenomenon, over 158,000 treaties or international agreements entered into by Members of the United Nations have

---

[726] *Ibid.*, Art. 18.

[727] *Ibid.*, Art. 19.

[728] *Ibid.*, Art. 21.

[729] *Ibid.*, Art. 22.

[730] *Ibid.*, Art. 7.

[731] *Ibid.*, Art. 9.

[732] *Ibid.*, Art. 23.

[733] *Ibid.*, Art. 12 (1).

[734] *Ibid.*, Art. 17.

[735] *Ibid.*, Art. 2 (3).

[736] *Ibid.*, Art. 16.

[737] *Ibid.*, Art. 25 (b) provides that every citizen has the right "[t]o vote and to be elected at genuine periodic elections which shall be by universal and equal suffrage and shall be held by secret ballot, guaranteeing the free expression of the will of the electors" and para. (c) guarantees the right "[t]o have access, on general terms of equality, to public service in his country."

been registered with the United Nations Secretariat since the entry into force of the *UN Charter* (Dec. 14th, 1946).[738] If the Attorney General for Canada's argument had prevailed, there would be about nothing left of provincial jurisdiction.

However, one might be tempted to point out that the end of the excerpt of the *Reference re Anti-Inflation Act* quoted earlier[739] suggests a possibility of "double aspect",[740] subject to a possible federal paramountcy rule. I would respond that in addition to the fact that it is clearly *obiter*, it is also very doubtful that it would be applicable to the two Covenants given as examples above. In effect, the powers, duties and responsibilities they establish are so broad and are so broadly put that if the legislative jurisdiction to implement them were given to the federal Parliament, one fails to see what place could be left to provincial legislation. Justice Beetz writing for a unanimous Supreme Court explained in *Bell Canada v. Québec (Commission de la santé et de la sécurité du travail)*, that for the double aspect doctrine to operate, there must be two *distinct* aspects of the matters in question to be regulated.[741] Because treaties are not ends in themselves but are rather legal instruments – like statutes and regulations – for the accomplishment of certain purposes, treaty implementation is not a purpose that can be distinguished from the substance of the treaty that is being implemented. That was clearly the logic followed by the Supreme Court in *Global Securities Corp. v. British Columbia (Securities Commission)*,[742] when it evaluated the validity of a provincial statute that was implementing an agreement between the securities commissions of British Columbia, Ontario and Québec and the United States Securities and Exchange Commission. The Court wrote that "… the mere fact that the province is co-operating with a foreign authority in the pursuit of that [clearly dominant intraprovincial] purpose will not change the law's pith and

---

[738] See *supra* note 608.

[739] See *supra* note 711 and accompanying text.

[740] As we have seen earlier, the Privy Council stated in *Hodge v. R.*, *supra* note 14 at 130 that "subjects which in one aspect and for one purpose fall within s. 92, may in another aspect and for another purpose fall within s. 91". See *supra* note 143 and accompanying text.

[741] *Bell Canada v. Québec (Commission de la santé et de la sécurité du travail)*, [1988] 1 S.C.R. 749 at para. 299:

> The exact correspondence of these two objectives indicates that there are not two aspects and two purposes depending on whether the legislation is federal or provincial. In my opinion, the two legislators have legislated for the same purpose and in the same aspect. Yet they do not have concurrent legislative jurisdiction in the case at bar, but mutually exclusive jurisdictions. (Emphasis in the original.)

[742] *Global Securities Corp. v. British Columbia (Securities Commission)*, *supra* note 610.

substance".[743] In fact, even when the Court found that one of the two main purposes of the impugned provision was "ensuring cooperation from other jurisdictions", it was understood as a mere means "enabling the Commission to carry out its domestic mandate effectively."[744] Thus, treaty implementation cannot be said to be an aspect distinct from the substantive aspect of a statute.

Moreover, if we were to find a "federal aspect" in treaty implementation, this would provoke a truly radical change in our constitutional framework. In effect, reversing the *Labour Conventions* case[745] and allowing the federal Parliament to legislatively implement any treaty would thus convert all exclusive provincial powers into concurrent ones,[746] allowing the federal Parliament to always have the last word on provincial matters by virtue of the federal paramountcy rule. Obviously, as Vincent C. MacDonald warned us, "jurisdiction is not to be denied by mere capacity for abuse by the federal government".[747] However, here, we are talking of something of another magnitude. To put it simply, provinces would lose their equal status with the federal power by becoming truly subordinated to Parliament and they would be reduced to a

---

[743] *Ibid.* at para. 38. This is an implicit repudiation of the thesis that Bora Laskin defended years before he was appointed to the bench. In his article B. Laskin, "The Provinces and International Agreements", *supra* note 40 at 111, Laskin argued that if a province purported to implement an agreement made with a foreign state on a matter otherwise within provincial competence, the implementing legislation would be vulnerable as being action taken under a non-existing power to enter into international commitments. The Supreme Court, like the Privy Council in the *Labour Conventions* case, *supra* note 19, expressly stated that it did not have to examine the constitutional validity of the agreement to decide on the validity of the legislation (see at para. 38).

[744] *Ibid.* at para. 32. The full citation is "I therefore agree with the Commission that one of the dominant purposes of s. 141(1)(b) is obtaining reciprocal cooperation from other securities regulators, thus enabling the Commission to carry out its domestic mandate effectively." The other dominant purpose of the impugned provision was "discovering wrongdoings by British Columbia registrants in other jurisdictions" (subtitle between para. 32 and para. 33).

This example also goes to show how impractical would be the suggestion made by Peter Hogg (P. Hogg, *Constitutional Law of Canada*, 1992, *supra* note 268 at 296) to confine the *Labour Conventions* case ruling to treaties concerned only with the harmonization of the domestic law of states or the promotion of shared values in domestic law – as opposed to treaties under which the parties undertake reciprocal obligations to each other. The problem is that states undertake reciprocal obligations in order to achieve internal purposes. The conceptual barrier between Hogg's two categories does not stand.

[745] *Labour Conventions* case, *supra* note 19.

[746] A.L.C. de Mestral, "L'évolution des rapports entre le droit canadien et le droit international un demi-siècle après l'affaire des conventions internationales de travail", *supra* note 112 at 307.

[747] V.C. MacDonald, "The Canadian Constitution Seventy Years Later", *supra* note 112 at 416.

status akin to municipalities. This would certainly not be a minor rein-
terpretation of the Constitution but rather an important amendment to
it[748]: it would change the very heart of the division of legislative powers.
Courts should certainly restrain themselves from making such a radical
amendment to the Constitution.

All of these consequences of claiming that Parliament has the power
to implement treaties related to provincial matters through the "national
concern" doctrine would obviously be dreadful for the Canadian federation. Fortunately, however, we need not to worry too much about those
potential consequences because, as we are about to see, treaty implementation simply does not meet the applicability criteria of the "national
concern" doctrine.

After having written a long analysis of the case law on the "Peace,
Order and good Government" powers, Justice Le Dain writing for the
majority in *R. v. Crown Zellerbach Canada*,[749] clearly approved Justice
Beetz's analysis of the "national concern" doctrine in *Reference re Anti-
Inflation Act*.[750] Indeed, Le Dain J. writes:

> For a matter to qualify as a matter of national concern in either sense it must
> have a singleness, distinctiveness and indivisibility that clearly distinguishes
> it from matters of provincial concern and a scale of impact on provincial
> jurisdiction that is reconcilable with the fundamental distribution of
> legislative power under the Constitution.[751]

There is no doubt that his opinion was shared not only by the three
judges concurring with his opinion (Chief Justice Dickson and McIntyre
and Wilson JJ.) but also by the dissenting judges (Beetz, Lamer and La
Forest JJ.). The latter dissented on the *application* of Beetz's method of
analysis by Le Dain J. *and not at all with the method itself*.[752] Writing
the dissenting opinion, La Forest J. expressly approved Justice Beetz's
analysis[753] and further added:

> The need to make such characterizations from time to time is readily appar-
> ent. From this necessary function, however, it is easy but, I say it with re-
> spect, fallacious to go further, and, taking a number of quite separate areas

---

[748] A.L.C. Mestral, "L'évolution des rapports entre le droit canadien et le droit international un demi-siècle après l'affaire des conventions internationales de travail", *supra*
note 112 at 307; J.-Y. Morin, "La personnalité internationale du Québec" *supra* note
41 at 296.

[749] *R. v. Crown Zellerbach Canada*, *supra* note 711.

[750] *Reference re Anti-Inflation Act*, *supra* note 691.

[751] *R. v. Crown Zellerbach Canada*, *supra* note 711 at 432.

[752] Le Dain J. held that salt waters, including intraprovincial ones, were a new subject-
matter and that the Parliament could control their quality.

[753] *R. v. Crown Zellerbach Canada*, *supra* note 711 at 453.

of activity, some under accepted constitutional values within federal, and some within provincial legislative capacity, consider them to be a single indivisible matter of national interest and concern lying outside the specific heads of power assigned under the Constitution. By conceptualizing broad social, economic and political issues in that way, one can effectively invent new heads of federal power under the national dimensions doctrine, thereby incidentally removing them from provincial jurisdiction or at least abridging the provinces' freedom of operation.[754]

The foregoing shows that the relevant question is this one: has the federal jurisdiction to implement treaties related to provincial matters the "singleness, distinctiveness and indivisibility" necessary to trigger the application of the peace, order and good government doctrine? In my opinion, the answer to that question is certainly "no" because such jurisdiction would be "an aggregate" of *exclusive provincial matters*. The fact that those matters would not be taken in isolation but would be seen in relation to the implementation of a treaty is insufficient to give them the required distinctiveness.

After the excerpt reproduced above,[755] Le Dain J. added the following:

> In determining whether a matter has attained the required degree of singleness, distinctiveness and indivisibility that clearly distinguishes it from matters of provincial concern it is relevant to consider what would be the effect on extra-provincial interests of a provincial failure to deal effectively with the control or regulation of the intra-provincial aspects of the matter.[756]

That test, generally referred to as the "provincial inability" test, possibly relevant for example in the case of pollution of interprovincial waterways, has obviously not the same relevance for the issue of federal implementation of treaties related to provincial matters. However, a closely related argument is sometimes put forward in support of such a federal power: the absence of extraterritorial provincial powers. I will now turn to that point in the next section.

C. Extra-Territoriality or the "Sufficient Connection" Doctrine

It is well-established that provincial legislatures' power to adopt extra-territorial statutes is limited.[757] For example, a majority of the Su-

---

[754] *Ibid.* at 452.

[755] *Supra* note 751 and accompanying text.

[756] *R. v. Crown Zellerbach Canada, supra* note 711 at 432.

[757] The introductory paragraph of s. 92 *Constitution Act, 1867, supra* note 39, reads: "*In each Province* the Legislature may exclusively make Laws in relation to Matters coming within the Classes of Subjects next hereinafter enumerated; that is to say ..." (em-

preme Court recently stated that "[t]his territorial restriction is fundamental to our system of federalism in which each province is obliged to
respect the sovereignty of the other provinces within their respective
legislative spheres, and expects the same respect in return."[758] The
question then is: When implementing a treaty dealing with a provincial
subject-matter, does a provincial legislature run afoul its constitutional
limitations against acting extra-territorially?

I am urged to ask this question by authors who argue that the *content*
of a treaty cannot be said to be "local" or "provincial" in nature and that,
consequently, treaty implementation is necessarily a federal matter.[759]
However, this argument is wrongheaded. After all, under what federal
heading of powers would such treaty *content* fall? For as we have just
seen, the power to implement treaties in relation to provincial subject-
matter cannot flow from the general and residuary powers of the "Peace,
Order and Good Government" clause of s. 91 *Constitution Act, 1867.*

However, one might attempt to reformulate the extra-territorial
argument to suggest that if treaty *implementation*, in itself, is by its very
nature an extra-territorial matter, then, maybe it could fall within
Parliament's exclusive jurisdiction. This argument would at least have
an air of plausibility in light of the fact that scholars of past generations
often explained provinces' inability to adopt extra-territorial statutes by
reason of an Imperial desire to avoid having colonial legislatures
violating international obligations binding on the Empire.[760] This would
lead to the following question: If a province were to adopt legislative
provisions inconsistent with a binding international treaty, could such
legislative provisions be declared unconstitutional on the basis of the
purportedly extra-territorial character of international violations?

---

phasis added). Also, the exercise of many of the most important powers granted to
provincial legislatures by virtue of that section is limited to "the province". For example, s. 92 (13) reads "Property and Civil Rights *in the Province*" (emphasis added).

I should note that until the adoption of s. 3 of the *Statute of Westminster, supra* note
67, in 1931, the Federal Parliament also lacked the capacity to adopt extraterritorial
statutes. The *Extra-Territorial Act, 1933*, S.C. 23-24 Geo.V., c.39 was adopted by the
federal Parliament to specify that this new power could also apply to federal statutes
adopted prior to 1931. Same is now to be found at *Interpretation Act*, R.S.C. 1985, c.
I-21, s. 8 (3). In *Society of Composers, Authors and Music Publishers of Canada v.
Canadian Assn. of Internet Providers*, [2004] 2 S.C.R. 427, 2004 SCC 45 at para. 54
[*S.O.C.A.M. v. C.A.I.P.*], the Court held that absent "clear words or necessary implica-
tion to the contrary", there was a presumption against the extraterritorial extension of
federal laws.

[758] *Unifund Assurance Co. v. Insurance Corp. of British Columbia, supra* note 661 at
para. 51 (Binnie J. for McLachlin C.J. and Iacobucci and LeBel JJ.).

[759] See *supra* notes 318-320.

[760] G.V. La Forest, "May the Provinces Legislate in Violation of International Law?",
supra note 41.

In that vein, Mark A. Luz and C. Marc Miller have recently argued that, in the context of the current globalization, new types of treaties have been adopted that create civil rights of an international nature and that, being of such international nature, they escape provincial jurisdiction on the basis of the extra-territorial doctrine.[761] They write:

> The premise that provinces are legislatively bound within their jurisdictions has important implications for their ability to deal with the realities of globalization. As typified by the NAFTA, subject matters that would have traditionally fallen into provincial power now take on an importance that transcends provincial boundaries. As outlined above, an investment or an

---

[761] Luz and Miller identify three "indicators" of how globalization has "permeated and transformed international law" (Mark A. Luz and C. Marc Miller, "Globalization and Canadian Federalism: Implications of the NAFTA's Investment Rules" (2002) 47 McGill L.J. 951 at 961ff [M.A. Luz and C.M. Miller, "Globalization and Canadian Federalism: Implications of the NAFTA's Investment Rules"]): the increase in number and scope of regulatory treaties, the degree of legal institutionalisation of international dispute resolution mechanisms and the individualisation of remedies. By their last indicator, they want to emphasise the extent to which states now not only grant substantive rights to non-state actors, but also procedural mechanisms to enforce them. In particular, they refer to the growth in the number of foreign direct investment ("FDI") treaties that allow for direct investor-state arbitration. Under those FDI treaties, foreign investors need no longer rely on the politically contingent espousal of their claim by their home state. This often means that (a) foreign investors will be able to directly sue the state that has deprived them of the rights recognized by a FDI treaty, (b) the state in question will already have accepted compulsory jurisdiction of an international arbitration board when it adhered to the FDI treaty, and (c) the arbitral decision will be enforceable in the domestic court of the state. Chapter 11 of the *North American Free Trade Agreement between the Government of Canada, the Government of Mexico and the Government of the United States*, 17 December 1992, Can. T.S. 1994 No. 2, 32 I.L.M. 289 & 605 (entered into force 1 January 1994) ("N.A.F.T.A.") is taken as a prime example of such mechanisms.

I note that these processes are often presented as processes of "depoliticisation" of trade in favour of predictability and efficiency. However, we have to understand that "depoliticisation" is a political tool of governance like many others. Rules are supposed to substitute for the discretion of domestic politicians and are made difficult to change or difficult to violate, therefore reassuring investors. However, under the veil of neutrality, depoliticisation often operates by shifting the decision-making powers to a different political arena. This is the case with FDI treaties and the arbitrations board attached to them. Once the system is in place, politicians can claim that they cannot be blamed for the depoliticised decisions but can benefit from any positive outcome by suggesting those outcomes are the product of other actions of their own. On the politics of depoliticisation, see Peter Burnham, "New Labour and the politics of depoliticisation" (2001) 3 *Brit. J. of Pol. and Int'l Rel.* 127 and on the risk of "accountability mismatch" caused by depoliticisation, see Mariana Mota Prado, "Independent Regulatory Agencies and the Electoral Accountability of the President" (Paper presented to the *Seminario en Latinoamérica de Teoría Constitucional y Política 2004*, Oaxaca, Mexico, 10-13 June, 2004), online: Seminario en Latinoamérica de Teoría Constitucional y Política <http://islandia.law.yale.edu/sela/SELA%202004/MotaPradoPaperEnglishSELA2004.pdf>.

investor covered by Chapter 11 can certainly be strictly intraprovincial. If Chapter 11 falls legitimately within the federal trade and commerce power, however, and incorporates principles of customary international law, investors in fact have civil rights that are "extra-provincial"; that is, they enjoy rights and privileges that exist by virtue of federal legislation and international law but operate in an intraprovincial context. The NAFTA has granted investors access to a new international mechanism of dispute resolution that is independent from the control of the respondent governments. This reality goes beyond their "foreign investor" status. However, for those investors who qualify under the terms of Chapter 11, their remedy is international, based on the NAFTA. The enforcement of any arbitral awards is based on international conventions (ICSID, *New York Convention, Inter-American Convention*), some of which have been directly adopted into domestic law. Thus, it can no longer be asserted that these are "local investors" in the sense that they are territorially bounded by provincial jurisdiction. The rules applicable to those individuals are in fact extraterritorial.[762]

Whether we try to recast the problem as one of the international law consequences of improper treaty *implementation* or one of substantive international rights, these are simply variations of the thesis mentioned earlier according to which anything that is "international" cannot be, at the same time, of a "local" or a "provincial" nature. To put it differently, the argument goes along this line: anything that flows from international law is *exogenous* and, consequently, extra-territorial. However, this is not the way extra-territoriality is conceived by Canadian constitutional law. It is thus worth examining more carefully exactly what that doctrine of extra-territoriality entails for provincial legislatures.

Let's begin with two very telling examples of the application of the so-called "extra-territorial" doctrine by the Supreme Court of Canada. First, in *Global Securities Corp. v. British Columbia (Securities Commission)*, the Supreme Court held that a province could use her investigative powers to order the production of documents in order "to assist in the administration of the securities laws of another jurisdiction", namely, in that case, the United States, and that a statute to that effect – even if it could seem at first sight extraterritorial – was perfectly valid.[763] In that case, the two valid objectives identified by the Court for the impugned provisions were "obtaining reciprocal cooperation from other securities regulators, thus enabling the [British Columbia Securities] Commission to carry out its domestic mandate effectively"[764] and "un-

---

[762] M.A. Luz and C.M. Miller, "Globalization and Canadian Federalism: Implications of the NAFTA's Investment Rules", *ibid.* at 985-986.

[763] *Global Securities Corp. v. British Columbia (Securities Commission)*, *supra* note 610.

[764] *Ibid.* at para. 32.

covering foreign violations of securities laws by domestic registrants".[765] The assistance provided by the province to foreign jurisdictions was thus deemed to have a sufficient connection with the provincial interests in question. In a somewhat similar way, the Supreme Court concluded in an earlier case, *Ontario (A.-G.) v. Scott*,[766] that Ontario was not legislating on civil rights outside her territory when she adopted a statute ordering Ontario husbands who had deserted their wives in England, to pay alimonies due to the latter who remained in England. The connection between that legislative measure and the province was held to be clearly sufficient because, on the one hand, the husbands targeted by the statute were Ontario residents and, on the other hand, the reciprocal nature of the legislative measure would help deserted wives in Ontario whose husbands fled to England. For those reasons, the help provided to the wives in England had a connection with the interests of the province of Ontario.

One could say – as François Chevrette and Herbert Marx did about twenty-five years ago – that in its most general sense, extra-territoriality entails an "absence de lien ou de connexité entre la mesure adoptée et les intérêts et pouvoirs de l'autorité publique qui l'adopte".[767] In a series of recent decisions, the Supreme Court of Canada recognized, and stated unequivocally, that what really matters here is the *sufficiency of the connection* between the province and the object being allegedly covered by the provincial authorities.[768] The reason for this is quite evident:

---

[765] *Ibid.* at para. 36.

[766] *Ontario (A.-G.) v. Scott*, [1956] S.C.R. 137 [*Ontario (A.-G.) v. Scott*].

[767] Chevrette and Marx, *Droit constitutionnel*, *supra* note 41 at 1176. On extraterritoriality, see also P. Hogg, *Constitutional Law of Canada*, 2002, *supra* note 217, ch. 13 and references found therein. We note that the *Canadian Charter of Rights and Freedoms*, supra note 81, raises many difficulties in relation to extraterritoriality. See *R. v. Hape*, *supra* note 398 and *Canada (Justice) v. Khadr*, 2008 SCC 28. It will not be necessary to address the complex issues raised by this problem here.

[768] I use the expression "provincial authorities" because issues of extra-territoriality might arise not only in relation to provincial legislatures but also in relation to courts. In effect, courts are often asked to take part in multi-jurisdictional litigations. That is why, both the common law and civil law have long developed rules to attribute jurisdiction and to choose which laws will be applicable in such cases. These rules are often imperfectly referred to as "conflict of laws" rules (an expression that unfortunately downplays the importance of jurisdictional issues) or "private international law" (an expression that eclipses the public nature of allocation rules and hides the reality of the regulatory government). They are in fact the rules developed by a legal system to specify its relations with other legal systems. Therefore those rules are necessary for any well-functioning legal system that has to interact with peers. And because of the principle of territoriality adopted by many legal systems, these relational rules often have an extra-territorial aspect in the sense that they are meant to deal with legal cases in which not all of the relevant elements are situated *within* their state.

Thus, for example, the rules meant to ensure that courts have jurisdiction to hear the cases brought before them – the doctrine of "jurisdiction *simpliciter*" – may include a reference to territoriality. This is the case for courts in Canada. In order to respect the purposes of the federation, courts must verify in inter-provincial cases that they have a "real and substantial connection" with the subject-matter of the litigation (see *Moran v. Pyle National (Canada) Ltd.*, [1975] 1 S.C.R. 393 [*Moran v. Pyle National (Canada)*]; *Morguard Investments Ltd. v. De Savoye*, [1990] 3 S.C.R. 1077 [*Morguard Investments Ltd. v. De Savoye*] at 1106; *Hunt v. T&N plc*, [1993] 4 S.C.R. 289 [*Hunt v. T&N plc*]; *Tolofson v. Jensen; Lucas (Litigation Guardian of) v. Gagnon*, [1994] 3 S.C.R. 1022 [*Tolofson v. Jensen; Lucas (Litigation Guardian of) v. Gagnon*]; *Holt Cargo Systems Inc. v. ABC Containerline N.V. (Trustees of)*, [2001] 3 S.C.R. 907, 2001 SCC 90 at para. 71; *Spar Aerospace Ltd. v. American Mobile Satellite Corp.*, [2002] 4 S.C.R. 205, 2002 SCC 78 [*Spar Aerospace Ltd. v. American Mobile Satellite Corp.*]; *Unifund Assurance Co. v. Insurance Corp. of British Columbia, supra* note 661 at para. 54 and *Beals v. Saldanha*, [2003] 3 S.C.R. 416, 2003 SCC 72). This evaluation is done through a flexible approach that cannot be reduced to an exhaustive set of rules to be mechanically applied (*Spar Aerospace Ltd. v. American Mobile Satellite Corp., ibid.* at para. 52 (LeBel J. for a unanimous court)). However, the Supreme Court hinted that there might not be any specific constitutional requirements applicable to the determination of jurisdiction *simpliciter* in international cases as opposed to inter-provincial ones (*Spar Aerospace Ltd. v. American Mobile Satellite Corp., ibid.* at para. 54).

Once jurisidiction *simpliciter* is established, the question of *forum conveniens* may arise: the court might have a "real and substantive connection" to the case but it might not be the best jurisdiction to hear a case. See for example Art. 3135 *C.C.Q.* ("Even though a Québec authority has jurisdiction to hear a dispute, it may exceptionally and on an application by a party, decline jurisdiction if it considers that the authorities of another country are in a better position to decide.") However, at common law, "the existence of a more appropriate forum must be <u>clearly</u> established to displace the forum selected by the plaintiff" (*Amchem Products Inc. v. British Columbia (Workers' Compensation Board)*, [1993] 1 S.C.R. 897 at 921 (Sopinka J., for the Court)).

Finally, once proper jurisdiction is established, there might still be an issue of "choice of law", that is, it is possible that the law to be applied by the local court might not be the *lex loci*. Thus, a series of rules usually exist to identify which laws pertaining to the case are applicable. Take for example, the *C.C.Q.*'s rule regarding legal persons: "[t]he status and capacity of a legal person are governed by the law of the country under which it was formed subject, with respect to its activities, to the law of the place where they are carried on." (Art. 3083 para. 2 *C.C.Q.*) Or, to take a different example, in *Castillo v. Castillo*, [2005] 3 S.C.R. 870, 2005 SCC 83, the Supreme Court decided that the substantive law to be applied by an Alberta court was the law of the jurisdiction where the car accident occurred – California – and that substantive law included the limitations law of that jurisdiction. That being the case, the Californian limitations period had extinguished the rights of action of the plaintiff.

At any rate, this also means that the law of a province may be applied by courts in other provinces to the extent that it satisfies the inter-systemic relational rules in place. This has not traditionally been seen as an "extra-territorial" application of a provincial law but simply as the application of the provincial law to a local issue by a foreign court. However, in this section, the immediate focus of our attention will not be on those jurisdictional issues but rather will be directed at the issue of the possible invalidity or inapplicability of provincial statutes by reason of insufficient territorial connection. That being said, to the extent that the inter-systemic relational rules in questions are so-called "conflict of laws" rules or "private international law" rules that aim

because law does not deal directly with tangible objects but deals with intangible things such as "rights", "duties", "corporations", etc., we cannot expect the territorial principle to apply in a purely physical sense. "Rights", "duties" and "corporations" are conceptual entities that do not occupy a physical space but rather are conceptual entities that exist in a shared understanding of the world. Thus, we must conventionally attribute a location to those entities. The location of the tangible thing to which those conceptual entities are related is just one of the ways in which we connect law with space. Thus, whether we locate those conceptual entities where the tangible thing to which they relate are situated[769] or we locate them where those entities were "created",[770] where the event to which they are attached occurred[771] or where those conceptual entities are meant to make a practical difference in people's actions, we are ultimately only looking to draw a *connection* between those entities and the physical world construed by the legal system. Thus, truly the most important thing to understand when we are dealing with the so-called "extra-territoriality" doctrine is that we are not first and foremost dealing with a rule *against* any external consequences of provincial actions as with a doctrine *requiring a sufficient connection* between the provincial interests and legislative measures adopted by that province.[772]

---

at ensuring that there is a sufficient territorial connection between local courts and the cases presented to them, those rules will not fall victim to the extra-territoriality doctrine.

[769] See for example: *British Columbia v. Imperial Tobacco Canada Ltd.*, [2005] 2 S.C.R. 473, 2005 SCC 49 at para. 30 [*British Columbia v. Imperial Tobacco*] where Justice Major wrote for the Court: "Where the pith and substance of legislation relates to a tangible matter — i.e., something with an intrinsic and observable physical presence — the question of whether it respects the territorial limitations in s. 92 is easy to answer. One need only look to the location of the matter. If it is in the province, the limitations have been respected, and the legislation is valid. If it is outside the province, the limitations have been violated, and the legislation is invalid."

[770] For example, the status and capacity of a legal person is governed, under Québec's inter-systemic relational rules (Art. 3083 para. 2 *C.C.Q.*), by the law of the location where it was formed.

[771] See for example, for a car accident: *Unifund Assurance Co. v. Insurance Corp. of British Columbia, supra* note 661.

[772] As we have seen earlier at note 757, because of the presumption *against* extra-territorial applications of federal statutes, courts also had to develop analytical tools to apply those statutes in a way that would respect the territoriality principle. It is interesting to note here that the Supreme Court used the exact same generous methodology in the case of the federal *Copyright Act*, R.S.C. 1985, c. C-42 as it did when dealing with provincial statutes. See for example *S.O.C.A.M. v. C.A.I.P., supra* note 757 at paras. 57 and 60:

The applicability of our *Copyright Act* to communications that have international participants will depend on whether there is a sufficient connection between this

This is reflected in the method of analysis established by the Supreme Court to deal with claims of territorial overreach by provincial legislatures. When examining the *validity* of a provincial statute in light of the territorial restrictions imposed on provincial legislatures, the Supreme Court states that one must follow these analytical steps:

> The first step is to determine the pith and substance, or dominant feature, of the impugned legislation, and to identify a provincial head of power under which it might fall. Assuming a suitable head of power can be found, the second step is to determine whether the pith and substance respects the territorial limitations on that head of power — i.e., whether it is in the province. If the pith and substance is tangible, whether it is in the province is simply a question of its physical location. If the pith and substance is intangible, the court must look to the *relationships among the enacting territory, the subject matter of the legislation and the persons made subject to it,* in order to determine whether the legislation, if allowed to stand, would respect *the dual purposes of the territorial limitations in s. 92 (namely, to ensure that provincial legislation has a meaningful connection to the enacting province and pays respect to the legislative sovereignty of other territories).* If it would, the pith and substance of the legislation should be regarded as situated in the province.[773]

The Court also notes that "[i]ncidental or ancillary extra-provincial aspects of such legislation are irrelevant to its validity."[774] Also, because

---

> country and the communication in question for Canada to apply its law consistent with the "principles of order and fairness... that ensure security of [cross-border] transactions with justice" ...
>
> The "real and substantial connection" test was adopted and developed by this Court in *Morguard Investments, supra,* at pp. 1108-9; *Hunt v. T&N plc,* [1993] 4 S.C.R. 289, at pp. 325-26 and 328; and *Tolofson, supra,* at p. 1049. The test has been reaffirmed and applied more recently in cases such as *Holt Cargo Systems Inc. v. ABC Containerline N.V. (Trustees of),* [2001] 3 S.C.R. 907, 2001 SCC 90, at para. 71; *Spar Aerospace Ltd. v. American Mobile Satellite Corp.,* [2002] 4 S.C.R. 205, 2002 SCC 78; *Unifund, supra,* at para. 54; and *Beals v. Saldanha,* [2003] 3 S.C.R. 416, 2003 SCC 72. From the outset, the real and substantial connection test has been viewed as an appropriate way to "prevent overreaching... and [to restrict] the exercise of jurisdiction over extraterritorial and transnational transactions" (La Forest J. in *Tolofson, supra,* at p. 1049). The test reflects the underlying reality of "the territorial limits of law under the international legal order" and respect for the legitimate actions of other states inherent in the principle of international comity (*Tolofson,* at p. 1047). A real and substantial connection to Canada is sufficient to support the application of our *Copyright Act* to international Internet transmissions in a way that will accord with international comity and be consistent with the objectives of order and fairness.

[773] *British Columbia v. Imperial Tobacco, supra* note 769 at para. 36 (emphasis added).

[774] *Ibid.* at para. 28, referring to *Reference re Upper Churchill Water Rights Reversion Act,* [1984] 1 S.C.R. 297 at 332 [*Reference re Upper Churchill Water Rights Reversion Act*], and *Global Securities Corp. v. British Columbia (Securities Commission),, supra* note 610 at para. 24.

the analysis is not a mechanical one, the analysis is highly context-dependent and the degree of connection required will vary according to the subject matter of the dispute,[775] the type of jurisdiction claimed,[776] the type of rights or duties involved,[777] etc.

However, it is true that when the issue is not one of constitutional validity *per se* but rather one of the *applicability* of an otherwise valid provincial statutes to matters that may have extra-territorial aspects, a majority of the Supreme Court held that what constitutes a "sufficient connection" is not entirely resolved by looking at "the relationship among the enacting jurisdiction, the subject matter of the legislation and the individual or entity sought to be regulated by it".[778] In effect, the majority states that "[t]he applicability of an otherwise competent provincial legislation to out-of-province defendants is conditioned by the requirements of order and fairness that underlie our federal arrangements" and that those principles, "being purposive, are applied flexibly according to the subject matter of the legislation".[779] The principles of

---

[775] *Unifund Assurance Co. v. Insurance Corp. of British Columbia, supra* note 661 at para. 65: "[i]t appears from the case law that different degrees of connection to the enacting province may be required according to the subject matter of the dispute."

[776] In *Unifund Assurance Co. v. Insurance Corp. of British Columbia, ibid.* at para. 80, the majority suggested that

> [t]he required strength of the relationship varies with the type of jurisdiction being asserted. A relationship that is inadequate to support the application of regulatory legislation may nevertheless provide a sufficient "real and substantial connection" to permit the courts of the forum to take jurisdiction over a dispute. This happens regularly.

This last-cited passage must be kept in mind when reading an earlier statement found in that opinion according to which, "[a]s will be seen, a "real and substantial connection" sufficient to permit the court of a province to take jurisdiction over a dispute may not be sufficient for the law of that province to regulate the outcome" ("*Unifund Assurance Co. v. Insurance Corp. of British Columbia, ibid.* at para. 58). In light of the quote that preceded it, that last statement should probably *not* be read as affirming that provincial legislatures cannot set up provincial courts that would have *inter alia* the power to settle issues that simply have a "real and substantial connection" to the province. After all, the Supreme Court recognized in *Ontario (A.-G.) v. Scott, supra* note 766, the power of the Ontario family court to make maintenance orders against an Ontario resident for the benefit of his deserted wife in England.

[777] For example, "[m]erely going through the air space over Manitoba" was judged to be an insufficient connection with the province to allow for the imposition of a provincial tax "within the Province" (*R. v. Air Canada*, [1980] 2 S.C.R. 303 at 316) However, for product liability purposes, the presence of the manufacturer in the province is not necessary; knowledge of the distribution within that province is sufficient (*Moran v. Pyle National (Canada), supra* note 768 at 409).

[778] *Unifund Assurance Co. v. Insurance Corp. of British Columbia, supra* note 661 at para. 56.

[779] *Ibid.* at para. 56. Similarly, in *Hunt v. T&N plc, supra* note 768 at para. 56, the Court wrote: "This does not mean, however, that a province is debarred from enacting any legis-

order and fairness are meant to "ensure security of transactions with justice",[780] to ensure that a province's autonomy will be respected[781] and that other provinces will not stop her from applying her own valid laws on her own territory,[782] that the overlap between provinces' laws will be limited[783] and that the choice of law applicable will not be unfair to the parties involved in a litigation.[784] But all this should in no way detract us from the fact that the driving force of the analysis is still the issue of the *sufficiency of the connection* between the province and the subject matter of the legislation and this is because comity between provinces that are members of an integrated federation requires mutual respect of provincial autonomy.[785]

A good illustration of how this doctrine of "sufficient connection" comes into play is provided by the recent *Unifund Assurance Co. v.*

---

lation that may have some effect on litigation in other provinces or indeed from enacting legislation respecting modalities for recognition of judgments of other provinces. But it does mean that it must respect the minimum standards of order and fairness addressed in *Morguard*."

[780] *Morguard Investments Ltd. v. De Savoye, supra* note 768 at 1097.

[781] *Unifund Assurance Co. v. Insurance Corp. of British Columbia, supra* note 661 at para. 51. See also *supra* note 758 and accompanying text.

[782] For example, by adopting a "blocking statute" prohibiting the production of business documents outside of the province: *Hunt v. T&N plc, supra* note 768. It is worth noting that the latter decision was rendered in the inter-provincial context and relied heavily on the idea that Canada was an integrated country. It is quite unclear whether a case involving a foreign country would yield the same result. The fact that the Court only declared the impugned act "constitutionally inapplicable to other provinces" (*ibid.* at para. 67) and did not declare it totally *invalid* may be an indication that one could expect a different result in a truly international case.

[783] *Tolofson v. Jensen, supra* note 768 at 1051: "Many activities within one state necessarily have impact in another, but a multiplicity of competing exercises of state power in respect of such activities must be avoided."

[784] See for example, *Unifund Assurance Co. v. Insurance Corp. of British Columbia, supra* note 661 at para. 72

[785] In *British Columbia v. Imperial Tobacco, supra* note 769 at para. 35, the Supreme Court seems to equate the "sufficient connection" doctrine to the respect for the two underlying purposes of s. 92 of the *Constitution Act, 1867* that it identified as being "... to ensure that provincial legislation both has a meaningful connection to the province enacting it, and pays respect to "the sovereignty of the other provinces within their respective legislative spheres"" (*ibid.* at para. 27.) In effect, the Court writes at para. 35: "In *Churchill Falls*, an examination of those relationships indicated that the intangible civil rights constituting the pith and substance of the Newfoundland legislation at issue were not meaningfully connected to the legislating province, and could properly be the subject-matter only of Québec legislation. Put slightly differently, if the impugned Newfoundland legislation had been permitted to regulate those civil rights, neither of the purposes underlying s. 92's territorial limitations would be respected."

Insurance Corp. of British Columbia case.[786] In that case, the Ontario *Insurance Act*[787] provided that Ontario insurers who paid the statutory no-fault accident benefits (SAB) to Ontario residents injured in motor vehicle accidents were entitled to seek indemnification from the insurers of any heavy commercial vehicle involved in the accidents according to fault determination rules set out by regulations. The SAB covered accidents occurring anywhere in North America. Unifund, having paid the SAB to two of its clients for an accident that occurred in British Columbia, requested the indemnification provided for by the Ontario *Insurance Act* from the Insurance Corporation of British Columbia (ICBC) which covered the negligent truck driver who had cause the accident. The ICBC is the only provider of motor vehicle insurance in the British Columbia and, probably for that reason, the British Columbia legislation does not contain loss transfer provisions. The ICBC refused to pay alleging that the Ontario scheme of loss transfer was inapplicable to accidents occurring in another province. Justice Binnie pointed out that the ICBC is not authorized and does not in fact carry business in Ontario and the accident occurred in British Columbia.[788] Justice Binnie wrote:

> The most that can be said for the respondent [Unifund Insurance] in this case is that the fact of a motor vehicle accident in British Columbia triggered certain payments in Ontario under Ontario law. However, the fact the Ontario legislature has chosen to attach legal consequences in Ontario to an event (the motor vehicle accident) taking place elsewhere does not extend its legislative reach to a resident of "elsewhere".

The Court thus decided that even if Ontarians had been injured in the accident, the connection between Ontario and the British Columbia insurer was insufficient to allow for the application of the Ontario *Insurance Act* to the ICBC. If it were otherwise, Ontario could have attached any benefits to an out-of-province accident and then could have asked outsiders to reimburse the Ontario insurers,[789] thus effectively regulating out-of-province behaviours. And the flipside of that would have been that British Columbia insurers could have been liable for whatever benefits other jurisdictions in Canada – and the rest of the world – decided to attach to events occurring *in British Columbia*, thus undermining that province's autonomy.

---

[786] *Unifund Assurance Co. v. Insurance Corp. of British Columbia, supra* note 661.

[787] *Insurance Act*, R.S.O. 1990, c. I.8.

[788] *Unifund Assurance Co. v. Insurance Corp. of British Columbia, supra* note 661 at para. 82.

[789] *Ibid.* at para. 101.

Now that I have looked more closely at the "sufficiency of connection" doctrine, I can come back to *Global Securities Corp. v. British Columbia (Securities Commission)* and *Ontario (A.-G.) v. Scott* to see how absurd it would be to pretend that the implementation of international agreements would, by nature, constitute an invalid extra-territorial provincial act. Whether or not those two cases were concerned with binding treaties as understood by orthodox international lawyers does not matter; what matters is that there were certainly international agreements concluded prior to the adoption of the reciprocal statutes. No one would have thought of making the argument that because those statutes were adopted *as a consequence* of those agreements – however informal they were – the statutes were of an extra-territorial nature. If a provincial statute implementing an international treaty fails to meet the requirements of the "sufficient connection" doctrine, it is because of its content, not because it is implementing a treaty.

Examining a case where a provincial law was deemed to fail the territoriality test will further help understand why treaty implementation, in itself, does not raise issues of extra-territoriality. A provincial statute that would modify contractual rights situated outside of the province would be judged to violate the "extra-territorial doctrine" – unless its extra-territorial effects were simply incidental. That is why the Supreme Court was of the opinion that a provincial law purporting to end a "Power Contract" for the purchase of hydro-electric power by an out-of-province buyer – a contract deemed by the provincial government too generous to the buyer – was *ultra vires* after concluding that the contractual rights in question were situated outside of that province.[790] In that case, the very purpose of the legislation was extra-territorial. The situation would be quite different if we were concerned with a vast provincial program to help ailing municipalities that contained incidentally, as one of its many components, lowering of the interest rates on the cities' bonds. Obviously, the modification of the interest rates may affect the out-of-province rights of creditors, however this incidental effect was judged constitutionally unproblematic by the Privy Council.[791]

It is important to highlight here that there is all the difference in the world between a right given by an international treaty and a right situ-

---

[790] *Reference re Upper Churchill Water Rights Reversion Act, supra* note 774. For other examples of provincial laws deemed *ultra vires* for unconstitutionally modifying out-of-province contractual rights, see: *Royal Bank of Canada v. R.*, [1913] A.C. 283; *Ottawa Valley Power Co. v. Hydro-Electric Power Commission*, [1937] O.R. 265 (C.A.); *Beauharnois Light, Heat and Power Co. v. Hydro-Electric Power Commission of Ontario*, [1937] O.R. 796 (C.A.) and *Credit-Foncier Franco-Canadien v. Ross*, [1937] 3 D.L.R. 365 (Alta. C.A.).

[791] *Ladore v. Bennett*, [1939] A.C. 468 (P.C.).

ated outside of a province. With regard to domestic law, the former is not effective as long as it has not been transformed and integrated. On this point, we have to remember that transnational or international laws are not directly constitutive of property law and basic market rules; they are meant to be second-order rules that apply to those primary constitutive rules. In other words, transnational and international laws are not functioning on the same plane as domestic laws; they recognize second-order rights.[792] As we have seen, provinces get into trouble when they attempt to legislate in ways that modify domestic (first order) rights that exist outside of their territorial jurisdiction. But the same reasoning does not apply to second-order rights and Luz and Miller seem to make a surprising mistake here. There are clearly strong territorial connections between the property and the civil rights situated within the province and that same province.

The so-called "extra-territoriality doctrine" thus has nothing to do with the idea that Canadian provinces lack jurisdiction on anything that is exogenous to them. If it were otherwise, this would lead to the self-defeating claim that provinces lack jurisdiction to adopt regulations aimed at social norms that have grown outside of the state.[793] The doctrine, as applied and interpreted by the case-law, also has nothing to do with a pretended impossibility of provinces to legislate against international law since the courts have clearly recognized that provinces can do so.[794] In fact, assimilating public international law to extra-territorial law

---

[792] See also L. Giroux, "La capacité internationale des provinces en droit constitutionnel canadien", *supra* note 23.

[793] If a provincial legislature were to be prohibited from regulating norms outside of itself it would fail to meet almost all of its purposes. Apart from regulating non-norm-guided behaviour, it would be forced into a recursive loop on itself.

[794] See for example, *Ordon Estate*, *supra* note 420 at 526 (Iacobucci and Major JJ. for a unanimous court): "Although international law is *not binding* upon Parliament or the *provincial legislatures*, a court must presume that legislation is intended to comply with Canada's obligations under international instruments and as a member of the international community." (Emphasis added). See also L. LeBel and G. Chao, "The Rise of International Law in Canadian Constitutional Litigation: Fugue or Fusion? Recent Developments and Challenges in Internalizing International Law", *supra* note 41 and Stéphane Beaulac, "Arrêtons de dire que les tribunaux au Canada sont 'liés' par le droit international" (2004) 38 R.J.T. 359. No one seriously claims today that a provincial statute would be constitutionally invalid by the mere fact that it goes against international law. None of the legal reasons advanced by those who argued that Parliament or provincial legislatures were not allowed to legislate against international law could stand today. For example, Vanek (D.C. Vanek, "Is International Law Part of the Law of Canada?", *supra* note 41) was of the view that neither Canada nor the provinces could legislate in violation of international law given the presumption that a power delegated by the Parliament in London does not, unless expressly stated, empower to legislate contrary to international law. Vanek's argument was that since the *Constitution Act, 1867*, does not contain any such mention, it follows that legisla-

and, following that, deducing that provinces lack jurisdiction to implement it demonstrates a clear lack of understanding of what is the so-called "extra-territoriality doctrine", if not of international law itself. It is not with this kind of weak arguments that one will be able to justify reversing the *Labour Conventions* case.

D. Constitutional Amendments

It is clear that the federal Parliament does not possess the power to implement treaties related to provincial matters and that courts could not make that constitutional amendment without stepping outside of their legitimate powers. As we have seen, changing the rules here would not be a minor evolutive adjustment; it would mean in-depth transformation of the Canadian constitutional structure. The only avenue remaining for those who would like to change the current division of powers is to go through the formal constitutional amendment process provided at Part V of the *Constitution Act, 1982*.[795] And, as we will see, the very demanding amending formulas applicable to those changes are there to buttress the argument that those changes would not simply be minor institutional

---

tion cannot be introduced in Canada in violation of international law. This argument cannot be defended in light of Canada's independence and it clearly ignores the fact that legislative powers possessed by Canada and by the provinces are not the result of "delegations" (see *Hodge v. R.*, *supra* note 14). While he was Dean, Rand J. claimed that provinces could not legislate contrary to international law since he claimed that jurisdiction on foreign affairs fell entirely upon the Dominion (I.C. Rand, "Some Aspects of Canadian Constitutionnalism", *supra* note 41 at 143-44). It is hard to reconcile this proposition with the decision rendered in the *Labour Conventions* case, *supra* note 19 at 348, where the Judicial Committee declared that powers of the federal Crown in the sphere of international relations had nothing to do with the way in which international obligations were implemented in Canada. Indeed, in the words of Lord Atkin: "The question is not how is the obligation formed, that is the function of the executive: but how is the obligation to be performed and that depends upon the authority of the competent Legislature or Legislatures". Finally, while he was professor, La Forest J. also defended the thesis that provinces could not legislate in violation of international law by invoking the constitutional doctrine of extra-territoriality and, alternatively, for the reason advanced by Vanek (G.V. La Forest, "May the Provinces Legislate in Violation of International Law?", *supra* note 41 at 81-87). The doctrine of extra-territoriality is not of great assistance here because, as La Forest J. put it, it "was developed to prevent violations of international law by the colonies" (*ibid.* at 82) which could attract the liability of the metropolitan state. Canada is no longer a British colony and it cannot be said that provinces are "colonies or dependencies" of the federal government. However unsatisfactory the *ad hoc* nature of responses to breaches of international obligation – customary or conventional – that flow from a lack of comprehensive agreement between the federal government and provinces over their mutual responsibility in such cases, this *ad hoc* nature does not justify a constitutional amendment limiting provincial legislative powers.

[795] *Constitution Act, 1982, supra* note 70.

adjustments and that courts would have no business making those sweeping changes.

What would be the relevant amending procedures here?

Because it would transfer to Parliament the powers to adopt laws that would otherwise be of provincial jurisdiction, this amendment would clearly "derogat[e] from the legislative powers, the proprietary rights or any other rights or privileges of the legislature or government of a province" and would seem therefore to require, according to s. 38 (2) of the *Constitution Act, 1982*, "a resolution supported by a majority of the members of each of the Senate, the House of Commons" and "resolutions of the legislative assemblies of at least two-thirds of the provinces that have, in the aggregate, according to the then latest general census, at least fifty per cent of the population of the provinces".[796] This is the default amending formula for matters affecting both federal and provincial powers (the "7/50" formula).[797] It is purposefully difficult to achieve because it involves changing the basic federal deal.

---

[796] Subss. 38 (1) and (2) of the *Constitution Act, 1982, ibid.* provide that:

38. (1) An amendment to the Constitution of Canada may be made by proclamation issued by the Governor General under the Great Seal of Canada where so authorized by	38. (1) La Constitution du Canada peut être modifiée par proclamation du gouverneur général sous le grand sceau du Canada, autorisée à la fois:
(a) resolutions of the Senate and the House of Commons; and	a) par des résolutions du Sénat et de la Chambre des communes;
(b) resolutions of the legislative assemblies of at least two-thirds of the provinces that have, in the aggregate, according to the then latest general census, at least fifty per cent of the population of the provinces.	b) par des résolutions des assemblées législatives d'au moins deux tiers des provinces dont la population confondue représente, selon le recensement général le plus récent à l'époque, au moins cinquante pour cent de la population de toutes les provinces.
(2) An amendment made under subsection (1) that derogates from the legislative powers, the proprietary rights or any other rights or privileges of the legislature or government of a province shall require a resolution supported by a majority of the members of each of the Senate, the House of Commons and the legislative assemblies required under subsection (1).	(2) Une modification faite conformément au paragraphe (1) mais dérogatoire à la compétence législative, aux droits de propriété ou à tous autres droits ou privilèges d'une législature ou d'un gouvernement provincial exige une résolution adoptée à la majorité des sénateurs, des députés fédéraux et des députés de chacune des assemblées législatives du nombre requis de provinces.

[797] Other aspects of the Canadian constitution that affect only one level of government are subject to less stringent rules. See for example, ss. 44 and 45 of the *Constitution Act, 1982, ibid.* that provide that

Moreover, assuming that the above amending formula is applicable, even if the federal government were to be able to garner the support of seven provinces representing more than 50% of the population, this would not be the end of the story. For s. 38 (3) of the *Constitution Act, 1982* also provides that

> (3) An amendment referred to in subsection (2) shall not have effect in a province the legislative assembly of which has expressed its dissent thereto by resolution supported by a majority of its members prior to the issue of the proclamation to which the amendment relates unless that legislative assembly, subsequently, by resolution supported by a majority of its members, revokes its dissent and authorizes the amendment.[798]

Therefore, the amendment would not be effective in the provinces that opposed the amendment. If, for example, Alberta and Québec decided to opt out of a constitutional amendment granting Parliament the powers to implement treaties in relation to provincial matters, the amendment would have no effect on the legislative powers of those two provinces.[799] That "opting-out" clause is there to ensure that no changes in the legislative powers of provinces would be forced upon an unwilling province. This was meant to protect the original deal of the federation. The fact that this is the only "opting-out" clause of the Constitution shows the importance of respecting provinces' powers.

---

44. Subject to sections 41 and 42, Parliament may exclusively make laws amending the Constitution of Canada in relation to executive government of Canada or the Senate and House of Commons.

44. Sous réserve des articles 41 et 42, le Parlement a compétence exclusive pour modifier les dispositions de la Constitution du Canada relatives au pouvoir exécutif fédéral, au Sénat ou à la Chambre des communes.

45. Subject to section 41, the legislature of each province may exclusively make laws amending the constitution of the province.

45. Sous réserve de l'article 41, une législature a compétence exclusive pour modifier la constitution de sa province.

[798] The equally authoritative French version reads:

> (3) La modification visée au paragraphe (2) est sans effet dans une province dont l'assemblée législative a, avant la prise de la proclamation, exprimé son désaccord par une résolution adoptée à la majorité des députés, sauf si cette assemblée, par résolution également adoptée à la majorité, revient sur son désaccord et autorise la modification.

[799] Also, to the extent that the amendment would have the effect of transferring "provincial legislative powers relating to education or other cultural matters from provincial legislatures to Parliament, Canada shall provide reasonable compensation to any province to which the amendment does not apply." (See *Constitution Act, 1982, ibid.*, s. 40. ("Le Canada fournit une juste compensation aux provinces auxquelles ne s'applique pas une modification faite conformément au paragraphe 38(1) et relative, en matière d'éducation ou dans d'autres domaines culturels, à un transfert de compétences législatives provinciales au Parlement.")

But that is not all. There are tricky aspects to the issue of transfer of the provincial Crown prerogative to conclude international agreements to the federal Crown. As we have seen earlier, Crown prerogatives were originally divided between the Crown in right of Canada and the Crown in right of each province *following the division of legislative powers.* Thus, the prerogatives vest in the *Crown* in right of each government. As we have seen earlier, provinces can delegate to the federal government the exercise of their Crown prerogative powers to conclude international agreements in relation to provincial matters. However, if the provincial governments were willing not only to *delegate* such powers but to go further and *operate a complete devolution* – i.e. completely taking away from the provincial Crown certain prerogatives and giving them to the federal Crown –, this could give rise to difficult amendment problems. Indeed, while provincial legislative powers can be transferred from the provinces to the Parliament through the "7/50" formula, according to s. 41 of the *Constitution Act, 1982,* any "amendment to the Constitution of Canada in relation" to the "office of the Queen, the Governor General and the Lieutenant Governor of a province" requires "resolutions of the Senate and House of Commons and of the legislative assemblies of *each* province".[800] The latter amending formula is known as the "unanimity" formula. Therefore, in order to adopt an amendment stripping the provincial Crown of some of its prerogatives and transferring them in the fullness of their original status to the federal Crown, unanimity would be required. But would that also affect the modification of the legislative powers?

A difficult question to answer here is whether or not a legislative transfer can indirectly do what it cannot do directly (i.e. modify the basic attributes of the Crown in right of the provinces without having gone through the s. 41 process). Again, let's remember, the question is

---

[800] Emphasis added. *Constitution Act, 1982, ibid.,* s. 41 reads:

41. An amendment to the Constitution of Canada in relation to the following matters may be made by proclamation issued by the Governor General under the Great Seal of Canada only where authorized by resolutions of the Senate and House of Commons and of the legislative assemblies of each province:	41. Toute modification de la Constitution du Canada portant sur les questions suivantes se fait par proclamation du gouverneur général sous le grand sceau du Canada, autorisée par des résolutions du Sénat, de la Chambre des communes et de l'assemblée législative de chaque province:
(*a*) the office of the Queen, the Governor General and the Lieutenant Governor of a province; ...	a) la charge de Reine, celle de gouverneur général et celle de lieutenant-gouverneur; [...]

not whether legislatures can or cannot limit or constrain the extent of Crown prerogatives through regular statutes. They obviously can. They can also delegate the exercise of the prerogatives. We are talking about something else here; we are talking about plucking out a Crown prerogative and vesting it in another entity. In *In re The Initiative and Referendum Act*,[801] the Privy Council declared invalid a provincial statute that amounted to a constitutional amendment that was giving away to a new entity (a popular legislature) the Crown power to veto certain bills. The Privy Council wrote

> The references their Lordships have already made to the character of the office of Lieutenant-Governor, and to his position as directly representing the Sovereign in the Province, renders natural the exclusion of his office from the power conferred on the Provincial Legislature to amend the constitution of the Province. The analogy of the British constitution is that on which the entire scheme is founded, and that analogy points to the impropriety, in the absence of clear and unmistakable language, of construing s. 92 as permitting the abrogation of any power which the Crown possesses through a person who directly represents it.[802]

Because it seems here that the only "clear and unmistakable language" "permitting the abrogation of [the] power which the Crown possesses through a person who directly represents it" is found in s. 41 of the *Constitution Act, 1982*, it is probable that unanimity would be required to transfer a Crown prerogative from one level of government to another.

At any rate, if such a transfer of prerogative powers could be achieved following the "7/50" formula, which I seriously doubt, again, I note that the dissenting provinces would not be affected according to s. 38 (3) of the *Constitution Act, 1982*.

Whether we refer to the stringent requirements of the "7/50" formula to transfer treaty implementation powers from provincial legislatures to Parliament, the provincial "opting-out" clause aimed at protecting the rights and powers of dissenting provinces or the unanimity requirement to transfer the provincial Crown prerogative to conclude international agreements related to provincial matters to the federal Crown, all three demonstrate how seriously such transformations are taken by the very text of the Canadian constitution. One thing should be clear by now:

---

[801] *In re The Initiative and Referendum Act, supra* note 233.

[802] *Ibid.* at 943. See also *Ontario Public Service Employees' Union v. Ontario (Attorney General)*, [1987] 2 S.C.R. 2 at 46 ("... it is uncertain, to say the least, that a province could touch upon the power of the Lieutenant Governor to dissolve the legislature, or his power to appoint and dismiss ministers, without unconstitutionally touching his office itself.")

reversing the *Labour Conventions* case[803] would not simply mean reversing a single precedent, it would mean reversing a long list of well-established constitutional rules and such reversals would have a dramatic impact on the many threads that compose the constitutional fabric of Canada. Again, this should give pause to judges who would be disposed to overturn any of the already well-established constitutional rules discussed in this essay. Bypassing the proper constitutional amendment procedure through a judicial amendment in the form of a reversal of the *Labour Conventions* case[804] would be tantamount to a constitutional coup. And what might be broken by the illegitimate stroke of a judicial pen might not be fixed without the right alignment of stars that has been eluding Canada since 1867.

---

[803] *Labour Conventions* case, *supra* note 19.
[804] *Ibid.*

Conclusion

This essay began by suggesting that the Canadian constitution was better seen not through the looking glass of "sovereignty" but rather through the constitutionally entrenched principle of federalism.

In the first chapter, I revisited the famous *Labour Conventions* case and put it back in its legal and political context. In particular, I highlighted how the "Canadian sovereignist" vision was articulated by the federal government, how it was rebutted by the federalist arguments presented by provinces and finally, how it was ultimately defeated by the Privy Council. That decision was thoroughly analysed to show how well it was integrated in an already formed body of constitutional law.

I then demonstrated in the second chapter that under current constitutional law, treaty-making powers are divided according to the same lines as the division of legislative competence. Thus, the federal government may make treaties in relation to federal legislative matters while provinces may do the same in relation to provincial matters. Therefore, only through a provincial delegation of powers is the federal government able to conclude treaties in relation to provincial matters. All other potential alternative sources for such a federal power have turned out to be empty. Strong policy reasons support those constitutional rules and nothing in international law prohibits such an arrangement. As we have seen, international law is not only open to a multitude of international players but it welcomes that diversity. Globalisation is not about the flattening out of international actors, it is about the development of networks of governance operating at all levels of government. This helped to explain why the recognition of provincial treaty-making powers entails no consequence whatsoever for any potential claim of independence because treaty-making power is no longer seen as solely the attribute of "independent states".

The third chapter focused on rebutting the claim made by certain scholars that the *Labour Conventions* case should be overturned. Most of the policy reasons for maintaining the *status quo* in relation to that case were presented in the previous chapter. Therefore, I concentrated my efforts on the purely constitutional arguments involved in the debate. I have shown clearly that reversing the *Labour Conventions* case would not merely entail reversing a simple precedent but would rather mean ripping apart large portions of the current Canadian constitutional fabric. In effect, the decision fits in a complex yet mostly coherent web of rules and precedents that would need to be overturned as well if the *Labour*

Conventions case was reversed. And whether that reversal were done through a resurrection of s. 132 or through a radical transformation of the "Peace, Order and Good Government" powers of s. 91, this would have tremendous consequences for the federation. If it were done through s. 91, for example, it would require transforming the "Peace, Order and good Government" powers so as to allow for the possibility of covering aggregates of exclusive provincial matters. If this were done, all formerly exclusive provincial powers could be turned into exclusive federal powers. I have also shown that the arguments based on the allegedly extraterritorial nature of treaty implementation displays a profound lack of understanding of the way that latter doctrine works in Canadian constitutional law. Finally, I have also shown that the Canadian constitution's amending procedures support the claim that the actual rules dealing with the division of powers over treaty-making and treaty implementation ought not to be modified lightly. In fact, those rules ensure that provinces' rights will be protected against any attempt by the federal government or by other provinces to impose a change on their powers. *A fortiori*, there are good reasons for not judicially trampling on those provincial rights. Bypassing the most deeply entrenched rules of the Canadian constitution would be out of character for a body that owes its existence to the respect of the rule of law.

Now that all these things have been said, nothing stops the federal government and the provinces from improving on the actual practices without violating the constitutional structure in which they operate. I have already suggested a series of ways in which the current practices could be improved by formalising in an intergovernmental agreement the general modalities of intervention on issues that are of common interest to the federal government and one or many provinces. Among other things, I have suggested the possible creation of an interprovincial coordinating body that would establish common positions – when possible – over provincial matters and that would be able to take the proper initiatives to achieve common goals. I suggested that this coordinating body should be open to the participation of civil society to prepare nuanced positions that will reflect the interests of the people it is supposed to serve. I also suggested that while provinces could represent themselves in the international arena to the extent that the host institutions are ready to accept them and that the unified voice of the provinces could speak for Canada in international institutions dealing with provincial matters, provinces could also decide, if they so wished, that the federal government could act as their mandatee in certain instances. The details would have to be worked out through negotiations between those governments interested in perfecting the actual system. However, if the federal government ever needed an incentive to participate in such negotiations, the fact that it might be able to conclude an agreement that would set the rules for the internal allocation of liability in case of international law violations should help.

In the remaining part of this conclusion, I want to open up two other avenues of reform. While this essay was mainly interested in the interplay between the constitutionally entrenched principle of federalism and treaty powers, other constitutional principles are at play here. I did mention briefly how the federalism principle is connected to the democratic principle[805] but my exploration of the links between the latter principle and treaty powers has been very limited. I will thus conclude this essay by adding a few remarks on how the exercise of treaty powers could better respect the democratic principle.

There have been many complaints about the lack of systematic democratic participation from the preparation phase of treaty negotiation (when issues and strategies are defined) to its conclusion and about the frequent lack of transparency of the process.[806] An obvious way in which we could increase the accountability of the executive in treaty-making is through the increased participation of parliamentarians in the process. This could be done in several ways. First, we could establish publicity rules to inform parliamentarians about the nature of the treaties being contemplated, the issues they raise and the likely consequences of the adoption of such treaties (e.g. obligations contemplated, budgetary impacts, need for legal reforms, etc.). This information would be provided in time for parliamentarians to examine the issues and influence the position that will be taken by the government during the negotiations. Second, we could increase executive accountability in treaty-making through the requirement of parliamentary "assent" prior to ratification. This could be done in different ways. For example, we could have a "positive assent" mechanism which would require parliamentarians to adopt a resolution supporting ratification for that ratifica-

---

[805] *Reference Re Secession of Québec, supra* note 76.

[806] See for example, J. Harrington, "Scrutiny and Approval: The Role for Westminster-style Parliaments in Treaty-Making", *supra* note 41; J. Harrington, "Redressing the Democratic Deficit in Treaty Law Making: (Re-)Establishing a Role for Parliament", *supra* note 41; G. van Ert, *Using International Law in Canadian Courts, supra* note 41 at 68-71; Daniel Turp, "Un nouveau défi démocratique: l'accentuation du rôle du parlement dans la conclusion et la mise en oeuvre des traités internationaux" in Canadian Council on International Law, *The Impact of International Law on the Practice of Law in Canada: Proceedings of the 27ᵗʰ Annual Conference of the Canadian Council on International Law, Ottawa, October 15-17, 1998 / L'influence du droit international sur la pratique du droit au Canada: travaux du 27ᵉ congrès annuel du Conseil canadien de droit international, Ottawa, 15-17 octobre, 1998* (The Hague: Kluwer Law International, 1999) 115 [Daniel Turp, "Un nouveau défi démocratique: l'accentuation du rôle du parlement dans la conclusion et la mise en oeuvre des traités internationaux"]. I owe most of the suggestions presented in this paragraph about parliamentary procedural reforms to Joanna Harrington.

tion to be effective. We could do the reverse with a "no-rejection" mechanism whereby contemplated treaties accompanied by an explanatory memorandum would be tabled and unless objections were raised by parliamentarians within a certain delay, the executive could go ahead and ratify the treaty. We could have a mixed system where "important" treaties would be subjected to "positive assent" while others would go through the "no-rejection" test.[807]

One might argue that the above was rejected by the Privy Council when it wrote in the *Labour Conventions* case that "Parliament, no doubt, … has a constitutional control over the executive: but it cannot be disputed that the creation of the obligations undertaken in treaties and the assent to their form and quality are the function of the *executive alone*."[808] However, this could certainly be read to mean only that the executive has an exclusive jurisdiction over the formal act of "creation of the obligations" through a formal assent to the "form and quality" of treaties. Also, let's remember that the issue here is one of executive *prerogative* and, by definition, prerogatives can be legislatively limited.[809] At the federal level, up until the late 1960s, important treaties were tabled for parliamentary approval before ratification.[810] At the provincial level, Québec offers an interesting model. The province has adopted simple procedures that allow for elected officials' input in relation to international agreements falling in its jurisdiction.[811] Among other things, the statute setting up the procedures provides that important international agreements[812] "must, to be valid, be signed by the

---

[807] This was the system proposed at the federal level by the defunct bill C-260, *An Act respecting the negotiation, approval, tabling and publication of treaties, supra* note 497.

[808] *Labour Conventions* case, *supra* note 19 at 348 (emphasis added).

[809] For example, *Constitution Act, 1867, supra* note 39, s. 15, entrenches certain military prerogatives: "The Command-in-Chief of the Land and Naval Militia, and of all Naval and Military Forces, of and in Canada, is hereby declared to continue and be vested in the Queen." On the distinction between limiting prerogatives and completely transferring them *qua* prerogatives to another entity, see section II.A.1.ii.

[810] See Daniel Turp, "Un nouveau défi démocratique: l'accentuation du rôle du parlement dans la conclusion et la mise en oeuvre des traités internationaux", *supra* note 806.

[811] *An Act respecting the Ministère des Relations internationales, supra* note 35.

[812] An "important international commitment" is defined at *An Act respecting the Ministère des Relations internationales, ibid.*, s. 22.2 al.2:

The expression "important international commitment" means an international agreement referred to in section 19 or an international accord referred to in section 22.1 and any instrument relating to either of them, which, in the opinion of the Minister,

1) requires, for its implementation by Québec, the passing of an Act or the making of a regulation, the imposition of a tax or the acceptance of an important financial obligation;

Minister, approved by the National Assembly and ratified by the Government."[813] Every "important international agreement" must first be tabled in the National Assembly with an explanatory note on the content and effects of the commitment[814] and (except in case of an emergency[815]) "... unless the Assembly, with the unanimous consent of its members, decides otherwise, the motion shall be the subject of a two-hour debate that may not begin before the lapse of 10 days after the tabling of the commitment."[816] Finally, "the ratification of an international agreement or the making of an order referred to in the third paragraph of section 22.1[817] shall not take place, where it concerns an important international commitment, until the commitment is approved by the National Assembly."[818]

These types of procedures involve legislative bodies only in the decision to ratify treaties and not necessarily in the implementation of them. However, the use of such procedures could help solve a debate that is

---

2) concerns human rights and freedoms;

3) concerns international trade; or

4) should be tabled in the National Assembly.

[813] *Ibid.*, s. 20 al. 3 provides: "Subject to section 22.5, international agreements referred to in section 22.2 must, to be valid, be signed by the Minister, approved by the National Assembly and ratified by the Government."

[814] *Ibid.*, s. 22.2 al.1.

[815] *Ibid*, s. 22.5 provides that:

The Government may, in case of urgency, ratify an important international agreement or make an order referred to in the third paragraph of section 22.1 relating to an important international accord before it is tabled in or approved by the National Assembly. The Minister shall table the agreement or accord in the National Assembly together with a statement setting out the reasons for the urgency within 30 days after the ratification or the making of the order or, if the National Assembly is not sitting on that date, within 30 days of resumption.

[816] The entire s. 22.3 of *An Act respecting the Ministère des Relations internationales, ibid.*, reads:

The Minister may present a motion proposing that an important international commitment tabled in the National Assembly be approved or rejected by the Assembly. No prior notice is required if the motion is presented immediately after the tabling of the commitment. Unless the Assembly, with the unanimous consent of its members, decides otherwise, the motion shall be the subject of a two-hour debate that may not begin before the lapse of 10 days after the tabling of the commitment. The only amendment that may be received is an amendment proposing to defer the approval or rejection of the commitment by the Assembly.

[817] *Ibid.*, 22.1 al.3 reads: "The Government must, in order to be bound by an international accord pertaining to any matter within the constitutional jurisdiction of Québec and to give its assent to Canada's expressing its consent to be bound by such an accord, make an order to that effect. The same applies in respect of the termination of such an accord."

[818] *Ibid.*, s. 22.4.

currently dividing courts and scholars in Canada over the issue of the "presumption of conformity to international law".[819] I will briefly say a few words about the debate and then conclude by offering a suggestion to solve the dispute.

On one side of the debate, we find those who want to maximize the use of the presumption of conformity to ensure that governments are respecting their international obligations as much as possible. Those people argue that courts must *always* choose the interpretation that is most in compliance with international law – or to put it in stronger terms: "In choosing among possible interpretations of a statute, the court should avoid interpretations that would put Canada in breach of such [international] obligations".[820] Prof. Kindred states clearly the rationale behind that general presumption: "States are bound to fulfill their treaty obligations and may not invoke domestic law as justification for their failure to do so. Courts will not purposefully place the state in breach of international law by their decisions if such a consequence can be avoided."[821] An *obiter* in the majority opinion in the recent *R. v. Hape* weights heavily in favour of this side of the debate.[822]

On the other side of the debate, we find those who believe that re-specting international obligations is important but that it should not be done at the expense of the democratic will of the people. They thus favour a more restrictive approach to the use of the presumption. They remind us that the Supreme Court also held that given the principle that clear legislation must take precedence over treaty law, an international agreement cannot dictate the interpretation to be given to a domestic statute unless the legislation in question contains an ambiguity.[823] The ambiguity requirement would serve to protect the democratic will of the people by telling courts to keep to the intention of the legislatures unless that intention is ambiguous. However, the Supreme Court relaxed its

---

[819] See *supra* note 413ff and accompanying text.

[820] *Ordon Estate, supra* note 420 at para. 137 (per Iacobucci and Major JJ for the Court). The full text reads:

> Although international law is not binding upon Parliament or the provincial legisla-tures, a court must presume that legislation is intended to comply with Canada's ob-ligations under international instruments and as a member of the international com-munity. In choosing among possible interpretations of a statute, the court should avoid interpretations that would put Canada in breach of such obligations ... (refer-ence omitted.)

[821] H. Kindred, "Canadians as Citizens of the International Community: Asserting Unimplemented Treaty Rights in the Courts", *supra* note 41 at 272.

[822] See *R. v. Hape, supra* note 398 at paras. 53-54 and cited at note 414 and accompany-ing text.

[823] *Schavernoch v. Foreign Claims Commission et al.*, [1982] 1 S.C.R. 1092 at 1092 and 1101.

position in 1990 in *National Corn Growers Association.*[824] In its ruling, the Court declared among other things that it is reasonable to refer to the international agreement in the process of determining the existence of such ambiguity and that patent ambiguity was not required.[825] The issue was recently raised again by the Supreme Court. [826] Despite the Court's *obiter* in *R. v. Hape,* [827] there might still be doubts about what is the precise rule.

While the goal of the second group is quite worthy, the way they propose to achieve it is impractical and normatively inconsistent. After all, every good lawyer knows that legal language can be made to look ambiguous or clear, depending on the needs of a client and the skills of the advocate. And if we were to examine the factual situations of the cases in which the courts have refused to look at the text of the treaties and compare them with those of the cases in which the courts used the international instrument to interpret the statute in question, we might be surprised to discern patterns that better explain these discrepancies than what might be predicted by formal legal doctrine. For example, it is possible that courts will be more sensitive to treaty obligations when they are aware of strong international enforcement mechanisms related to the treaty in question. It might be the case that courts are effectively more careful with bilateral treaties where there is a possibility of "tit for tat" than with multilateral treaties where enforcement often raises "collective action" problems. All that is to say that if the goal is to ensure that it is the elected members of legislative bodies who will decide whether or not a treaty obligation is to be respected, then this method fails because it leaves it entirely to the discretion of the judges through their ability to characterise a statute as being ambiguous or not.

Also, by casting this debate as one over whether or not courts need to find an "ambiguity" to invoke the presumption of conformity, the groups are artificially pitting themselves one against the other. And that is because it is clearly possible to achieve the objectives of both groups without having to invoke the impractical need to find an ambiguity before applying the presumption of conformity. This is where ratification approval by the relevant legislative assembly could come into play. If the presumption of conformity only applied to situations where ratification had been approved by the relevant legislative assembly, there

---

[824] *National Corn Growers Association, supra* note 413.

[825] *Ibid.* at 1371-1372.

[826] See the analysis by Stéphane Beaulac of *Schreiber* v. *Canada, supra* note 413 in Stéphane Beaulac, "Recent Developments on the Role of International Law in Canadian Statutory Interpretation" (2004) 25 Stat. L. Rev. 19.

[827] See *R. v. Hape, supra* note 398 at paras. 53-54 and cited at note 414 and accompanying text.

would be no need anymore to argue over the futile question as to whether a specific provision is ambiguous or not and international law would have received the democratic imprimatur required. It is much easier to verify whether or not an assembly has adopted a motion supporting the ratification of a treaty than determining whether or not a judge or another will find a statutory disposition ambiguous. Of course, this modest proposal does not have to affect the rule to the effect that treaty implementation, to the extent that it would requires alteration of domestic law, requires proper legislation.

Finally, as I mentioned earlier, this essay stayed very close to well-established constitutional law precedents to examine how Canadian federalism could meet the current needs of existential communities that recognize themselves in Canada and in Québec. However, conspicuously absent from this narrative – as it has sadly been too often the case in the history of the last few hundred years – were the Aboriginal groups. Out of respect for their desire for self-definition, I preferred not to try and to force them in any of my own conceptual categories. In particular, many of the arguments presented here referred to the Crown as the symbol of the public authority and the logic of the argument was almost entirely intrasystemic. The issue of an Aboriginal *jus tractatum* will quite possibly have to be examined on a different basis. But we will have to wait for someone else to write that story.

In the meantime, I hope that I have been able to present a few useful ideas about the interconnectness of our current world and the call for a world federalism that is no longer based on sovereignty but rather on the harmony of overlapping existential communities and functional regimes.

Bibliography

Constitutional Documents

Austrian Federal Chancellery, *Österreichische Bundesverfassungsgesetze (Auswahl) / Austrian Federal Constitutional Laws (selection) / Lois constitutionnelles de l'Autriche (une sélection)*, English transl. by Charles Kessler and Peter Krauth (Vienna: Herausgegeben vom Bundespressedienst, 2000) online: Legal Information System of the Republic of Austria (RIS) <http://www.ris.bka.gv.at/info/bvg_eng.pdf>)..154

Basic Law for the Federal Republic of Germany, (Berlin: German Bundestag – Administration – Public Relations section, 2001), online: German Bundestag <http://www.bundestag.de/htdocs_e/parliament/function/legal/germanbasic law.pdf> 154

British North America (No. 2) Act, 1949 (U.K.), 13 Geo. VI, c. 81. 105

Canadian Charter of Rights and Freedoms, Part I of the *Constitution Act, 1982*, being Schedule B to the *Canada Act 1982* (U.K.), 1982, c.11 .... 144, 145, 146, 222, 243

Colonial Laws Validity Act, 1865 (U.K.), 28 & 29 Vict., c. 63 220

Constitución Nacional De La República Argentina, Convención Nacional Constituyente, ciudad de Santa Fe, 22 de agosto de 1994 154

Constitution Act, 1867 (U.K.), 30 & 31 Vict., c. 3, reprinted in R.S.C. 1985, App. II, No. 5118, 124, 125, 128, 129, 135, 143, 181, 194, 198, 199, 211, 218, 220, 221, 222, 225, 226, 227, 228, 239, 240, 248, 251, 262

Constitution Act, 1871 (U.K.), 34 & 35 Vic., c. 28, s. 3 118

Constitution Act, 1982, being Schedule B to the *Canada Act 1982* (U.K.), 1982, c. 11 ....37, 41, 48, 105, 111, 135, 145, 146, 252, 253, 254, 255, 256

Constitution fédérale de la Confédération suisse du 18 avril 1999.................154

Constitution of Bosnia and Herzegovina, English transl., online: Constitutional Court of Bosnia and Herzegovina < http://www.ustavnisud.ba/public/down/ USTAV_BOSNE_I_HERCEGOVINE_engl.pdf >) 155

Constitution of the United States of America...34, 38

Global Securities Corp. v. British Columbia (Securities Commission), [2000] 1 S.C.R. 494 .... 89, 202, 236, 237, 242, 243, 246, 250

Grundgesetz für die Bundesrepublik Deutschland 154

Inter-Imperial Relations Committee, Report, *Proceedings And Memoranda (Balfour Declaration)*, E (I.R./26) Series, p. 2 ....36, 67, 87, 88, 120

Letters Patent Constituting the Office of the Governor General of Canada, reproduced at R.S.C. 1985, Appendix II, no. 31................................37, 104, 105

Legislation

Jurisprudence

The Ship "North" v. The King, (1906) 37 S.C.R. 385 .... 137, 141

Thomson v. Thomson, [1994] 3 S.C.R. 551 .... 101, 102, 103, 217

Tolofson v. Jensen; Lucas (Litigation Guardian of) v. Gagnon, [1994] 3 S.C.R. 1022 .... 244, 246, 248

Toronto Electric Commissioners v. Snider, [1925] A.C. 396 .... 95, 96

Trendtex Trading Corporation Ltd v. Central Bank of Nigeria, [1977] 1 All E.R. 881 .... 137, 139

Triquet v. Bath, (1774) 3 Burr. 1478 137

Unifund Assurance Co. v. Insurance Corp. of British Columbia, [2003] 2 S.C.R. 63, 2003 SCC 40 .... 223, 240, 244, 245, 246, 247, 248, 249

United Kingdom (A.-G.) v. DeKeyser's Royal Hotel, [1920] A.C. 508.... 108, 113

United States v. Burns, [2001] 1 S.C.R. 283, 2001 SCC 7 44

Vancouver Island Peace Society v. Canada, [1994] 1 F.C. 102, 64 F.T.R. 127 (T.D.), aff'd (1995), 16 C.E.L.R. (N.S.) 24, 179 N.R. 106 (F.C.A.) 108

Governmental Documents

ALBERTA, *Framework for Alberta's International Strategies* (Edmonton: Alberta International and Intergovernmental Relations, 2000) reproduced online: Government of Alberta <http://www.iir.gov.ab.ca/international_relations/pdfs/3.1.1-%20AB_International_Strategies.pdf> 188

ALBERTA, Ministry of International and Intergovernmental Relations, "Alberta Washington Office", online: Government of Alberta <http://www.iir.gov.ab.ca/international_relations/alberta_washington_office. asp> 188

ALBERTA, Ministry of International and Intergovernmental Relations, "Our Mission – International Relations", online: Government of Alberta <http://www.iir.gov.ab.ca/international_relations/our_mission.asp> 188

ALBERTA, Ministry of International and Intergovernmental Relations, "Twinning Relations", online: Government of Alberta <http://www.iir.gov. ab.ca/international_relations/twinning_relations.asp> 188

BRITISH COLUMBIA, Intergovernmental Relations Secretariat, "International Section", online: Government of British Columbia <http://www.gov.bc. ca/igrs/prgs/#inter> 187, 188

CANADA, Canada School of Public Service, CSPS Action-Research Round-table on Managing Canada-US Relations, *Building Cross-Border Links: A Compendium of Canada-US Government Collaboration* by Dieudonné Mouafo, Nadia Ponce Morales, Jeff Heynen, eds. (Ottawa: CSPS Action-Research Roundtable on Managing Canada-US Relations, 2004) (Chair: Louis Ranger) 170, 196

CANADA, Department of Foreign Affairs, *Federalism and International Relations* by Paul Martin, Sr. (Ottawa: Queen's Printer, 1968) 26, 101

CANADA, Department of Justice, *The Department: Our Work*, online: Department of Justice <http://www.justice.gc.ca/en/dept/work.html> 169

NEW BRUNSWICK, Department of Intergovernmental Affairs, "International Relations": Government of New Brunswick <http://www.gnb.ca/0056/International/index-e.asp>. 193

NEWFOUNDLAND & LABRADOR, Intergovernmental Affairs Secretariat, "Overview", online: Government of Newfoundland & Labrador <http://www.exec.gov.nl.ca/exec/iga/iga-ovr.htm> 194

NORTHWEST TERRITORIES, Department of Aboriginal Affairs and Intergovernmental Relations, "Intergovernmental Relations", online: Government of the Northwest Territories <http://www.daair.gov.nt.ca/who-we-are/intergovernmental-relations.html> 196

NORTHWEST TERRITORIES, Department of the Executive, "Department of the Executive", online: Government of the Northwest Territories <http://www.executive.gov.nt.ca/>; archived online at Internet Archive, *Wayback Machine*, online: Internet Archive <http://web.archive.org/web/20051231153516/http://www.executive.gov.nt.ca/>................................. 195

NOVA SCOTIA, Department of Intergovernmental Affairs, "About Us", online: Government of Nova Scotia <http://www.gov.ns.ca/iga/aboutus.htm> 194

NOVA SCOTIA, Department of Intergovernmental Affairs, "Welcome to the Department of Intergovernmental Affairs", online: Government of Nova Scotia <http://www.gov.ns.ca/iga/> 194

NOVA SCOTIA, Department of Intergovernmental Affairs, "Welcome to the Department of Intergovernmental Affairs", online: Government of Nova Scotia <http://www.gov.ns.ca/iga/>; archived online at Internet Archive, *Wayback Machine*, online: Internet Archive <http://web.archive.org/web/20051228064032/http://www.gov.ns.ca/iga/>................................. 194

NUNANVUT, Executive and Intergovernmental Affairs, "Intergovernmental Affairs", online: Government of Nunavut <http://www.gov.nu.ca/Nunavut/English/departments/EIA/ia.shtml>... 196

ONTARIO, Ministry of Economic Development and Trade, "In-Market Support", online: Government of Ontario <http://www.ontarioexports.com/oei/redirect.jsp?page=English/Target_Your_Market/Ontario_Abroad.html>. 190

ONTARIO, Ministry of Economic Development and Trade, "International Marketing Centres", online: Government of Ontario <http://www.ontarioexports.com/oei/redirect.jsp?page=English/Target_Your_Market/IMC.html> 190

ONTARIO, Ministry of Intergovernmental Affairs, "About the Ministry", online: website: Government of Ontario <http://www.mia.gov.on.ca/english/about/aboutmia_en.html>.. 190

ONTARIO, Ministry of Natural Resources, "About the Ministry of Natural Resources", online: Government of Ontario <http://www.mnr.gov.on.ca/MNR/>... 190

ONTARIO, Ministry of Natural Resources, "Great Lakes-St. Lawrence River Basin Sustainable Water Resources Agreement", online: Government of

QUÉBEC, Secrétariat aux affaires intergouvernementales, Bureau des ententes, Ententes intergouvernementales canadiennes déposées au bureau des en- tentes, *Entente Canada-Québec concernant la participation du Québec aux programmes de l'agence de coopération culturelle et technique (ACCT)*, 1971-024; reproduced as *Modalités selon lesquelles le gouvernement du Québec est admis comme gouvernement participant aux institutions, aux activités et aux programmes de l'Agence de coopération, culturelle et technique, convenues le 1er octobre 1971, entre le gouvernement du Canada et le gouvernement du Québec* in Jaques-Yvan Morin, Francis Rigaldies and Daniel Turp, eds., *Droit international public: Notes et documents*, t. 2, 3rd ed. (Montréal: Thémis, 1997) at 462, Doc. No. 114A 185

SASKATCHEWAN, Government Relations, "Intergovernmental Affairs", online: Government of Saskatchewan <http://www.gr.gov.sk.ca/ intergovernmental.htm> 188, 189

International Instruments

Charter of the United Nations, 26 June 1945, Can. T.S. 1945 No. 7 106

Convention on the Continental Shelf, 29 April 1958, 499 U.N.T.S. 311 (entered into force 10 June 1964. Accession by Canada 08 March 1970) 119

Convention on the Protection and Promotion of the Diversity of Cultural Expressions, 20 October, 2005 online: UNESCO site: <http://unesdoc. unesco.org/images/0014/001429/142919e.pdf> 29

Convention on the Recognition and Enforcement of Foreign Arbitral Awards, 10 June 1958, 330 U.N.T.S. 3 150

European Convention on the Recognition of the Legal Personality of Inter- national Non-governmental Organizations, 24 April 1986, Europ. T.S. No. 124 148

Geneva Convention on the Territorial Sea and the Contiguous Zone, 29 April 1958, 516 U.N.T.S. 7477 117

Great Lakes—St. Lawrence River Basin Sustainable Water Resources Agree- ment, Illinois, Indiana, Michigan, Minnesota, New York, Ohio, Ontario, Québec, Pennsylvania and Wisconsin, 13 December 2005, online: Council of Great Lakes Governors < http://www.cglg.org/projects/water/ docs/12-13- 05/Great_Lakes-St_Lawrence_River_Basin_Sustainable_Water_ Resources_ Agreement.pdf>. 191

Halibut Fisheries Convention 1923, 1923, 32 L.N.T.S. no. 93 35

ILO Convention Concerning the Application of the Weekly Rest in Industrial Undertakings, 17 November 1921, 38 U.N.T.S. 187 .... 62, 63

ILO Convention Concerning the Creation of Minimum Wage-Fixing Machinery, 16 June 1928, 39 U.N.T.S. 3 62

ILO Convention Limiting the Hours of Work in Industrial Undertakings to Eight in the Day and Fourty-Eight in the Week, 3 November 1919, 38 U.N.T.S. 17 62

International Materials (Documents)

International Materials (Decisions)

Monographies

BICKEL, Alexander, *The Least Dangerous Branch: The Supreme Court at the Bar of Politics* (Indianapolis: Bobbs-Merrill, 1962)..40

BLACKSTONE, William, *Commentaries on the Laws of England* (1765), Vol. 1 (Buffalo (N.Y.): William S. Hein & Co, 1992) 140

BOORSTIN, Daniel J., *The Genius of American Politics* (Chicago: University of Chicago Press, 1953)..45, 46

BORK, Robert, *Slouching Toward Gomorrah: Modern Liberalism And American Decline* (New York: Regan Books, 1996) 40

BROSSARD, Jacques, André PATRY and Elisabeth WEISER, eds., *Les pouvoirs extérieurs du Québec* (Montréal: Presses Universitaires de l'Université de Montréal, 1967) 26

BROWNLIE, Ian, *Principles of Public International Law*, 5th ed. (Oxford: Oxford University Press, 1998)..146

BRUN, Henri and Guy TREMBLAY, *Droit constitutionnel*, 4th ed. (Cowansville (Qc): Yvon Blais, 2002)..83, 116

CARTER, Barry E. and Philip R. TRIMBLE, *International Law* (Boston: Little, Brown, 1991)..148

CHEVRETTE, François and Herbert MARX, *Droit constitutionnel: notes et jurisprudence* (Montréal: Presses de l'Université de Montréal, 1982) 26, 88, 112, 243

CLEMENT, William H.P., *The Law of the Canadian Constitution*, 3rd ed. (Toronto: Carswell, 1916) 109

CÔTÉ, P.-A., *The Interpretation of Legislation in Canada*, 3rd ed., (Scarborough: Carswell, 2000)..141

CRAWFORD, James, *The Creation of States in International Law* (Oxford: Clarendon Press, 1979)..152

D'AMATO, Anthony A., *The Concept of Custom in International Law* (Ithaca (N.Y.): Cornell University Press, 1971) 146

DEHOUSSE, Renaud, *Fédéralisme et relations internationales* (Bruxelles: Bruylant, 1991) 171

DETTER, Ingrid, *The International Legal Order* (Brookfield (VT): Dartmouth, 1994) 152

DICEY, Albert V., *An Introduction to the Study of the Constitution*, 10th ed. with an introduction of Emlyn C.S. Wade (London: MacMillan, 1967) 43, 108, 113

DINH, Nguyen Quoc, Patrick DAILLIER, Alain PELLET, *Droit International Public*, 3rd ed. (Paris: Librairie générale de droit et de jurisprudence, 1994) 151

DUCHACEK, Ivo, Daniel LATOUCHE and Garth STEVENSON, eds., *Perforated Sovereignties and International Relations: Trans-sovereign Contacts of Subnational Governments* (New York: Greenwood Press, 1988) 153

DUGUIT, Léon, *Les transformations du droit public* (Paris: Librairie Armand Colin, 1913)..54

HOGG, Peter W., *Meech Lake Constitutional Accord Annotated* (Toronto: Carswell, 1988) 223

HOGG, Peter, *Constitutional Law of Canada*, 3rd ed., Carswell, Scarborough, 1992.. 101, 104, 107, 133, 237

HOGG, Peter, *Constitutional Law of Canada: Student Edition 2002* (Toronto: Carswell, 2002) 88, 232, 243

HOOGHE, Liesbet, ed., *Cohesion Policy and European Integration: Building Multi-Level Governance* (Oxford: Oxford University Press, 1996) 153

JACOMY-MILLETTE, Anne-Marie, *L'introduction et l'application des traités internationaux au Canada* (Paris: Librairie générale de droit et de jurisprudence, 1971)..114

JACOMY-MILLETTE, Anne-Marie, *Treaty Law in Canada*, trans. by Thomas V. Helwig (Ottawa: University of Ottawa Press, 1975) 26, 114

JENNINGS, Sir Robert and Sir Arthur WATTS, eds., *Oppenheim's International Law*, 9th ed., Vol. 1 (Harlow (U.K.): Longman, 1992) 148

KAHN, Paul W., *Legitimacy and History: Self-Government In American Constitutional Theory* (New Haven: Yale University Press, 1992) 39, 40, 47

KAHN, Paul W., *The Reign Of Law: Marbury v. Madison and the Construction of America* (New Haven: Yale University Press, 1997) 38

KANTOROWICZ, Ernst, *The Kings Two Bodies: A Study in Mediaeval Political Theology* (Princeton: Princeton University Press, 1957) 42

KEATING, Michael and John LOUGHLIN, eds., *The Political Economy of Regionalism* (London (U.K.): Frank Cass, 1997).......................................153

KELSEN, Hans, *General Theory of Law and State*, trans. by Anders Wedberg (Cambridge (MA): Harvard University Press, 1949) 148

KENNEDY, William P. M., *The Constitution of Canada: An Introduction to Its Development and Law* (London UK: Oxford University Press, 1922)..........55

LACHAPELLE, Guy and Stéphane PAQUIN, eds., *Mastering Globalization: New Sub-States' Governance and Strategies* (London (U.K.): Frank Routledge, 2005) 153

LANGAN, Peter St. J., ed., *Maxwell on the Interpretation of Statutes*, 12th ed. (London (U.K.), Sweet and Maxwell, 1969)...141

LARDY, Pierre, La force obligatoire du droit international en droit interne – Étude de droit constitutionnel comparé (Paris: Librairie générale de droit et de jurisprudence, 1966) 138

LASKIN, Bora, *Canadian Constitutional Law*, 4th ed. by Albert S. Abel and John I. Laskin (Toronto: Carswell, Toronto, 1975)......................................26

LASKIN, Bora, Laskin's Canadian Constitutional Law: Cases, Text and Notes on Distribution of Legislative Power, rev. 4th ed. by Albert S. Abel and John I. Laskin (Toronto: Carswell, 1975) 227

LAUTERPACHT, Hersch, *Recognition in International Law* (Cambridge (U.K.): Cambridge University Press, 1947) 158

RUBENFELD, Jed, *Freedom And Time: A Theory Of Self-Government* (New Haven: Yale University Press, 2001) 40

RUBIN, Edward L., *Beyond Camelot: Rethinking Politics and Law for the Modern State* (Princeton: Princeton Universtity Press, 2005) 178

SALISBURY, John of, *Policraticus (1159)*, transl. and ed. by Cary J. Nederman (Cambridge: Cambridge University Press, 1990) 42

SCHABAS, William A., *International Human Rights Law and the Canadian Charter – A Manual for the Practitioner*, 1ˢᵗ ed. (Toronto: Carswell, 1991) 137

SCHABAS, William and BEAULAC, Stéphane, *International Human Rights and Canadian Law — Legal Commitment, Implementation and the Charter* (Toronto: Thomson Carswell, 2007) 26

SCHABAS, William, *International Human Rights Law and the Canadian Charter*, 2ⁿᵈ ed. (Toronto: Carswell, 1996) 26

SCHMITT, Carl, *Political Theology: Four Chapters on the Concept of Sovereignty*, trans. by George Schwab (London: MIT Press, 1985.) 70, 109

SEIDL-HOHENVELDERN, Ignaz, *Corporations in and Under International Law* (Cambridge (U.K.): Grotius Publications, 1987) 147

SHAW, Malcolm N., *International Law*, 5ᵗʰ ed. (Cambridge: Cambridge University Press, 1997) 148, 149

SHEARER, Ivan A., ed., *Starke's International Law*, 11ᵗʰ ed. (London: Butterworths, 1994) 152

STARKE, Joseph G., *Introduction to International Law*, 9ᵗʰ ed. (London: Butterworths, 1984) 90

SULLIVAN, Ruth, ed., *Driedger on the Construction of Statutes.* 3ʳᵈ ed. (Toronto: Butterworths, 1994) 142

SULLIVAN, Ruth, *Sullivan and Driedger on the Construction of Statutes.* 4ᵗʰ ed. (Markham (Ont.):Butterworths, 2002) 141

UNGER, Roberto Mangabeira, *What Should Legal Analysis Become* (London (U.K.): Verso, 1996) 175

van ERT, Gibran, *Using International Law in Canadian Courts* (New York: Kluwer Law International, 2002) 26, 104, 105, 106, 131, 133, 134, 136, 144, 182, 199, 201, 261

VARCOE, Frederick P., *The Constitution of Canada* (Toronto: Carswell, 1965) 26

von NEUMANN, John and Oskar MORGENSTERN, *Theory of Games and Economic Behavior*, 60ᵗʰ—anniversary ed., introduction by Harold Kuhn and afterword by Ariel Rubinstein (Princeton: Princeton University Press, 2004). 203

WATSON, Samuel J., *The Powers of Canadian Parliaments* (Toronto: Carswell, 1880) 135

WHEARE, Kenneth C., *Federal Government*, 3ʳᵈ ed. (London: Oxford University Press, 1953) 26

BEAULAC, Stéphane, "National Application of International Law: The Statutory Interpretation Perspective" (2004) Can. Y.B. of Int'l L. 225 25

BEAULAC, Stéphane, "Recent Developments on the Role of International Law in Canadian Statutory Interpretation" (2004) 25 Stat. L. Rev. 19 ....25, 265

BEAULAC, Stéphane, "The Canadian Federal Constitutional Framework and the Implementation of the Kyoto Protocol" (2005) 5 R.J.P. 125 26

BONENFANT, Jean-Charles, "L'étanchéité de l'A.A.N.B. est-elle menacée ?" (1977) C. de D. 383 56

BRADLEY, Curtis A., "The Treaty Power and American Federalism II" (2000) 99 Mich. L. Rev. 98 29

BRADLEY, Curtis A., "The Treaty Power and American Federalism" (1998) 97 Mich. L. Rev. 390 29

BURNHAM, Peter, "New Labour and the politics of depoliticisation" (2001) 3 Brit. J. of Pol. and Int'l Rel. 127 241

CARTER, Janet R., "Commandeering Under the Treaty Power", Note, (2001) 76 N.Y.U.L. Rev. 598 30

CHARNEY, Jonathan I., "Transnational Corporations and Developing International Law" (1983) 1983 Duke L.J. 748 148

CHARNEY, Jonathan, "The Persistent Objector Rule and the Development of Customary International Law" (1986) 56 Brit. Y.B. Int'l L. 1 146

CHARNEY, Jonathan, "Universal International Law" (1993) 87 Am J Intl L 529 146

CHEVRETTE, François, "*Dominium* et *imperium:* l'État propriétaire et l'État puissance publique en droit constitutionnel canadien" in Benoît Moore, ed., *Mélanges Jean Pineau* (Montréal, Éditions Thémis, 2003) 665 112

CLAYDON, John, "The Application of International Human Rights Law by Canadian Courts" (1981) 30 Buff. L. R. 727 24

COHEN, Maxwell and Anne BAYEFSKY, "The Canadian Charter of Rights and Freedoms and International Law" (1983) 61 Can. Bar Rev. 26525,   137, 140, 141

CRAWFORD, James, (1976-77) 48 Brit. Y.B. Int. L. 357 137

CRONKITE, Frederick C., "The Social Legislation References" (1937) Can. Bar Rev. 495 56

CYR, Hugo, "L'interprétation constitutionnelle, un exemple de postpluralisme" (1998) 43 McGill L.J. 565 ....75, 219

CYR, Hugo, "La conjugalité dans tous ses états: la validité constitutionnelle de \'l'union civile'\ sous l'angle du partage des compétences législatives" in Pierre-Claude Lafond et Brigitte Lefebre, eds., *L'union civile nouveaux modèles de conjugalité et de parentalité au 21ᵉ siècle* (Cowansville: Yvon Blais, 2003) 193 ....222, 223

DAWSON, William F., "Parliamentary Privilege in the Canadian House of Commons"(1959) 25 R.C.E.S.P. 462 135

Interstate Commerce": Recognizing the Realities of the New Federalism" (2004) 22 Va. Envtl. L.J. 167 30

GIROUX, Lorne, "La capacité internationale des provinces en droit constitutionnel canadien" (1967-1968) 9 C. de D. 241 ....18, 116, 149

GOLDSMITH, Jack L., "Federal Courts, Foreign Affairs, and Federalism" (1997) 83 Va. L. Rev. 1617..29

GOLOVE, David M., "Treaty-Making and the Nation: The Historical Foundations of the Nationalist Conception of the Treaty Power" (2000) 98 Mich. L. Rev. 1075 29

GRANT, Thomas D., "Defining Statehood: The Montevideo Convention and Its Discontents" (1999) 37 Colum. J. Transnat'l L. 403 ....147, 148, 151, 152

GRENON, Jean-Yves, "De la conclusion des traités et de leur mise en oeuvre au Canada" (1962) 40 Can. Bar Rev. 151 ....23, 24, 136, 147

GRENON, Jean-Yves, "De la mise œuvre du futur Pacte international des droits de l'homme dans l'État fédératif canadien" (1951-52) 1-2 R.J.T. 195..........24

HARRINGTON, Joanna, "Redressing the Democratic Deficit in Treaty Law Making" (2005) 50 McGill L.J. 465..26, 82, 261

HARRINGTON, Joanna, "Scrutiny and Approval: The Role for Westminster-style Parliaments in Treaty-Making" (2006) 55 I.C.L.Q 121 ....26, 261

HARRINGTON, Joanna, "The Role for Parliament in Treaty-Making" in Oonagh Fitzgerald, *et al*, eds., *The Globalized Rule of Law: Relationships between International and Domestic Law* (Toronto: Irwin Law, 2006) 159 26

HEALY, Thomas, "Is Missouri v. Holland Still Good Law? Federalism and the Treaty Power", Note, (1998) 98 Colum. L. Rev. 1726....................................29

HEARD, Andrew, "Canada's Independence" (1990) online: Constitutional Law of Canada <http://www.sfu.ca/~aheard/324/Independence.html>. 108

HENKIN, Louis, "International Law: Politics, Values, Functions" (1990) 216 Rec. des Cours 13..53

HOULE, France, "La légitimité constitutionnelle de la réception directe des normes du droit international des droits de la personne en droit interne canadien" (2004) 45 C. de D. 295 25

HOULE, France, "La réception du droit international des droits de la personne en droit interne canadien: de la théorie de la séparation des pouvoirs vers une approche fondée sur les droits fondamentaux" in Patricia Hughes and Patrick Molinari, eds., *Justice et participation dans un monde global: la nouvelle règle de droit? / Participatory Justice in a Global Economy: The New Rule of Law? Proceedings of the Canadian Institute for the Administration of Justice Conference, Banff, 2003* (Montréal: Thémis, 2004)) 173..............................26

HOULE, France, "L'arrêt Baker: Le rôle des règles administratives dans la réception du droit international des droits de la personne en droit interne" (2002) 27 Queen's L.J. 511..25

HUMPHREY, John, "The Canadian Charter of Rights and Freedoms and International Law" (1985-86) 50 Sask. L. Rev. 13....................................25

La FOREST, Gerald V., "May the Provinces Legislate in Violation of International Law?" (1961) 39 Can. Bar Rev. 78 .... 24, 142, 143, 240, 252

La FOREST, Gerald V., "The Labour Conventions Case Revisited" (1974), 12 Can. Y.B. Int'l L. 137...56, 218

LASKIN, Bora, "The Provinces and International Agreements" in Ontario, Ontario Advisory Committee on Confederation, *Background Papers and Reports*, Vol. 1 (Toronto: Queen's Printer, 1967) at 108 .... 23, 24, 104, 115, 116, 147, 150, 197, 212, 237

LeBEL, Louis and Gloria CHAO, "The Rise of International Law in Canadian Constitutional Litigation: Fugue or Fusion? Recent Developments and Challenges in Internalizing International Law" (2002) 16 *Sup. Ct. L. Rev. (2nd)* 23 ....25, 251

LEBEL, Michel, "L'interprétation de la Charte canadienne des droits et libertés au regard du droit international des droits de la personne – Critique de la démarche suivie par la Cour suprême du Canada" (1988) 48 R. du B. 743 25

LECLAIR, Jean, "Federal Constitutionalism and Aboriginal Difference" (2006) 31 Queen's L. J. 521..43

LECLAIR, Jean, "Jane Austen and the Council of the Federation" (2006) 15 Const. Forum 51 161

LECLAIR, Jean, "The Elusive Quest for the Quintessential 'National Interest'" (2005) 38 U.B.C. L. Rev. 353 75

LEVY, Thomas A., "Provincial International Status Revisited" (1976-77) 3 Dal. L.J. 70..24, 82

L'HEUREUX-DUBÉ, Claire, "From Many Different Stones: A House of Justice" (2003) 41 Alta. L. Rev. 659 144

Lord WRIGHT OF DURLEY, *Commentaire*, (1955) 33 Can. Bar Rev. 1123..56

LUZ, Mark A. and C. Marc MILLER, "Globalization and Canadian Federalism: Implications of the NAFTA's Investment Rules" (2002) 47 McGill L.J. 951...241, 242

LYSYK, Kenneth, "The Constitutional Reform and the Introductory Clause of Section 91: Residual and Emergency Law-Making Authority" (1979) 57 Can. Bar Rev. 531..75

MACDONALD, Roderick, "Kaleidoscopic Federalism" in Jean-François Gaudreault-DesBiens and Fabien Gélinas, eds, *Le fédéralisme dans tous ses états / The States and Moods of Federalism* (Cowansville (Qc): Yvon Blais, 2005) 261 175

MacDONALD, Vincent C., "Canada's Power to Perform Treaty Obligations" (1933) 11 Can. Bar Rev. 581..66

MacDONALD, Vincent C., "The Canadian Constitution Seventy Years Later" (1937) 15 Can. Bar Rev. 401 .... 56, 115, 116, 218, 232

MACKENZIE, Norman A.M., "Canada and the Treaty-Making Power" (1937) 15 Can. Bar Rev. 436 24

MANSERGH, Nicholas, "The Commonwealth at the Queen's Accession" (1953) 29 International Affairs 277 at 280 110

MATAS, Richard J., "Treaty Making in Canada" (1947) 25 Can. Bar Rev. 458 24

MAZER, Brian M., "Sovereignty and Canada: An Examination of Canadian Sovereignty from a Legal Perspective" (1977-78) 42 Sask. L.R. 1 24

McGINNIS, John O., "The Decline of the Western Nation State and the Rise of the Regime of International Federalism" (1996) 18 Cardozo L. Rev. 903...53, 174

McGREGOR, Gaile, "The International Covenant on Social, Economic, and Cultural Rights: Will It Get Its Day in Court?" (2002) 28 Man. L.J. 321 ...144

McRAE, Donald M. and CURRIE, John H., "Treaty-Making and Treaty Implementation: The Kyoto Protocol" (2003) 29:2 Canadian Council on International Law Bulletin..83

McWHINNEY, Edward, "Canadian Federalism and the Foreign Affairs and Treaty Power: The Impact of Québec's Quiet Revolution" (1969) 7 Can. Y.B. Int'l. Law 3 ....24, 182

McWHINNEY, Edward, "The Constitutional Competence within Federal Systems as to International Agreements" (1964-68) 1 Can. Legal Stud. 145...24, 82

McWHINNEY, Edward, Book Review of *Les États Fédéraux dans les Relations Internationales: actes du colloque de Bruxelles, Institut de sociologie, 26-27 février 1982 / Société belge de droit international (S.B.D.I.)* (1984) 80 A.J.I.L. 998 157

MENON, P.K., "The International Personality of Individuals in International Law: A Broadening of the Traditional Doctrine" (1992) 1 J. Transnat'l L. & Pol'y 151..148

MERICO-STEPHENS, Ana Maria, "Of Federalism, Human Rights, and the Holland Caveat: Congressional Power To Implement Treaties" (2004) 25 Mich. J. Int'l L. 265 30

MORIN, Jacques-Yvan, "La conclusion d'accords internationaux par les provinces canadiennes à la lumière du droit comparé" (1965) 3 Can. Y.B. Int'l Law 127...14, 18, 24

MORIN, Jacques-Yvan, "La personnalité internationale du Québec" (1984) 1 R.Q.D.I. 163 ....25, 82, 186, 238

MORRIS, Gerald L., "Canadian Federalism and International Law" in Ronald St. John MacDonald, Gerald L. Morris and Douglas M. Johnston, eds., *Canadian Perspectives on International Law and Organization* (Toronto: University of Toronto Press, 1974) 55 24

MORRIS, Gerald R.,"The Treaty-Making Power: A Canadian Dilemma" (1967) 45 Can. Bar Rev. 478..18, 23, 24, 114, 115, 116, 130, 136, 159, 165, 198, 214

NETTL, John Peter, "The Treaty Enforcement Power in Federal Constitutions" (1950) 28 Can. Bar Rev. 1051 24

NEUMAN, Gerald L., "The Global Dimension of RFRA" (1997) 14 Const. Commentary 33 29

NIJMAN, Janneke, "Leibniz's Theory of Relative Sovereignty and International Legal Personality: Justice and Stability or the Last Great Defence of the Holy Roman Empire" IILJ Working Paper 2004/2 (History and Theory of International Law Series) online: New York School of Law, Institute for International Law and Justice (I.I.L.J.) <http://www.iilj.org/papers/2004/2004.2%20Nijman.pdf> 183, 184

NORMAN, Ken, "Practising What We Preach in Human Rights: A Challenge in Rethinking for Canadian Courts" (1991) 55 Sask. L. Rev. 289 144

OLIVER, Covey T., "The Enforcement of Treaties by a Federal State" (1974) 14 Can.Y.B. Int'l. Law 331 24

PAQUIN, Stéphane, "La paradiplomatie identitaire en Catalogne et les relations Barcelone-Madrid" (2002) 33 Études internationales 57 153

PAQUIN, Stéphane, "Quelle place pour les provinces canadiennes dans les organisations et les négociations internationales du Canada à la lumière des pratiques au sein d'autres fédérations?" (2005) 48 Administration publique du Canada/Canadian Public Administration 477 162

PASCOE, James J., "Time for a New Approach? Federalism and Foreign Affairs After Crosby v. National Foreign Trade Council" (2002) 35 Vand. J. Transnat'l L. 291 30

PATENAUDE, Pierre, "L'érosion graduelle de la règle d'étanchéité: une nouvelle menace à l'autonomie du Québec" (1977) 20 C. de D. 229 56

PATTON, Ryan, "Federal Preemption in an Age of Globalization", Note, (2005) 37 Case W. Res. J. Int'l L. 111 30

PEEBLES, Thomas H., "A Call To High Debate: The Organic Constitution in its Formative Era, 1890-1920" (1980-1981) 52 U. Colo. L. Rev. 49 47

PHILIPPART, Éric, "Le Comité des Régions confronté à la 'paradiplomatie' des régions de l'Union européenne", in Jacques Bourrinet, ed., *Le Comité des Régions de l'Union européenne* (Paris: Editions économica, 1997) 153

POCOCK, John G.A., "Burke and the Ancient Constitution: A Problem in the History of Ideas" in John G.A. Pocock, *Politics, Language & Time: Essays on Political Thought and History* (Chicago: University of Chicago Press, 1989), 202 44

POOLE, Thomas, "Back to the Future? Unearthing the Theory of Common Law Constitutionalism" (2003) 23 O.J.L.S. 435 47

POOLE, Thomas, "Dogmatic Liberalism? T.R.S. Allan and Common Law Constitutionalism" (2002) 65 Modern L. Rev. 463 47

POOLE, Thomas, "Questioning Common Law Constitutionalism" (2005) 25 L.S. 142 47

RAMSEY, Michael D., "The Power of the States in Foreign Affairs: The Original Understanding of Foreign Policy Federalism" (1999) 75 Notre Dame L. Rev. 341 29

RAND, Ivan C., "Some Aspects of Canadian Constitutionnalism" (1960) 38 Can. Bar Rev. 135 .... 24, 114, 143, 213, 252

St. JOHN MacDONALD, Ronald, "The Relationship between International Law and Domestic Law in Canada" in Ronald St. John MacDonald, Gerald L. Morris and Douglas M. Johnston, eds., *Canadian Perspectives on International Law and Organization* (Toronto: University of Toronto Press, 1974) 88 ....24, 82, 90, 137

STAIRS, Denis, "The Conduct of Canadian Foreign Policy and the Interests of Newfoundland and Labrador" in *Collected Research Papers of the Royal Commission on Renewing and Strengthening Our Place in Canada*, Vol. 2 (St. John's (NL): Royal Commission on Renewing and Strengthening Our Place in Canada, 2003) 147, online: Newfoundland & Labrador, Research Papers <http://www.gov.nf.ca/publicat/royalcomm/research/ Stairs.pdf>. 169, 170

STANFORD, J. S., "United Nations Law of Treaties Conference: First Session" (1969) 19 U.T.L.J. 59..157

STEIN, Ted L. Stein, "The Approach of a Different Drummer: The Principle of the Persistent Objector in International Law" (1985) 26 Harv. Int'l L.J. 457..146

STRAUSS, David A., "Common Law Constitutional Interpretation" (1996) 63 U. Chi. L. Rev. 877 47

STRAUSS, David A., "Constitutions, Written and Otherwise" (2000) 19 Law and Philosophy 451 47

STRAUSS, David A., "The Irrelevance of Constitutional Amendments" (2001) 114 Harv. L. Rev. 1457 47

STRAUSS, David A., "Tragedies Under the Common Law Constitution" in William Eskridge and Sanford Levinson, eds. Constitutional Stupidities, Constitutional Tragedies (New York: New York University Press, 1998)....47

STROM, Torsten H. and Peter FINKLE, "Treaty Implementation: The Canadian Game Needs Australian Rules" (1993) 25 Ottawa L. Rev. 39 218

SWAIN, Edward T., "Does Federalism Constrain the Treaty Power?" (2003) 103 Colum. L. Rev. 403 30

SWAINE, Edward T., "Negotiating Federalism: State Bargaining and the Dormant Treaty Power" (2000) 49 Duke L.J. 1127 29

SYKES, Alan O., "The Economics of Public International Law" (July 2004) U Chicago Law & Economics, Olin Working Paper No. 216, at 19-20, online: Social Science Research Network <http://ssrn.com/abstract=564383> 205

Symposium, *Federal Courts and Foreign Affairs*, (2002) 42 Va. J. Int'l L. 365. 30

Symposium, *Foreign Affairs Law at the End of the Century*, (1999) 70 U. Colo. L. Rev. 1089 30

Symposium, *New Voices on the New Federalism*, (2001) 46 Vill. L. Rev. 907 30

SZABLOWSKI, George J., "Creation and Implementation of Treaties in Canada" (1956) 34 Can. Bar Rev. 28 24

TOOPE, Stephen J., "Inside and Out: The Stories of International Law and Domestic Law" (2001) 50 U.N.B L.J. 11 25

WILLIAMSON, Oliver E., "Credible Commitments: Using Hostages to Support Exchange" (1983) 73 American Economic Review 519 206

WRIGHT, Quincy, "Sovereignty of the Mandates" (1923) 17 Am. J. Int'l L. 691 148

Unpublished Manuscripts

CYR, Hugo, "Why The Rules Governing The Division Of Legislative Powers Over Marriage And Divorce Favour The Recognition Of Same-Sex Marriages", brief presented to the House of Commons Standing Committee on Justice and Human Rights (Ottawa: 8 April 2003) 222

Addresses and Papers Delivered at Conferences

CHAREST, Jean, Québec, Cabinet du Premier ministre, "Pour redécouvrir l'esprit fédéral" (Address pronounced at the occasion of the 40th anniversary of the Confederation Centre of the Arts in Charlottetown (P.E.I.), November 8th, 2004,), online: Premier ministre <http://www.premier.gouv.qc.ca/general/discours/2004/novembre/dis20041108.htm>. 21

GÉRIN-LAJOIE, Paul, Québec, *Ministère des Relations internationales*, *Paul Gérin-Lajoie's speech delivered at the Montreal to the Consular Corps on April 12, 1965*, trans. by *Ministère des Relations internationales*, online: *Ministère des Relations internationales* <http://www.mri.gouv.qc.ca/en/ministere/documentation/textes/discours_paul_gerin_lajoie.asp> (English translation) 15, 16, 17, 18, 19, 208

PRADO, Mariana Mota, "Independent Regulatory Agencies and the Electoral Accountability of the President" (Paper presented to the *Seminario en Latinoamérica de Teoría Constitucional y Política 2004*, Oaxaca, Mexico, 10-13 June, 2004), online: Seminario en Latinoamérica de Teoría Constitucional y Política <http://islandia.law.yale.edu/sela/SELA%202004/MotaPradoPaperEnglishSELA2004.pdf> 241

Newspaper Articles

Aird, Robert, "La magie canadienne" *Le Devoir* (9 September 2005) A9 31

Aird, Robert, "Signé André Patry" *Le Devoir* (9 March 2005) C4 31

Aubry, Jack, "Ottawa set to discuss Quebec's world role: Seeks increased profile" National Post (1 September 2005) A9 32

Authier, Philip, "Bouchard says no to partition" The [Montreal] Gazette (28 January 1996) A1 175

Beaudoin, Louise, "Remettre le Québec à sa place" *La Presse* (19 November 2004) A14 30

Beaudouin, Louise, "Mensonges et reculs" *Le Devoir* (9 September 2005) A9 31

Bellavance, Joël-Denis, "Harper promet de laisser le Québec s'exprimer sur la scène internationale" *La Presse* (28 November 2005) A3 30

Block, Irwin and Mike de Souza, "Pelletier makes pitch for greater Quebec role" The Gazette (18 March 2005) A8..32

Brand, Constant, "Charest réclame un plus grand rôle international pour le Québec" *La Presse* (5 March 2005) A14 30

Brooke, Jeffrey, *et al.*, "With the Liberal Party holding a policy convention this weekend, the Globe and Mail asked a sampling of members for their views on three issues" The Globe and Mail (5 March 2005) A4..............................32

Buzzetti, Hélène, "La bonne vieille méthode" *Le Devoir* (21 September 2005) A3..31

Castonguay, Alec, "Paul Martin envoie des renforts à Sgro et Frulla" *Le Devoir* (3 December 2004) A3 31

Castonguay, Alec, Diversité culturelle: dernière ligne droit à l'UNESCO *Le Devoir* (3 October 2005) A1...31

Chouinard, Tommy, "Relations internationales" *La Presse* (15 September 2005) A10..30

Chouinard, Tommy and Joël-Denis Bellavance, "Conseil de la fédération" *La Presse* (10 August 2005) A9 30

Clément, Éric, "Le Québec et la France main dans la main" *La Presse* (8 January 2005) A6...30

Cloutier, Mario, "Mission au Mexique" *La Presse* (20 November 2004) A19..30

Cloutier, Mario, "Rencontre Charest-Fox" *La Presse* (29 October 2004) A8...30

David, Michel, "La doctrine Charest" *Le Devoir* (23 November 2004) A3 31

David, Michel, "Le prix de la mollesse" *Le Devoir* (30 June 2005) A3............31

David, Michel, "Les slogans creux" *Le Devoir* (19 March 2005) B3................31

Dawson, Anne, "Belgium" plan might be tough sell in Ontario" The Gazette (22 October 2004) A14..32

Dawson, Anne, "Harper backs ADQ program" The Gazette (19 October 2004) A.12...32

Dawson, Anne, "Harper's Canada: Belgium: Calls for devolved powers, backs Dumont's Quebec plan" National Post (19 October 2004) A1 32

de Souza, Mike, "Canada should play bigger international role: Pettigrew" The Gazette (19 February 2005) A11...32

de Souza, Mike, "Charest as little to say on anti-missile shield" The Gazette (1 December 2004) A12 32

de Souza, Mike, "Ex-ambassador challenges Quebec's international role" The Gazette (18 February 2005) A9...32

de Souza, Mike, "Harper touts Belgium as a Federal model" The Gazette (16 October 2004) A13...32

de Souza, Mike, "Quebec bids to improve international presence" National Post (18 February 2005) A8 32

Descôteaux, Bernard, "Le corset de M. Pettigrew" *Le Devoir* (6 September 2005) A6..31

Descôteaux, Bernard, "Les sophismes de Pettigrew" *Le Devoir* (10 September 2005) B4 31

Desrosiers, Éric, "Se mêler de ses affaires" *Le Devoir* (19 March 2005) C3 31

Dougherty, Kevin, "Deal signed in Quebec to resume Vietnamese adoptions" The Gazette (16 September 2005) A9 32

Dougherty, Kevin, "Feds, province end Vietnam adoption spat" The Gazette (13 September 2005) A17 32

Dougherty, Kevin, "Our man in London" The Gazette (5 December 2004) D.1.BRE 32

Dougherty, Kevin, "Vietnam orphans caught in war of words: Accord scuttled Ottawa, Quebec in jurisdiction fight" The Gazette (2 July 2005) A12.........32

Dougherty, Kevin, "Wider role sought on world stage: Provincial minister takes hard line with Pettigrew" The Gazette (15 September 2005) A11 32

Dumont, Jean-Guillaume, "Faute de leadership, le Québec stagne" *Le Devoir* (5 February 2005) G5 31

Dumont, Jean-Guillaume, "Le gouvernement doit agir pour préserver l'identité québécoise" *Le Devoir* (9 March 2005) C5 31

Dutrisac, Robert, "Le Canada doit parler d'une seule voix" *Le Devoir* (2 September 2005) A1 31

Dutrisac, Robert, "Ottawa se crispe, Québec s'alarme" *Le Devoir* (2 July 2005) A1 31

Dutrisac, Robert, "Québec entend renforcer la doctrine Gérin-Lajoie" *Le Devoir* (3 September 2005) A5 31

Dutrisac, Robert, "Québec fera sa place dans le monde après entente avec Ottawa" *Le Devoir* (15 September 2005) A3 31

Fife, Robert, "PM threatens 'one Canada', Liberal says: Asymmetrical federalism" National Post (21 October 2004) A4...32

Freeman, Alan, "Premiers raise fear over border plans. Charest, McGuinty talk to US official" The Globe and Mail (19 April 2005) A18............................32

Gagnon, Lysiane, "Howard Dean à Montréal" *La Presse* (28 October 2004) A21...30

Gagnon-Tremblay, Monique, "C'est la meilleure entente qui soit" *Le Devoir* (23 September 2005) A8 31

Gagnon-Tremblay, Monique, "L'action internationale du Québec et les droits de la personne: des efforts réels" *Le Devoir* (31 August 2005) A7...................31

Gagnon-Tremblay, Monique, "Quebec and America" National Post (14 March 2005) A17...32

Gagnon-Tremblay, Monique, "Quebec needs place at table" The Gazette (3 September 2005) A21 32

Gauthier, Michel, "Le parti libéral n'a pas de leçon à donner à personne" *La Presse* (16 September 2005) A21..30

Gotlieb, Allan and Eli Lederman, "Ignoring the provinces is not Canada's way" National Post (3 January 2003) A14...212

Gotlieb, Allan, "Only one voice speaks for Canada" The Globe and Mail (5 October 2005) A23...213

Gunter, Lorne, "Who may speak for Canada?" National Post (12 September 2005) A11..32

Hachey, Isabelle, "Le début d'un temps nouveau" *La Presse* (6 February 2005) PLUS 5...30

Hamilton, Graeme, "'Country' of Quebec" National Post (15 November 2004) A6...32

Harel, Louise and Gilles Duceppe, "Le Québec n'est plus libre de ses choix" *Le Devoir* (18 August 2005) A7...31

Harper, Stephen, "My plan for 'open' federalism" National Post (27 October 2004) A19...32

Harvey, Réginald, "Concertation et coopération" *Le Devoir* (9 octobre 2004) G3 31

Hébert, Chantal, "Pettigrew Kamikaze" *Le Devoir* (12 September 2005) A3...31

Joyal, Serge, "La fin du Canada ? D'une asymétrie à l'autre, il risque de rester bien peu de la fédération" *La Presse* (22 October 2004) A19.....................30

Lamarche, Lucie, "La place du Québec sur la scène internationale: qu'en est-il des droits de la personne?" *Le Devoir* (24 August 2005) A7.....................31

Larocque, Sylvain, "Désaccord sur le rôle du Québec sur la scène internationale" (5 October 2005) A5...31

Larocque, Sylvain, "Pettigrew fait baisser les attentes" *Le Devoir* (3 October 2005) A3...31

Leblanc, Daniel, "Guité: 'When you're at war you drop... the rules'" Globe and Mail (Saturday, April 03, 2004) A1 179

Legault, Josée, "Pettigrew makes me pine for the Stephane Dion days" The Gazette (16 September 2005) A21 32

Léger Marketing, The [Montreal] Gazette and Le journal de Montréal, Press Release, "Quebec Survey" (14 May 2005), online: Léger Marketing <http://legermarketing.com/documents/SPCLM/050516ENG.pdf>...........176

Léger Marketing, The Globe and Mail, Le Devoir, Press Release, "Québec Poll" (27 April 2005), online: Léger Marketing: <http://legermarketing.com/ documents/spclm/050427ENG.pdf>)...176

Lemieux, Marie-Claude, "Boisclair veut faire mieux que René Lévesque" *La Presse* (19 September 2005) A1...30

Macdonald, Don, "Charest outlines goals of trip to China" The Gazette (14 September 2005) B1..32

Macpherson, Don, "Quebec, Ottawa spar over foreign affairs" The Gazette (17 September 2005) A31 32

McCarthy, Shawn, "Chretien defends handling of ad scandal" The Globe and Mail (30 April 2005) A19 32

McWhinney, Edward, "Point de départ d'un dialogue fructueux" *Le Devoir* (12-13 July 2003) B5 185

Menninger, Tomy, "Les États fédérés et la scène internationale" *Le Devoir* (28 September 2005) A6 31

Morin, Claude, "L'obstacle oublié" *Le Devoir* (9 March 2005) C6 31

National Post, "Firewall folly, take two" National Post (20 October 2004) A23 32

Normand, Gilles, "Conseil de la fédération" *La Presse* (27 December 2004) A16...30

Paquin, Stéphane, "La réforme proposée par le gouvernement du Québec est plus nécessaire que jamais" *Le Devoir* (9 September 2005) A9...................31

Paquin, Stéphane, "Une réforme indispensable" *Le Devoir* (9 March 2005) C6...31

Parenteau, Danic and Ian Parenteau, "La question de l'identité québécoise à l'heure de l'altermondialisme" *Le Devoir* (22 August 2005) A6 31

Pelletier, Benoît, "To refuse provincial input in international negotiations is to condemn our federation to a state of perpetual stagnation" The Globe and Mail (12 October 2005), online: The Globe and Mail (update) <http://www.theglobeandmail.com/servlet/story/RTGAM.20051011.wwebex 1012/BNStory> 213

Pelletier, Benoit, "Un rôle accru" *La Presse* (1 December 2004) A21..............30

Pelletier, Benoit and Monique Gagnon-Tremblay, "La doctrine Gérin-Lajoie: un cadre de référence toujours d'actualité" *Le Devoir* (10 September 2005) B5..31

Pratte, André, "Deux doctrines" *La Presse* (19 September 2005) A16 30

Presse Canadienne et Le Devoir, "Québec hausse le ton" (10 September 2005) \A1...31

Presse Canadienne, "Line Beauchamp parlera pour le Canada" *La Presse* (4 October 2005) A7 30

Presse Canadienne, "Pettigrew et Pelletier se parleront" *Le Devoir* (13 September 2005) A3..31

Richer, Jocelyne, "Jean Charest souhaite rencontrer Hilary Clinton à Washington" *La Presse* (12 March 2005) A18 30

Richer, Jocelyne, "Québec veut contribuer au succès des élections en Haïti" *La Presse* (5 February 2005) A8 30

Richer, Jocelyne, "Québec veut s'avancer sur la scène internationale" *Le Devoir* (9 August 2005) A3...31

Rioux, Christian, "Québec veut participer aux négociations avec l'Europe" *Le Devoir* (4 March 2005) A2..31

Robitaille, Antoine, "C'est à Ottawa de parler de droits de l'homme, dit l'entourage de Charest" *Le Devoir* (30 September 2005) A4......................31

Robitaille, Antoine, "La goutte d'eau de trop dans le vase asymétrique" *Le Devoir* (16 October 2004) B4...31

Robitaille, Antoine, "Le débat sur la place du Québec continue de faire rage" Le Devoir (5 October 2005) A2..31

Rodrigue, Isabelle, "Pettigrew craint une récupération par les \'fanatiques de l'indépendance'" *Le Devoir* (9 September 2005) A1 31

Rodrigue, Isabelle, "Pettigrew et Pelletier bientôt face à face" *La Presse* (13 September 2005) A23 30

Rodrigue, Isabelle, "Pettigrew tient son bout face à Charest" *La Presse* (9 September 2005) A11 30

Sauvé, Robert, "Americans' view of Quebecers" National Post (15 March 2005) A17..32

Séguin, Rhéal, "Quebec will work with Ottawa in representing Canada abroad" The Globe and Mail (15 September 2005) A4. 32

Simpson, Jeffrey, "Ottawa, please stop trying to please" The Globe and Mail (15 October 2004) A23..32

The Gazette "Canada must speak in one united voice" The Gazette (19 September 2005) A22 32

The Gazette, "Ex-MNA Christos Sirros named as Quebec's man in Brussels" The Gazette (7 October 2004) A16 31

The Gazette, "Who wants a more complicated Canada" The Gazette (20 October 2004) A30..32

The Globe and mail, "France and Quebec plan joint mission" The Globe and Mail (14 October 2004) A1 32

The Globe and Mail, "Martin chats with Globe's editorial board. Sweeping conversation covers successes, economy, NDP, Darfur and Gomery probe" The Globe and Mail (26 April 2005) A6..32

Thériault, Normand, "Au cœur des nations" *Le Devoir* (9 March 2005) C1 31

Thompson, Elizabeth, "Feds set to work with Quebec" The Gazette (6 March 2005) A6...32

Thompson, Elizabeth, "Province, feds jockey over roles in world: Quebec minister to read part of UNESCO speech" The Gazette (4 October 2005) A10..32

Toupet, Gilles, "Rejet du projet de loi sur la consultation des provinces" *La Presse* (30 September 2005) A7..30

Toupin, Gilles, "Martin reçoit l'aval de Chirac pour son G20" *La Presse* (15 October 2004) A21..30

Tremblay, Mylène, "Retour sur la doctrine Gérin-Lajoie" *Le Devoir* (9 March 2005) C7..31

Turp, Daniel, "Je ne suis pas candidat et j'appuie André Boisclair" *Le Devoir* (26 August 2005) A9..31

Yakabuski, Konrad, "Big dreams in Canada's city that never sleeps. The mayor is working overtime to help Montreal get its groove back" The Globe and Mail (16 July 2005) A3 32

Yelden, Max, "Quebec Already Speaks for Canada" The Globe and Mail (17 October 2005), online: The Globe and Mail (web-exclusive comment)

<http://www.theglobeandmail.com/servlet/story/RTGAM.20051017.wcomm
ent1017/BNStory/National/>..213

Internet Instruments

Internet Archive, *Wayback Machine*, online: Internet Archive <http://www.
archive.org/web/web.php.> 13

Diversitas

The aim of this series is to study diversity by privileging an interdisciplinary approach, through political, legal, cultural and social frameworks. The proposed method of inquiry will be to appeal, at once, to the fields of political philosophy, law, political science, history and sociology. In a period characterized by the increasing diversity of contemporary societies, the authors published in this series will explore avenues for the accommodation and management of pluralism and identity. Such studies will not be limited to assessments of federal states, but will include states that are on the path to federalization as well as non-federal states. Serious efforts will be undertaken to enrich our comprehension of so-called 'nations without states', most notably Catalonia, Scotland, Flanders and Quebec. A point of emphasis will also be placed on extracting lessons from experiences with civil law relative to those cases marked by the common law tradition. Monist and competing models will be compared in order to assess the relative capacity of each model to provide responses to the question of political instability, while pursuing the quest for justice in minority societies. The series also addresses the place of cities in the management of diversity, as well as the question of migration more generally and the issue of communities characterized by overlapping and hybrid identities. A profound sensitivity to historical narratives is also expected to enrich the proposed scientific approach. Finally, the works published in this series will reveal a common aspiration to advance social and political debates without privileging any particular school of thought.

Series editor: Alain-G. Gagnon, Canada Research Chair in Quebec and Canadian Studies (CRÉQC) and Director of the *Centre de recherche interdisciplinaire sur la diversité au Québec* (CRIDAQ).

Scientific Committee:
Alain Dieckhoff, Institut d'Études Politiques, Paris
Avigail Eisenberg, University of Victoria, Victoria
Montserrat Guibernau, University of London, London
Will Kymlicka, Queen's University, Kingston, Canada
Bernard Jouve, Université de Lyon, Lyon
Ramon Maïz, University of Santiago de Compostela, Santiago de Compostela
Marco Martiniello, Université de Liège, Liège
Ferran Requejo, Universidad Pompeu Fabra, Barcelona
Michel Seymour, Université de Montréal, Montréal
James Tully, University of Victoria, Victoria
Stephen Tierney, University of Edinburgh, Edinburgh

Series titles

Peter Lang—The website

Discover the general website of the Peter Lang publishing group:

www.peterlang.com